The Bible Unearthed

Archaeology's New Vision of Ancient Israel
and the Origin of Its Sacred Texts

ISRAEL FINKELSTEIN
and
NEIL ASHER SILBERMAN

A TOUCHSTONE BOOK
PUBLISHED BY SIMON AND SCHUSTER
NEW YORK   LONDON   TORONTO   SYDNEY

TOUCHSTONE
Rockefeller Center
1230 Avenue of the Americas
New York, NY 10020

First Touchstone Edition 2002

For information regarding special discounts for bulk purchases,
please contact Simon & Schuster Special Sales at 1-800-456-6798
or business@simonandschuster.com

TOUCHSTONE and colophon are trademarks
of Simon & Schuster Inc.

Designed by Charles B. Hames
Manufactured in the United States of America

27   29   30   28   26

The Library of Congress has cataloged the Free Press edition as follows:
Finkelstein, Israel:
The Bible unearthed : archaeology's new vision of ancient Israel and the origin
of its sacred texts / by Israel Finkelstein and Neil Asher Silberman.
p. cm.
Includes bibliographical references and index.
1. Bible. O.T.—Antiquities.   2. Bible. O.T.—Evidences, authority, etc.
1. Silberman, Neil Asher   II. Title.
BS621.F56 2001
221.9'5—dc21   00-057311
ISBN-13: 978-0-684-86912-4
ISBN-10:   0-684-86912-8
ISBN-13: 978-0-684-86913-1 (Pbk)
ISBN-10:   0-684-86913-6 (Pbk)

Acknowledgments

Almost eight years ago—during a peaceful summer weekend with our families on the coast of Maine—the idea for this book was born. The debate about the historical reliability of the Bible was again beginning to attract considerable attention outside scholarly circles and we came to the realization that an updated book on this subject for general readers was needed. In it, we would set out what we believed to be the compelling archaeological and historical evidence for a new understanding of the rise of ancient Israel and the emergence of its sacred historical texts.

Over the intervening years, the archaeological battle over the Bible has grown increasingly bitter. It has sunk—in some times and places—to personal attacks and accusations of hidden political motives. Did the Exodus happen? Was there a conquest of Canaan? Did David and Solomon actually rule over a vast empire? Questions like these have attracted the attention of journalists and commentators all over the world. And the public discussion of each of these questions has often gone far beyond the confines of academic archaeology and biblical criticism into the hotly contested realms of theology and religious belief.

Despite the passions aroused by this subject, we believe that a reassessment of finds from earlier excavations and the continuing discoveries by new digs have made it clear that scholars must now approach the problems of biblical origins and ancient Israelite society from a completely new perspective. In the following chapters, we will present evidence to bolster that contention and to reconstruct a very different history of ancient Israel. Readers must judge for themselves if our reconstruction fits the evidence.

Before beginning, we must note a few items regarding sources and transliterations. Our direct quotations from the biblical text all come from the Revised Standard Version translation of the Hebrew Bible. Although we have followed the RSV in referring to the names of the God of Israel within the quotations, we have used the name YHWH in *our* text to designate the tetragrammaton or explicit name of God. In the RSV it is represented by the word "LORD," while *Elohim* or *Elohei* is represented by the word "God."

Regarding biblical chronology, with its many uncertainties and pitfalls, we have decided that a combination of dating systems provides the best match with the emerging archaeological reality: from the beginning of the Israelite monarchy to the time of Ahab, we follow the dates determined in Gershon Galil, *The Chronology of the Kings of Israel and Judah* (Leiden: 1996). For the dates of the subsequent reigns of Israelite and Judahite kings, we follow Mordecai Cogan's article on "Chronology" in the *Anchor Bible Dictionary* (New York: 1992). Of course many uncertainties (relating to the precise dates of the earliest kings, later coregencies, and contradictions within the biblical material) remain, but we feel that in general, this chronological scheme is reliable for the purposes of this general work.

The renewed excavations of Tel Megiddo, undertaken by Tel Aviv University in partnerhip with Pennsylvania State University, have offered a unique opportunity for thinking, reflecting, and discussing with colleagues the material contained in this book. We would like to extend special thanks to the other co-directors of the Megiddo Expedition, Professors David Ussishkin and Baruch Halpern, and to the many staff members and team members of the Megiddo Expedition who have, over the years, played such an important role in the excavations and in the wider scholarly work of biblical archaeology.

The research and initial writing of this book was carried out by Israel Finkelstein during a sabbatical year in Paris and by Neil Asher Silberman in New Haven. Colleague and friend Professor Pierre de Miroschedji helped to make possible a productive and enjoyable time in Paris. During the writing of this book, the library of the Institute of Archaeology at Tel Aviv University; of the Institut Catholique, the Centre d'Archéologie Orientale in the Sorbonne, and the Section des Etudes Sémitiques of the Collège de France in Paris; and, at Yale, the Sterling Memorial Library and the library of the Yale Divinity School all provided excellent research faciletes.

Our deep appreciation goes to Judith Dekel of the Institute of Archaeology of Tel Aviv University who prepared the maps, diagrams, and drawings that appear in this book.

Professors Baruch Halpern, Nadav Naaman, Jack Sasson, and David Ussishkin have been generous with their advice and knowledge. We have been greatly helped by questions posed (and answered) in many late-night phone calls to Nadav Naaman and Baruch Halpern, who helped us to sort out the complex problems of biblical redactions and biblical history. Baruch also read and discussed with us early drafts of many of the chapters. We are grateful to these and all other friends and colleagues with whom we have consulted, even as we acknowledge that the responsibility for the final result is entirely ours.

In New York, our literary agent Carol Mann skillfully guided the project from initial idea to publication. At the Free Press, we want to thank assistant editor Daniel Freedberg for his efficiency and continuing help at every stage of the work. Senior editor Bruce Nichols has been an enthusiastic and tireless supporter of this book from the very beginning. Thanks to his perceptive insights and editorial skill, our evolving manuscript has been immeasurably improved.

Lastly, our families—Joëlle, Adar, and Sarai Finkelstein and Ellen and Maya Silberman—deserve a great share of the credit for their love, patience, and willingness to forgo many weekend outings and family events while this book took shape. We can only hope that the result of our efforts justifies their confidence in us—and in our idea of a book about archaeology and the Bible that first took shape in their presence just a few years ago.

I.F.
N.A.S.

Contents

PART THREE
Judah and the Making of Biblical History

The Bible Unearthed

PROLOGUE

In the Days of King Josiah

The world in which the Bible was created was not a mythic realm of great cities and saintly heroes, but a tiny, down-to-earth kingdom where people struggled for their future against the all-too-human fears of war, poverty, injustice, disease, famine, and drought. The historical saga contained in the Bible—from Abraham's encounter with God and his journey to Canaan, to Moses' deliverance of the children of Israel from bondage, to the rise and fall of the kingdoms of Israel and Judah—was not a miraculous revelation, but a brilliant product of the human imagination. It was first conceived—as recent archaeological findings suggest—during the span of two or three generations, about twenty-six hundred years ago. Its birthplace was the kingdom of Judah, a sparsely settled region of shepherds and farmers, ruled from an out-of-the-way royal city precariously perched in the heart of the hill country on a narrow ridge between steep, rocky ravines.

During a few extraordinary decades of spiritual ferment and political agitation toward the end of the seventh century BCE, an unlikely coalition of Judahite court officials, scribes, priests, peasants, and prophets came together to create a new movement. At its core was a sacred scripture of unparalleled literary and spiritual genius. It was an epic saga woven together from an astonishingly rich collection of historical writings, memories, leg-

ends, folk tales, anecdotes, royal propaganda, prophecy, and ancient poetry. Partly an original composition, partly adapted from earlier versions
and sources, that literary masterpiece would undergo further editing and
elaboration to become a spiritual anchor not only for the descendants of
the people of Judah but for communities all over the world.

The historical core of the Bible was born in the bustle of the crowded
streets of Jerusalem, in the courts of the royal palace of the Davidic dynasty,
and in the Temple of the God of Israel. In stark contrast to the countless
other sanctuaries of the ancient Near East, with their ecumenical readiness
to conduct international relations through the honoring of allies' deities
and religious symbols, Jerusalem's Temple stood insistently alone. In reaction to the pace and scope of the changes brought to Judah from the outside, the seventh-century leaders in Jerusalem, headed by King Josiah—a
sixteenth-generation descendant of King David—declared all traces of
foreign worship to be anathema, and indeed the cause of Judah's current
misfortunes. They embarked on a vigorous campaign of religious purification in the countryside, ordering the destruction of rural shrines, declaring
them to be sources of evil. Henceforth, Jerusalem's Temple, with its inner
sanctuary, altar, and surrounding courtyards at the summit of the city
would be recognized as the *only* legitimate place of worship for the people
of Israel. In that innovation, modern monotheism* was born. At the
same time, Judah's leaders' political ambitions soared. They aimed to make
the Jerusalem Temple and royal palace the center of a vast Pan-Israelite
kingdom, a realization of the legendary united Israel of David and
Solomon.

How strange it is to think that Jerusalem only belatedly—and suddenly—rose to the center of Israelite consciousness. Such is the power of
the Bible's own story that it has persuaded the world that Jerusalem was always central to the experience of all Israel and that the descendants of
David were always blessed with special holiness, rather than being just an-

---

* By Israelite "monotheism" we refer to the biblically mandated worship of one God in one place—the
Jerusalem Temple—that was imbued with a special holiness. The modern scholarly literature has identified
a wide spectrum of modes of worship in which a single god is central but not exclusive (i.e., accompanied by
secondary deities and various heavenly beings). We recognize that during the late monarchic period and
for a long time afterward the worship of the God of Israel was regularly accompanied by the veneration of
divine attendants and other heavenly beings. But we suggest that a decisive move toward modern monotheism was made in the time of Josiah, with the Deuteronomic ideas.

other aristocratic clan fighting to remain in power despite internal strife and unprecedented threats from outside.

How tiny their royal city would have appeared to a modern observer! The built-up area of Jerusalem in the seventh century BCE covered an area of no more than one hundred and fifty acres, about half the size of the present Old City of Jerusalem. Its population of around fifteen thousand would have made it seem hardly more than a small Middle Eastern market town huddling behind walls and gates, with bazaars and houses clustered to the west and south of a modest royal palace and Temple complex. Yet Jerusalem had never before been even as large as this. In the seventh century it was bursting at the seams with a swollen population of royal officials, priests, prophets, refugees, and displaced peasants. Few other cities in any historical eras have been so tensely self-conscious of their history, identity, destiny, and direct relationship with God.

These new perceptions of ancient Jerusalem and the historical circumstances that gave birth to the Bible are due in large measure to the recent discoveries of archaeology. Its finds have revolutionized the study of early Israel and have cast serious doubt on the historical basis of such famous biblical stories as the wanderings of the patriarchs, the Exodus from Egypt and conquest of Canaan, and the glorious empire of David and Solomon.

This book aims to tell the story of ancient Israel* and the birth of its sacred scriptures from a new, archaeological perspective. Our goal will be to attempt to separate history from legend. Through the evidence of recent discoveries, we will construct a new history of ancient Israel in which some of the most famous events and personalities mentioned in the Bible play unexpectedly different roles. Yet our purpose, ultimately, is not mere deconstruction. It is to share the most recent archaeological insights—still largely unknown outside scholarly circles—not only on *when,* but also *why* the Bible was written, and why it remains so powerful today.

---

* Throughout this book we use the name "Israel" in two distinct and alternative senses: as the name of the northern kingdom and as a collective name for the community of all Israelites. In most cases, we refer to the northern kingdom as "the kingdom of Israel" and the wider community as "ancient Israel" or "the people of Israel."

INTRODUCTION

Archaeology and the Bible

The story of how and why the Bible was written—and how it fits into the extraordinary history of the people of Israel—is closely linked to a fascinating tale of modern discovery. The search has centered on a tiny land, hemmed in on two sides by desert and on one side by the Mediterranean, that has, over the millennia, been plagued by recurrent drought and almost continual warfare. Its cities and population were minuscule in comparison to those of the neighboring empires of Egypt and Mesopotamia. Likewise, its material culture was poor in comparison to the splendor and extravagance of theirs. And yet this land was the birthplace of a literary masterpiece that has exerted an unparalleled impact on world civilization as both sacred scripture and history.

More than two hundred years of detailed study of the Hebrew text of the Bible and ever more wide-ranging exploration in all the lands between the Nile and the Tigris and Euphrates Rivers have enabled us to begin to understand when, why, and how the Bible came to be. Detailed analysis of the language and distinctive literary genres of the Bible has led scholars to identify oral and written sources on which the present biblical text was based. At the same time, archaeology has produced a stunning, almost encyclopedic knowledge of the material conditions, languages, societies, and historical developments of the centuries during which the traditions of ancient Israel gradually crystallized, spanning roughly six hundred years—from about 1000 to 400 BCE. Most important of all, the textual insights and the archaeological evidence have combined to help us to distinguish between the power and poetry of biblical saga and the more down-to-earth events and processes of ancient Near Eastern history.

Not since ancient times has the world of the Bible been so accessible and so thoroughly explored. Through archaeological excavations we now know what crops the Israelites and their neighbors grew, what they ate, how they built their cities, and with whom they traded. Dozens of cities and towns mentioned in the Bible have been identified and uncovered. Modern excavation methods and a wide range of laboratory tests have been used to date and analyze the civilizations of the ancient Israelites and their neighbors the Philistines, Phoenicians, Arameans, Ammonites, Moabites, and Edomites. In a few cases, inscriptions and signet seals have been discovered that can be directly connected with individuals mentioned in the biblical text. But that is not to say that archaeology has proved the biblical narrative to be true in all of its details. Far from it: it is now evident that many events of biblical history did not take place in either the particular era or the manner described. Some of the most famous events in the Bible clearly never happened at all.

Archaeology has helped us to reconstruct the history behind the Bible, both on the level of great kings and kingdoms and in the modes of everyday life. And as we will explain in the following chapters, we now know that the early books of the Bible and their famous stories of early Israelite history were first codified (and in key respects composed) at an identifiable place and time: Jerusalem in the seventh century BCE.

What Is the Bible?

First, some basic definitions. When we speak of the Bible we are referring primarily to the collection of ancient writings long known as the Old Testament—now commonly referred to by scholars as the Hebrew Bible. It is a collection of legend, law, poetry, prophecy, philosophy, and history, written almost entirely in Hebrew (with a few passages in a variant Semitic dialect called Aramaic, which came to be the lingua franca of the Middle East after 600 BCE). It consists of thirty-nine books that were originally divided by subject or author—or in the case of longer books like 1 and 2 Samuel, 1 and 2 Kings, and 1 and 2 Chronicles, by the standard length of parchment or papyrus rolls. The Hebrew Bible is the central scripture of Judaism, the first part of Christianity's canon, and a rich source of allusions and ethical teachings in Islam conveyed through the text of the Quran. Traditionally the Hebrew Bible has been divided into three main parts (Figure 1).

The *Torah*—also known as the Five Books of Moses, or the Pentateuch ("five books" in Greek)—includes Genesis, Exodus, Leviticus, Numbers, and Deuteronomy. These narrate the story of the people of Israel from the creation of the world, through the period of the flood and the patriarchs, to the Exodus from Egypt, the wanderings in the desert, and the giving of the Law at Sinai. The Torah concludes with Moses' farewell to the people of Israel.

The next division, the *Prophets,* is divided into two main groups of scriptures. The Former Prophets—Joshua, Judges, 1 and 2 Samuel, 1 and 2 Kings—tell the story of the people of Israel from their crossing of the river Jordan and conquest of Canaan, through the rise and fall of the Israelite kingdoms, to their defeat and exile at the hands of the Assyrians and Babylonians. The Latter Prophets include the oracles, social teachings, bitter condemnations, and messianic expectations of a diverse group of inspired individuals spanning a period of about three hundred and fifty years, from the mid-eighth century BCE to the end of the fifth century BCE.

Finally, the *Writings* are a collection of homilies, poems, prayers, proverbs, and psalms that represent the most memorable and powerful expressions of the devotion of the ordinary Israelite at times of joy, crisis, worship, and personal reflection. In most cases, they are extremely difficult to link to any specific historical events or authors. They are the products of a continuous process of composition that stretched over hundreds of years. Although the earliest material in this collection (in Psalms and Lamentations) may have been assembled in late monarchic times or soon after the destruction of Jerusalem in 586 BCE, most of the Writings were apparently composed much later, from the fifth to the second century BCE—in the Persian and Hellenistic periods.

This book examines the main "historical" works of the Bible, primarily the Torah and the Former Prophets, which narrate the saga of the people of Israel from its beginnings to the destruction of the Temple of Jerusalem in

THE TORAH

Genesis Exodus
Leviticus Numbers
Deuteronomy

THE PROPHETS

THE FORMER PROPHETS

Joshua Judges
1 Samuel 2 Samuel
1 Kings 2 Kings

THE LATTER PROPHETS

Isaiah Jeremiah Ezekiel
Hosea Joel Amos Obadiah
Jonah Micah Nahum Habbakkuk
Zephaniah Haggai Zechariah Malachi

THE WRITINGS

POETRY

Psalms Proverbs Job

THE FIVE SCROLLS

Song of Solomon Ruth Lamentations
Ecclesiastes Esther

PROPHECY

Daniel

HISTORY

I Chronicles II Chronicles
Ezra Nehemiah

Figure 1: Books of the Hebrew Bible.

586 BCE. We compare this narrative with the wealth of archaeological data that has been collected over the last few decades. The result is the discovery of a fascinating and complex relationship between what *actually* happened in the land of the Bible during the biblical period (as best as it can be determined) and the well-known details of the elaborate historical narrative that the Hebrew Bible contains.

From Eden to Zion

The heart of the Hebrew Bible is an epic story that describes the rise of the people of Israel and their continuing relationship with God. Unlike other ancient Near Eastern mythologies, such as the Egyptian tales of Osiris, Isis, and Horus or the Mesopotamian Gilgamesh epic, the Bible is grounded firmly in earthly history. It is a divine drama played out before the eyes of humanity. Also unlike the histories and royal chronicles of other ancient Near Eastern nations, it does not merely celebrate the power of tradition and ruling dynasties. It offers a complex yet clear vision of *why* history has unfolded for the people of Israel—and indeed for the entire world—in a pattern directly connected with the demands and promises of God. The people of Israel are the central actors in this drama. Their behavior and their adherence to God's commandments determine the direction in which history will flow. It is up to the people of Israel—and, through them, all readers of the Bible—to determine the fate of the world.

The Bible's tale begins in the garden of Eden and continues through the stories of Cain and Abel and the flood of Noah, finally focusing on the fate of a single family—that of Abraham. Abraham was chosen by God to become the father of a great nation, and faithfully followed God's commands. He traveled with his family from his original home in Mesopotamia to the land of Canaan where, in the course of a long life, he wandered as an outsider among the settled population and, by his wife, Sarah, begot a son, Isaac, who would inherit the divine promises first given to Abraham. It was Isaac's son Jacob—the third-generation patriarch—who became the father of twelve distinct tribes. In the course of a colorful, chaotic life of wandering, raising a large family, and establishing altars throughout the land, Jacob wrestled with an angel and received the name Israel (meaning "He who struggled with God"), by which all his descendants would be known. The Bible relates how Jacob's twelve sons fought among one another, worked together, and eventually left their homeland to seek shelter in Egypt at the time of a great famine. And the patriarch Jacob declared in his last will and testament that the tribe of his son Judah would rule over them all (Genesis 49:8–10).

The great saga then moves from family drama to historical spectacle. The God of Israel revealed his awesome power in a demonstration against the pharaoh of Egypt, the mightiest human ruler on earth. The children of Israel had grown into a great nation, but they were enslaved as a despised minority, building the great monuments of the Egyptian regime. God's intention to make himself known to the world came through his selection of Moses as an intermediary to seek the liberation of the Israelites so that they could begin their true destiny. And in perhaps the most vivid sequence of events in the literature of the Western world, the books of Exodus, Leviticus, and Numbers describe how through signs and wonders, the God of Israel led the children of Israel out of Egypt and into the wilderness. At Sinai, God revealed to the nation his true identity as YHWH (the Sacred Name composed of four Hebrew letters) and gave them a code of law to guide their lives as a community and as individuals.

The holy terms of Israel's covenant with YHWH, written on stone tablets and contained in the Ark of the Covenant, became their sacred battle standard as they marched toward the promised land. In some cultures, a founding myth might have stopped at this point—as a miraculous explanation of how the people arose. But the Bible had centuries more of history to recount, with many triumphs, miracles, unexpected reverses, and much collective suffering to come. The great triumphs of the Israelite conquest of Canaan, King David's establishment of a great empire, and Solomon's construction of the Jerusalem Temple were followed by schism, repeated lapses into idolatry, and, ultimately, exile. For the Bible describes how, soon after the death of Solomon, the ten northern tribes, resenting their subjugation to Davidic kings in Jerusalem, unilaterally seceded from the united monarchy, thus forcing the creation of two rival kingdoms: the kingdom of Israel, in the north, and the kingdom of Judah, in the south.

For the next two hundred years, the people of Israel lived in two separate kingdoms, reportedly succumbing again and again to the lure of foreign deities. The leaders of the northern kingdom are described in the Bible as all irretrievably sinful; some of the kings of Judah are also said to have strayed from the path of total devotion to God. In time, God sent outside invaders and oppressors to punish the people of Israel for their sins. First the Arameans of Syria harassed the kingdom of Israel. Then the mighty Assyrian empire brought unprecedented devastation to the cities of the northern kingdom and the bitter fate of destruction and exile in 720 BCE for a significant portion of the ten tribes. The kingdom of Judah survived more than a century longer, but its people could not avert the inevitable judgment of God. In 586 BCE, the rising, brutal Babylonian empire decimated the land of Israel and put Jerusalem and its Temple to the torch.

With that great tragedy, the biblical narrative dramatically departs in yet another characteristic way from the normal pattern of ancient religious epics. In many such stories, the defeat of a god by a rival army spelled the end of his cult as well. But in the Bible, the power of the God of Israel was seen to be even *greater* after the fall of Judah and the exile of the Israelites. Far from being humbled by the devastation of his Temple, the God of Israel was seen to be a deity of unsurpassable power. He had, after all, manipulated the Assyrians and the Babylonians to be his unwitting agents to punish the people of Israel for their infidelity.

Henceforth, after the return of some of the exiles to Jerusalem and the reconstruction of the Temple, Israel would no longer be a monarchy but a religious community, guided by divine law and dedicated to the precise fulfillment of the rituals prescribed in the community's sacred texts. And it would be the free choice of men and women to keep or violate that divinely decreed order—rather than the behavior of its kings or the rise and fall of great empires—that would determine the course of Israel's subsequent history. In this extraordinary focus on human responsibility lay the Bible's great power. Other ancient epics would fade over time. The impact of the Bible's story on Western civilization would only grow.

Who Wrote the Pentateuch, and When?

For centuries, Bible readers took it for granted that the scriptures were both divine revelation and accurate history, conveyed directly from God to a wide variety of Israelite sages, prophets, and priests. Established religious authorities, both Jewish and Christian, naturally assumed that the Five

Books of Moses were set down in writing by Moses himself—just before
his death on Mount Nebo as narrated in the book of Deuteronomy. The
books of Joshua, Judges, and Samuel were all regarded as sacred records
preserved by the venerable prophet Samuel at Shiloh, and the books of
Kings were seen as the product of the prophet Jeremiah's pen. Likewise,
King David was believed to be the author of the Psalms, and King
Solomon, of Proverbs and the Song of Solomon. Yet by the dawn of the
modern era, in the seventeenth century, scholars who devoted themselves
to the detailed literary and linguistic study of the Bible found that it was
not quite so simple. The power of logic and reason applied to the text of the
holy scriptures gave rise to some very troubling questions about the Bible's
historical reliability.

The first question was whether Moses could really have been the author
of the Five Books of Moses, since the last book, Deuteronomy, described in
great detail the precise time and circumstances of Moses' own death. Other
incongruities soon became apparent: the biblical text was filled with literary asides, explaining the ancient names of certain places and frequently
noting that the evidences of famous biblical events were still visible "to this
day." These factors convinced some seventeenth century scholars that the
Bible's first five books, at least, had been shaped, expanded, and embellished by later, anonymous editors and revisers over the centuries.

By the late eighteenth century and even more so in the nineteenth,
many critical biblical scholars had begun to doubt that Moses had any
hand in the writing of the Bible whatsoever; they had come to believe that
the Bible was the work of later writers exclusively. These scholars pointed
to what appeared to be different versions of the same stories *within* the
books of the Pentateuch, suggesting that the biblical text was the product
of several recognizable hands. A careful reading of the book of Genesis, for
example, revealed two conflicting versions of the creation (1:1–2:3 and
2:4–25), two quite different genealogies of Adam's offspring (4:17–26 and
5:1–28), and two spliced and rearranged flood stories (6:5–9:17). In addition, there were dozens more doublets and sometimes even triplets of the
same events in the narratives of the wanderings of the patriarchs, the Exodus from Egypt, and the giving of the Law.

Yet there was a clear order in this seemingly chaotic repetition. As observed as early as the nineteenth century (and clearly explained by the

American biblical scholar Richard Elliott Friedman in his book *Who Wrote the Bible?),* the doublets occurring primarily in Genesis, Exodus, and Numbers were not arbitrary variations or duplications of the same stories. They maintained certain readily identifiable characteristics of terminology and geographical focus, and—most conspicuously—used different names in narration to describe the God of Israel. Thus one set of stories consistently used the tetragrammaton—the four-letter name YHWH (assumed by most scholars to have been pronounced *Yahweh*)—in the course of its historical narration and seemed to be most interested in the tribe and territory of Judah in its various accounts. The other set of stories used the names *Elohim* or *El* for God and seemed particularly concerned with the tribes and territories in the north of the country—mainly Ephraim, Manasseh, and Benjamin. In time, it became clear that the doublets derived from two distinct sources, written in different times and different places. Scholars gave the name "J" to the Yahwist source (spelled Jahvist in German) and "E" to the Elohist source.

The distinctive uses of geographical terminology and religious symbols and the roles played by the various tribes in the two sources convinced scholars that the J text was written in Jerusalem and represented the perspective of the united monarchy or the kingdom of Judah, presumably at or soon after the time of King Solomon (c. 970–930 BCE). Likewise, the E text seemed to have been written in the north and represented the perspective of the kingdom of Israel, and would have been composed during the independent life of that kingdom (c. 930–720 BCE). The book of Deuteronomy, in its distinctive message and style, seemed to be an independent document, "D." And among the sections of the Pentateuch that could not be ascribed to J, E, or D were a large number of passages dealing with ritual matters. In time, these came to be considered part of a long treatise called "P," or the Priestly source, which displayed a special interest in purity, cult, and the laws of sacrifice. In other words, scholars gradually came to the conclusion that the first five books of the Bible as we now know them were the result of a complex editorial process in which the four main source documents—J, E, P, and D—were skillfully combined and linked by scribal compilers or "redactors," whose literary traces (called by some scholars "R" passages) consisted of transitional sentences and editorial asides. The latest of these redactions took place in the post-exilic period.

In the last few decades scholarly opinions about the dates and author-
ship of these individual sources have varied wildly. While some scholars
argue that the texts were composed and edited during the existence of the
united monarchy and the kingdoms of Judah and Israel (c. 1000–586 BCE),
others insist that they were late compositions, collected and edited by
priests and scribes during the Babylonian exile and the restoration (in the
sixth and fifth centuries), or even as late as the Hellenistic period
(fourth–second centuries BCE). Yet all agree that the Pentateuch is not a
single, seamless composition but a patchwork of different sources, each
written under different historical circumstances to express different religious or political viewpoints.

Two Versions of Israel's Later History

The first four books of the Bible—Genesis, Exodus, Leviticus, and Numbers—seemed to be the result of a skillful interweaving of the J, E, and P
sources. Yet the fifth, the book of Deuteronomy, was an entirely different
case. It bears a distinctive terminology (shared by none of the other
sources) and contains an uncompromising condemnation of worship of
other gods, a new view of God as completely transcendent, and the ab-
solute prohibition of the sacrificial worship of the God of Israel in any
place but the Temple in Jerusalem. Scholars long ago recognized this book's
possible connection to the otherwise mysterious "book of the Law" discovered by the high priest Hilkiah in the course of renovations to the Temple
during the reign of King Josiah—in 622 BCE. As narrated in 2 Kings
22:8–23:24, this document became the inspiration for a religious reform of
unprecedented severity.

The impact of the book of Deuteronomy on the ultimate message of the
Hebrew Bible goes far beyond its strict legal codes. The connected historical narrative of the books that follow the Pentateuch—Joshua, Judges, 1
and 2 Samuel, 1 and 2 Kings—is so closely related to Deuteronomy lin-
guistically and theologically that it has come to be called by scholars since
the middle of the 1940s the "Deuteronomistic History." This is the second
great literary work on the history of Israel in the Bible. It continues the
story of Israel's destiny from the conquest of the promised land to the
Babylonian exile and expresses the ideology of a new religious movement

that arose among the people of Israel at a relatively late date. This work too was edited more than once. Some scholars argue that it was compiled during the exile in an attempt to preserve the history, culture, and identity of the vanquished nation after the catastrophe of the destruction of Jerusalem. Other scholars suggest that in the main, the Deuteronomistic History was written in the days of King Josiah, to serve his religious ideology and territorial ambitions, and that it was finished and edited a few decades later in exile.

The books of Chronicles—the third great historical work in the Bible, dealing with pre-exilic Israel—were put in writing only in the fifth or fourth century BCE, several centuries after the events they describe. Their historical perspective is sharply slanted in favor of the historical and political claims of the Davidic dynasty and Jerusalem; they almost entirely ignore the north. In many ways Chronicles uniquely reflects the ideology and needs of Second Temple Jerusalem, for the most part reshaping an historical saga that already existed in written form. For these reasons we will make minimal use of Chronicles in this book, keeping our focus on the earlier Pentateuch and Deuteronomistic History.

As we shall see in the coming chapters, archaeology has provided enough evidence to support a new contention that the historical core of the Pentateuch and the Deuteronomistic History was substantially shaped in the seventh century BCE. We will therefore put the spotlight on late eighth and seventh century BCE Judah, when this literary process began in earnest, and shall argue that much of the Pentateuch is a late monarchic creation, advocating the ideology and needs of the kingdom of Judah, and as such is intimately connected to the Deuteronomistic History. And we shall side with the scholars who argue that the Deuteronomistic History was compiled, in the main, in the time of King Josiah, aiming to provide an ideological validation for particular political ambitions and religious reforms.

History, or Not History?

Archaeology has always played a crucial role in the debates about the composition and historical reliability of the Bible. At first, archaeology seemed to refute the more radical critics' contention that the Bible was a rather late composition, and that much of it is unreliable historically. From the end of the nineteenth century, as the modern exploration of the lands of the Bible got underway, a series of spectacular discoveries and decades of steady archaeological excavation and interpretation suggested to many that the Bible's accounts were basically trustworthy in regard to the main outlines of the story of ancient Israel. Thus it seemed that even if the biblical text was set down in writing long after the events it describes, it must have been based on a substantial body of accurately preserved memories. This conclusion was based on several new classes of archaeological and historical evidence.

Geographical Identifications

Although Western pilgrims and explorers had roamed over the land of the Bible since the Byzantine period, it was only with the rise of modern historical and geographical studies, in the late eighteenth and early nineteenth centuries, that scholars well versed in both the Bible and other ancient sources began to reconstruct the landscape of ancient Israel on the basis of topography, biblical references, and archaeological remains, rather than relying on the ecclesiastical traditions of the various holy places. The pioneer in this field was the American Congregationalist minister Edward Robinson, who undertook two long explorations through Ottoman Palestine in 1838 and in 1852, in an effort to refute the theories of the biblical critics by locating and identifying authentic, historically verified biblical sites.

While some of the main locales of Biblical history, such as Jerusalem, Hebron, Jaffa, Beth-shean, and Gaza, had never been forgotten, hundreds of additional places mentioned in the Bible were unknown. By using the geographical information contained in the Bible and carefully studying the modern Arabic place-names of the country, Robinson found it was possible to identify dozens of ancient mounds and ruins with previously forgotten biblical sites.

Robinson and his successors were able to identify the extensive ruins at places like el-Jib, Beitin, and Seilun, all north of Jerusalem, as the likely sites of biblical Gibeon, Bethel, and Shiloh. This process was particularly effective in regions that had been inhabited continuously throughout the centuries and where the site's name had been preserved. Yet subsequent generations of scholars realized that in other places, where the modern names bore no relation to those of biblical sites in the vicinity, other criteria such as size and datable pottery types could be utilized to make identifications. Thus Megiddo, Hazor, Lachish, and dozens of other biblical locations were gradually added to the evolving reconstruction of biblical geography. In the late nineteenth century, the British Royal Engineers of the Palestine Exploration Fund undertook this work in a highly systematic manner, compiling detailed topographical maps of the entire country, from the sources of the Jordan River in the north to Beersheba in the Negev in the south.

More important even than the specific identifications was the growing familiarity with the major geographical regions of the land of the Bible (Figure 2): the broad and fertile coastal plain of the Mediterranean, the foothills of the Shephelah rising to the central hill country in the south, the arid Negev, the Dead Sea region and Jordan valley, the northern hill country, and the broad valleys in the north. The biblical land of Israel was an area with extraordinary climatic and environmental contrasts. It also served as a natural land bridge between the two great civilizations of Egypt and Mesopotamia. Its characteristic landscapes and conditions proved in virtually every case to be reflected quite accurately in the descriptions of the biblical narrative.

Monuments and Archives from Egypt and Mesopotamia

During the Middle Ages and the Renaissance, repeated attempts were made to establish a standard chronology for the events described in the Bible. Most were dutifully literal. Outside sources were needed to verify the Bible's inner chronology, and they were eventually found among the archaeological remains of two of the most important—and most literate— civilizations of the ancient world.

Egypt, with its awesome monuments and vast treasure of hieroglyphic inscriptions, began to be intensively explored by European scholars in the late eighteenth century. But it was only with the decipherment of Egyptian hieroglyphics (on the basis of the trilingual Rosetta Stone) by the French scholar Jean-François Champollion in the 1820s that the historical value of Egyptian remains for dating and possibly verifying historical events in the

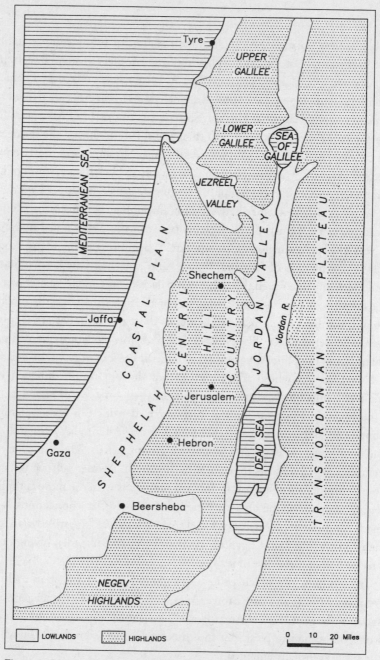

Figure 2: Geographical zones of the Land of Israel.

Bible became apparent. Although identification of the specific pharaohs mentioned in the stories of Joseph and of the Exodus remained uncertain, other direct connections became clear. A victory stele erected by Pharaoh Merneptah in 1207 BCE mentioned a great victory over a people named Israel. In a slightly later era, Pharaoh Shishak (mentioned in 1 Kings 14:25 as having come up against Jerusalem to demand tribute during the fifth year of the reign of Solomon's son) was identified as Sheshonq I of the Twenty-second Dynasty, who ruled from 945 to 924 BCE. He left an account of his campaign on a wall in the temple of Amun at Karnak, in Upper Egypt.

Another rich source of discoveries for chronology and historical identifications came from the broad plains between the Tigris and Euphrates Rivers, the ancient region of Mesopotamia. Beginning in the 1840s, scholarly representatives of England, France, and eventually the United States and Germany uncovered the cities, vast palaces, and cuneiform archives of the empires of Assyria and Babylonia. For the first time since the biblical period, the main monuments and cities of those powerful Eastern empires were uncovered. Places like Nineveh and Babylon, previously known primarily from the Bible, were now seen to be the capitals of powerful and aggressive empires whose artists and scribes thoroughly documented the military campaigns and political events of their time. Thus references to a number of important biblical kings were identified in Mesopotamian cuneiform archives—the Israelite kings Omri, Ahab, and Jehu and the Judahite kings Hezekiah and Manasseh, among others. These outside references allowed scholars to see biblical history in a wider perspective, and to synchronize the reigns of the biblical monarchs with the more complete dating systems of the ancient Near East. Slowly the connections were made, and the regnal dates of Israelite and Judahite kings, Assyrian and Babylonian rulers, and Egyptian pharaohs were set in order, giving quite precise dates for the first time.

In addition, the much earlier Mesopotamian and Egyptian archives from the Middle and Late Bronze Ages (c. 2000–1150 BCE) at ancient sites such as Mari, and Tell el-Amarna and Nuzi, shed important light on the world of the ancient Near East and thus on the cultural milieu from which the Bible eventually emerged.

Scattered inscriptions would also be found in areas closer to the land of Israel that offered even more specific links. A triumphal description by the

Moabite king Mesha, discovered in the nineteenth century in Transjordan, mentioned Mesha's victory over the armies of Israel and provided an outside testimony to a war between Israel and Moab that was reported in 2 Kings 3:4–27. The single most significant inscription for historical validation was discovered in 1993 at the site of Tel Dan in northern Israel, apparently recording the victory of the Aramean king Hazael over the king of Israel and the king of the "house of David" in the ninth century BCE. Like the Moabite inscription, it provides an extrabiblical anchor for the history of ancient Israel.

Excavations of Biblical Sites

By far the most important source of evidence about the historical context of the Bible has come from more than a hundred years of modern archaeological excavations in Israel, Jordan, and the neighboring regions. Closely tied to advances in archaeological technique worldwide, biblical archaeology has been able to identify a long sequence of readily datable architectural styles, pottery forms, and other artifacts that enable scholars to date buried city levels and tombs with a fair degree of accuracy. Pioneered by the American scholar William F. Albright in the early twentieth century, this branch of archaeology concentrated mostly on the excavation of large city mounds (called "tells" in Arabic, "tels" in Hebrew), composed of many superimposed city levels, in which the development of society and culture can be traced over millennia.

After decades of excavation, researchers have been able to reconstruct the vast archaeological context into which biblical history must be fit (Figure 3). Beginning with the first evidence of agriculture and settled communities in the region at the very end of the Stone Age, archaeologists have gone on to delineate the rise of urban civilization in the Bronze Age (3500–1150 BCE) and its transformation into territorial states in the succeeding period, the Iron Age (1150–586 BCE), when most of the historical events described in the Bible presumably occurred.

By the end of the twentieth century, archaeology had shown that there were simply too many material correspondences between the finds in Israel and in the entire Near East and the world described in the Bible to suggest that the Bible was late and fanciful priestly literature, written with no his-

ARCHAEOLOGICAL PERIODS*

Early Bronze Age	3500–2200 BCE
Intermediate Bronze Age	2200–2000 BCE
Middle Bronze Age	2000–1550 BCE
Late Bronze Age	1550–1150 BCE
Iron Age I	1150–900 BCE
Iron Age II	900–586 BCE
Babylonian Period	586–538 BCE
Persian Period	538–333 BCE

* The dates follow the system in this book. Dates for the Early Bronze through the Middle Bronze Ages are approximate and depend mainly on cultural considerations. Dates for the Late Bronze Age through the Persian Period depend in the main on historical events.

KINGS OF ISRAEL AND JUDAH*

Saul ca. 1025–1005 BCE
David ca. 1005–970
Solomon ca. 970–931

Judah		Israel	
Rehoboam	931–914	Jeroboam I	931–909
Abijam	914–911	Nadab	909–908
Asa	911–870	Baasha	908–885
Jehoshaphat	870–846**	Elah	885–884
Jehoram	851–843**	Zimri	884
Ahaziah	843–842	Tibni	884–880***
Athaliah	842–836	Omri	884–873
Jehoash	836–798	Ahab	873–852
Amaziah	798–769	Ahaziah	852–851
Azariah	785–733**	Joram	851–842
Jotham	743–729**	Jehu	842–814
Ahaz	743–727**	Jehoahaz	817–800**
Hezekiah	727–698	Joash	800–784
Manasseh	698–642	Jeroboam II	788–747**
Amon	641–640	Zechariah	747
Josiah	639–609	Shallum	747
Jehoahaz	609	Menahem	747–737
Jehoiakim	608–598	Pekahiah	737–735
Jehoiachin	597	Pekah	735–732
Zedekiah	596–586	Hoshea	732–724

* According to the *Anchor Bible Dictionary*, Volume I, Page 1010 and Galil's *The Chronology of the Kings of Israel and Judah*.
** Including coregencies.
*** Rival rule

Figure 3: Main archaeological periods and the chronology of Judahite and Israelite kings.

torical basis at all. But at the same time there were too many contradictions between archaeological finds and the biblical narratives to suggest that the Bible provided a precise description of what actually occurred.

From Biblical Illustration to the Anthropology of Ancient Israel

So long as the biblical textual critics and the biblical archaeologists maintained their basically conflicting attitudes about the historical reliability of the Bible, they continued to live in two separate intellectual worlds. The textual critics continued to view the Bible as an object of dissection that could be split up into ever tinier sources and subsources according to the distinctive religious or political ideas each was supposed to express. At the same time, the archaeologists often took the historical narratives of the Bible at face value. Instead of using archaeological data as an independent source for the reconstruction of the history of the region, they continued to rely on the biblical narratives—particularly the traditions of the rise of Israel—to interpret their finds. Of course, there were new understandings of the rise and development of Israel as the excavations and surveys proceeded. Questions were raised about the historical existence of the patriarchs and on the date and scale of the Exodus. New theories were also developed to suggest that the Israelite conquest of Canaan may not have occurred, as the book of Joshua insists, as a unified military campaign. But for biblical events beginning at the time of David—around 1000 BCE— the archaeological consensus, at least until the 1990s, was that the Bible could be read as a basically reliable historical document.

By the 1970s, however, new trends began to influence the conduct of biblical archaeology and eventually to change its major focus and completely reverse the traditional relationship between artifact and biblical text. For the first time, archaeologists working in the lands of the Bible did not seek to use excavated finds as illustrations of the Bible; in a dramatic shift to the methods of the social sciences, they sought to examine the human realities that lay *behind* the text. In excavating ancient sites, emphasis was no longer put only on a site's biblical associations. Excavated artifacts, architecture, and settlement patterns, as well as animal bones, seeds, chemical analysis of soil samples, and long-term anthropological models drawn from many world cultures, became the keys to perceiving wider changes in the economy, political history, religious practices, population density, and the very structure of ancient Israelite society. Adopting methods used by archaeologists and anthropologists in other regions, a growing number of scholars attempted to understand how human interaction with the complex, fragmented natural environment of the land of Israel influenced the development of its unique social system, religion, and spiritual legacy.

A New Vision of Biblical History

Recent developments in archaeology have finally allowed us to bridge the gap between the study of biblical texts and the archaeological finds. We can now see that the Bible is—along with distinctive pottery forms, architectural styles, and Hebrew inscriptions—a characteristic artifact that tells a great deal about the society in which it was produced.

That is because it is now clear that phenomena like record keeping, administrative correspondence, royal chronicles, and the compiling of a national scripture—especially one as profound and sophisticated as the Bible—are linked to a particular stage of social development. Archaeologists and anthropologists working all over the world have carefully studied the context in which sophisticated genres of writing emerge, and in almost every case they are a sign of state formation, in which power is centralized in national institutions like an official cult or monarchy. Other traits of this stage of social development include monumental building, economic specialization, and the presence of a dense network of interlocked communities ranging in size from large cities to regional centers to medium-sized towns and small villages.

Until recently both textual scholars and archaeologists have assumed that ancient Israel reached the stage of full state formation at the time of the united monarchy of David and Solomon. Indeed, many biblical specialists continue to believe that the earliest source of the Pentateuch is the J, or Yahwist, document—and that it was compiled in Judah in the era of David and Solomon, in the tenth century BCE. We will argue in this book that such a conclusion is highly unlikely. From an analysis of the archaeological evidence, there is no sign whatsoever of extensive literacy or any other attributes of full statehood in Judah—and in particular, in Jerusalem—until more than two and a half centuries later, toward the end of the eighth century BCE. Of course, no archaeologist can deny that the Bible contains legends, characters, and story fragments that reach far back in time. But archaeology can show that the Torah and the Deuteronomistic History bear unmistakable hallmarks of their initial compilation in the seventh century BCE. Why this is so and what it means for our understanding of the great biblical saga is the main subject of this book.

We will see how much of the biblical narrative is a product of the hopes, fears, and ambitions of the kingdom of Judah, culminating in the reign of King Josiah at the end of the seventh century BCE. We will argue that the historical core of the Bible arose from clear political, social, and spiritual conditions and was shaped by the creativity and vision of extraordinary women and men. Much of what is commonly taken for granted as accurate history—the stories of the patriarchs, the Exodus, the conquest of Canaan, and even the saga of the glorious united monarchy of David and Solomon—are, rather, the creative expressions of a powerful religious reform movement that flourished in the kingdom of Judah in the Late Iron Age. Although these stories may have been based on certain historical kernels, they primarily reflect the ideology and the world-view of the writers. We will show how the narrative of the Bible was uniquely suited to further the religious reform and territorial ambitions of Judah during the momentous concluding decades of the seventh century BCE.

But suggesting that the most famous stories of the Bible did not happen as the Bible records them is far from implying that ancient Israel had no genuine history. In the following chapters we will reconstruct the history of ancient Israel on the basis of archaeological evidence—the only source of information on the biblical period that was not extensively emended, edited, or censored by many generations of biblical scribes. Assisted by archaeological finds and extrabiblical records, we will see how the biblical narratives are themselves part of the story, not the unquestioned historical framework into which every particular find or conclusion must fit. Our story will depart dramatically from the familiar biblical narrative. It is a story not of one, but *two* chosen kingdoms, which together comprise the historical roots of the people of Israel.

One kingdom—the kingdom of Israel—was born in the fertile valleys and rolling hills of northern Israel and grew to be among the richest, most cosmopolitan, and most powerful in the region. Today it is almost totally forgotten, except for the villainous role it plays in the biblical books of Kings. The other kingdom—the kingdom of Judah—arose in the rocky, inhospitable southern hill country. It survived by maintaining its isolation and fierce devotion to its Temple and royal dynasty. These two kingdoms represent two sides of ancient Israel's experience, two quite different societies with different attitudes and national identities. Step by step we will trace the stages by which the history, memory, and hopes of both kingdoms were merged powerfully into a single scripture, that, more than any other document ever written, shaped—and continues to shape—the face of Western society.

PART ONE

The Bible as History?

Searching for the Patriarchs

In the beginning was a single family, with a special relationship to God. In time, that family was fruitful and multiplied greatly, growing into the people of Israel. That is the first great saga of the Bible, a tale of immigrant dreams and divine promises that serves as a colorful and inspiring overture to the subsequent history of the nation of Israel. Abraham was the first of the patriarchs and the recipient of a divine promise of land and plentiful descendants that was carried forward across the generations by his son Isaac, and Isaac's son Jacob, also known as Israel. Among Jacob's twelve sons, each of whom would become the patriarch of a tribe of Israel, Judah is given the special honor of ruling them all.

The biblical account of the life of the patriarchs is a brilliant story of both family and nation. It derives its emotional power from being the record of the profound human struggles of fathers, mothers, husbands, wives, daughters, and sons. In some ways it is a typical family story, with all its joy and sadness, love and hatred, deceit and cunning, famine and prosperity. It is also a universal, philosophical story about the relationship between God and humanity; about devotion and obedience; about right and wrong; about faith, piety, and immorality. It is the story of God choosing a nation; of God's eternal promise of land, prosperity, and growth.

From almost every standpoint—historical, psychological, spiritual—

the patriarchal narratives are powerful literary achievements. But are they reliable annals of the birth of the people of Israel? Is there any evidence that patriarchs Abraham, Isaac, and Jacob—and matriarchs Sarah, Rebecca, Leah, and Rachel—actually lived?

A Saga of Four Generations

The book of Genesis describes Abraham as the archetypal man of faith and family patriarch, originally coming from Ur in southern Mesopotamia and resettling with his family in the town of Haran, on one of the tributaries of the upper Euphrates (Figure 4). It is there that God appeared to him and commanded him, "Go from your country and your kindred and your father's house to the land I will show you. And I will make of you a great nation, and I will bless you and make your name great so that you will be a blessing" (Genesis 12: 1–2). Obeying God's words, Abram (as he was then called) took his wife, Sarai, and his nephew Lot, and departed for Canaan. He wandered with his flocks among the central hill country, moving mainly between Shechem in the north, Bethel (near Jerusalem), and Hebron in the south, but also moving into the Negev, farther south (Figure 5).

During his travels, Abram built altars to God in several places and gradually discovered the true nature of his destiny. God promised Abram and his descendants all the lands from "the river of Egypt to the great river, the river Euphrates" (Genesis 15:18). And to signify his role as the patriarch of many people, God changed Abram's name to Abraham—"for I have made you the father of a multitude of nations" (Genesis 17:5). He also changed his wife Sarai's name to Sarah to signify that her status had changed as well.

The family of Abraham was the source of all the nations of the region. During the course of their wandering in Canaan, the shepherds of Abraham and the shepherds of Lot began to quarrel. In order to avoid further family conflict, Abraham and Lot decided to partition the land. Abraham and his people remained in the western highlands while Lot and his family went eastward to the Jordan valley and settled in Sodom near the Dead Sea. The people of Sodom and the nearby city of Gomorrah proved to be wicked and treacherous, but God rained brimstone and fire on the sinful cities, utterly destroying them. Lot then went off on his own to the eastern hills to become the ancestor of the Transjordanian peoples of Moab and

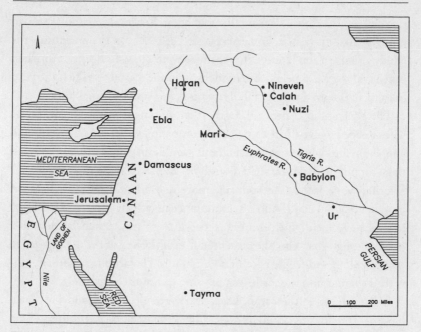

Figure 4: Mesopotamian and other ancient Near Eastern sites connected with the patriarchal narratives.

Ammon. Abraham also became the father of several other ancient peoples. Since his wife, Sarah, at her advanced age of ninety, could not produce children, Abraham took as his concubine Hagar, Sarah's Egyptian slave. Together they had a child named Ishmael, who would in time become the ancestor of all the Arab peoples of the southern wilderness.

Most important of all for the biblical narrative, God promised Abraham another child, and his beloved wife, Sarah, miraculously gave birth to a son, Isaac, when Abraham was a hundred years old. One of the most powerful images in the Bible occurs when God confronts Abraham with the ultimate test of his faith, commanding him to sacrifice his beloved son Isaac on a mountain in the land of Moriah. God halted the sacrifice but rewarded Abraham's display of faithfulness by renewing his covenant. Not only would Abraham's descendants grow into a great nation—as numerous as the stars in the heavens and the sand on the seashore—but in the future all the nations of the world would bless themselves by them.

Isaac grew to maturity and wandered with his own flocks near the southern city of Beersheba, eventually marrying Rebecca, a young woman brought from his father's homeland far to the north. In the meantime, the family's roots in the land of the promise were growing deeper. Abraham purchased the Machpelah cave in Hebron in the southern hill country for burying his beloved wife, Sarah. He would also later be buried there.

The generations continued. In their encampment in the Negev, Isaac's wife, Rebecca, gave birth to twins of completely different characters and temperaments, whose own descendants would carry on a struggle between them for hundreds of years. Esau, a mighty hunter, was the elder and Isaac's favorite, while Jacob, the younger, more delicate and sensitive, was his mother's beloved child. And even though Esau was the elder, and the legitimate heir to the divine promise, Rebecca disguised her son Jacob with a cloak of rough goatskin. She presented him at the bed of the dying Isaac so that the blind and feeble patriarch would mistake Jacob for Esau and unwittingly grant him the birthright blessing due to the elder son.

On returning to the camp, Esau discovered the ruse—and the stolen blessing. But nothing could be done. His aged father, Isaac, promised Esau only that he would become the father of the desert-dwelling Edomites: "Behold, away from the fatness of the earth your dwelling shall be" (Genesis 27:39). Thus another of the peoples of the region was established and in time, as Genesis 28:9 reveals, Esau would take a wife from the family of his uncle Ishmael and beget yet other desert tribes. And these tribes would always be in conflict with the Israelites—namely, the descendants of his brother, Jacob, who snatched the divine birthright from him.

Jacob soon fled from the wrath of his aggrieved brother and journeyed far to the north to the house of his uncle Laban in Haran, to find a wife for himself. On his way north God confirmed Jacob's inheritance. At Bethel Jacob stopped for a night's rest and dreamed of a ladder set up on the earth, with its top reaching heaven and angels of God going up and down. Standing above the ladder, God renewed the promise he had given Abraham:

I am the LORD, the God of Abraham your father and the God of Isaac; the land on which you lie I will give to you and to your descendants; and your descendants shall be like the dust of the earth, and you shall spread abroad to the west and to the east and to the north and to the south; and by you and your descendants shall all the families of the earth bless themselves. Behold, I am with you and will keep you wherever you go, and will bring you back to this land; for I will not leave you until I have done that of which I have spoken to you. (GENESIS 28:13–15)

Jacob continued northward to Haran and stayed with Laban several years, marrying his two daughters, Leah and Rachel, and fathering eleven sons—Reuben, Simeon, Levi, Judah, Dan, Naphtali, Gad, Asher, Issachar, Zebulun, and Joseph—from his two wives and from their two maid-servants. God then commanded Jacob to return to Canaan with his family. Yet on his way, while crossing the river Jabbok in Transjordan, he was forced to wrestle with a mysterious figure. Whether it was an angel or God, the mysterious figure changed Jacob's name to Israel (literally, "He who struggled with God"), "for you have striven with God and with men, and have prevailed" (Genesis 32:28). Jacob then returned to Canaan, setting up an encampment near Shechem and building an altar at Bethel—in the same place where God had revealed himself to him on his way to Haran. As they moved farther south, Rachel died in childbirth near Bethlehem as she gave birth to Benjamin, the last of Jacob's sons. Soon afterward Jacob's father, Isaac, died and was buried in the cave of Machpelah in Hebron.

Slowly the family was becoming a clan on the way to becoming a nation. Yet the children of Israel were at this stage still a family of squabbling brothers, among whom Joseph, Jacob's favored son, was detested by all the others because of his bizarre dreams that predicted he would reign over his family. Though most of the brothers wanted to murder him, Reuben and Judah dissuaded them. Instead of slaying Joseph, the brothers sold him to a group of Ishmaelite merchants going down to Egypt with a caravan of camels. The brothers feigned sadness and explained to the patriarch Jacob that a wild beast had devoured Joseph. Jacob mourned his beloved son.

But Joseph's great destiny would not be averted by his brothers' jealousy. Settling in Egypt, he rose quickly in wealth and status because of his ex-traordinary abilities. After interpreting a dream of the pharaoh predicting seven good years followed by seven bad years, he was appointed the pharaoh's grand vizier. In that high position he reorganized the economy of Egypt by storing surplus food from good years for future bad years. Indeed, when the bad years finally commenced, Egypt was well prepared. In nearby Canaan, Jacob and his sons suffered from famine and Jacob sent ten of his eleven remaining sons to Egypt for food. In Egypt, they went to see the

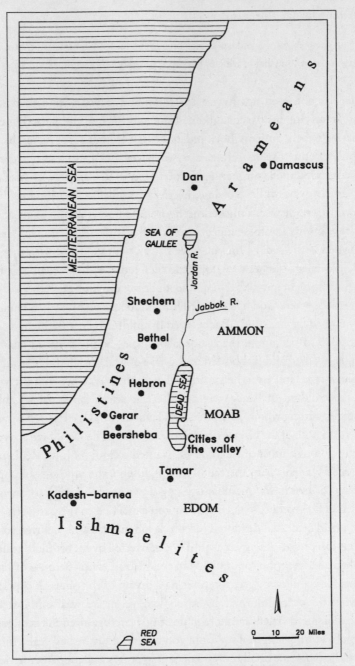

Figure 5: Main places and peoples in Canaan mentioned in the Patriarchal narratives.

vizier Joseph—now grown to adulthood. Jacob's sons did not recognize their long-lost brother and Joseph did not initially reveal his identity to them. Then, in a moving scene, Joseph revealed to them that he was the scorned brother whom they sold away into slavery.

The children of Israel were at last reunited, and the aged patriarch Jacob came to live with his entire family near his great son, in the land of Goshen. On his deathbed, Jacob blessed his sons and his two grandsons, Joseph's sons Manasseh and Ephraim. Of all the honors, Judah received the royal birthright:

> Judah, your brothers shall praise you; your hand shall be on the neck of your enemies; your father's sons shall bow down before you. Judah is a lion's whelp; from the prey, my son, you have gone up. He stooped down, he couched as a lion, and as a lioness; who dares rouse him up? The scepter shall not depart from Judah, nor the ruler's staff from between his feet, until he comes to whom it belongs; and to him shall be the obedience of the peoples. (GENESIS 49:8–10)

And after the death of Jacob, his body was taken back to Canaan—to the territory that would someday become Judah's tribal inheritance—and was buried by his sons in the cave of Machpelah in Hebron. Joseph died too, and the children of Israel remained in Egypt where the next chapter of their history as a nation would unfold.

The Failed Search for the Historical Abraham

Before we describe the likely time and historical circumstances in which the Bible's patriarchal narrative was initially woven together from earlier sources, it is important to explain why so many scholars over the last hundred years have been convinced that the patriarchal narratives were at least in outline historically true. The pastoral lifestyle of the patriarchs seemed to mesh well in very general terms with what early twentieth century archaeologists observed of contemporary bedouin life in the Middle East. The scholarly idea that the bedouin way of life was essentially unchanged over millennia lent an air of verisimilitude to the biblical tales of wealth measured in sheep and goats (Genesis 30:30–43), clan conflicts with settled villagers over watering wells (Genesis 21:25–33), and disputes over grazing lands (Genesis 13:5–12). In addition, the conspicuous references to Meso-

potamian and Syrian sites like Abraham's birthplace, Ur, and Haran on a
tributary of the Euphrates (where most of Abraham's family continued to
live after his migration to Canaan) seemed to correspond with the findings
of archaeological excavations in the eastern arc of the Fertile Crescent,
where some of the earliest centers of ancient Near Eastern civilization had
been found.

Yet there was something much deeper, much more intimately connected with modern religious belief, that motivated the scholarly search for
the "historical" patriarchs. Many of the early biblical archaeologists had
been trained as clerics or theologians. They were persuaded by their faith
that God's promise to Abraham, Isaac, and Jacob—the birthright of the
Jewish people and the birthright passed on to Christians, as the apostle
Paul explained in his letter to the Galatians—was real. And if it was real, it
was presumably given to real people, not imaginary creations of some
anonymous ancient scribe's pen.

The French Dominican biblical scholar and archaeologist Roland de
Vaux noted, for example, that "if the historical faith of Israel is not founded
in history, such faith is erroneous, and therefore, our faith is also." And the
doyen of American biblical archaeology, William F. Albright, echoed the
sentiment, insisting that "as a whole, the picture in Genesis is historical,
and there is no reason to doubt the general accuracy of the biographical details." Indeed, from the early decades of the twentieth century, with the
great discoveries in Mesopotamia and the intensification of archaeological
activity in Palestine, many biblical historians and archaeologists were convinced that new discoveries could make it likely—if not completely
prove—that the patriarchs were historical figures. They argued that the
biblical narratives, even if compiled at a relatively late date such as the period of the united monarchy, preserved at least the main outlines of an authentic, ancient historical reality.

Indeed, the Bible provided a great deal of specific chronological information that might help, first of all, pinpoint exactly when the patriarchs lived.
The Bible narrates the earliest history of Israel in sequential order, from the
patriarchs to Egypt, to Exodus, to the wandering in the desert, to the conquest of Canaan, to the period of the judges, and to the establishment of the
monarchy. It also provided a key to calculating specific dates. The most important clue is the note in 1 Kings 6:1 that the Exodus took place four-

hundred eighty years before the construction of the Temple began in Jerusalem, in the fourth year of the reign of Solomon. Furthermore, Exodus 12:40 states that the Israelites endured four-hundred thirty years of slavery in Egypt *before* the Exodus. Adding a bit over two hundred years for the overlapping life spans of the patriarchs in Canaan before the Israelites left for Egypt, we arrive at a biblical date of around 2100 BCE for Abraham's original departure for Canaan.

Of course, there were some clear problems with accepting this dating for precise historical reconstruction, not the least of which were the extraordinarily long life spans of Abraham, Isaac, and Jacob, which all far exceeded a hundred years. In addition, the later genealogies that traced Jacob's descendants were confusing, if not plainly contradictory. Moses and Aaron, for example, were identified as *fourth*-generation descendants of Jacob's son Levi, while Joshua, a contemporary of Moses and Aaron, was declared to be a *twelfth* generation descendant of Joseph, another of Jacob's sons. This was hardly a minor discrepancy.

The American scholar Albright, however, argued that certain unique details in the stories in Genesis might hold the key to verifying their historical basis. Elements such as personal names, unusual marriage customs, and land-purchase laws might be identified in the records of second millennium BCE Mesopotamian societies, from which the patriarchs reportedly came. No less important, the patriarchs were realistically described as carrying on a bedouin lifestyle, moving with their flocks throughout the central hill country of Canaan, between Shechem, Bethel, Beersheba, and Hebron. All these elements convinced Albright that the age of the patriarchs was a real one. He and his colleagues thus began to search for evidence for the presence of pastoral groups of Mesopotamian origin roaming throughout Canaan around 2000 BCE.

Yet the search for the historical patriarchs was ultimately unsuccessful, since none of the periods around the biblically suggested date provided a completely compatible background to the biblical stories. (See Appendix A for additional details.) The assumed westward migration of groups from Mesopotamia toward Canaan—the so-called Amorite migration, in which Albright placed the arrival of Abraham and his family—was later shown to be illusory. Archaeology completely disproved the contention that a sudden, massive population movement had taken place at that time.

And the seeming parallels between Mesopotamian laws and customs of the second millennium BCE and those described in the patriarchal narratives were so general that they could apply to almost any period in ancient Near Eastern history. Juggling dates did not help the matter. Subsequent attempts by de Vaux to place the narratives of the patriarchs in the Middle Bronze Age (2000–1550 BCE), by the American scholars Speiser and Gordon to place them against the background of a fifteenth century BCE archive found in Nuzi in northern Iraq, and by the Israeli biblical historian Benjamin Mazar to place them in the Early Iron Age also failed to establish a convincing link. The highlighted parallels were so general that they could be found in many periods.

The whole enterprise created something of a vicious circle. Scholarly theories about the age of the patriarchs (whose historical existence was never doubted) changed, according to the discoveries, from the mid-third millennium BCE to the late third millennium, to the early second millennium, to the mid-second millennium, to the Early Iron Age. The main problem was that the scholars who accepted the biblical accounts as reliable mistakenly believed that the patriarchal age must be seen, one way or the other, as the earliest phase in a *sequential* history of Israel.

Some Telltale Anachronisms

The critical textual scholars who had identified distinct sources underlying the text of Genesis insisted that the patriarchal narratives were put into writing at a relatively late date, at the time of the monarchy (tenth–eighth centuries BCE) or even later, in exilic and post-exilic days (sixth–fifth centuries BCE). The German biblical scholar Julius Wellhausen argued that the stories of the patriarchs in both the J and E documents reflected the concerns of the later Israelite monarchy, which were projected onto the lives of legendary fathers in a largely mythical past. The biblical stories should thus be regarded as a national mythology with no more historical basis than the Homeric saga of Odysseus's travels or Virgil's saga of Aeneas's founding of Rome.

In more recent decades, the American biblical scholars John Van Seters and Thomas Thompson further challenged the supposed archaeological evidence for the historical patriarchs in the second millennium BCE. They argued that even if the later texts contained some early traditions, the selection and arrangement of stories expressed a clear message by the biblical editors at the time of compilation, rather than preserving a reliable historical account.

But when did that compilation take place? The biblical text reveals some clear clues that can narrow down the time of its final composition. Take the repeated mention of camels, for instance. The stories of the patriarchs are packed with camels, usually herds of camels; but as in the story of Joseph's sale by his brothers into slavery (Genesis 37:25), camels are also described as beasts of burden used in caravan trade. We now know through archaeological research that camels were not domesticated as beasts of burden earlier than the late second millennium and were not widely used in that capacity in the ancient Near East until well after 1000 BCE. And an even more telling detail—the camel caravan carrying "gum, balm, and myrrh," in the Joseph story—reveals an obvious familiarity with the main products of the lucrative Arabian trade that flourished under the supervision of the Assyrian empire in the eighth–seventh centuries BCE.

Indeed, excavations at the site of Tell Jemmeh in the southern coastal plain of Israel—a particularly important entrepôt on the main caravan route between Arabia and the Mediterranean—revealed a dramatic increase in the number of camel bones in the seventh century. The bones were almost exclusively of mature animals, suggesting that they were from traveling beasts of burden, not from locally raised herds (among which the bones of young animals would also be found). Indeed, precisely at this time, Assyrian sources describe camels being used as pack animals in caravans. It was only then that camels became a common enough feature of the landscape to be included as an incidental detail in a literary narrative.

Then there is the issue of the Philistines. We hear of them in connection with Isaac's encounter with "Abimelech, king of the Philistines," at the city of Gerar (Genesis 26:1). The Philistines, a group of migrants from the Aegean or eastern Mediterranean, had not established their settlements along the coastal plain of Canaan until sometime after 1200 BCE. Their cities prospered in the eleventh and tenth centuries and continued to dominate the area well into the Assyrian period. The mention of Gerar as a Philistine city in the narratives of Isaac and the mention of the city (without the Philistine attribution) in the stories of Abraham (Genesis 20:1) suggest that it had a special importance or at least was widely known at the time of the composition of the patriarchal narratives. Gerar is today identified with Tel Haror northwest of Beersheba, and excavations there have shown that in the Iron Age I—the early phase of Philistine history—it was no more than a small, quite insignificant village. But by the late eighth and seventh century BCE, it had become a strong, heavily fortified Assyrian administrative stronghold in the south, an obvious landmark.

Were these incongruous details merely late insertions into early traditions or were they indications that *both* the details and the narrative were late? Many scholars—particularly those who supported the idea of the "historical" patriarchs—considered them to be incidental details. But as Thomas Thompson put it as early as the 1970s, the specific references in the text to cities, neighboring peoples, and familiar places are precisely those aspects that distinguish the patriarchal stories from completely mythical folk-tales. They are crucially important for identifying the date and message of the text. In other words, the "anachronisms" are far more important for dating and understanding the meaning and historical context of the stories of the patriarchs than the search for ancient bedouin or mathematical calculations of the patriarchs' ages and genealogies.

So the combination of camels, Arabian goods, Philistines, and Gerar—as well as other places and nations mentioned in the patriarchal stories in Genesis—are highly significant. All the clues point to a time of composition many centuries after the time in which the Bible reports the lives of the patriarchs took place. These and other anachronisms suggest an intensive period of writing the patriarchal narratives in the eighth and seventh centuries BCE.

A Living Map of the Ancient Near East

It becomes evident when we begin to examine the genealogies of the patriarchs and the many nations that arose from their trysts, marriages, and family relations, that they offer a colorful human map of the ancient Near East from the unmistakable viewpoint of the kingdom of Israel and the kingdom of Judah in the eighth and seventh centuries BCE. These stories offer a highly sophisticated commentary on political affairs in this region in the Assyrian and Neo-Babylonian periods. Not only can many of the ethnic terms and place-names be dated to this time, but their characterizations mesh perfectly with what we know of the relationships of neighboring peoples and kingdoms with Judah and Israel.

Let us start with the Arameans, who dominate the stories of Jacob's marriage with Leah and Rachel and his relationship with his uncle Laban. The Arameans are not mentioned as a distinct ethnic group in ancient Near Eastern texts before c. 1100 BCE. They became a dominant factor on the northern borders of the Israelites in the early ninth century BCE, when a number of Aramean kingdoms arose throughout the area of modern Syria. Among them, the kingdom of Aram-Damascus was a sometime ally, sometime rival of the kingdom of Israel for control of the rich agricultural territories that lay between their main centers—in the upper Jordan valley and Galilee. And, in fact, the cycle of stories about Jacob and Laban metaphorically expresses the complex and often stormy relations between Aram and Israel over many centuries.

On the one hand, Israel and Aram were frequent military rivals. On the other, much of the population of the northern territories of the kingdom of Israel seems to have been Aramean in origin. Thus, the book of Deuteronomy goes so far as to describe Jacob as "a wandering Aramean" (26:5), and the stories of the relations between the individual patriarchs and their Aramean cousins clearly express the consciousness of shared origins. The biblical description of the tensions between Jacob and Laban and their eventual establishment of a boundary stone east of the Jordan to mark the border between their peoples (Genesis 31:51–54, significantly an E, or "northern," story) reflects the territorial partition between Aram and Israel in the ninth–eighth centuries BCE.

The relationships of Israel and Judah with their eastern neighbors are also clearly reflected in the patriarchal narratives. Through the eighth and seventh centuries BCE their contacts with the kingdoms of Ammon and Moab had often been hostile; Israel, in fact, dominated Moab in the early ninth century BCE. It is therefore highly significant—and amusing—how the neighbors to the east are disparaged in the patriarchal genealogies. Genesis 19:30–38 (significantly, a J text) informs us that those nations were born from an incestuous union. After God overthrew the cities of Sodom and Gomorrah, Lot and his two daughters sought shelter in a cave in the hills. The daughters, unable to find proper husbands in their isolated situation—and desperate to have children—served wine to their father until he became drunk. They then lay with him and eventually gave birth to two sons: Moab and Ammon. No seventh century Judahite looking across the Dead Sea toward the rival kingdoms would have been able to suppress a smile of contempt at a story of such a disreputable ancestry.

The biblical stories of the two brothers Jacob and Esau provide an even clearer case of seventh century perceptions presented in ancient costume. Genesis 25 and 27 (southern, J texts) tell us about the twins—Esau and Jacob—who are about to be born to Isaac and Rebecca. God says to the pregnant Rebecca: "Two nations are in your womb, and two peoples, born of you, shall be divided; the one shall be stronger than the other, the elder shall serve the younger" (25:23). As events unfold, we learn that Esau is the elder and Jacob the younger. Hence the description of the two brothers, the fathers of Edom and Israel, serves as a divine legitimation for the political relationship between the two nations in late monarchic times. Jacob-Israel is sensitive and cultured, while Esau-Edom is a more primitive hunter and man of the outdoors. But Edom did not exist as a distinct political entity until a relatively late period. From the Assyrian sources we know that there were no real kings and no state in Edom before the late eighth century BCE. Edom appears in ancient records as a distinct entity only after the conquest of the region by Assyria. And it became a serious rival to Judah only with the beginning of the lucrative Arabian trade. The archaeological evidence is also clear: the first large-scale wave of settlement in Edom accompanied by the establishment of large settlements and fortresses may have started in the late eighth century BCE but reached a peak only in the seventh and early sixth century BCE. Before then, the area was sparsely populated. And excavations at Bozrah—the capital of Late Iron II Edom—revealed that it grew to become a large city only in the Assyrian period.

Thus here too, the stories of Jacob and Esau—of the delicate son and the mighty hunter—are skillfully fashioned as archaizing legends to reflect the rivalries of late monarchic times.

The Peoples of the Desert and the Empires to the East

During the eighth and seventh centuries the lucrative caravan trade in spices and rare incense from southern Arabia, winding through the deserts and the southern frontier of Judah to the ports of the Mediterranean, was a significant factor in the entire region's economic life. For the people of Judah, a number of peoples of nomadic origins were crucial to this long-range trade system. Several of the genealogies included in the patriarchal stories offer a detailed picture of the peoples of the southern and eastern deserts during late monarchic times and they explain—again through the metaphor of family relationships—what role they played in Judah's contemporary history. In particular, Ishmael, the scorned son of Abraham and Hagar, is described in Genesis as having been the ancestor of many of the Arab tribes who inhabited the territories on the southern fringe of Judah. The portrait is far from flattering. He is described as a perpetual wanderer, "a wild ass of a man, his hand against every man and every man's hand against his" (Genesis 16:12, not surprisingly a J document). Among his many children are the various southern tribes who established new contact with Judah in the Assyrian period.

Among the descendants of Ishmael listed in Genesis 25:12–15, for example, are the Q(K)edarites (from his son Kedar) who are mentioned for the first time in Assyrian records of the late eighth century BCE and are frequently referred to during the reign of the Assyrian king Ashurbanipal in the seventh century BCE. Before that time, they lived beyond the area of Judah's and Israel's immediate interest, occupying the western fringe of the Fertile Crescent. Likewise, Ishmael's sons Adbeel and Nebaioth represent north Arabian groups that are also first mentioned in late eighth and seventh century Assyrian inscriptions. And finally Ishmael's son Tema is probably linked with the great caravan oasis of Tayma in northwest Arabia, mentioned in Assyrian and Babylonian sources of the eighth and sixth centuries BCE. It was one of the two major urban centers in north Arabia from c. 600 BCE through the fifth century BCE. The group named Sheba, which is mentioned in another list of southern people (Genesis 25:3), also lived in northern Arabia. Since none of these specific names were relevant or even present in the experience of the people of Israel before the Assyrian period,

there seems little doubt that these genealogical passages were crafted between the late eighth and sixth centuries BCE.*

Other place-names mentioned in the patriarchal narratives relating to
the desert and surrounding wilderness serve further to confirm the date of
the composition. Genesis 14, the story of the great war waged by invaders
from the north (led by the mysterious Chedorlaomer from Elam in
Mesopotamia) with the kings of the cities of the plain is a unique source in
Genesis, which may be dated to exilic or post-exilic times. But it provides
interesting geographical information relevant *only* to the seventh century
BCE. "En-mishpat, that is, Kadesh" (Genesis 14:7) is most likely a reference
to Kadesh-barnea, the great oasis in the south that would play an important role in the Exodus narratives. It is identified with Ein el-Qudeirat in
eastern Sinai, a site that has been excavated and shown to have been occupied primarily in the seventh and early sixth century BCE. Likewise, the site
referred to as Tamar in the same biblical verse should most probably be
identified with Ein Haseva in the northern Arabah, where excavations have
uncovered a large fortress that also functioned mainly in the Late Iron Age.
Thus the geography and even the basic situation of frightening conflict
with a Mesopotamian invader would have seemed ominously familiar to
the people of Judah in the seventh century BCE.

And this is not all. The Genesis narratives also reveal unmistakable familiarity with the location and reputation of the Assyrian and Babylonian
empires of the ninth–sixth centuries BCE. Assyria is specifically mentioned
in relation to the Tigris River in Genesis 2:14, and two of the royal capitals
of the Assyrian empire—Nineveh (recognized as the capital of the empire
in the seventh century BCE) and Calah (its predecessor)—are mentioned
in Genesis 10:11 (both are J documents). The city of Haran plays a dominant role in the patriarchal stories. The site, still called Eski Harran ("old
Haran"), is located in southern Turkey, on the border with Syria; it prospered in the early second millennium BCE and again in the Neo-Assyrian

---

* It is important to note that some of this genealogical material in Genesis, such as the list of the sons of Ishmael, belongs to the P source, which is dated, in the main, to postexilic times. While some scholars argue
that P has a late monarchic layer, and therefore may very well reflect interests and realities of seventh century
Judah, it is possible that some allusions may also reflect realities of the sixth century BCE. But in no case is
there any convincing explanation for the mention of all these desert dwelling peoples in the patriarchal
genealogies except as late literary attempts to incorporate them in a systematic way into the early history of
Israel.

period. Finally, Assyrian texts mention towns in the area of Haran that carry names resembling the names of Terah, Nahor, and Serug—Abraham's forefathers (Genesis 11:22–26, a P source). It is possible that they were the eponymous ancestors of these towns.

Judah's Destiny

The German biblical scholar Martin Noth long ago argued that the accounts of the events of Israel's earliest periods of existence—the stories of the patriarchs, the Exodus, and the wandering in Sinai—were not originally composed as a single saga. He theorized that they were the separate traditions of individual tribes that were assembled into a unified narrative to serve the cause of the political unification of a scattered and heterogeneous Israelite population. In his opinion, the geographical focus of each of the cycles of stories, particularly of the patriarchs, offers an important clue to where the composition—not necessarily the events—of the story took place. Many the stories connected with Abraham are set in the southern part of the hill country, specifically the region of Hebron in southern Judah. Isaac is associated with the southern desert fringe of Judah, in particular the Beersheba region. In contrast, Jacob's activities take place for the most part in the northern hill country and Transjordan—areas that were always of special interest to the northern kingdom of Israel. Noth therefore suggested that the patriarchs were originally quite separate regional ancestors, who were eventually brought together in a single genealogy in an effort to create a united history.

It is now evident that the selection of Abraham, with his close connection to Hebron, Judah's earliest royal city, and to Jerusalem ("Salem" in Genesis 14:18), was meant also to emphasize the primacy of Judah even in the earliest eras of Israel's history. It is almost as if an American scripture describing pre-Columbian history placed inordinate attention on Manhattan Island or on the tract of land that would later become Washington, D.C. The pointed political meaning of the inclusion of such a detail in a larger narrative at least calls into question its historical credibility.

As we will see in much greater detail in the chapters to follow, Judah was a rather isolated and sparsely populated kingdom until the eighth century BCE. It was hardly comparable in territory, wealth, and military might to

the kingdom of Israel in the north. Literacy was very limited and its capital, Jerusalem, was a small, remote hill country town. Yet after the northern
kingdom of Israel was liquidated by the Assyrian empire in 720 BCE, Judah
grew enormously in population, developed complex state institutions, and
emerged as a meaningful power in the region. It was ruled by an ancient
dynasty and possessed the most important surviving Temple to the God of
Israel. Hence in the late eighth century and in the seventh century, Judah
developed a unique sense of its own importance and divine destiny. It saw
its very survival as evidence of God's intention, from the time of the patriarchs, that Judah should rule over all the land of Israel. As the only surviving Israelite polity, Judah saw itself in a more down-to-earth sense as the
natural heir to the Israelite territories and the Israelite population that had
survived the Assyrian onslaught. What was needed was a powerful way to
express this understanding both to the people of Judah and to the scattered
Israelite communities under Assyrian rule. Thus the Pan-Israelite idea,
with Judah in its center, was born.

The patriarchal narratives thus depict a unified ancestry of the Israelite
people that leads back to the most Judean of patriarchs—Abraham. Yet
even though the Genesis stories revolve mainly around Judah, they do
not neglect to honor northern Israelite traditions. In that respect it is significant that Abraham builds altars to YHWH at Shechem and Bethel
(Genesis 12:7–8), the two most important cult centers of the northern
kingdom—as well as at Hebron (Genesis 13:18), the most important center
of Judah after Jerusalem. The figure of Abraham therefore functions as the
unifier of northern and southern traditions, bridging north and south. The
fact that Abraham is credited with establishing the altars at Bethel and
Shechem is clear testimony to the Judahites' claim that even the places of
worship polluted by idolatry during the time of the Israelite kings were
once legitimately sacred sites connected to the southern patriarch.*

---

* Another example of the unification of northern and southern traditions under Judahite supremacy is
the location of the tombs of the patriarchs. This sacred place—where Abraham and Isaac (southern heroes)
as well as Jacob (a northern hero) were buried—is located at Hebron, traditionally the second most important city in the hill country of Judah. The story of the purchase of the tomb of the patriarchs is generally ascribed to the Priestly (P) source, which seems to have more than one compositional layer to it. If this
tradition is late monarchic in origin (though its final version came later), it is a clear expression of the centrality of Judah and its superiority over the North. The specific land transaction described in the story has
strong parallels in the Neo-Babylonian period—another clue to the late realities underlying the patriarchal
narratives.

It is entirely possible and even probable that the individual episodes in the patriarchal narratives are based on ancient local traditions. Yet the use to which they are put and the order in which they are arranged transform them into a powerful expression of seventh century Judahite dreams. Indeed, the superiority of Judah over all the others could not be emphasized more strongly than in the last blessing of Jacob to his sons quoted earlier. Though enemies might be pressing on all sides, Judah, it is promised, will never be overthrown.

The patriarchal traditions therefore must be considered as a sort of pious "prehistory" of Israel in which Judah played a decisive role. They describe the very early history of the nation, delineate ethnic boundaries, emphasize that the Israelites were outsiders and not part of the indigenous population of Canaan, and embrace the traditions of both the north and the south, while ultimately stressing the superiority of Judah.* In the admittedly fragmentary evidence of the E version of the patriarchal stories, presumably compiled in the northern kingdom of Israel before its destruction in 720 BCE, the tribe of Judah plays almost no role. But by the late eighth and certainly seventh century BCE, Judah was the center of what was left of the Israelite nation. In that light, we should regard the J version of the patriarchal narratives primarily as a literary attempt to redefine the unity of the people of Israel—rather than as an accurate record of the lives of historical characters living more than a millennium before.

The biblical story of the patriarchs would have seemed compellingly familiar to the people of Judah in the seventh century BCE. In the stories, the familiar peoples and threatening enemies of the present were ranged around the encampments and grazing grounds of Abraham and his offspring. The landscape of the patriarchal stories is a dreamlike romantic vision of the pastoral past, especially appropriate to the pastoral background of a large proportion of the Judahite population. It was stitched together from memory, snatches of ancient customs, legends of the birth of peoples, and the concerns aroused by contemporary con-

---

* Since the Priestly (P) source in the Pentateuch is dated by most scholars to post-exilic times, and the final redaction of the Pentateuch was also undertaken in that period, we face a serious question of whether we can also identify a post-exilic layer in the stories in Genesis. In many ways, the needs of the post-exilic community were quite similar to the necessities of the late monarchic state. Yet, as we try to demonstrate here, the basic framework and initial elaboration of the patriarchal narratives point clearly to a seventh century origin.

flicts.* The many sources and episodes that were combined are a testimony
to the richness of the traditions from which the biblical narrative was
drawn—and the diverse audience of Judahites and Israelites to whom it
was aimed.

Genesis as Preamble?

Though the Genesis stories revolve around Judah—and if they were written in the seventh century BCE, close to the time of the compilation of the
Deuteronomistic History—how is it that they are so far from Deuteronomistic ideas, such as the centralization of cult and the centrality of
Jerusalem? They even seem to promote northern cult places such as Bethel
and Shechem and describe the establishment of altars in many places other
than Jerusalem. Perhaps we should see here an attempt to present the
patriarchal traditions as a sort of a pious prehistory, before Jerusalem,
before the monarchy, before the Temple, when the fathers of the nations
were monotheists but were still allowed to sacrifice in other places. The
portrayal of the patriarchs as shepherds or pastoralists may indeed have
been meant to give an atmosphere of great antiquity to the formative
stages of a society that had only recently developed a clear national consciousness.

The meaning of all this is that both J of the Pentateuch and the Deuteronomistic History were written in the seventh century BCE in Judah, in
Jerusalem, when the northern kingdom of Israel was no more. The ideas,
basic stories, and even characters behind both compositions were probably

* The territorial ambitions of seventh-century Judah to reclaim Israelite lands conquered by the Assyrians
are also expressed in the Abraham traditions. In the story of the great war in Genesis 14, Abraham pursues
the Mesopotamian kings who captured his nephew Lot, chasing them all the way to Damascus and Dan
(14:14–15). In this act he liberates his kinsman from Mesopotamian bondage and ejects foreign forces from
the later northern boundary of the kingdom of Israel.

Also relevant to Judah's territorial ambitions in this period is the special focus on the "Joseph" tribes—
Ephraim and Manasseh—and the strong message of separation of the Israelites from the Canaanites in the
patriarchal narratives. The immediate agenda for Judah after the fall of the northern kingdom was expansion into the former Israelite territories in the highlands directly north of Judah—namely the territories of
Ephraim and Manasseh. The Assyrians, after destroying Samaria, settled deportees from Mesopotamia in
the territories of the vanquished northern kingdom. Some were settled in the area of Bethel, close to the
northern border of Judah. The Pan-Israelite idea had to take into consideration this situation of new
"Canaanites" living in the territories Judah saw as its inheritance. The patriarchal narratives, which place
strong emphasis on the importance of marriage with kinfolk and avoidance of marriage with the other peoples of the land also perfectly fit this situation.

widely known. The J source describes the very early history of the nation, while the Deuteronomistic History deals with events of more recent centuries, with special emphasis on the Pan-Israelite idea, on the divine protection of the Davidic lineage, and on centralization of cult in the Temple in Jerusalem.

The great genius of the seventh century creators of this national epic was the way in which they wove the earlier stories together without stripping them of their humanity or individual distinctiveness. Abraham, Isaac, and Jacob remain at the same time vivid spiritual portraits and the metaphorical ancestors of the people of Israel. And the twelve sons of Jacob were brought into the tradition as junior members of more complete genealogy. In the artistry of the biblical narrative, the children of Abraham, Isaac, and Jacob were indeed made into a single family. It was the power of legend that united them—in a manner far more powerful and timeless than the fleeting adventures of a few historical individuals herding sheep in the highlands of Canaan could ever have done.

[2]

Did the Exodus Happen?

The heroic figure of Moses confronting the tyrannical pharaoh, the ten plagues, and the massive Israelite Exodus from Egypt have endured over the centuries as the central, unforgettable images of biblical history. Through a divinely guided leader—not a father—who represented the nation to God and God to the nation, the Israelites navigated the almost impossible course from hopeless slave status back to the very borders of their Promised Land. So important is this story of the Israelites' liberation from bondage that the biblical books of Exodus, Leviticus, Numbers, and Deuteronomy—a full four-fifths of the central scriptures of Israel—are devoted to the momentous events experienced by a single generation in slightly more than forty years. During these years occurred the miracles of the burning bush, the plagues, the parting of the Red Sea, the appearance of manna in the wilderness, and the revelation of God's Law on Sinai, all of which were the visible manifestations of God's rule over both nature and humanity. The God of Israel, previously known only by private revelations to the patriarchs, here reveals himself to the nation as a universal deity.

But is it history? Can archaeology help us pinpoint the era when a leader named Moses mobilized his people for the great act of liberation? Can we trace the path of the Exodus and the wandering in the wilderness? Can we even determine if the Exodus—as described in the Bible—ever occurred? Two hundred years of intensive excavation and study of the remains of ancient Egyptian civilization have offered a detailed chronology of the events, personalities, and places of pharaonic times. Even more than descriptions of the patriarchal stories, the Exodus narrative is filled with a wealth of detailed and specific geographical references. Can they provide a reliable historical background to the great epic of the Israelites' escape from Egypt and their reception of the Law on Sinai?

Israel in Egypt: The Biblical Saga

The Exodus story describes two momentous transitions whose connection is crucial for the subsequent course of Israelite history. On the one hand, the twelve sons of Jacob and their families, living in exile in Egypt, grow into a great nation. On the other, that nation undergoes a process of liberation and commitment to divine law that would have been impossible before. Thus the Bible's message highlights the potential power of a united, pious nation when it begins to claim its freedom from even the greatest kingdom on earth.

The stage was set for this dramatic spiritual metamorphosis at the end of the book of Genesis, with the sons of Jacob living in security under the protection of their brother Joseph, who had come to power as an influential official in the Egyptian hierarchy. They were prosperous and content in the cities of the eastern Nile delta and had free access back and forth to their Canaanite homeland. After the death of their father, Jacob, they brought his body to the tomb that had been prepared for him—alongside his father Isaac and grandfather Abraham in the cave of Machpelah in Hebron. And over a period of four-hundred thirty years, the descendants of the twelve brothers and their immediate families evolved into a great nation—just as God had promised—and were known to the Egyptian population as Hebrews. "They multiplied and grew exceedingly strong, so that the land was filled with them" (Exodus 1:7). But times changed and eventually a new pharaoh came to power "who knew not Joseph." Fearing that the Hebrews would betray Egypt to one of its enemies, this new pharaoh enslaved them, forcing them into construction gangs to build the royal cities of Pithom and Raamses. "But the more they were oppressed, the more they multiplied" (Exodus 1:12). The vicious cycle of oppression continued to deepen:

the Egyptians made the Hebrews' life ever more bitter as they were forced into hard service "with mortar and brick and in all kinds of work in the field" (Exodus 1:14).

Fearing a population explosion of these dangerous immigrant workers, the pharaoh ordered that all Hebrew male infants be drowned in the Nile. Yet from this desperate measure came the instrument of the Hebrews' liberation. A child from the tribe of Levi—set adrift in a basket of bulrushes—was found and adopted by one of the pharaoh's daughters. He was given the name Moses (from the Hebrew root "to draw out" of the water) and raised in the royal court. Years later, when Moses had grown to adulthood, he saw an Egyptian taskmaster flaying a Hebrew slave and his deepest feelings rose to the surface. He slew the taskmaster and "hid his body in the sand." Fearing the consequences of his act, Moses fled to the wilderness—to the land of Midian—where he adopted a new life as a desert nomad. And it was in the course of his wandering as a solitary shepherd near Horeb, "the mountain of God," that he received the revelation that would change the world.

From the brilliant, flickering flames of a bush in the desert, which was burning yet was not consumed, the God of Israel revealed himself to Moses as the deliverer of the people of Israel. He proclaimed that he would free them of their taskmasters and bring them to a life of freedom and security in the Promised Land. God identified himself as the God of Abraham, Isaac, and Jacob—and now also revealed to Moses his mysterious, mystical name, YHWH, "I am who I am." And he solemnly commissioned Moses, with the assistance of his brother Aaron, to return to Egypt to confront the pharaoh with a demonstration of miracles and to demand freedom for the house of Israel.

But the pharaoh's heart was hardened and he responded to Moses by intensifying the suffering of the Hebrew slaves. So God instructed Moses to threaten Egypt with a series of terrible plagues if the pharaoh still refused to respond to the divine injunction to "Let my people go" (Exodus 7:16). The pharaoh did not relent and the Nile turned to blood. Frogs, then gnats, then flies swarmed throughout the country. A mysterious disease decimated the Egyptians' livestock. Boils and sores erupted on their skin and the skin of their surviving animals. Hail pounded down from the heavens, ruining the crops. And yet the pharaoh still refused to relent. Plagues of locusts and darkness then came upon Egypt—and finally a terrible plague of the killing of the firstborn, both human and animal, from all the land of the Nile.

In order to protect the Israelite firstborn, God instructed Moses and Aaron to prepare the congregation of Israel for a special sacrifice of lambs, whose blood should be smeared on the doorpost of every Israelite dwelling so that each would be passed over on the night of the slaying of the Egyptian sons. He also instructed them to prepare provisions of unleavened bread for a hasty exodus. When the pharaoh witnessed the horrible toll of the tenth plague, the killing of the firstborn, including his own, he finally relented, bidding the Israelites to take their flocks and herds and be gone.

Thus the multitude of Israel, numbering "about six hundred thousand men on foot, besides women and children" (Exodus 12:37), set out from the cities of the eastern delta toward the wilderness of Sinai. But "when the Pharaoh let the people go, God did not lead them by the way of the land of the Philistines, although that was near; for God said, 'Lest the people repent when they see war, and return to Egypt.' But God led the people round by the way of the wilderness toward the Red Sea" (Exodus 13:17–18). And when the pharaoh, regretting his decision, sent a force of "six hundred picked chariots and all the other chariots of Egypt" after the fleeing Israelites, the Red Sea parted to allow the Israelites to cross over to Sinai on dry land. And as soon as they had made the crossing, the towering waters engulfed the pursuing Egyptians in an unforgettable miracle that was commemorated in the biblical Song of the Sea (Exodus 15:1–18).

Guided by Moses, the Israelite multitude passed through the wilderness, following a carefully recorded itinerary of places at which they thirsted, hungered, and murmured their dissatisfaction, but were calmed and fed through Moses' intercession with God. Finally reaching the mountain of God where Moses had received his first great revelation, the people of Israel gathered as Moses climbed to the summit to receive the Law under which the newly liberated Israelites should forever live. Though the gathering at Sinai was marred by the Israelites' worship of a golden calf while Moses was on the mountain (and in anger Moses smashed the first set of stone tablets), God conveyed to the people through Moses the ten commandments and then the complex legislation of worship, purity, and dietary laws. The sacred Ark of the Covenant, containing the tablets of God's Law, would henceforth be the battle standard and most sacred national symbol, accompanying the Israelites in all of their wanderings.

Setting off from their camp at the wilderness of Paran, the Israelites sent spies to collect intelligence on the people of Canaan (Numbers 13). But those spies returned with reports so frightening about the strength of the Canaanites and the towering fortifications of their cities that the multitude of Israelites lost heart and rebelled against Moses, begging to return to Egypt, where at least their physical safety could be ensured. Seeing this, God determined that the generation that had known slavery in Egypt would not live to inherit the Promised Land, and the Israelites must remain wanderers in the wilderness for another forty years. Therefore, they did not enter Canaan directly, but by a winding route through Kadesh-barnea and into the Arabah, across the lands of Edom and Moab to the east of the Dead Sea.

The final act of the Exodus story took place on the plains of Moab in Transjordan, in sight of the Promised Land. The now elderly Moses revealed to the Israelites the full terms of the laws they would be required to obey if they were truly to inherit Canaan. This second code of law is contained in the book of Deuteronomy (named from the Greek word *deuteronomion*, "second law"). It detailed the mortal dangers of idolatry, set the calendar of festivals, listed a wide range of social legislation, and mandated that once the land was conquered the God of Israel could be worshiped in a single sanctuary, "the place that the LORD your God will choose." (Deuteronomy 26:2). Then, after the appointment of Joshua, son of Nun, to lead the Israelites on their campaign of swift conquest, the 120-year-old Moses ascended to the summit of Mount Nebo and died. The transition from family to nation was complete. Now the nation faced the awesome challenge of fulfilling its God-given destiny.

The Lure of Egypt

One thing is certain. The basic situation described in the Exodus saga—the phenomenon of immigrants coming down to Egypt from Canaan and settling in the eastern border regions of the delta—is abundantly verified in the archaeological finds and historical texts. From earliest recorded times throughout antiquity, Egypt beckoned as a place of shelter and security for the people of Canaan at times when drought, famine, or warfare made life unbearable or even difficult. This historical relationship is based on the basic environmental and climatic contrasts between Egypt and Canaan, the two neighboring lands separated by the Sinai desert. Canaan, possessing a typical Mediterranean climate, is dry in the summer and gets its rain only in the winter, and the amount of rainfall in any given year can vary widely. Because agriculture in Canaan was so dependent on the climate, years with plentiful rainfall brought prosperity, but years of low precipitation usually resulted in drought and famine. Thus the lives of the people of Canaan were profoundly affected by fluctuations between years of good, average, and poor rainfall, which directly translated into years of prosperity, hardship, or outright famine. And in times of severe famine there was only one solution: to go down to Egypt. Egypt did not depend on rainfall but received its water from the Nile.

There were good years and bad years in Egypt too—determined by the fluctuating level of the Nile in the flood season, due to the very different rainfall patterns at its sources in central Africa and the Ethiopian highlands—but there was rarely outright famine. The Nile, even if low, was still a dependable source of water for irrigation, and in any case Egypt was a well-organized state and thus prepared for better or worse years by the storage of grain in government warehouses. The Nile delta, in particular, presented a far more inviting landscape in antiquity than is evident today. Today, because of silting and geological change, the Nile splits into only two main branches just north of Cairo. But a wide variety of ancient sources, including two maps from the Roman-Byzantine period, report that the Nile once split into as many as *seven* branches and created a vastly larger area of well-watered land. The easternmost branch extended into what is now the marshy, salty, arid zone of northwestern Sinai. And man-made canals flowing from it carried freshwater to the entire area, making what are now the arid, salty swamps of the Suez Canal area into green, fertile, densely inhabited land. Both the eastern branch of the Nile and the man-made canals have been identified in recent years in geological and topographical studies in the delta and the desert to its east.

There is good reason to believe that in times of famine in Canaan—just as the biblical narrative describes—pastoralists and farmers alike would go to Egypt to settle in the eastern delta and enjoy its dependable fertility. Yet archaeology has provided a far more nuanced picture of the large communities of Semites who came in the Bronze Age from southern Canaan to settle in the delta for a wide variety of reasons and achieved different levels of success. Some of them were conscripted as landless laborers in the construction of public works. In other periods they may have come simply because Egypt offered them the prospect of trade and better economic opportunities. The famous Beni Hasan tomb painting from Middle Egypt, dated to the nineteenth century BCE, portrays a group from Transjordan coming down to Egypt with animals and goods—presumably as traders, not as conscripted laborers. Other Canaanites in the delta may have been brought there by the armies of the pharaohs as prisoners of war, taken in punitive campaigns against the rebellious city-states of Canaan. We know that some were assigned as slaves to cultivate lands of temple estates. Some found their way up the social ladder and eventually became government officials, soldiers, and even priests.

These demographic patterns along the eastern delta—of Asiatic people immigrating to Egypt to be conscripted to forced work in the delta—are not restricted to the Bronze Age. Rather, they reflect the age-old rhythms in the region, including later centuries in the Iron Age, closer to the time when the Exodus narrative was put in writing.

The Rise and Fall of the Hyksos

The tale of Joseph's rise to prominence in Egypt, as narrated in the book of Genesis, is the most famous of the stories of Canaanite immigrants rising to power in Egypt, but there are other sources that offer essentially the same picture—from the Egyptian point of view. The most important of them was written by the Egyptian historian Manetho in the third century BCE; he recorded an extraordinary immigrant success story, though from his patriotic Egyptian perspective it amounted to a national tragedy. Basing his accounts on unnamed "sacred books" and "popular tales and legends," Manetho described a massive, brutal invasion of Egypt by foreigners from the east, whom he called Hyksos, an enigmatic Greek form of an Egyptian word that he translated as "shepherd kings" but that actually means "rulers of foreign lands." Manetho reported that the Hyksos established themselves in the delta at a city named Avaris. And they founded a dynasty there that ruled Egypt with great cruelty for more than five hundred years.

In the early years of modern research, scholars identified the Hyksos with the kings of the Fifteenth Dynasty of Egypt, who ruled from about 1670 to 1570 BCE. The early scholars accepted Manetho's report quite literally and sought evidence for a powerful foreign nation or ethnic group that came from afar to invade and conquer Egypt. Subsequent studies showed that inscriptions and seals bearing the names of Hyksos rulers were West Semitic—in other words, Canaanite. Recent archaeological excavations in the eastern Nile delta have confirmed that conclusion and indicate that the Hyksos "invasion" was a gradual process of immigration from Canaan to Egypt, rather than a lightning military campaign.

The most important dig has been undertaken by Manfred Bietak, of the University of Vienna, at Tell ed-Daba, a site in the eastern delta identified as Avaris, the Hyksos capital (Figure 6, p. 58). Excavations there show a gradual increase of Canaanite influence in the styles of pottery, architecture, and tombs from around 1800 BCE. By the time of the Fifteenth Dynasty, some 150 years later, the culture of the site, which eventually became a huge city, was overwhelmingly Canaanite. The Tell ed-Daba finds are evidence for a long and gradual development of Canaanite presence in the delta, and a peaceful takeover of power there. It is a situation that is uncannily similar, at least in its broad outlines, to the stories of the visits of the patriarchs to Egypt and their eventual settlement there. The fact that Manetho, writing almost fifteen hundred years later, describes a brutal invasion rather than a gradual, peaceful immigration should probably be understood on the background of his own times, when memories of the invasions of Egypt by the Assyrians, Babylonians, and Persians in the seventh and sixth centuries BCE were still painfully fresh in the Egyptian consciousness.

But there is an even more telling parallel between the saga of the Hyksos and the biblical story of the Israelites in Egypt, despite their drastic difference in tone. Manetho describes how the Hyksos invasion of Egypt was finally brought to an end by a virtuous Egyptian king who attacked and defeated the Hyksos, "killing many of them and pursuing the remainder to the frontiers of Syria." In fact, Manetho suggested that after the Hyksos were driven from Egypt, they founded the city of Jerusalem and constructed a temple there. Far more trustworthy is an Egyptian source of the sixteenth century BCE that recounts the exploits of Pharaoh Ahmose, of the Eighteenth Dynasty, who sacked Avaris and chased the remnants of the Hyksos to their main citadel in southern Canaan—Sharuhen, near Gaza—which he stormed after a long siege. And indeed, around the middle of the sixteenth century BCE, Tell ed-Daba was abandoned, marking the sudden end of Canaanite influence there.

So, independent archaeological and historical sources tell of migrations of Semites from Canaan to Egypt, and of Egyptians forcibly expelling them. This basic outline of immigration and violent return to Canaan is parallel to the biblical account of Exodus. Two key questions remain: First, who were these Semitic immigrants? And second, how does the date of their sojourn in Egypt square with biblical chronology?

A Conflict of Dates and Kings

The expulsion of the Hyksos is generally dated, on the basis of Egyptian records and the archaeological evidence of destroyed cities in Canaan, to around 1570 BCE. As we mentioned in the last chapter in discussing the dating of the age of the patriarchs, 1 Kings 6:1 tells us that the start of the construction of the Temple in the fourth year of Solomon's reign took place 480 years after the Exodus. According to a correlation of the regnal dates of Israelite kings with outside Egyptian and Assyrian sources, this would roughly place the Exodus in 1440 BCE. That is more than a hundred years after the date of the Egyptian expulsion of the Hyksos, around 1570 BCE. But there is an even more serious complication. The Bible speaks explicitly about the forced labor projects of the children of Israel and mentions, in particular, the construction of the city of Raamses (Exodus 1:11). In the fifteenth century BCE such a name is inconceivable. The first pharaoh named Ramesses came to the throne only in 1320 BCE—more than a century after the traditional biblical date. As a result, many scholars have tended to dismiss the literal value of the biblical dating, suggesting that the figure 480 was little more than a symbolic length of time, representing the life spans of twelve generations, each lasting the traditional forty years. This highly schematized chronology puts the building of the Temple about halfway between the end of the first exile (in Egypt) and the end of the second exile (in Babylon).

However, most scholars saw the specific biblical reference to the name Ramesses as a detail that preserved an authentic historical memory. In other words, they argued that the Exodus must have occurred in the thirteenth century BCE. And there were other specific details of the biblical Exodus story that pointed to the same era. First, Egyptian sources report that the city of Pi-Ramesses ("The House of Ramesses") was built in the delta in the days of the great Egyptian king Ramesses II, who ruled 1279–1213 BCE, and that Semites were apparently employed in its construction. Second, and perhaps most important, the earliest mention of Israel in an extrabiblical text was found in Egypt in the stele describing the campaign of Pharaoh Merneptah—the son of Ramesses II—in Canaan at the very end of the thirteenth century BCE. The inscription tells of a destructive Egyptian campaign into Canaan, in the course of which a people named Israel were decimated to the extent that the pharaoh boasted that Israel's "seed is not!" The boast was clearly an empty one, but it did indicate that some group known as Israel was already in Canaan by that time. In fact, dozens of settlements that were linked with the early Israelites appeared in the hill country of Canaan around that time. So if a historical Exodus took place, scholars have argued, it must have occurred in the late thirteenth century BCE.

The Merneptah stele contains the first appearance of the name Israel in any surviving ancient text. This again raises the basic questions: Who were the Semites in Egypt? Can they be regarded as Israelite in any meaningful sense? No mention of the name Israel has been found in any of the inscriptions or documents connected with the Hyksos period. Nor is it mentioned in later Egyptian inscriptions, or in an extensive fourteenth century BCE cuneiform archive found at Tell el-Amarna in Egypt, whose nearly four hundred letters describe in detail the social, political, and demographic conditions in Canaan at that time. As we will argue in a later chapter, the Israelites emerged only gradually as a distinct group in Canaan, beginning at the end of the thirteenth century BCE. There is no recognizable archaeological evidence of Israelite presence in Egypt immediately before that time.

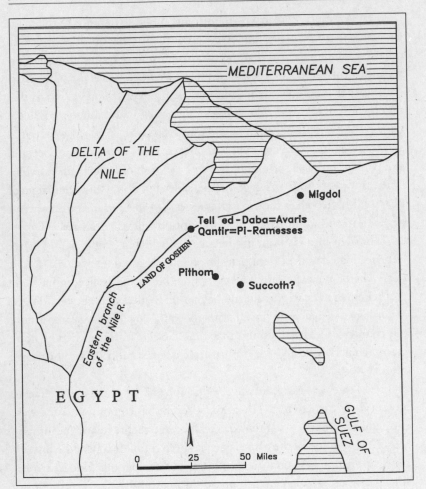

Figure 6: The Nile delta: Main sites mentioned in the Exodus story.

Was a Mass Exodus Even Possible in the Time of Ramesses II?

We now know that the solution to the problem of the Exodus is not as simple as lining up dates and kings. The expulsion of the Hyksos from Egypt in 1570 BCE ushered in a period when the Egyptians became extremely wary of incursions into their lands by outsiders. And the negative impact of the memories of the Hyksos symbolizes a state of mind that is also to be seen in the archaeological remains. Only in recent years has it become clear that from the time of the New Kingdom onward, beginning after the expulsion of the Hyksos, the Egyptians tightened their control over the flow of immigrants from Canaan into the delta. They established a system of forts along the delta's eastern border and manned them with garrison troops and administrators. A late thirteenth century papyrus records how closely the commanders of the forts monitored the movements of foreigners: "We have completed the entry of the tribes of the Edomite Shasu [i.e., bedouin] through the fortress of Merneptah-Content-with-Truth, which is in *Tjku*, to the pools of *Pr-Itm* which [are] in *Tjku* for the sustenance of their flocks."

This report is interesting in another connection: it names two of the most important sites mentioned in the Bible in connection with the Exodus (Figure 6). *Succoth* (Exodus 12:37; Numbers 33:5) is probably the Hebrew form of the Egyptian *Tjku*, a name referring to a place or an area in the eastern delta that appears in the Egyptian texts from the days of the Nineteenth Dynasty, the dynasty of Ramesses II. *Pithom* (Exodus 1:11) is the Hebrew form of *Pr-Itm*—"House [i.e., Temple] of the God Atum." This name appears for the first time in the days of the New Kingdom in Egypt. Indeed, two more place-names that appear in the Exodus narrative seem to fit the reality of the eastern delta in the time of the New Kingdom. The first, which we have already mentioned above, is the city called Raamses—Pi-Ramesses, or "The House of Ramesses," in Egyptian. This city was built in the thirteenth century as the capital of Ramesses II in the eastern delta, very close to the ruins of Avaris. Hard work in brick making, as described in the biblical account, was a common phenomenon in Egypt, and an Egyptian tomb painting from the fifteenth century BCE portrays this specialized building trade in detail. Finally, the name Migdol, which appears in the Exodus account (Exodus 14:2), is a common name in the New Kingdom for Egyptian forts on the eastern border of the delta and along the international road from Egypt to Canaan in northern Sinai.

The border between Canaan and Egypt was thus closely controlled. If a great mass of fleeing Israelites had passed through the border fortifications of the pharaonic regime, a record should exist. Yet in the abundant Egyptian sources describing the time of the New Kingdom in general and the thirteenth century in particular, there is no reference to the Israelites, not even a single clue. We know of nomadic groups from Edom who entered

Egypt from the desert. The Merneptah stele refers to Israel as a group of people already living in Canaan. But we have no clue, not even a single word, about early Israelites *in* Egypt: neither in monumental inscriptions on walls of temples, nor in tomb inscriptions, nor in papyri. Israel is absent—as a possible foe of Egypt, as a friend, or as an enslaved nation. And there are simply no finds in Egypt that can be directly associated with the notion of a distinct foreign ethnic group (as opposed to a concentration of migrant workers from many places) living in a distinct area of the eastern delta, as implied by the biblical account of the children of Israel living together in the Land of Goshen (Genesis 47:27).

There is something more: the escape of more than a tiny group from Egyptian control at the time of Ramesses II seems highly unlikely, as is the crossing of the desert and entry into Canaan. In the thirteenth century, Egypt was at the peak of its authority—the dominant power in the world. The Egyptian grip over Canaan was firm; Egyptian strongholds were built in various places in the country, and Egyptian officials administered the affairs of the region. In the el-Amarna letters, which are dated a century before, we are told that a unit of fifty Egyptian soldiers was big enough to pacify unrest in Canaan. And throughout the period of the New Kingdom, large Egyptian armies marched through Canaan to the north, as far as the Euphrates in Syria. Therefore, the main overland road that went from the delta along the coast of northern Sinai to Gaza and then into the heart of Canaan was of utmost importance to the pharaonic regime.

The most potentially vulnerable stretch of the road—which crossed the arid and dangerous desert of northern Sinai between the delta and Gaza—was the most protected. A sophisticated system of Egyptian forts, granaries, and wells was established at a day's march distance along the entire length of the road, which was called the Ways of Horus. These road stations enabled the imperial army to cross the Sinai peninsula conveniently and efficiently when necessary. The annals of the great Egyptian conqueror Thutmose III tell us that he marched with his troops from the eastern delta to Gaza, a distance of about 250 kilometers, in ten days. A relief from the days of Ramesses II's father, Pharaoh Seti I (from around 1300 BCE), shows the forts and water reservoirs in the form of an early map that traces the route from the eastern delta to the southwestern border of Canaan (Figure 7). The remains of these forts were uncovered in the course of archaeologi-

Figure 7: A relief from the time of Pharaoh Seti I (ca. 1300 BCE). Engraved on a wall in the temple of Amun at Karnak, the relief depicts the international road from Egypt to Canaan along the northern coast of the Sinai Peninsula. Egyptian forts with water reservoirs are designated in the lower register.

cal investigations in northern Sinai by Eliezer Oren of Ben-Gurion University, in the 1970s. Oren discovered that each of these road stations, closely corresponding to the sites designated on the ancient Egyptian relief, comprised three elements: a strong fort made of bricks in the typical Egyptian military architecture, storage installations for food provisions, and a water reservoir.

Putting aside the possibility of divinely inspired miracles, one can hardly accept the idea of a flight of a large group of slaves from Egypt through the heavily guarded border fortifications into the desert and then into Canaan in the time of such a formidable Egyptian presence. Any group escaping Egypt against the will of the pharaoh would have easily been tracked down not only by an Egyptian army chasing it from the delta but also by the Egyptian soldiers in the forts in northern Sinai and in Canaan.

Indeed, the biblical narrative hints at the danger of attempting to flee by the coastal route. Thus the only alternative would be to turn into the desolate wastes of the Sinai peninsula. But the possibility of a large group of people wandering in the Sinai peninsula is also contradicted by archaeology.

Phantom Wanderers?

According to the biblical account, the children of Israel wandered in the desert and mountains of the Sinai peninsula, moving around and camping in different places, for a full forty years (Figure 8). Even if the number of fleeing Israelites (given in the text as six hundred thousand) is wildly exaggerated or can be interpreted as representing smaller units of people, the text describes the survival of a great number of people under the most challenging conditions. Some archaeological traces of their generation-long wandering in the Sinai should be apparent. However, except for the Egyptian forts along the northern coast, not a single campsite or sign of occupation from the time of Ramesses II and his immediate predecessors and successors has ever been identified in Sinai. And it has not been for lack of trying. Repeated archaeological surveys in all regions of the peninsula, including the mountainous area around the traditional site of Mount Sinai, near Saint Catherine's Monastery (see Appendix B), have yielded only neg-

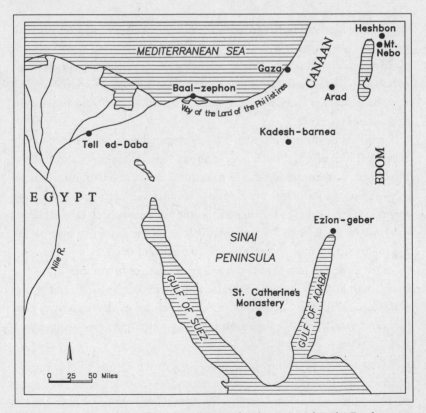

Figure 8: The Sinai Peninsula, showing main places mentioned in the Exodus story.

ative evidence: not even a single sherd, no structure, not a single house, no trace of an ancient encampment. One may argue that a relatively small band of wandering Israelites cannot be expected to leave material remains behind. But modern archaeological techniques are quite capable of tracing even the very meager remains of hunter-gatherers and pastoral nomads all over the world. Indeed, the archaeological record from the Sinai peninsula discloses evidence for pastoral activity in such eras as the third millennium BCE and the Hellenistic and Byzantine periods. There is simply no such evidence at the supposed time of the Exodus in the thirteenth century BCE.

The conclusion—that the Exodus did not happen at the time and in the manner described in the Bible—seems irrefutable when we examine the evidence at specific sites where the children of Israel were said to have camped for extended periods during their wandering in the desert (Numbers 33) and where some archaeological indication—if present—would almost certainly be found. According to the biblical narrative, the children of Israel camped at Kadesh-barnea for thirty eight of the forty years of the wanderings. The general location of this place is clear from the description of the southern border of the land of Israel in Numbers 34. It has been identified by archaeologists with the large and well-watered oasis of Ein el-Qudeirat in eastern Sinai, on the border between modern Israel and Egypt. The name Kadesh was probably preserved over the centuries in the name of a nearby smaller spring called Ein Qadis. A small mound with the remains of a Late Iron Age fort stands at the center of this oasis. Yet repeated excavations and surveys throughout the entire area have not provided even the slightest evidence for activity in the Late Bronze Age, not even a single sherd left by a tiny fleeing band of frightened refugees.

Ezion-geber is another place reported to be a camping place of the children of Israel. Its mention in other places in the Bible as a later port town on the northern tip of the Gulf of Aqaba has led to its identification by archaeologists at a mound located on the modern border between Israel and Jordan, halfway between the towns of Eilat and Aqaba. Excavations here in the years 1938–1940 revealed impressive Late Iron Age remains, but no trace whatsoever of Late Bronze occupation. From the long list of encampments in the wilderness, Kadesh-barnea and Ezion-geber are the only ones that can safely be identified, yet they revealed no trace of the wandering Israelites.

And what of other settlements and peoples mentioned in the account of the Israelites' wanderings? The biblical narrative recounts how the Canaanite king of Arad, "who dwelt in the Negeb," attacked the Israelites and took some of them captive—enraging them to the point that they appealed for divine assistance to destroy all the Canaanite cities (Numbers 21:1–3). Almost twenty years of intensive excavations at the site of Tel Arad east of Beersheba have revealed remains of a great Early Bronze Age city, about twenty-five acres in size, and an Iron Age fort, but no remains whatsoever from the Late Bronze Age, when the place was apparently deserted. The same holds true for the entire Beersheba valley. Arad simply did not exist in the Late Bronze Age.

The same situation is evident eastward across the Jordan, where the wandering Israelites were forced to do battle at the city of Heshbon, capital of Sihon, king of the Amorites, who tried to block the Israelites from passing in his territory on their way to Canaan (Numbers 21:21–25; Deuteronomy 2:24–35; Judges 11:19–21). Excavations at Tel Hesban south of Amman, the location of ancient Heshbon, showed that there was no Late Bronze city, not even a small village there. And there is more here. According to the Bible, when the children of Israel moved along the Transjordanian plateau they met and confronted resistance not only in Moab but also from the full-fledged states of Edom and Ammon. Yet we now know that the plateau of Transjordan was very sparsely inhabited in the Late Bronze Age. In fact, most parts of this region, including Edom, which is mentioned as a state ruled by a king in the biblical narrative, were not even inhabited by a sedentary population at that time. To put it simply, archaeology has shown us that there were no kings of Edom there for the Israelites to meet.

The pattern should have become clear by now. Sites mentioned in the Exodus narrative are real. A few were well known and apparently occupied in much earlier periods and much later periods—after the kingdom of Judah was established, when the text of the biblical narrative was set down in writing for the first time. Unfortunately for those seeking a historical Exodus, they were unoccupied precisely at the time they reportedly played a role in the events of the wandering of the children of Israel in the wilderness.

Back to the Future: The Clues to the Seventh Century BCE

So where does this leave us? Can we say that the Exodus, the wandering, and—most important of all—the giving of the Law on Sinai do not possess even a kernel of truth? So many historical and geographical elements from so many periods may have been embedded in the Exodus story that it is hard to decide on a single unique period in which something like it might have occurred. There is the timeless rhythm of migrations to Egypt in antiquity. There is the specific incident of the Hyksos domination of the delta in the Middle Bronze Age. There are the suggestive parallels to elements of the Ramesside era relating to Egypt—together with the first mention of Israel (in Canaan, not Egypt). Many of the place-names in the book of Exodus, such as the Red Sea (in Hebrew Yam Suph), the river Shihor in the eastern delta (Joshua 13:3), and the Israelites' stopping place at Pi-ha-hiroth, seem to have Egyptian etymologies. They are all related to the geography of the Exodus, but they give no clear indication that they belong to a specific period in Egyptian history.

The historical vagueness of the Exodus story includes the fact that there is no mention *by name* of any specific Egyptian New Kingdom monarch (while later biblical materials do mention pharaohs by their names, for example Shishak and Necho). The identification of Ramesses II as the pharaoh of the Exodus came as the result of modern scholarly assumptions based on the identification of the place-name Pi-Ramesses with Raamses (Exodus 1:11; 12:37). But there are few indisputable links to the seventh century BCE. Beyond a vague reference to the Israelites' fear of taking the coastal route, there is no mention of the Egyptian forts in northern Sinai or their strongholds in Canaan. The Bible may reflect New Kingdom reality, but it might just as well reflect later conditions in the Iron Age, closer to the time when the Exodus narrative was put in writing.

And that is precisely what the Egyptologist Donald Redford has suggested. The most evocative and consistent geographical details of the Exodus story come from the seventh century BCE, during the great era of prosperity of the kingdom of Judah—six centuries after the events of the Exodus were supposed to have taken place. Redford has shown just how many details in the Exodus narrative can be explained in this setting, which was also Egypt's last period of imperial power, under the rulers of the Twenty-sixth Dynasty.

The great kings of that dynasty, Psammetichus I (664–610 BCE) and his son Necho II (610–595 BCE), modeled themselves quite consciously on Egypt's far more ancient pharaohs. They were active in building projects throughout the delta in an attempt to restore the faded glories of their state and increase its economic and military power. Psammetichus established his capital in Sais in the western delta (thus the name Saite as an alternative for the Twenty-sixth Dynasty). Necho was engaged in an even more ambitious public works project in the eastern delta: cutting a canal through the isthmus of Suez in order to connect the Mediterranean with the Red Sea through the easternmost tributaries of the Nile. Archaeological exploration of the eastern delta has revealed the initiation of some of these extraordinary building activities by the Saite Dynasty—and the presence of large numbers of foreign settlers there.

In fact, the era of the Saite Dynasty provides us with one of the best historical examples for the phenomenon of foreigners settling in the delta of the Nile. In addition to Greek commercial colonies, which were established there from the second half of the seventh century BCE, many migrants from Judah were present in the delta, forming a large community by the early sixth century BCE (Jeremiah 44:1; 46:14). In addition, the public works initiated in this period mesh well with the details of the Exodus account. Though a site carrying the name Pithom is mentioned in a late thirteenth century BCE text, the more famous and prominent city of Pithom was built in the late seventh century BCE. Inscriptions found at Tell Maskhuta in the eastern delta led archaeologists to identify this site with the later Pithom. Excavations there revealed that except for a short occupation in the Middle Bronze Age, it was not settled until the time of the Twenty-sixth Dynasty, when a significant city developed there. Likewise, Migdol (mentioned in Exodus 14:2) is a common title for a fort in the time of the New Kingdom, but a specific, very important Migdol is known in the eastern delta in the seventh century BCE. It is not a coincidence that the prophet Jeremiah, who lived in the late seventh and early sixth centuries BCE, tells us (44:1; 46:14) about Judahites living in the delta, specifically mentioning Migdol. Finally, the name Goshen—for the area where the Israelites settled in the eastern delta (Genesis 45:10)—is not an Egyptian name but a Semitic one. Starting with the seventh century BCE the Qedarite Arabs expanded to the fringe of the settled lands of the Levant, and in the sixth century reached the delta. Later, in the fifth century, they became a dominant factor in the delta. According to Redford, the name Goshen derives from Geshem—a dynastic name in the Qedarite royal family.

A seventh century BCE background is also evident in some of the peculiar Egyptian names mentioned in the Joseph story. All four names—Zaphenath-paneah (the grand vizier of the pharaoh), Potiphar (a royal officer), Potiphera (a priest), and Asenath (Potiphera's daughter), though used occasionally in earlier periods of Egyptian history, achieve their greatest popularity in the seventh and sixth centuries BCE. An additional seemingly incidental detail seems to clinch the case for the biblical story having integrated many details from this specific period: the Egyptian fear of invasion from the east. Egypt was never invaded from that direction before the attacks by Assyria in the seventh century. Yet in the Joseph story, dramatic tension is heightened when he accuses his brothers, newly arrived from Canaan, of being spies who "come to see the weakness of the land" (Genesis 42:9). And in the Exodus story, the pharaoh fears that the departing Israelites will collaborate with an enemy. These dramatic touches would make sense only *after* the great age of Egyptian power of the Ramesside period, against the background of the invasions of an Egypt greatly weakened by the Assyrians, Babylonians, and Persians in the seventh and sixth centuries.

Lastly, all the major places that play a role in the story of the wandering of the Israelites were inhabited in the seventh century; in some cases they were occupied *only* at that time. A large fort was established at Kadesh-barnea in the seventh century. There is a debate about the identity of the builders of the fort—whether it served as a far southern outpost of the kingdom of Judah on the desert routes in the late seventh century or was built in the early seventh century under Assyrian auspices. Yet in either case the site so prominent in the Exodus narrative as the main camping place of the Israelites was an important and perhaps famous desert outpost in the late monarchic period. The southern port city of Ezion-geber also flourished at this time. Likewise, the kingdoms of Transjordan were populous, well-known localities in the seventh century. Most relevant is the case of

Edom. The Bible describes how Moses sent emissaries from Kadesh-barnea to the king of Edom to ask permission to pass through his territory on the way to Canaan. The king of Edom refused to grant the permission and the Israelites had to bypass his land. According to the biblical narrative, then, there was a kingdom in Edom at that time. Archaeological investigations indicate that Edom reached statehood only under Assyrian auspices in the seventh century BCE. Before that period it was a sparsely settled fringe area inhabited mainly by pastoral nomads. No less important, Edom was destroyed by the Babylonians in the sixth century BCE, and sedentary activity there recovered only in Hellenistic times.

All these indications suggest that the Exodus narrative reached its final form during the time of the Twenty-sixth Dynasty, in the second half of the seventh and the first half of the sixth century BCE. Its many references to specific places and events in this period quite clearly suggest that the author or authors integrated many contemporary details into the story. (It was in much the same way that European illuminated manuscripts of the Middle Ages depicted Jerusalem as a European city with turrets and battlements in order to heighten its direct impact on contemporary readers.) Older, less formalized legends of liberation from Egypt could have been skillfully woven into the powerful saga that borrowed familiar landscapes and monuments. But can it be just a coincidence that the geographical and ethnic details of both the patriarchal origin stories and the Exodus liberation story bear the hallmarks of having been composed in the seventh century BCE? Were there older kernels of historical truth involved, or were the basic stories first composed then?

Challenging a New Pharaoh

It is clear that the saga of liberation from Egypt was not composed as an original work in the seventh century BCE. The main outlines of the story were certainly known long before, in the allusions to the Exodus and the wandering in the wilderness contained in the oracles of the prophets Amos (2:10; 3:1; 9:7) and Hosea (11:1 13:4) a full century before. Both shared a memory of a great event in history that concerned liberation from Egypt and took place in the distant past. But what kind of memory was it?

The Egyptologist Donald Redford has argued that the echoes of the great events of the Hyksos occupation of Egypt and their violent expulsion from the delta resounded for centuries, to become a central, shared memory of the people of Canaan. These stories of Canaanite colonists established in Egypt, reaching dominance in the delta and then being forced to return to their homeland, could have served as a focus of solidarity and resistance as the Egyptian control over Canaan grew tighter in the course of the Late Bronze Age. As we will see, with the eventual assimilation of many Canaanite communities into the crystallizing nation of Israel, that powerful image of freedom may have grown relevant for an ever widening community. During the time of the kingdoms of Israel and Judah, the Exodus story would have endured and been elaborated as a national saga—a call to national unity in the face of continual threats from great empires.

It is impossible to say whether or not the biblical narrative was an expansion and elaboration of vague memories of the immigration of Canaanites to Egypt and their expulsion from the delta in the second millennium BCE. Yet it seems clear that the biblical story of the Exodus drew its power not only from ancient traditions and contemporary geographical and demographic details but even more directly from contemporary political realities.

The seventh century was a time of great revival in both Egypt and Judah. In Egypt, after a long period of decline and difficult years of subjection to the Assyrian empire, King Psammetichus I seized power and transformed Egypt into a major international power again. As the rule of the Assyrian empire began to crumble, Egypt moved in to fill the political vacuum, occupying former Assyrian territories and establishing permanent Egyptian rule. Between 640 and 630 BCE, when the Assyrians withdrew their forces from Philistia, Phoenicia, and the area of the former kingdom of Israel, Egypt took over most of these areas, and political domination by Egypt replaced the Assyrian yoke.

In Judah, this was the time of King Josiah. The idea that YHWH would ultimately fulfill the promises given to the patriarchs, to Moses, and to King David—of a vast and unified people of Israel living securely in their land—was a politically and spiritually powerful one for Josiah's subjects. It was a time when Josiah embarked on an ambitious attempt to take advantage of the Assyrian collapse and unite all Israelites under his rule. His program was to expand to the north of Judah, to the territories where Israelites

were still living a century after the fall of the kingdom of Israel, and to real-
ize the dream of a glorious united monarchy: a large and powerful state
of all Israelites worshiping one God in one Temple in one capital—
Jerusalem—and ruled by one king of Davidic lineage.

The ambitions of mighty Egypt to expand its empire and of tiny Judah
to annex territories of the former kingdom of Israel and establish its independence were therefore in direct conflict. Egypt of the Twenty-sixth Dynasty, with its imperial aspirations, stood in the way of the fulfillment of
Josiah's dreams. Images and memories from the past now became the am-
munition in a national test of will between the children of Israel and the
pharaoh and his charioteers.

We can thus see the composition of the Exodus narrative from a striking
new perspective. Just as the written form of the patriarchal narratives wove
together the scattered traditions of origins in the service of a seventh century national revival in Judah, the fully elaborated story of conflict with
Egypt—of the great power of the God of Israel and his miraculous rescue
of his people—served an even more immediate political and military end.
The great saga of a new beginning and a second chance must have resonated in the consciousness of the seventh century's readers, reminding
them of their own difficulties and giving them hope for the future.

Attitudes towards Egypt in late monarchic Judah were always a mixture
of awe and revulsion. On one hand, Egypt had always provided a safe
haven in time of famine and an asylum for runaways, and was perceived as
a potential ally against invasions from the north. At the same time there
had always been suspicion and animosity toward the great southern neigh-
bor, whose ambitions from earliest times were to control the vital overland
passage through the land of Israel northward to Asia Minor and Mesopotamia. Now a young leader of Judah was prepared to confront the great
pharaoh, and ancient traditions from many different sources were crafted
into a single sweeping epic that bolstered Josiah's political aims.

New layers would be added to the Exodus story in subsequent centuries—during the exile in Babylonia and beyond. But we can now see
how the astonishing composition came together under the pressure of a
growing conflict with Egypt in the seventh century BCE. The saga of Israel's
Exodus from Egypt is neither historical truth nor literary fiction. It is a
powerful expression of memory and hope born in a world in the midst of

change. The confrontation between Moses and pharaoh mirrored the momentous confrontation between the young King Josiah and the newly crowned Pharaoh Necho. To pin this biblical image down to a single date is to betray the story's deepest meaning. Passover proves to be not a single event but a continuing experience of national resistance against the powers that be.

[3]

The Conquest of Canaan

Israel's national destiny could be fulfilled only in the land of Canaan. The book of Joshua tells the story of a lightning military campaign during which the powerful kings of Canaan were defeated in battle and the Israelite tribes inherited their land. It is a story of the victory of God's people over arrogant pagans, a timeless epic of new frontiers conquered and cities captured, in which the losers must suffer the ultimate punishments of dispossession and death. It is a stirring war saga, with heroism, cunning, and bitter vengeance, narrated with some of the most vivid stories in the Bible—the fall of the walls of Jericho, the sun standing still at Gibeon, and the burning of the great Canaanite city of Hazor. It is also a detailed geographical essay about the landscape of Canaan and a historical explanation of how each of the twelve Israelite tribes came into its traditional territorial inheritance within the promised land.

Yet if, as we have seen, the Israelite Exodus did not take place in the manner described in the Bible, what of the conquest itself? The problems are even greater. How could an army in rags, traveling with women, children, and the aged, emerging after decades from the desert, possibly mount an effective invasion? How could such a disorganized rabble overcome the great fortresses of Canaan, with their professional armies and well-trained corps of chariots?

Did the conquest of Canaan really happen? Is this central saga of the Bible—and of the subsequent history of Israel—history, or myth? Despite the fact that the ancient cities of Jericho, Ai, Gibeon, Lachish, Hazor, and nearly all the others mentioned in the conquest story have been located and excavated, the evidence for a historical conquest of Canaan by the Israelites is, as we will see, weak. Here too, archaeological evidence can help disentangle the events of history from the powerful images of an enduring biblical tale.

Joshua's Battle Plan

The saga of the conquest begins with the last of the Five Books of Moses— the book of Deuteronomy—when we learn that Moses, the great leader, would not live to lead the children of Israel into Canaan. As a member of the generation that had personally experienced the bitterness of life in Egypt, he too had to die without entering the Promised Land. Before his death and burial on Mount Nebo in Moab, Moses stressed the importance of the observance of God's laws as a key to the coming conquest and, according to God's instructions, gave his long-time lieutenant Joshua command over the Israelites. After generations of slavery in Egypt and forty years of wandering in the desert, the Israelites were now standing on the very border of Canaan, across the river from the land where their forefathers Abraham, Isaac, and Jacob had lived. God now commanded that the land be cleansed of all traces of idolatry—and that would entail a complete extermination of the Canaanites.

Led by Joshua—a brilliant general with a flair for tactical surprise—the Israelites soon marched from one victory to another in a stunning series of sieges and open field battles. Immediately across the Jordan lay the ancient city of Jericho, a place that would have to be taken if the Israelites were to establish a bridgehead. As the Israelites were preparing to cross the Jordan, Joshua sent two spies into Jericho to gain intelligence on the enemy preparations and the strength of the fortifications. The spies returned with the encouraging news (provided to them by a harlot named Rahab) that the inhabitants had already become fearful at the news of the Israelite approach. The people of Israel immediately crossed the Jordan with the Ark of the Covenant leading the camp. The story of the subsequent conquest of Jeri-

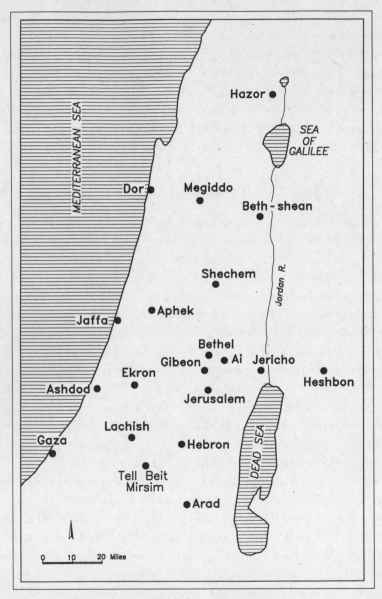

Figure 9: Main sites connected with the conquest narratives.

cho is almost too familiar to bear recounting: the Israelites followed the command of God as conveyed to them by Joshua, marching solemnly around the high walls of city, and on the seventh day, with a deafening blast of the Israelites' war trumpets, the mighty walls of Jericho came tumbling down (Joshua 6).

The next objective was the city of Ai, near Bethel, located in the highlands of Canaan at a strategic place on one of the main roads leading from the Jordan valley to the hill country. This time the city was taken by Joshua's brilliant tactics, worthy of the Greek warriors at Troy, rather than by a miracle. While Joshua arranged the bulk of his troops in the open field to the east of the city, taunting Ai's defenders, he secretly set an ambush on the western side. And when the warriors of Ai stormed out of the city to engage the Israelites and pursue them into the desert, the hidden ambush unit entered the undefended city and set it ablaze. Joshua then reversed his retreat and slaughtered all of Ai's inhabitants, taking all the cattle and spoil of the city as booty, and ignominiously hanging the king of Ai from a tree (Joshua 8:1–29).

Panic now began to spread among the inhabitants of other cities in Canaan. Hearing what had happened to the people of Jericho and Ai, the Gibeonites, who inhabited four cities north of Jerusalem, sent emissaries to Joshua to plead for mercy. Since they insisted that they were foreigners to the country, not natives (whom God had ordered to be exterminated), Joshua agreed to make peace with them. But when it was revealed that the Gibeonites had lied and were indeed native to the land, Joshua punished them by declaring that they would always serve as "hewers of wood and drawers of water" for the Israelites (Joshua 9:27).

The initial victories of the Israelite invaders in Jericho and in the towns of the central hill country became an immediate cause for concern among the more powerful kings of Canaan. Adonizedek, the king of Jerusalem, quickly forged a military alliance with the king of Hebron in the southern highlands and the kings of Jarmuth, Lachish, and Eglon in the Shephelah foothills to the west. The Canaanite kings marshaled their combined forces around Gibeon, but in a lightning movement, marching all night from the Jordan valley, Joshua surprised the army of the Jerusalem coalition. The Canaanite forces fled in panic along the steep ridge of Beth-horon to the west. As they fled, God pummeled them with great stones from heaven. In fact, the Bible tells us, "there were more who died because of the hailstones than the men of Israel killed with the sword" (Joshua 10:11). The sun was setting, but the righteous killing was not over, so Joshua turned to God in the presence of the entire Israelite army and bid that the sun stand still until the divine will was fulfilled. The sun then

> stayed in the midst of heaven, and did not hasten to go down for about a whole day. There has been no day like it before or since, when the LORD hearkened to the voice of a man; for the LORD fought for Israel." (JOSHUA 10:13–14)

The fleeing kings were finally captured and put to the sword. Joshua then continued the campaign and destroyed the Canaanite cities of the southern parts of the country, completely conquering that region for the people of Israel.

The final act took place in the north. A coalition of Canaanite kings headed by Jabin of Hazor, "a great host, in number like the sand that is upon the seashore, with very many horses and chariots" (Joshua 11:4), met the Israelites in an open field battle in Galilee that ended with the complete destruction of the Canaanite forces. Hazor, the most important city in Canaan, "the head of all those kingdoms" (Joshua 11:10), was conquered and set ablaze. Thus with this victory the entire promised land, from the southern desert to the snowy peak of Mount Hermon in the north, came into Israelite possession. The divine promise had indeed been fulfilled. The Canaanite forces were annihilated and the children of Israel settled down to divide the land among the tribes as their God-given inheritance.

A Different Kind of Canaan

As with the Exodus story, archaeology has uncovered a dramatic discrepancy between the Bible and the situation within Canaan at the suggested date of the conquest, between 1230 and 1220 BCE.* Although we know that a group named Israel was already present somewhere in Canaan by 1207 BCE, the evidence on the general political and military landscape of Canaan suggests that a lightning invasion by this group would have been impractical and unlikely in the extreme.

---

* This date, as we saw in the last chapter, was suggested by presumed references to the Ramesside pharaohs in the Exodus narratives and by the date of the Merneptah Stele (1207 BCE) that indicated "Israel" was present in Canaan by that time.

There is abundant evidence from Egyptian texts of the Late Bronze Age (1550–1150 BCE) on affairs in Canaan, in the form of diplomatic letters, lists of conquered cities, scenes of sieges engraved on the walls of temples in Egypt, annals of Egyptian kings, literary works, and hymns. Perhaps the most detailed source of information on Canaan in this period is provided by the Tell el-Amarna letters. These texts represent part of the diplomatic and military correspondence of the powerful pharaohs Amenhotep III and his son Akhenaten, who ruled Egypt in the fourteenth century BCE.

The almost four hundred Amarna tablets, now scattered in museums around the world, include letters sent to Egypt by rulers of powerful states, such as the Hittites of Anatolia and the rulers of Babylonia. But most were sent from rulers of city-states in Canaan, who were vassals of Egypt during this period. The senders included the rulers of Canaanite cities that would later become famous in the Bible, such as Jerusalem, Shechem, Megiddo, Hazor, and Lachish. Most important, the Amarna letters reveal that Canaan was an Egyptian province, closely controlled by Egyptian administration. The provincial capital was located in Gaza, but Egyptian garrisons were stationed at key sites throughout the country, like Beth-shean south of the Sea of Galilee and at the port of Jaffa (today part of the city of Tel Aviv).

In the Bible, no Egyptians are reported outside the borders of Egypt and none are mentioned in any of the battles within Canaan. Yet contemporary texts and archaeological finds indicate that they managed and carefully watched over the affairs of the country. The princes of the Canaanite cities (described in the book of Joshua as powerful enemies) were, in actuality, pathetically weak. Excavations have shown that the cities of Canaan in this period were not regular cities of the kind we know in later history. They were mainly administrative strongholds for the elite, housing the king, his family, and his small entourage of bureaucrats, with the peasants living scattered throughout the surrounding countryside in small villages. The typical city had only a palace, a temple compound, and a few other public edifices—probably residences for high officials, inns, and other administrative buildings. But there were no city walls. The formidable Canaanite cities described in the conquest narrative were not protected by fortifications!

The reason apparently was that with Egypt firmly in charge of security for the entire province, there was no need of massive defensive walls. There

was also an economic reason for the lack of fortifications at most Canaanite cities. With the imposition of heavy tribute to be paid to the pharaoh by
the princes of Canaan, local petty rulers may not have had the means (or
the authority) to engage in monumental public works. In fact, Late Bronze
Age Canaan was a mere shadow of the prosperous society that it had been
several centuries before, in the Middle Bronze Age. Many cities were abandoned and others shrank in size, and the total settled population could not
have greatly exceeded one hundred thousand. One demonstration of the
small scale of this society is the request in one of the Amarna letters sent by
the king of Jerusalem to the pharaoh that he supply fifty men "to protect
the land." The miniscule scale of the forces of the period is confirmed by
another letter, sent by the king of Megiddo, who asks the pharaoh to send
a hundred soldiers to guard the city from an attack by his aggressive neigh-
bor, the king of Shechem.

The Amarna letters describe the situation during the fourteenth century
BCE, a hundred or so years before the supposed date of the Israelite conquest. We have no such detailed source of information about affairs in
Canaan during the thirteenth century BCE. Yet Pharaoh Ramesses II, who
ruled during most of the thirteenth century, was not likely to have slack-
ened his military oversight of Canaan. He was a strong king, possibly the
strongest of all pharaohs, who was deeply interested in foreign affairs.

Other indications—both literary and archaeological—seem to show
that in the thirteenth century BCE, the grip of Egypt on Canaan was
stronger than ever. At times of reported unrest, the Egyptian army would
cross the Sinai desert along the Mediterranean coast and march against
rebel cities or troublesome people. As mentioned, the military route in
northern Sinai was protected by a series of forts and supplied with freshwater sources. After crossing the desert, the Egyptian army could easily rout
any rebel forces and impose its will on the local population.

Archaeology has uncovered dramatic evidence of the extent of Egyptian
presence in Canaan itself. An Egyptian stronghold was excavated at the site
of Beth-shean to the south of the Sea of Galilee in the 1920s. Its various
structures and courtyards contained statues and inscribed hieroglyphic
monuments from the days of the pharaohs Seti I (1294–1279 BCE),
Ramesses II (1279–1213 BCE), and Ramesses III (1184–1153 BCE). The ancient Canaanite city of Megiddo disclosed evidence for strong Egyptian in-

fluence as late as the days of Ramesses VI, who ruled toward the end of the twelfth century BCE. This was long after the supposed conquest of Canaan by the Israelites.

It is highly unlikely that the Egyptian garrisons throughout the country would have remained on the sidelines as a group of refugees (from Egypt) wreaked havoc throughout the province of Canaan. And it is inconceivable that the destruction of so many loyal vassal cities by the invaders would have left absolutely no trace in the extensive records of the Egyptian empire. The only independent mention of the name Israel in this period—the victory stele of Merneptah—announces only that this otherwise obscure people, living in Canaan, had suffered a crushing defeat. Something clearly doesn't add up when the biblical account, the archaeological evidence, and the Egyptian records are placed side by side.

In the Footsteps of Joshua?

There are, however—or at least there have been—counterarguments to the Egyptian evidence. First of all, it was clear that the book of Joshua was not a completely imaginary fable. It accurately reflected the geography of the land of Israel. The course of Joshua's campaign followed a logical geographical order. At the beginning of the twentieth century, a number of scholars selected sites that could be confidently identified with the progress of the Israelite conquest and began digging—to see if any evidence of fallen walls, burnt beams, and wholesale destruction could be found.

The most prominent figure in this quest was again the American scholar William Foxwell Albright, of Johns Hopkins University in Baltimore, a brilliant linguist, historian, biblical scholar, and field archaeologist, who had argued that the patriarchs were authentic historical personalities. On the basis of his reading of the archaeological evidence he believed that Joshua's exploits were also historical. Albright's most famous excavation took place between 1926 and 1932 at a mound named Tell Beit Mirsim, located in the foothills southwest of Hebron (Figure 9, p.74). On the basis of its geographical position, Albright identified the site with the Canaanite city of Debir, whose conquest by the Israelites is mentioned in three different stories in the Bible: twice in the book of Joshua (10:38–39; 15:15–19) and once in the book of Judges (1:11–15). Though the identification was later challenged, the archaeological finds from Tell Beit Mirsim remain central to the historical debate.

The excavations revealed a small and relatively poor unwalled town that was destroyed by a sudden catastrophic fire toward the end of the Late Bronze Age—according to Albright, around 1230 BCE. Over the ashes of this burnt city, Albright perceived what he thought was evidence for the arrival of new settlers: a scattering of coarse pottery that he knew from other sites in the highlands and that he intuitively identified as Israelite. The evidence seemed proof of the historicity of the biblical narratives: a Canaanite city (mentioned in the Bible) was set ablaze by the Israelites, who then inherited it and settled on its ruins.

Indeed, Albright's results seemed to be reproduced everywhere. At the ancient mound at the Arab village of Beitin, identified with the biblical city of Bethel, about nine miles north of Jerusalem, excavations revealed a Canaanite city inhabited in the Late Bronze. It was destroyed by fire in the late thirteenth century BCE and apparently resettled by a different group in the Iron Age I. It matched the biblical story of the Canaanite city of Luz, which was taken by members of the house of Joseph, who resettled it and changed its name to Bethel (Judges 1:22–26). Farther south, at the imposing mound of Tell ed-Duweir in the Shephelah, a site identified with the famous biblical city of Lachish (Joshua 10:31–32), a British expedition in the 1930s uncovered remains of yet another great Late Bronze Age city destroyed in a conflagration.

The discoveries continued in the 1950s, after the establishment of the state of Israel, when Israeli archaeologists began to concentrate on the question of the conquest of the promised land. In 1956, the leading Israeli archaeologist, Yigael Yadin, initiated excavations at the ancient city of Hazor, described in the book of Joshua as "the head of all those kingdoms" (Joshua 11:10). It was an ideal testing ground for the archaeological search for the Israelite conquest. Hazor, identified with the huge mound of Tell el-Waqqas in upper Galilee on the basis of its location and prominence, proved to be the largest city of Late Bronze Canaan. It covered an area of eighty hectares, eight times larger than such prominent sites as Megiddo and Lachish.

Yadin discovered that although Hazor's peak of prosperity occurred in the Middle Bronze Age (2000–1550 BCE), it continued to prosper well into the Late Bronze Age. It was a fabulous city, with temples and a huge palace. That palace's opulence in architectural style, statuary, and other small finds—already hinted at by the results of Yadin's excavations—has since been uncovered in the 1990s in the course of the renewed excavations at Hazor led by Amnon Ben-Tor of the Hebrew University. A number of cuneiform tablets hint at the presence of a royal archive. One of the recovered tablets bears the royal name Ibni, and a king of Hazor named Ibni-Addu is mentioned in the Mari archive. Though both date to much earlier times (in the Middle Bronze Age), they may relate etymologically to the name of Jabin, the king of Hazor mentioned in the Bible. The suggestive recurrence of this name may indicate that it was a dynastic name associated with Hazor for centuries—and remembered long after the city was destroyed.

The Hazor excavations showed that the splendor of the Canaanite city, like that of so many other cities in various parts of the country, came to a brutal end in the thirteenth century BCE. Suddenly, with no apparent alarm and little sign of decline, Hazor was attacked, destroyed, and set ablaze. The mud brick walls of the palace, which were baked red from the terrible conflagration, are still preserved today to a height of six feet. After a period of abandonment, a poor settlement was established in one part of the vast ruins. Its pottery resembled that of the early Israelite settlements in the central hill country to the south.

Thus, for much of the twentieth century, archaeology seemed to confirm the Bible's account. Unfortunately the scholarly consensus would eventually dissolve.

Did the Trumpets Really Blast?

In the midst of the euphoria—almost at the very moment when it seemed that the battle of the conquest was won for Joshua—some troubling contradictions emerged. Even as the world press was reporting that Joshua's conquest had been confirmed, many of the most important pieces of the archaeological puzzle simply did not fit.

Jericho was among the most important. As we have noted, the cities of Canaan were unfortified and there were no walls that could have come tumbling down. In the case of Jericho, there was no trace of a settlement

of any kind in the thirteenth century BCE, and the earlier Late Bronze settlement, dating to the fourteenth century BCE, was small and poor, almost
insignificant, and unfortified. There was also no sign of a destruction. Thus
the famous scene of the Israelite forces marching around the walled town
with the Ark of the Covenant, causing Jericho's mighty walls to collapse by
the blowing of their war trumpets was, to put it simply, a romantic mirage.

A similar discrepancy between archaeology and the Bible was found at
the site of ancient Ai, where, according to the Bible, Joshua carried out his
clever ambush. Scholars identified the large mound of Khirbet et-Tell, located on the eastern flank of the hill country northeast of Jerusalem, as the
ancient site of Ai. Its geographical location, just to the east of Bethel, closely
matched the biblical description. The site's modern Arabic name, et-Tell,
means "the ruin," which is more or less equivalent to the meaning of the
biblical Hebrew name Ai. And there was no alternative Late Bronze Age site
anywhere in the vicinity. Between 1933 and 1935, the French-trained Jewish
Palestinian archaeologist Judith Marquet-Krause carried out a large-scale
excavation at et-Tell and found extensive remains of a huge Early Bronze
Age city, dated over a millennium before the collapse of Late Bronze
Canaan. Not a single pottery sherd or any other indication of settlement
there in the Late Bronze Age was recovered. Renewed excavations at the site
in the 1960s produced the same picture. Like Jericho, there was no settlement at the time of its supposed conquest by the children of Israel.

And what about the saga of the Gibeonites with their pleading for
protection? Excavations at the mound in the village of el-Jib, north of
Jerusalem, which a scholarly consensus identified as the site of biblical
Gibeon, revealed remains from the Middle Bronze Age and from the Iron
Age, but none from the Late Bronze Age. And archaeological surveys at
the sites of the other three "Gibeonite" towns of Chephirah, Beeroth, and
Kiriath-jearim revealed the same picture: at none of the sites were there any
Late Bronze Age remains. The same holds true for other towns mentioned
in the conquest narrative and in the summary list of the kings of Canaan
(Joshua 12). Among them we find Arad (in the Negev) and Heshbon (in
Transjordan), which we mentioned in the last chapter.

Passionate explanations and complex rationalizations were not long in
coming, because there was so much at stake. Regarding Ai, Albright suggested that the story of its conquest originally referred to nearby Bethel, be-

cause Bethel and Ai were so closely associated both geographically and traditionally. In the case of Jericho, some scholars sought environmental explanations. They suggested that the entire stratum representing Jericho at the time of the conquest, including the fortifications, had been eroded away.

Only recently has the consensus finally abandoned the conquest story. As for the destruction of Bethel, Lachish, Hazor, and other Canaanite cities, evidence from other parts of the Middle East and the eastern Mediterranean suggests that the destroyers were not necessarily Israelites.

The Mediterranean World of the Thirteenth Century BCE

The Bible's geographical focus is almost entirely on the land of Israel, but in order to understand the magnitude of the events that took place at the end of the Late Bronze Age, one must look far beyond the borders of Canaan, to the entire eastern Mediterranean region (Figure 10). Digs in Greece, Turkey, Syria, and Egypt reveal a stunning story of upheaval, war, and widespread social breakdown. In the last years of the thirteenth century BCE and the beginning of the twelfth, the entire ancient world went through a dramatic transformation, as a devastating crisis swept away the Bronze Age kingdoms and a new world began to emerge. This was one of the most dramatic and chaotic periods in history, with old empires falling and new forces rising to take their place.

Beforehand—as late as the mid-thirteenth century BCE—two great empires ruled the region. In the south, Egypt was at its peak. Ruled by Ramesses II, it controlled Canaan, including the territories of modern Lebanon and southwestern Syria. In the south it dominated Nubia, and in the west it ruled over Libya. The Egyptian empire was engaged in monumental building activity and participated in lucrative trade in the eastern Mediterranean. Emissaries and merchants from Crete, Cyprus, Canaan, and Hatti frequented Egypt and brought gifts to the pharaoh. Turquoise and copper mines in Sinai and the Negev were exploited by Egyptian expeditions. There had never been such an expansive or powerful empire in Egypt. One needs only to stand before the Abu Simbel temple in Nubia or the famous temples of Karnak and Luxor to feel the grandeur of Egypt in the thirteenth century BCE.

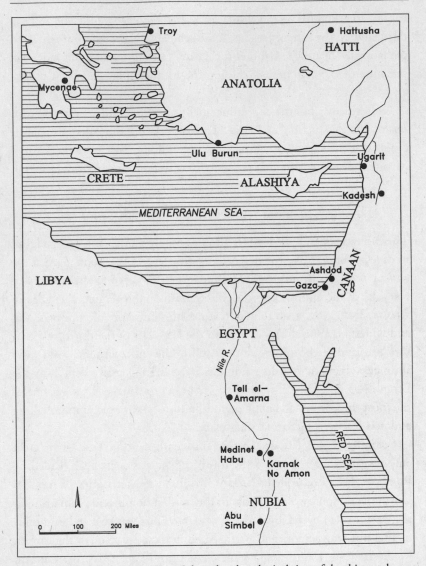

Figure 10: The Ancient Near East: Selected archaeological sites of the thirteenth century BCE.

The other great empire of the region was centered in Anatolia. This was the mighty Hittite state, which was ruled from its capital, Hattusha, east of the modern Turkish capital of Ankara. The Hittites controlled Asia Minor and northern Syria. They reached remarkable heights in architecture, literature, and warfare. The immense city of Hattusha, with its stupendous fortifications and rock-cut temple, gives modern visitors a sense of the Hittites' greatness.

The two empires—Egyptian and Hittite—bordered each other in Syria. The inevitable clash between them came at the beginning of the thirteenth century. The two formidable armies met at Kadesh on the Orontes River in western Syria. On one side was Muwatallis, the Hittite king; on the other side stood the then young and inexperienced Ramesses II. We have records of the battle from both sides and both claim victory. The truth was somewhere in the middle. Apparently the battle ended with no clear winner and the two great powers had to compromise. The new Hittite king, Hattusilis III, and the now battle-hardened Ramesses II soon signed a peace treaty that pronounced friendship between the two powers and renounced hostilities "forever." It was sealed with the symbolic act of Ramesses taking a Hittite princess as his bride.

The world created by this Egyptian-Hittite stalemate offered increasing opportunities for another great power, in the West. It was a strong force not because of military might but because of maritime skills. This was the Mycenaean world, which produced the famous citadels of Mycenae and Tiryns and the opulent palaces of Pylos and Thebes. It was the world that apparently provided the romantic background to the *Iliad* and the *Odyssey;* the world that produced the famous figures of Agamemnon, Helen, Priam, and Odysseus. We are not sure if the Mycenaean world was ruled by one center, such as Mycenae. More probably it was a system of several centers that each ruled large territories: something like the city-states of Canaan or the polis system of classical Greece, but on a much bigger scale.

The Mycenaean world, which was first revealed in the dramatic excavations of Heinrich Schliemann in Mycenae and Tiryns in the late nineteenth century, started revealing its secrets years later, when its Linear B script was deciphered. The tablets found in the Mycenaean palaces proved that the Mycenaeans spoke Greek. Their power and wealth apparently came from trade in the eastern Mediterranean.

The island of Cyprus—known at that time as Alashiya—also played an important role in this world of the thirteenth century BCE. It was the main producer of copper in the eastern Mediterranean and a gateway to the trade with the Levant. Impressive structures built with ashlar blocks show how prosperous the island became at that time.

The Late Bronze Age world was characterized by great power, wealth, and active trade. The now famous shipwreck of Ulu Burun, found off the coast of southern Turkey, gives a hint of the boom times. A ship carrying a cargo of ingots of copper and tin, logs of ebony, terebinth resin, hippopotamus and elephant ivory, ostrich eggshells, spices, and other goods was sailing along the coast of Asia Minor sometime around 1300 BCE when it apparently went down in a storm. Underwater excavations of the wreck and recovery of its rich cargo have shown that this small vessel—certainly not exceptional at the time—plied the lucrative routes of trade in the entire eastern Mediterranean, with lavish artifacts and consumer goods picked up in every port of call.

It is important to keep in mind that this world was not just an ancient version of a modern Common Market, with each nation trading freely with all the rest. It was a world that was tightly controlled by the kings and princes of every political region, and carefully watched over by Egypt and the other great powers of the time. In this world of order and prosperity for the Bronze Age elites, the suddenness and violence of their downfall would have certainly made a lasting impression—in memory, legend, and poetry.

The Great Upheaval

The view from the palaces of the city-states of Canaan may have looked peaceful, but there were problems on the horizon, problems that would bring the whole economy and social structure of the Late Bronze Age crashing down. By 1130 BCE, we see a whole different world, so different that an inhabitant of Mycenae, or of No Amon (the capital of Egypt, today's Luxor), or of Hattusha from 1230 BCE would not be able to recognize it. By then, Egypt was a poor shadow of its past glory and had lost most of its foreign territories. Hatti was no more, and Hattusha lay in ruins. The Mycenaean world was a fading memory, its palatial centers destroyed. Cyprus was transformed; its trade in copper and other goods had

ceased. Many large Canaanite ports along the Mediterranean coast including the great maritime emporium of Ugarit in the north were burnt to
ashes. Impressive inland cities, such as Megiddo and Hazor, were abandoned fields of ruins.

What happened? Why did the old world disappear? Scholars who have
worked on this problem have been convinced that a major cause was the
invasions of mysterious and violent groups named the Sea Peoples, migrants who came by land and sea from the west and devastated everything
that stood in their way. The Ugaritic and Egyptian records of the early
twelfth century BCE mention these marauders. A text found in the ruins of
the port city of Ugarit provides dramatic testimony for the situation
around 1185 BCE. Sent by Ammurapi, the last king of Ugarit, to the king of
Alashiya (Cyprus), it frantically describes how "enemy boats have arrived,
the enemy has set fire to the cities and wrought havoc. My troops are in
Hittite country, my boats in Lycia, and the country has been left to its own
devices." Likewise, a letter of the same period from the great king of Hatti
to the prefect of Ugarit expresses his anxiety about the presence of a group
of Sea People called Shiqalaya, "who live on boats."

Ten years later, in 1175 BCE, it was all over in the north. Hatti, Alashiya,
and Ugarit lay in ruins. But Egypt was still a formidable power, determined
to make a desperate defense. The monumental inscriptions of Ramesses III
at the temple of Medinet Habu in Upper Egypt recount the Sea People's
purported conspiracy to ravage the settled lands of the eastern Mediterranean: "The foreign countries made a conspiracy in their islands. . . . No
land could stand before their arms. . . . They were coming forward toward
Egypt, while the flame was prepared before them. Their confederation was
the Philistines, Tjeker, Shekelesh, Denyen, and Weshesh, lands united.
They laid their hands upon the lands as far as the circuit of the earth, their
hearts confident and trusting: 'Our plans will succeed!' "

Vivid depictions of the subsequent battles cover an outside wall of the
temple (Figure 11). In one, a tangle of Egyptian and foreign ships are shown
in the midst of a chaotic naval engagement, with archers poised to strike
the ships of their enemies, and dying warriors falling into the sea. The
seaborne invaders look very different from the Egyptians, or from repre-
sentations of Asiatic people in Egyptian art. The most striking feature in
their appearance is their distinctive headgear: some wear horned helmets,

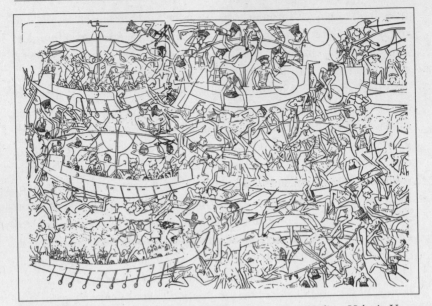

Figure·11: Relief from the mortuary temple of Ramesses III at Medinet Habu in Upper
Egypt, showing the naval battle with the Sea Peoples.

others strange feathered headdresses. Nearby, depictions of an intense land
battle show Egyptians engaging the Sea People warriors, while families of
men, women, and children riding wooden ox carts for an overland migration watch helplessly. The outcome of the land and sea battles, according to
Pharaoh Ramesses III's description, was decisive: "Those who reached my
frontier, their seed is not, their heart and their soul are finished forever and
ever. Those who came forward together on the sea, the full flame was in
front of them. . . . They were dragged in, enclosed, and prostrated on the
beach, killed, and made into heaps from tail to head."

Who were these threatening Sea Peoples? There is a continuing scholarly
debate about their origin and the factors that set them in motion toward
the south and east. Some say they were Aegean; others look to southern
Anatolia for their origin. But what set thousands of uprooted people onto
the land and sea routes in search of new homes? One possibility is that they
were a ragtag confederation of freebooters, rootless sailors, and dispos-
sessed peasants driven by famine, population pressure, or scarcity of land.
By moving eastward and destroying the fragile network of international

trade in the eastern Mediterranean, they disrupted the Bronze Age economies and sent the great empires of the time to oblivion. More recent theories have offered dramatically different explanations. Some point to sudden climatic change that devastated agriculture and caused widespread famine. Others hypothesize a complete breakdown of societies throughout the eastern Mediterranean that had become too specialized to survive economic change or social stress. In both these possible scenarios, the sudden migrations of the Sea Peoples were not the cause but the effect. In other words, the breakdown of the palace economies of the Late Bronze Age sent hordes of uprooted people roaming across the eastern Mediterranean to find new homes and livelihoods.

The truth is, we really don't know the precise cause of the Late Bronze Age collapse throughout the region. Yet the archaeological evidence for the outcome is clear. The most dramatic evidence comes from southern Israel—from Philistia, the land of the Philistines, who were one of the Sea Peoples mentioned in the inscription of Ramesses III. Excavations in two of the major Philistine centers—Ashdod and Ekron—uncovered evidence about these troubled years. In the thirteenth century BCE, Ashdod in particular was a prosperous Canaanite center under Egyptian influence. Both Ashdod and Ekron survived at least until the days of Ramesses III and at least one of them, Ashdod, was then destroyed by fire. The Philistine immigrants founded cities on the ruins, and by the twelfth century BCE, Ashdod and Ekron had become prosperous cities, with a new material culture. The older mix of Egyptian and Canaanite features in architecture and ceramics was replaced by something utterly new in this part of the Mediterranean: Aegean-inspired architecture and pottery styles.

In other parts of the country, the Late Bronze Age order was disrupted by spreading violence whose source is not entirely clear. Because of the long period of time—nearly a century—during which the Canaanite city-state system collapsed, it is possible that the intensifying crisis led to conflicts between neighboring Canaanite cities over control of vital agricultural land and peasant villages. In some cases the increasingly hard-pressed peasants and pastoral population may have attacked the wealthy cities in their midst. One by one, the old Canaanite centers fell in sudden, dramatic conflagrations or went into gradual decline. In the north, Hazor was set on fire, with the statues of gods in its royal palace decapitated and smashed.

On the coastal plain, Aphek was destroyed in a terrible fire; a cuneiform tablet dealing with a vital wheat transaction between Ugarit and Egypt was found in the thick destruction debris. Farther south, the imposing Canaanite city of Lachish was torched and abandoned. And in the rich Jezreel valley, Megiddo was set aflame and its palace was buried under six feet of burnt brick debris.

It should be stressed that this great transformation was not sudden in every place. The archaeological evidence indicates that the destruction of Canaanite society was a relatively long and gradual process. The pottery types found in the rubble of Late Bronze Age Hazor lack the characteristic shapes of the late thirteenth century, so it must have been devastated somewhat earlier. At Aphek, the cuneiform letter in the layer of destruction bears names of officials from Ugarit and Egypt who are known from other sources—and can be thus dated to around 1230 BCE. The Egyptian stronghold there could have been devastated at any time in the two or three decades that followed. The excavators at Lachish found in the destruction layer a metal fragment—probably a fitting for the main gate of the city—bearing the name of Pharaoh Ramesses III. This find tells us that Lachish must have been destroyed no earlier than the reign of this monarch, who ruled between 1184 and 1153 BCE. Finally, a metal base of a statue carrying the name of Ramesses VI (1143–1136 BCE) was found in the ruins of Megiddo, indicating that the great Canaanite center of the Jezreel valley was probably destroyed in the second half of the twelfth century.

The kings of each of these four cities—Hazor, Aphek, Lachish, and Megiddo—are reported to have been defeated by the Israelites under Joshua. But the archaeological evidence shows that the destruction of those cities took place over a span of more than a century. The possible causes include invasion, social breakdown, and civil strife. No single military force did it, and certainly not in one military campaign.

Memories in Transition

Even before the archaeological findings had called the historical basis of Joshua's conquest of Canaan into question, a small circle of German biblical scholars had been speculating about the development of Israelite literary traditions rather than battlefield strategies. As heirs to the tradition of the higher criticism of the nineteenth century, they pointed out the inner inconsistencies of the biblical text, which contains at least two distinct and mutually contradictory versions of the conquest of Canaan.

The German scholars had always considered the book of Joshua to be a complex collection of legends, hero tales, and local myths, from various parts of the country, that had been composed over centuries. The biblical scholars Albrecht Alt and Martin Noth, in particular, argued that many of the tales preserved within the book of Joshua were no more than etiological traditions—that is to say, they were legends about how famous landmarks or natural curiosities came to be. For example, the people living in and around the Iron Age town of Bethel undoubtedly noticed the huge mound of Early Bronze Age ruins just to the east. This ruin was almost ten times bigger than their own town and the remains of its fortifications were still impressive. So—argued Alt and Noth—legends might have started growing around the ruins, tales of the victory of ancient heroes that explained how it was possible for such a great city to be destroyed.

In another region of the country, the people living in the foothills of the Shephelah may have been impressed by the sheer size of a stone blocking the entrance to a mysterious cave near the town of Makkedah. So stories could have arisen that linked the huge stone with heroic acts in their own hazy past: the stone sealed the cave where five ancient kings hid and were later buried, as explained in Joshua 10:16–27. According to this view, the biblical stories that concluded with the observation that a certain landmark could still be seen "to this very day" were probably legends of this kind. At a certain point these individual stories were collected and linked to the single campaign of a great mythical leader of the conquest.

In contrast to their estimation of the largely legendary character of the book of Joshua, Alt and Noth regarded the first chapter of the book of Judges as possessing a possible reliable nucleus of memories of ancient victories by widely scattered hill country militias over the various cities that had dominated them. Indeed, the chaotic situation of the destruction of Canaanite cities in some places and their survival in others corresponds more closely to the archaeological evidence. Yet there is no reason why the conquest narrative of the book of Joshua cannot also include folk memories and legends that commemorated this epoch-making historical transformation. They may offer us highly fragmentary glimpses of the violence, the passion, the euphoria at the destruction of cities and the horrible slaughter of their inhabitants that clearly occurred. Such searing experiences are not likely to have been totally forgotten, and indeed, their once-vivid memories, growing progressively vaguer over the centuries, may have become the raw material for a far more elaborate retelling. Thus there is no reason to suppose that the burning of Hazor by hostile forces, for example, never took place. But what was in actuality a chaotic series of upheavals caused by many different factors and carried out by many different groups became—many centuries later—a brilliantly crafted saga of territorial conquest under God's blessing and direct command. The literary production of that saga was undertaken for purposes quite different from the commemoration of local legends. It was, as we will see, an important step toward the creation of a Pan-Israelite identity.

Back to the Future Again?

This basic picture of the gradual accumulation of legends and stories—and their eventual incorporation into a single coherent saga with a definite theological outlook—was a product of that astonishingly creative period of literary production in the kingdom of Judah in the seventh century BCE. Perhaps most telling of all the clues that the book of Joshua was written at this time is the list of towns in the territory of the tribe of Judah, given in detail in Joshua 15:21–62. The list precisely corresponds to the borders of the kingdom of Judah during the reign of Josiah. Moreover, the place-names mentioned in the list closely correspond to the seventh-century BCE settlement pattern in the same region. And some of the sites were occupied *only* in the final decades of the seventh century BCE.

But geography is not the only link to the age of Josiah. The ideology of religious reform and territorial aspirations characteristic of the period are also evident. Biblical scholars have long seen the book of Joshua as part of the so-called Deuteronomistic History, the seven-book compilation of biblical material from Deuteronomy to 2 Kings that was compiled during the reign of Josiah. The Deuteronomistic History repeatedly returns to the idea that the entire land of Israel should be ruled by the divinely chosen leader of the entire people of Israel, who strictly follows the laws handed down at Sinai—and the even stricter warnings against idolatry given by

Moses in the book of Deuteronomy. The language, style, and uncompromising theological messages conveyed by the book of Deuteronomy are found throughout the book of Joshua—particularly in passages where the stories of individual battles are woven together in the larger narrative. And the overall battle plan of the book of Joshua fits seventh century realities far better than the situation of the Late Bronze Age.

The first two battles in the book of Joshua, at Jericho and Ai (that is, the area of Bethel), were fought in territories that were the first target of Josianic expansionism after the withdrawal of Assyria from the province of Samaria. Jericho was the southeasternmost outpost of the northern Kingdom of Israel and the later Assyrian province, situated opposite a strategic ford in the Jordan River. Bethel was the main, much-hated cult center of the northern kingdom and a focus of Assyrian resettlement of non-Israelite peoples.* Both places were later targets of Josianic activity: Jericho and its region flourished after the Judahite takeover, and the northern temple at Bethel was completely destroyed.

So too, the story of the conquest of the Shephelah parallels the renewed Judahite expansion into this very important and fertile region. This area— the traditional breadbasket of Judah—was conquered by the Assyrians a few decades earlier and given to the cities of Philistia. Indeed, 2 Kings 22:1 tells us that Josiah's mother came from a town named Bozkath. This place is mentioned only one more time in the Bible—in the list of the towns of the tribe of Judah, that date to the time of Josiah. (Joshua 15:39). There Bozkath appears between Lachish and Eglon—the two Canaanite cities that play a major role in the narrative of Joshua's conquest of the Shephelah.

The saga of Joshua's campaign then turns toward the north, expressing a seventh century vision of future territorial conquest. The reference to Hazor calls to mind not only its reputation in the distant past as the most prominent of the Canaanite city-states but also the realities of only a cen-

---

* The story of the Gibeonites, who had "come from a far country" and sought to make a covenant with the invading Israelites (Joshua 9:3–27), may also reflect an adaptation of an old tradition to a seventh century reality. Expanding northward into the area of Bethel after the retreat of Assyria, Judah faced a problem of how to integrate the descendants of the deportees brought by the Assyrians from afar and settled there a few decades earlier. The mention of Avvim in this area in Joshua 18:23 recalls the name Avva—one of the places of origin of the deportees listed in 2 Kings 17:24. Especially crucial in the Josianic era was the question of how to absorb those who were sympathetic to Judah into the community. The old story of the Gibeonites could provide a "historical" context in which the Deuteronomist explained how this might be done.

tury before, when Hazor was the most important center of the kingdom of
Israel, in the north, and a bit later an important regional center of the Assyrian empire, with an impressive palace and a fortress. No less meaningful
is the mention of Naphot Dor, possibly alluding to the days when the
coastal city of Dor served as the capital of an Assyrian province.

In sum, the northern territories described in the book of Joshua correspond to the vanquished kingdom of Israel and later Assyrian provinces
that Judah believed were the divinely determined inheritance of the people
of Israel, soon to be reclaimed by a "new" Joshua.

A New Conquest of the Promised Land?

By the time of Josiah's coronation in 639 BCE, the idea of the sanctity and
unity of the land of Israel—a concept that would be stressed with such
great passion by the book of Deuteronomy—was far from realization. Except for the tiny heartland of the kingdom of Judah (the traditional
birthright of the tribes of Judah and Simeon and a narrow sliver of the traditional land of Benjamin, just to the north), the vast majority of the
promised land had lain under the rule of a foreign power, Assyria, for almost a century. And Judah, too, was a vassal of Assyria.

The Bible's explanation for this unhappy situation was as grim as it was
simple. In recent times, the people of Israel had not fulfilled the laws of the
covenant that were the central prerequisite for their possession of the land.
They had not eradicated every trace of pagan worship. They had not ceased
to offer praise to the gods of other peoples in their attempts to gain wealth
through trade or political alliances. They had not faithfully followed the
laws of purity in personal life. And they had not cared even to offer the
slightest relief to their fellow Israelites who had found themselves destitute,
enslaved, or deeply in debt. In a word, they had ceased to be a holy
community. Only scrupulous adherence to the legislation in the recently
discovered "book of the Law" would overcome the sins of previous generations and allow them to regain possession of the entire land of Israel.

A few years later the Assyrians withdrew and the unification of all Israelites seemed possible. The book of Joshua offered an unforgettable epic
with a clear lesson—how, when the people of Israel *did* follow the Law of
the covenant with God to the letter, no victory could be denied to them.

That point was made with some of the most vivid folktales—the fall of the walls of Jericho, the sun standing still at Gibeon, the rout of Canaanite kings down the narrow ascent at Beth-horon—recast as a single epic against a highly familiar and suggestive seventh century background, and played out in places of the greatest concern to the Deuteronomistic ideology. In reading and reciting these stories, the Judahites of the late seventh century BCE would have seen their deepest wishes and religious beliefs expressed.

In that sense, the book of Joshua is a classic literary expression of the yearnings and fantasies of a people at a certain time and place. The towering figure of Joshua is used to evoke a metaphorical portrait of Josiah, the would-be savior of all the people of Israel. Indeed, the American biblical scholar Richard D. Nelson has demonstrated how the figure of Joshua is described in the Deuteronomistic history in terms usually reserved for a king. God's charge to Joshua at his assumption of leadership (Joshua 1:1–9) is framed in the phraseology of a royal installation. The loyalty pledge of the people for complete obedience to Joshua as the successor of Moses (Joshua 1:16–18) recalls the custom of public obeisance to a newly crowned king. And Joshua leads a ceremony of covenant renewal (Joshua 8:30–35), a role that became the prerogative of the kings of Judah. Even more telling is the passage in which God commands Joshua to meditate on the "book of the Law" day and night (Joshua 1:8–9), in uncanny parallelism to the biblical description of Josiah as a king uniquely concerned with the study of the Law, one who "turned to the Lord with all his heart and with all his soul and with all his might, according to all the Law of Moses" (2 Kings 23:25).

These are not simply conventional parallels between righteous biblical characters, but direct parallels in phraseology and ideology—not to mention Joshua's and Josiah's identical territorial goals. Of course, Josiah's expansion, or desire for annexation of the territories of the northern kingdom in the highlands, raised great hopes, but at the same time posed severe practical difficulties. There was the sheer military challenge. There was the need to prove to the native residents of the northern highlands that they were indeed part of the great people of Israel who fought together with the people of Judah to inherit their Promised Land. And there was also the problem of intermarriage with foreign women, which must have been a common practice among the Israelites who survived in the territories of the northern kingdom, among whom the Assyrians had settled foreign deportees.

It is King Josiah who lurks behind the mask of Joshua in declaring that the people of Israel must remain entirely apart from the native population of the land. The book of Joshua thus brilliantly highlights the deepest and most pressing of seventh-century concerns. And as we will later see, the power of this epic was to endure long after King Josiah's ambitious and pious plan to reconquer the land of Canaan had tragically failed.

[4]

Who Were the Israelites?

The Bible leaves little room for doubt or ambiguity about the unique origins of the people of Israel. As direct, lineal descendants of the patriarchs Abraham, Isaac, and Jacob, the twelve tribes of Israel are the biological offspring, over many generations, of the twelve sons of Jacob. Despite 430 years of bondage in Egypt, the Israelites are described as never having forgotten their roots in Canaan or their common heritage. Indeed the Bible stresses that Israel's strict maintenance of its distinctive way of life and special relationship with God would be the key to its future. In Deuteronomy, Moses had promised the Israelite nation that if they strictly observed the laws of the covenant, shunned intermarriage with their neighbors, and scrupulously avoided entanglement in the pagan ways of Canaan, they would be forever secure in their possession of the promised land. Once the great conquest of Canaan was completed, the book of Joshua related in great detail how the Israelite leader divided the land—now mostly cleared of the indigenous Canaanite population—among the victorious Israelite tribes as their eternal inheritances.

Yet within the book of Joshua and the following book of Judges are some serious contradictions to this picture of the tribes inheriting the entire land of Israel. Although the book of Joshua at one point declares that the Israelites had taken possession of all the land God promised and had defeated all their enemies (Joshua 21:43–44), other passages in the book of Joshua and in the book of Judges make it clear that many Canaanites and Philistines lived in close proximity to the Israelites. As in the case of Samson, intermarriage was not unheard of. And there were also problems within the family. In the book of Judges, the tribes of Israel combine to wage war on the tribe of Benjamin, vowing that they would never intermarry with them (Judges 19–21). Finally, it seems that the different tribes were left to solve their own local problems under the leadership of their own charismatic leaders. The Song of Deborah (Judges 5) even enumerates which particular tribes were faithful and heeded the call to rally for the cause of all Israel—and which tribes preferred to remain in their homes.

If, as archaeology suggests, the sagas of the patriarchs and the Exodus were legends, compiled in later periods, and if there is no convincing evidence of a unified invasion of Canaan under Joshua, what are we to make of the Israelites' claims for ancient nationhood? Who were these people who traced their traditions back to shared historical and cultic events? Once again archaeology can provide some surprising answers. Excavations of early Israelite villages, with their pottery, houses, and grain silos, can help us reconstruct their day-to-day life and cultural connections. And archaeology surprisingly reveals that the people who lived in those villages were indigenous inhabitants of Canaan who only gradually developed an ethnic identity that could be termed Israelite.

Inheriting the Promised Land

Once the great conquest of Canaan was over, the book of Joshua informs us, "the land had rest from war" (Joshua 11:23). All the Canaanites and other indigenous peoples of Canaan had been utterly destroyed. Joshua convened the tribes to divide the land. Reuben, Gad, and half the tribe of Manasseh received territories east of the Jordan River, while all the others received their portions to the west. Naphtali, Asher, Zebulun, and Issachar were to dwell in the highlands and valleys of Galilee. The other half of the tribe of Manasseh, and Ephraim and Benjamin, received the bulk of the central highlands, extending from the Jezreel valley in the north to Jerusalem in the south. Judah was allotted the southern highlands from Jerusalem to the Beersheba valley in the south. Simeon inherited the arid zone of the Beersheba valley and the adjoining coastal plain. Although Dan initially received an inheritance on the coastal plain, the tribe shifted its home to an area in the north of the country. With that last migration, the map of the holy land was set.

Or was it? In a puzzling contradiction to the proclamations of total victory, the book of Joshua reports that large territories within Canaan, situated outside the tribal inheritances, remained to be conquered. They included "all the regions of the Philistines" along the southern coast of the country, the Phoenician coast farther north, and the area of the Beqa valley in the northeast (Joshua 13:1–6). The book of Judges goes even further, listing important unconquered Canaanite enclaves in the territory of over half of the tribes. The great Canaanite cities of the coastal plain and the northern valleys, such as Megiddo, Beth-shean, Dor, and Gezer, were listed in the book of Judges as uncaptured—even though their rulers were included in the book of Joshua in its list of defeated Canaanite kings. In addition, the Ammonites and Moabites dwelling across the Jordan River remained hostile. And the violent Midianites and Amalekite camel raiders from the desert were always a threat to the people of Israel. Thus the menace that faced the newly settled Israelites was both military and religious. External enemies threatened the Israelites' physical safety and the Canaanites remaining in the land posed the mortal danger of luring the Israelites into apostasy—and thereby shattering the power of Israel's solemn covenant with God.

The stage was set for many years of protracted struggle. Following the book of Joshua, the book of Judges presents an extraordinarily rich collection of thrilling war stories and tales of individual heroism in the battles between the Israelites and their neighbors. It contains some of the Bible's most colorful characters and most unforgettable images. Othniel, a Calebite, single-handedly beats back the forces of the mysterious foe Cushan-rishathaim, "king of Mesopotamia" (Judges 3:7–11). Ehud the Benjaminite fearlessly assassinates Eglon, the powerful yet comically obese king of Moab, in his private apartment. (3:12–30). Shamgar slays six hundred Philistines with an ox goad (3:31). Deborah and Barak rouse the Israelite tribes against the threat of the remaining Canaanite kings in the north, and the heroic Yael, wife of Heber the Kenite, slays the Canaanite general Sisera by driving a stake into his head while he sleeps (4:1–5:31). Gideon the Manassite purifies the land from idolatry and protects his people from the desert-raiding Midianites (6:1–8:28). And of course, there is the famous saga of Samson, the hero of Dan, betrayed and shorn by the Philistine temptress Delilah, who goes to his death in Gaza, blinded and humbled, by pulling down the pillars of the great Philistine temple of Dagon (13:1–16:31).

The theological meaning of this early period of settlement is made clear at the very beginning of the book of Judges, in its sobering calculus of apostasy and punishment. If the people of Israel remain apart from the indigenous population, they will be rewarded. Should they be tempted to assimilate, divine punishment will be swift and severe. But they do not listen. Only the intervention of divinely inspired righteous leaders, called "judges," saves the people of Israel at least temporarily from losing everything:

> And the people of Israel did what was evil in the sight of the LORD and served the Baals; and they forsook the LORD, the God of their fathers, who had brought them out of the land of Egypt; they went after other gods, from among the gods of the peoples who were round about them, and bowed down to them; and they provoked the LORD to anger. They forsook the LORD, and served the Baals and the Ashtaroth. So the anger of the LORD was kindled against Israel, and he gave them over to plunderers, who plundered them; and he sold them into the power of their enemies round about, so that they could no longer withstand their enemies. Whenever they marched out, the hand of the LORD was against them for evil, as the LORD had warned, and as the LORD had sworn to them; and they were in sore straits. Then the LORD raised up judges, who saved them out of the power of those who plundered them. And yet they did not listen to their judges; for they played the harlot after other gods and bowed down to them; they soon turned aside from the way in which their fathers had walked, who had obeyed the commandments of the LORD, and they did not do so. Whenever the LORD raised up judges for them, the LORD was with the judge, and he saved them from the hand of their enemies all the days of the judge; for the LORD was moved to pity by their groaning because of those who afflicted and oppressed them. But whenever the judge died, they turned back and behaved worse than their fathers, going after other gods, serving them and bowing down to them; they did not drop any of their practices or their stubborn ways.
>
> (JUDGES 2:11–19)

Is the Bible relating a version of history as it really happened? Did the Israelites worship one God for centuries, but sometimes slip into the polytheism of their neighbors? More generally, how did they live? What was their culture like? Beyond the tales of ongoing struggle with idolatry, the Bible tells us very little of the day-to-day life of the Israelites. From the book of Joshua we learn mostly about the precise borders of the various tribal allotments. In Judges we read about the battles with Israel's enemies, but we hear very little about the kind of settlements the Israelites chose to establish and how they supported themselves. After centuries as immigrant laborers in Egypt and forty years' wandering in the desolate wilderness of Sinai, they could not have been well prepared to begin farming the narrow valleys and rugged upland fields of Canaan. How did they learn to become settled farmers and so quickly adapt to the routines and struggles of settled village life?

Immigrants from the Desert?

We know from the Merneptah stele that there was a people named Israel living in Canaan by 1207 BCE. Until very recently, despite doubts about the historical accuracy of the Exodus and the conquest stories, few biblical historians or archaeologists doubted that the Israelites were an immigrant people who entered Canaan from the outside.

The apparent difference between Canaanites and Israelites was clearest in the realm of material culture. Immediately above the destruction layers at the various Late Bronze Age Canaanite cities, archaeologists regularly found a scatter of haphazardly dug pits and coarse pottery—the apparent remains of what they interpreted as the temporary tent encampments of "seminomads." Many scholars believed they recognized a familiar pattern in this archaeological situation, namely the mass movement of displaced desert dwellers who invaded the settled land, then started to settle down, and gradually adopted a sedentary way of life. Scholars familiar with bedouin raids on agricultural regions in the Middle East believed that there had always been a conflict between desert nomads and settled peasants—a constant struggle between the desert and the sown. Though the Israelites might not have marched into Canaan as a unified army, the signs of their arrival seemed to be clear. In comparison to the monumental buildings, imported luxury items, and fine ceramic vessels uncovered in the levels of the preceding Canaanite cities, the rough encampments and implements of the arriving Israelites seemed to be on a far lower level of civilization than the remains of the population they replaced.

This comparison of lifestyles gave rise to what came to be called the "peaceful-infiltration" model, first put forward by the German biblical scholar Albrecht Alt in the 1920s. Alt suggested that the Israelites were pastoralists who wandered with their flocks in fixed seasonal migrations between the fringe of the desert and the settled lands. At some time near the end of the Late Bronze Age—for reasons that were not entirely clear to him—they started settling down in the sparsely settled highlands of Canaan.

According to Alt, the process was actually gradual and quite peaceful at the beginning. The arriving Israelite pastoralists cleared the forests and began to practice small-scale seasonal farming along with herding. In time, they adopted a more settled lifestyle, establishing permanent villages and concentrating more of their energy on agriculture. It was only in later days, when the new settlers' numbers grew and their need of ever more land and water increased—so ran the theory—that the Israelites' problems with the Canaanites began. Conflicts over land and water rights eventually led to local skirmishes that were the *real* background to the struggles between Israelites and their neighbors that the book of Judges so vividly conveys. (For a detailed description of the peaceful-infiltration theory, see Appendix C.)

It was thus assumed that the Israelites were scattered groups of arriving pastoralists rather than a unified army. The "Israel" stele of Merneptah offered no additional information about the exact location, size, or nature of this people. Yet other surviving Egyptian records—though providing only a small glimpse at what must have been a much fuller account—mention two groups of outsiders who chose to live or were pushed to live on the margins of the Canaanite urban society. Both are of particular interest in the search for the early Israelites.

The first are the Apiru, a group described in the Tell el-Amarna letters of the fourteenth century BCE (as well as other Bronze Age texts) in a variety of unflattering ways. Living outside mainstream Canaanite society, uprooted from their homes by war, famine, or heavy taxation, they are sometimes described as outlaws or brigands, sometimes as soldiers for hire. In one case they are even reported to be present in Egypt itself as hired laborers working on government building projects. In short, they were refugees or rebellious runaways from the system, living on the social fringe of urban society. No one in power seemed to like them; the worst thing that a local petty king could say about a neighboring prince was that "he joined the Apiru." In the past, scholars have suggested that the word *Apiru* (and its alternative forms, *Hapiru* and *Habiru*) had a direct linguistic connection to the word *Ibri*, or Hebrew, and that therefore the Apiru in the Egyptian sources were the early Israelites. Today we know that this association is not so simple. The widespread use of the term over many centuries and throughout the entire Near East suggests that it had a socioeconomic meaning rather than signifying a specific ethnic group. Nonetheless, a connection cannot be completely dismissed. It is possible that the phenomenon of the Apiru may have been remembered in later centuries and thus incorporated into the biblical narratives.

The second group mentioned in the Egyptian texts were the Shosu. They were apparently pastoral nomads, herders of sheep and goats who lived mainly in the frontier regions of Canaan and Transjordan. An account of an Egyptian raid against rebels in southern Canaan in the days of Ramesses III, in the early twelfth century BCE, provides a good description of these people. The Egyptian writer describes the plunder of their "tent camps of people and possessions and their cattle likewise, their being without number." They were obviously a problematic and uncontrollable element with an especially large presence in the wilderness and the highland frontiers. They were also known to have occasionally migrated to the eastern delta of Egypt, as the thirteenth century papyrus reporting their movements through the Egyptian border fortresses testifies.

Could either of these have been the mysterious "Israel" simply called by another name?

Uprooted Peasants?

Alt's peaceful-infiltration theory came under fierce attack in the 1970s because of new and far more detailed ethnographic data and anthropological theories on the relationship between pastoral nomads and sedentary communities in the Middle East. The main criticism of the earlier ideas of the struggle between the desert and the sown was that farmers and herders were much more integrated and less alien to each other. They were essentially components of a single society. And so, during the 1960s and 1970s, another unique theory of Israelite origins arose.

First put forward by the American biblical scholar George Mendenhall and later elaborated by the American biblical historian and sociologist Norman Gottwald, this theory suggested that the early Israelites were neither invading raiders nor infiltrating nomads, but peasant rebels who fled from the cities of Canaan to the empty highlands. Mendenhall and Gottwald argued, on the basis of the evidence contained in the Egyptian documents (mainly the Tell el-Amarna tablets), that Late Bronze Age Canaan was a highly stratified society with social tension and economic inequality on the rise. The urban elite controlled land, wealth, and commerce; the peasants in the villages were deprived of both wealth and rights. With the deteriorating situation in Canaan in the later phase of the Late Bronze Age, heavy taxation, mistreatment by landlords, and constant molestation by the authorities—both local and Egyptian—became unbearable.

Thus Mendenhall and Gottwald theorized that for many there was no other solution but to leave their homes and look for new frontiers. Some of them may have become Apiru, that is, people living on the fringe of the society, causing troubles to the authorities. Many resettled in the relatively empty forests of the highlands, far from Canaanite and Egyptian control. And in their new homeland these peasant rebels established a more equal society—less stratified and less rigid. In doing so, they became "Israelites."

Gottwald further suggested that the new ideas of equality were imported into Canaan by a small group of people who came from Egypt and settled in the highlands. This group may have been influenced by unorthodox Egyptian ideas on religion, like those that stimulated the monotheistic revolution of Akhenaten in the fourteenth century BCE. This new group would therefore have been the nucleus around which the new settlers in the highlands crystallized. The rise of early Israel was therefore a social revolution of the underprivileged against their feudal lords, energized by the arrival of a visionary new ideology.

Unfortunately, this theory has no archaeological evidence to support it—and indeed, much of the evidence flatly contradicts it. As we have seen, the material culture of the new villages was completely distinct from the culture of the Canaanite lowlands; if the settlers had been refugees from the lowlands, we would expect to see at least more similarity in architecture and pottery styles. More important, it has become clear in recent archaeological studies of the Late Bronze Age cities that the rural sector of the Canaanite society had begun to be impoverished as early as the sixteenth century BCE. In fact, this weakened and less populous countryside—and the consequent drop in agricultural production—may have played a role in the collapse of the urban culture. But it surely could not have supplied the energy behind a vigorous new wave of settlement in the highlands. Finally, even after the end of the Late Bronze Age and the destruction of the Canaanite urban centers, most of the lowland villages—few as they were—managed to survive and continued their existence much as before. This is evident in the heartland of Canaanite culture: the Jezreel and Jordan valleys and the southern coastal plain of Philistia.

Hence we really do not see hordes of uprooted people leaving their villages in the lowlands in search of new life on the highland frontier. The answer to the question "Who were the Israelites?" had to come from somewhere else.

A Sudden Archaeological Breakthrough

The early identifications and wider sociological theories about the early Israelites were based on the decipherment of scattered, fragmentary inscriptions and on the subjective interpretation of the biblical narrative—not primarily on archaeology. The sad fact was that for decades, archaeologists had been looking in all the wrong places for clues to the origins of the Israelites. Because many of them took the Joshua narrative at face value, they concentrated nearly all their efforts digging the major tells of Canaanite cities—such as Jericho, Bethel, Lachish, and Hazor. Today we know that this strategy was mistaken, for while these major tells revealed a great deal about Late Bronze Age urban culture, they told us next to nothing about the Israelites.

These major Canaanite cities were located along the coastal plain and in the valleys—far from the wooded hill country regions where early Israel emerged. Before the late 1960s, only one comprehensive archaeological survey was ever undertaken to search for evidence of purely Israelite sites. It was conducted by the Israeli archaeologist Yohanan Aharoni in a marginal region—at the very northern edge of the later area of Israelite control in the rugged and wooded mountains of upper Galilee. Aharoni discovered that the area was empty of Late Bronze sites and that it was settled on a score of small, poor Iron Age I (c. twelfth–eleventh centuries BCE) sites, which he identified with the early settlers of the tribes of Naphtali and Asher. Aharoni's fieldwork in upper Galilee seemed therefore to provide support for the peaceful-infiltration theory. The only problem was that his survey was far to the north of the heartland of Israelite settlement.

Surprising as it may seem, that Israelite heartland in the highlands of western Palestine between the Jezreel and the Beersheba valleys was virtually an archaeological terra incognita. The lack of archaeological exploration in the central hill country was not due to scholarly preferences alone. From the 1920s to 1967, war and political unrest in the Middle East discouraged thorough archaeological investigation in the heart of the hill country. But later, after the 1967 war, the archaeological landscape changed completely. A young generation of Israeli archaeologists, influenced by new trends in world archaeology, took to the field with a new method of investigation: their goal was to explore, map, and analyze the ancient landscape of the hill country—rather than only dig.

Beginning in the 1940s, archaeologists had recognized the importance of regional studies that examined settlement patterns over time. Excavations at single sites produce highly localized pictures of the material culture of ancient populations—uncovering the sequence of styles of pottery, jewelry, weapons, houses, and tombs of a particular community. But regional surveys, in which the ancient sites of a large area are mapped and dated by the characteristic pottery sherds collected on the surface, exchange depth for breadth. These surveys reveal where ancient people settled and the size of their settlements. The choice of certain topographic niches (such as hilltops rather than valleys) and certain economic niches (such as grain growing rather than horticulture), and ease of access to main roads and water sources, reveals a great deal about the lifestyle and, ultimately, social identity of populations of large areas rather than individual communities. No less important, surveys in which sites from many different periods are mapped allow archaeologists to track changes in the demographic history of a given region over long periods of time.

In the years since 1967, the heartland of the Israelite settlement—the traditional territories of the tribes of Judah, Benjamin, Ephraim, and Manasseh—have been covered by intensive surveys. Teams of archaeologists and students have combed virtually every valley, ridge, and slope, looking for traces of walls and scatters of pottery sherds. The work in the field was slow, with a day's work covering, on the average, about one square mile. Information on any signs of occupation from the Stone Age to the Ottoman period was recorded, in order to study the highlands' long-term settlement history. Statistical methods were used to estimate the size of each settlement in each of its periods of occupation. Environmental information on each site was collected and analyzed to reconstruct the natural landscape in various eras. In a few promising cases, excavations were undertaken as well.

These surveys revolutionized the study of early Israel. The discovery of the remains of a dense network of highland villages—all apparently established within the span of a few generations—indicated that a dramatic social transformation had taken place in the central hill country of Canaan around 1200 BCE. There was no sign of violent invasion or even the infiltration of a clearly defined ethnic group. Instead, it seemed to be a revolution in lifestyle. In the formerly sparsely populated highlands from the Judean hills in the south to the hills of Samaria in the north, far from the Canaanite cities that were in the process of collapse and disintegration, about two-hundred fifty hilltop communities suddenly sprang up. Here were the first Israelites.*

Life on the Highland Frontier

Excavations of some of the small Iron Age I sites discovered in the course of the surveys showed how surprisingly uniform the sudden wave of highland settlement was. The typical village was usually located on a hilltop or on a steep ridge, with a commanding view of the surrounding landscape. It was set in an open area surrounded by natural forests comprised mainly of oak and terebinth trees. In some cases, villages were founded on the edge of nar-

---

* Although there is no way to know if ethnic identities had been fully formed at this time, we identify these distinctive highland villages as "Israelite" since many of them were continuously occupied well into the period of the monarchies—an era from which we have abundant sources, both biblical and extrabiblical, testifying that their inhabitants consciously identified themselves as Israelites.

row valleys between the mountains—presumably for easier access to agricultural fields. In many cases they were built on the easternmost possible
fertile land overlooking the desert, close to good pastureland. In every case,
the villages seemed to be self-sufficient. Their inhabitants drew water from
nearby springs or stored winter rainwater in rock-cut, plastered cisterns for
use all year round. Most surprising of all was the tiny scale of these settlements. In most cases they were no more than a single acre in size and contained, according to estimates, about fifty adults and fifty children. Even

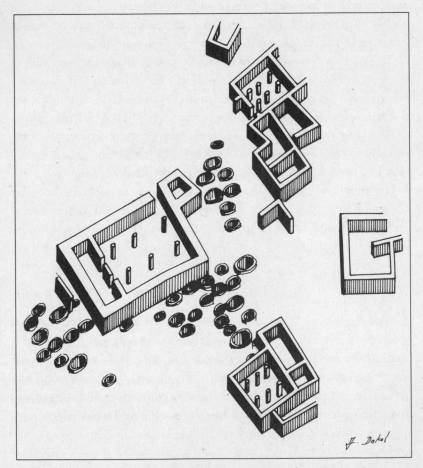

Figure 12: An excavated sector of Izbet Sartah, a Late Iron Age I village in the western
foothills featuring pillared houses and grain silos.

the largest settlements in the highlands reached only three or four acres in size, with a population of a few hundred people. The entire population of these hill country villages at the peak of the settlement process, around 1000 BCE, could not have been much more than forty-five thousand.

In contrast to the culture of the Canaanite cities and villages in the lowlands, the highland villages contained no public buildings, palaces, storehouses, or temples. Signs of any sophisticated kind of record keeping, such as writing, seals, and seal impressions, are almost completely absent. There are almost no luxury items: no imported pottery and almost no jewelry. Indeed, the village houses were all quite similar in size, suggesting that wealth was distributed quite evenly among the families. The houses were built of unworked fieldstones, with rough stone pillars propped up to provide support for the roof or upper story. The average building, around six hundred square feet in size, presumably housed four to five people—the size of a nuclear family. In many cases, stone-lined pits for storage of grain were dug between the houses (Figure 12). These silos, and a large number of sickle blades and grinding stones found in every house, indicate that grain growing was one of the villagers' main concerns. Yet herding was still important; fenced courtyards near the houses were apparently used for keeping animals secure at night.

The amenities of life were simple. Pottery was rough and basic, with no fancy or highly decorated vessels. Houseware included mainly storage jars and cooking pots—the basic utensils for everyday life. The jars were apparently used to store water, oil, and wine. We know almost nothing about burial customs, apparently because graves were simple and the dead were interred without offerings. Likewise, there is almost no indication for cult. No shrines were found in the villages, so their specific religious beliefs are unknown. In one case, at a tiny hilltop site in the northern hill country excavated by Amihai Mazar of the Hebrew University, a bronze bull figurine was discovered, suggesting the worship of traditional Canaanite deities. At another site, on Mount Ebal, Adam Zertal, of Haifa University, discovered an unusual stone structure that he identified as an early Israelite altar, but the precise function of that site and its surrounding walled enclosures is disputed.

It is also noteworthy—in contrast to the Bible's accounts of almost continual warfare between the Israelites and their neighbors—that the villages were not fortified. Either the inhabitants felt secure in their remote settlements and did not need to invest in defenses or they did not have the means or proper organization to undertake such work. No weapons, such as swords or lances, were uncovered—although such finds are typical of the cities in the lowlands. Nor were there signs of burning or sudden destruction that might indicate a violent attack.

One Iron Age I village—Izbet Sartah—located on the western margins of the highlands overlooking the coastal plain, was almost fully excavated and therefore provided enough information for a reliable reconstruction of its subsistence economy. A detailed analysis of the excavated data by Baruch Rosen, an Israeli specialist in ancient agricultural production and nutrition, suggested that the village (with an estimated population of about one hundred) was probably supported by about eight hundred acres of surrounding land, four-hundred fifty of which were cultivated and the rest used for pasture. Under the conditions of the Early Iron Age, those fields could have produced up to fifty-three tons of wheat and twenty-one tons of barley per year, with the help of about forty oxen for plowing. In addition, the inhabitants apparently maintained a herd of about three hundred sheep and goats. (It should be noted, though, that this village was located in a fertile area of the foothills. Most villages in the highlands were not as "rich.")

All this shows that the main struggles of the early Israelites were not with other peoples but with the stony terrain, the dense forests of the highlands, and the harsh and sometimes unpredictable environment. Yet they seem to have lived relatively peacefully and were able to maintain a self-sufficient economy. They were quite isolated from regional trade routes and also seem to have been quite remote from one another; there is no indication that any trade goods were exchanged between the highland villages. It comes as no surprise therefore that there is no evidence of significant social stratification in these villages, no sign of administrative buildings for officials, large residences of dignitaries, or the specialized products of highly skilled artisans.

The early Israelites appeared around 1200 BCE, as herders and farmers in the hills. Their culture was a simple one of subsistence. This much we know. But where did they come from?

New Clues to Israelite Origins

As it turned out, the answer to the question of Israelite origins lay in the remains of their earliest settlements. Most of the villages excavated in the highlands offered evidence about Israelite life several decades or even a century after they were founded. Houses and courtyards had been expanded and remodeled over those years. In only a very few cases were the remains of the initial settlement preserved intact beneath the later buildings. One such case was at the site of Izbet Sartah, already mentioned.

The earliest phase at the site had a highly unusual plan, very different from the later cluster of rectangular, pillared houses that later arose on the site. The first settlement was built in the shape of an oval, with a row of rooms surrounding a large open courtyard (Figure 13). Those outer rooms were connected to one another in a way that formed a kind of continuous belt protecting the inner courtyard. The large, enclosed courtyard hints that the inhabitants had herds, probably flocks of sheep and goats. The discovery of a few silos, sickle blades, and grinding stones indicates that they practiced a bit of grain farming as well.

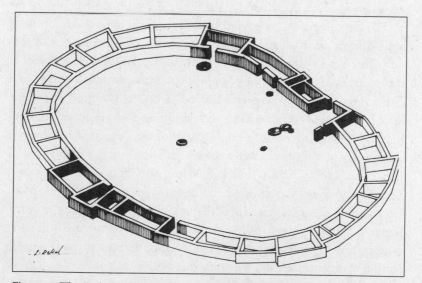

Figure 13: The Early Iron Age I phase at Izbet Sartah. The oval layout indicates the pastoral origins of the inhabitants.

Figure 14: An oval bedouin encampment near Jericho as shown in a nineteenth century drawing.

Similar oval sites have been discovered in the central highlands and in the highlands of the Negev in the south. Comparable sites, which date to other periods, have been found in the Sinai, Jordan, and other areas of the Middle East. In general, this type of enclosure seems to be characteristic of settlements in the highlands and on desert frontiers. The plan of this very early Iron Age I village is similar not only to Bronze and Iron Age sites in the steppe lands, but also to bedouin tent encampments described and even photographed by travelers in the Judean desert, Transjordan, and the Sinai at the end of the nineteenth and beginning of the twentieth century (Figure 14). In this type of encampment, a row of tents encircled an open courtyard, where the flocks were kept at night. The Iron Age highlands and Negev sites are uncannily similar in shape, size, and number of units. Though in the ancient settlements stone walls replaced the portable tents, form clearly suggests function in both kinds of settlements. The people living in these sites—both past and present—were pastoralists primarily concerned with protecting their flocks. All this indicates that a large proportion of the first Israelites were once pastoral nomads.

But they were pastoral nomads undergoing a profound transformation. The presumed shift from the earlier tent encampments to villages of similar layout in stone construction, and, later, to more permanent, rectangular pillared houses indicates that they abandoned their migratory lifestyle, gave up most of their animals, and shifted to permanent agriculture. Transformations like this can still be seen in the Middle East. Bedouin in the process of settling down often replace their tents with similarly shaped stone or brick structures. They also tend to maintain the layout of the traditional tent encampment in the layout of their first permanent settlement. Later they gradually depart from this tradition and shift to regular sedentary villages. A very similar evolution is apparent in the remains of the Iron Age highland villages.

There is another clue that points in the same direction: the kinds of places the Iron I settlers chose for their first permanent settlements suggest a background in pastoral nomadism. Many of the settlements from the beginning of Iron Age activity in the highlands were located in the eastern part of the region, not far from the desert fringe. Establishing settlements in this area enabled the villagers to continue sheep and goat herding, while gradually shifting to farming as their main means of support. Only later did they begin to expand to the west, which is less hospitable to farming and herding and more fitted to the cultivation of olive groves and grapevines.

Many of the early Israelites were thus apparently nomads who gradually became farmers. Still, nomads have to come from somewhere. Here too, recently uncovered archaeological evidence has something to say.

Canaan's Hidden Cycles

The extensive highland surveys of recent decades have collected data on the nature of human occupation in this region over many millennia. One of the biggest surprises was that the dramatic wave of pastoralists settling down and becoming permanent farmers in the twelfth century BCE was not a unique event. In fact, the archaeological evidence indicated that before the twelfth century BCE there were two previous waves of similar highland settlement, both of which were followed by an eventual return of the inhabitants to a dispersed, pastoral way of life.

We now know that the first occupation of the highlands took place in the Early Bronze Age, beginning over two thousand years before the rise of

TABLE ONE

WAVES OF SETTLEMENT IN THE HIGHLANDS

PERIOD	DATES	MAIN CHARACTERISTICS
Early Bronze Age	3500–2200 BCE	*First wave* of settlement; about 100 sites recorded
Intermediate Bronze Age	2200–2000 BCE	Settlement crisis; most of the sites deserted
Middle Bronze Age	2000–1550 BCE	*Second wave* of settlement; about 220 sites recorded
Late Bronze Age	1550–1150 BCE	Settlement crisis; only about 25 sites recorded
Iron Age I	1150–900 BCE	*Third wave* of settlement; about 250 sites recorded
Iron Age II	900–586 BCE	Settlement system develops and reaches over 500 sites (eighth century BCE)

early Israel, in around 3500 BCE. At the peak of this wave of settlement, there were almost a hundred villages and larger towns scattered throughout the central ridge. More than a thousand years later, around 2200 BCE, most of the highland settlements were abandoned and the highlands became a frontier area again. Yet a second wave of settlement, stronger than the first, began to gain momentum in the Middle Bronze Age, shortly after 2000 BCE. This wave began with the establishment of small, scattered villages that gradually grew into a complex network of about 220 settlements, ranging from villages to towns to fortified regional centers. The population of this second settlement wave has been estimated at about forty thousand. Many of the major, fortified centers of this period—Hebron, Jerusalem, Bethel, Shiloh, and Shechem—would become important centers at the time of the Israelites. Yet the second wave of highland settlement came to an end sometime in the sixteenth century BCE. And this time, the highlands would remain a sparsely populated frontier zone for four centuries.

Finally—as a third major wave—the early Israelite settlement began around 1200 BCE (Figure 15). Like its predecessors, it commenced with mainly small, rural communities with an initial population of approximately 45,000 in 250 sites. It gradually developed into a mature system with large cities, medium-sized regional market centers, and small villages. By the highpoint of this settlement wave in the eighth century BCE, after the establishment of the kingdoms of Judah and Israel, it encompassed over five hundred sites, with a population of about 160,000.

This dramatic population growth was made possible by the full utilization of the region's agricultural potential. The highlands offer excellent terrain for olive and vine growing—the most profitable sectors of the traditional Middle Eastern economy. In all three periods of extensive highland settlement, surplus wine and olive oil seem to have been sent to the lowlands and even exported beyond the borders of Canaan, especially to Egypt. Early Bronze Age storage vessels found in Egypt have been analyzed and found to have been made from clay from the Canaanite highlands. In one extraordinary case, a jar from Canaan still contained remains of grape seeds.

The similarities between the settlement patterns of the three major waves are thus clear. In many cases particular sites were occupied in all three periods. No less important, the overall settlement patterns in all the waves shared certain characteristics. First, it seems that the southern part of the highlands was always less populated than the northern part, which, as we will see, was the result of their very different natural environments. Second, it appears that each wave of demographic growth started in the east and gradually expanded to the west. Finally, each of the three waves is characterized by a roughly similar material culture—pottery, architecture, and village plan—that was probably a result of similar environmental and economic conditions.

In the periods between the peaks of highland settlement, when the cities, towns, and even most of the villages were abandoned, the highlands were far from deserted. Important evidence for this comes from an unexpected source—not inscriptions or excavated buildings, but a close analysis of excavated animal bones. Bones collected at sites that flourished during periods of intense settlement in the highlands contain a relatively large proportion of cattle—which generally indicates extensive field farming and the use of the plow. Indeed, these proportions are similar to what we see in traditional village farming communities in the Middle East today.

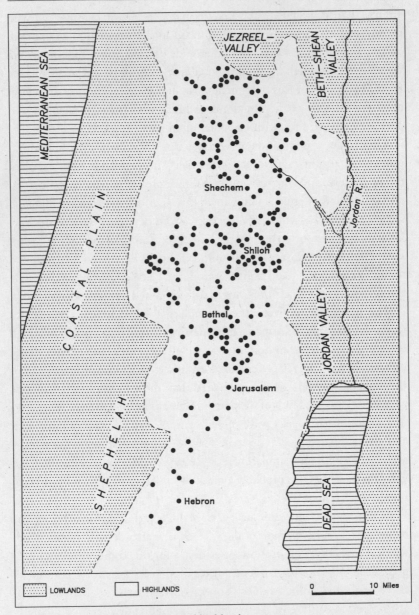

Figure 15: Iron Age I sites in the central highlands

However, a dramatic difference can be seen in the bones collected at the few sites in the highlands that continued to be occupied in the periods *between* the major settlement waves. The number of cattle is minimal, but there is an exceptionally large proportion of sheep and goats. This is similar to the composition of herds among bedouin groups. For pastoralists who engage in only marginal seasonal agriculture and spend much of the year seeking fresh pastureland, heavy, slow-moving cattle are a burden. They cannot move as fast and as far as sheep and goats. Thus in the periods of intense highland settlement, more people were engaged in farming; in the crisis years, people practiced sheep and goat herding.

Are such dramatic fluctuations common? In the Middle East, people have always had the know-how to rapidly change from village life to animal husbandry—or back from pastoralism to settled agriculture—according to evolving political, economic, or even climatic conditions. Many groups throughout the region have been able to shift their lifestyle according to the best interest of the moment, and the avenue connecting village life and pastoral nomadism has always been a two-way street. Anthropological studies of settlement history in Jordan, southwestern Syria, and the middle Euphrates valley in the nineteenth and early twentieth century show just that. Increasingly heavy taxation and the threat of conscription into the Ottoman army were among the factors that drove countless village families to abandon their houses in the agricultural regions and disappear into the desert. There they engaged in animal husbandry, which has always been a more resilient, if less comfortable, way of life.

An opposite process operates in times when security and economic conditions improve. Sedentary communities are founded or joined by former nomads, who take on a specialized role in a two-part, or dimorphic, society. One segment of this society specializes in agriculture while the other continues the traditional herding of sheep and goats.

This pattern has special meaning for the question, who were the first Israelites? That is because the two components of Middle Eastern society—farmers and pastoral nomads—have always maintained an interdependent economic relationship, even if there was sometimes tension between the two groups. Nomads need the marketplaces of settled villages in order to obtain grain and other agricultural products, while farmers are dependent on the nomads for a regular supply of meat, dairy products, and hides.

However, the two sides of the exchange are not entirely equal: villagers can rely on their own produce for survival, while pastoral nomads cannot exist entirely on the products of their herds. They need grain to supplement and balance their high-fat diet of meat and milk. As long as there are villagers to trade with, the nomads can continue to concentrate on animal husbandry. But when grain cannot be obtained in exchange for animal products, the pastoral nomads are forced to produce it for themselves.

And that is apparently what caused the sudden wave of highland settlement. In Late Bronze Age Canaan, in particular, the existence of large populations of pastoral nomads in the highlands and desert fringes was possible only as long as the Canaanite city-states and villages could produce an adequate grain surplus to trade. This was the situation during three centuries of Egyptian rule over Canaan. But when that political system collapsed in the twelfth century BCE, its economic networks ceased functioning. It is reasonable to assume that the villagers of Canaan were forced to concentrate on local subsistence and no longer produced a significant surplus of grain over and above what they needed for themselves. Thus the highland and desert-fringe pastoralists had to adapt to the new conditions and produce their own grain. Soon, the requirements of farming would cause a reduction in the range of seasonal migrations. Flocks would then have to be reduced as the period of migrations grew shorter, and with more and more effort invested in agriculture, a permanent shift to sedentarization occurred.

The process that we describe here is, in fact, the opposite of what we have in the Bible: the emergence of early Israel was an outcome of the collapse of the Canaanite culture, not its cause. And most of the Israelites did not come from outside Canaan—they emerged from within it. There was no mass Exodus from Egypt. There was no violent conquest of Canaan. Most of the people who formed early Israel were local people—the same people whom we see in the highlands throughout the Bronze and Iron Ages. The early Israelites were—irony of ironies—themselves originally Canaanites!

In What Sense Was Ancient Israel Unique?

In the more fertile areas of the highlands east of the Jordan, we see the same ups and downs in sedentary activity, the same crisis in the Late Bronze Age, and exactly the same wave of settlement in the Iron Age I. Archaeological surveys carried out in Jordan have revealed that the settlement history of the territories of Ammon, Moab, and Edom was broadly similar to those of early Israel. We could take our archaeological description of a typical Iron Age I Israelite village in the highlands west of the Jordan and use it as a description of an early Moabite village with almost no change. These people lived in the same kind of villages, in similar houses, used similar pottery, and led an almost identical way of life. Yet from the Bible and other historical sources, we know that the people who lived in the villages of the Iron Age I east of the Jordan did not become Israelites; instead, they later formed the kingdoms of Ammon, Moab, and Edom. So, is there anything specific in the villages of the people who formed early Israel that distinguished them from their neighbors? Can we say how their ethnicity and nationality crystallized?

Today, as in the past, people demonstrate their ethnicity in many different ways: in language, religion, customs of dress, burial practices, and elaborate dietary taboos. The simple material culture left by the highland herders and farmers who became the first Israelites offers no clear indication of their dialect, religious rituals, costume, or burial practices. But one very interesting detail about their dietary habits has been discovered. Bones recovered from the excavations of the small early Israelite villages in the highlands differ from settlements in other parts of the country in one significant respect: there are no pigs. Bone assemblages from earlier highlands settlements *did* contain the remains of pigs and the same is true for later (post–Iron Age) settlements there. But throughout the Iron Age—the era of the Israelite monarchies—pigs were not cooked and eaten, or even raised in the highlands. Comparative data from the coastal Philistine settlements of the same period—the Iron Age I—show a surprisingly large number of pigs represented among the recovered animal bones. Though the early Israelites did not eat pork, the Philistines clearly did, as did (as best we can tell from the sketchier data) the Ammonites and Moabites east of the Jordan.

A ban on pork cannot be explained by environmental or economic reasons alone. It may, in fact, be the only clue that we have of a specific, shared identity among the highland villagers west of the Jordan. Perhaps the proto-Israelites stopped eating pork merely because the surrounding peoples—their adversaries—did eat it, and they had begun to see themselves as different. Distinctive culinary practices and dietary customs are two of the ways in which ethnic boundaries are formed. Monotheism and the traditions of Exodus and covenant apparently came much later. Half a millennium before the composition of the biblical text, with its detailed laws and dietary regulations, the Israelites chose—for reasons that are not entirely clear—not to eat pork. When modern Jews do the same, they are continuing the oldest archaeologically attested cultural practice of the people of Israel.

The Book of Judges and Judah in the Seventh Century

We will never know to what extent the stories in the book of Judges are based on authentic memories of local heroes and village conflicts preserved over the centuries in the form of epic poems or popular folktales. Yet the historical reliability of the book of Judges cannot be assessed by the possible inclusion of heroic tales from earlier eras. Its most significant feature is an overall literary pattern that describes Israel's history in the period after the conquest as a repeating cycle of sin, divine retribution, and salvation (2:11–19). Only in the last verse (21:25) is there a hint that the cycle can be broken—with the establishment of a monarchy.

It is clear that this theological interpretation of the tales in the book of Judges was developed centuries after the events it purportedly describes. Though the individual stories of Israelite conflict against the Philistines, Moabites, Midianites, and Ammonites feature many different settings and characters, they are all used to illustrate an uneasy relationship between God and his people. YHWH is depicted as an angry, disappointed deity, who had delivered the Israelites from slavery in Egypt and had given them the promised land as an eternal inheritance, only to find them to be a sinful, ungrateful people. Time and again they betrayed YHWH by running after foreign gods. Thus YHWH punished them by giving them to the hands of their enemies so that they might feel the pain of violence and suffering—and cry to YHWH for help. Accepting their repentance, YHWH would then save them by commissioning a righteous leader among them to lead them to triumph against their adversaries. Theology, not history, is central. Covenant, promise, apostasy, repentance, and redemption constitute the cyclical sequence that runs throughout the book of Judges. And so it must have seemed to the people of Judah in the seventh century BCE that the same cyclical sequence applied to them.

Biblical scholars have long recognized that the book of Judges is part of the Deuteronomistic History, which, as we have argued, is the great expression of Israelite hopes and political aspirations compiled in Judah in the time of King Josiah, in the seventh century BCE. The stories of early Israelite settlement in the highlands offered a lesson to the people, with direct relevance to contemporary affairs. As Josiah and his supporters looked northward with visions of uniting the land of Israel, they stressed that conquest alone was worthless without a continuous and exclusive obedience to YHWH. The Deuteronomistic movement saw the pagan population within the land of Israel and in all the neighboring kingdoms as a mortal danger. Deuteronomy's law-codes and the historical lessons of the Deuteronomistic history made it clear that the people of Israel had to resist the temptation of idolatry, lest they suffer new calamities.

The chapter that opens the book of Judges makes a clear connection between past and present. Though many scholars have regarded it as a later addition, the biblical historian Baruch Halpern assigns it to the original Deuteronomistic History. This chapter tells us how the tribes that made up the core of the Southern Kingdom—Judah and Simeon—perfectly fulfilled their sacred mission in conquering all the Canaanite cities in their territories. The kingdom of Judah was therefore protected from the immediate danger of idolatry in its midst. But this was not the case with the tribes that later composed the core of the northern kingdom of Israel. All of them are reported to have failed in their quest to eliminate the Canaanites, and the Canaanite enclaves that persisted in each one of their tribal territories are listed in detail (Judges 1:21, 27–35). No wonder then, that pious Judah survived and apostate Israel was vanquished. Indeed, most of the tales of the book of Judges deal with the sin and punishment of the northern tribes. Not a single story explicitly accuses Judah of idolatry.

But the book of Judges implicitly offers a way out of the endless cycle of sin and divine retribution. It hints that the cycle had already been broken once before. Again and again, like a mantra, it repeats the sentence "In those days there was no king in Israel; every man did what was right in his own eyes" (Judges 21:25). This is a reminder that soon after the period of the judges came a great king to rule over all the tribes of Israel—the pious David, who established an eternal covenant with God. This king would banish the influence of foreign gods from the hearts and daily practices of the Israelites. He would establish a single capital in Jerusalem and designate a permanent place for the Ark of the Covenant. One God, worshipped in one Temple, located in the one and only capital, under one king of the Davidic dynasty were the keys to the salvation of Israel—both in David's time and in the time of the new David, King Josiah. By eradicating every trace of the worship of the same foreign gods that led Israel to sin in the past, Josiah would put an end to the seemingly endless cycle of apostasy and disaster and would lead Judah into a new Golden Age of prosperity and hope.

As we now know, however, the Bible's stirring picture of righteous Israelite judges—however powerful and compelling—has very little to do with what *really* happened in the hill country of Canaan in the Early Iron Age. Archaeology has revealed that complex social transformations among the pastoral people of the Canaanite highlands were—far more than the later biblical concepts of sin and redemption—the most formative forces in the birth of Israel.

[5]

Memories of a Golden Age?

In the Temple and royal palace of Jerusalem, biblical Israel found its permanent spiritual focus after centuries of struggle and wandering. As the books of Samuel narrate, the anointing of David, son of Jesse, as king over all the tribes of Israel finalized the process that had begun with God's original promise to Abraham so many centuries before. The violent chaos of the period of the Judges now gave way to a time in which God's promises could be established securely under a righteous king. Though the first choice for the throne of Israel had been the brooding, handsome Saul from the tribe of Benjamin, it was his successor David who became the central figure in early Israelite history. Of the fabled King David, songs and stories were nearly without number. They told of his slaying the mighty Goliath with a single sling stone; of his adoption into the royal court for his skill as a harpist; of his adventures as a rebel and freebooter; of his lustful pursuit of Bathsheba; and of his conquests of Jerusalem and a vast empire beyond. His son Solomon, in turn, is remembered as the wisest of kings and the greatest of builders. Stories tell of his brilliant judgments, his unimaginable wealth, and his construction of the great Temple in Jerusalem.

For centuries, Bible readers all over the world have looked back to the era of David and Solomon as a golden age in Israel's history. Until recently many scholars have agreed that the united monarchy was the first biblical period that could truly be considered historical. Unlike the hazy memories of the patriarchs' wanderings, or the miraculous Exodus from Egypt, or the bloody visions of the books of Joshua and Judges, the story of David was a highly realistic saga of political maneuvering and dynastic intrigue. Even though many details of David's early exploits are certainly legendary elaborations, scholars long believed that the story of his rise to power meshed well with the archaeological reality. The initial, dispersed settlement of the Israelites in their hill country villages slowly coalesced into more centralized forms of organization. And the threat posed to the Israelites by the coastal Philistine cities would have provided the crisis that precipitated the rise of the Israelite monarchy. Indeed, archaeologists have identified clear levels of destruction of former Philistine and Canaanite cities that they believed marked the path of David's wide-ranging conquests. And the impressive city gates and palaces uncovered at several important sites in Israel were seen as evidence of Solomon's building activities.

Yet many of the archaeological props that once bolstered the historical basis of the David and Solomon narratives have recently been called into question. The actual extent of the Davidic "empire" is hotly debated. Digging in Jerusalem has failed to produce evidence that it was a great city in David or Solomon's time. And the monuments ascribed to Solomon are now most plausibly connected with other kings. Thus a reconsideration of the evidence has enormous implications. For if there were no patriarchs, no Exodus, no conquest of Canaan—and no prosperous united monarchy under David and Solomon—can we say that early biblical Israel, as described in the Five Books of Moses and the books of Joshua, Judges, and Samuel, ever existed at all?

A Royal Dynasty for Israel

The biblical epic of Israel's transformation from the period of the judges to the time of the monarchy begins with a great military crisis. As described in 1 Samuel 4–5, the massed Philistine armies routed the Israelite tribal levies in battle and carried off the holy Ark of the Covenant as booty of war. Under the leadership of the prophet Samuel, a priest in the sanctuary at Shiloh (located halfway between Jerusalem and Shechem), the Israelites later recovered the ark, which was brought back and installed in the village of Kiriyat Yearim west of Jerusalem. But the days of the judges were clearly over. The military threats now faced by the people of Israel required full-time leadership. The elders of Israel assembled at Samuel's home in Ramah, north of Jerusalem, and asked him to appoint a king for Israel, "like all the nations." Though Samuel warned against the dangers of kingship in one of the most eloquent antimonarchic passages in the Bible (1 Samuel 8:10–18), God instructed him to do as the people requested. And God revealed his selection to Samuel: the first king of Israel would be Saul, son of Kish, from the tribe of Benjamin. Saul was a handsome young man and a brave warrior, yet one whose inner doubts and naive violations of the divine laws of sacrifice, war booty, and other sacred injunctions (1 Samuel 15:10–26) would lead to his ultimate rejection and eventual tragic suicide at Mount Gilboa, when the Israelites were routed by the Philistines.

Even as Saul still reigned as king of Israel he was unaware that his successor had already been chosen. God instructed Samuel to go to the family of Jesse from Bethlehem, "for I have provided for myself a king among his sons" (1 Samuel 16:1). The youngest of those sons was a handsome, red-haired shepherd named David, who would finally bring salvation to Israel. First came an awesome demonstration of David's battlefield prowess. The Philistines gathered again to wage war against Israel, and the two armies faced each other in the valley of Elah in the Shephelah. The Philistines' secret weapon was the giant warrior Goliath, who mocked the God of Israel and challenged any Israelite warrior to engage in single combat with him. Great fear fell upon Saul and his soldiers, but the young David, sent by his father to bring provisions to his three older brothers serving in Saul's army, took up the challenge fearlessly. Shouting to Goliath—"You come to me with a sword and with a spear and with a javelin; but I come to you in the name of the LORD" (1 Samuel 17:45)—David took a small stone from his shepherd's pouch and slung it with deadly aim at Goliath's forehead, killing him on the spot. The Philistines were routed. David, the new hero of Israel, befriended Saul's son Jonathan and married Michal, the daughter of the king. David was popularly acclaimed Israel's greatest hero—greater even than the king. The enthusiastic cries of his admirers, "Saul has slain his thousands, and David his ten thousands!" (1 Samuel 18:7), made King Saul jealous. It was only a matter of time before David would have to contest Saul's leadership and claim the throne of all Israel.

Escaping Saul's murderous fury, David became leader of a band of fugitives and soldiers of fortune, with people in distress or deep in debt flocking to him. David and his men roamed in the foothills of the Shephelah, in the Judean desert, and in the southern margins of the Judean hills—all regions located away from the centers of power of Saul's kingdom to the north of Jerusalem. Tragically, in battle with the Philistines far to the north at Mount Gilboa, Saul's sons were killed by the enemy and Saul took his own life. David proceeded quickly to the ancient city of Hebron in Judah, where the people of Judah declared him king. This was the beginning of the great Davidic state and lineage, the beginning of the glorious united monarchy.

Once David and his men overpowered the remaining pockets of opposition among Saul's supporters, representatives of all the tribes duly convened in Hebron to declare David king over all Israel. After reigning seven years in Hebron, David moved north to conquer the Jebusite stronghold of Jerusalem—until then claimed by none of the tribes of Israel—to make it his capital. He ordered that the Ark of the Covenant be brought up from Kiriyath-jearim.

David then received an astonishing, unconditional promise from God:

Thus says the LORD of hosts, I took you from the pasture, from following the sheep, that you should be prince over my people Israel; and I have been with you wherever you went, and have cut off all your enemies from before you; and I will make for you a great name, like the name of the great ones of the earth. And I will appoint a place for my people Israel, and will plant them, that they may dwell in their own place, and be disturbed no more; and violent men shall afflict them no more, as formerly, from the time that I appointed judges over my people Israel; and I will give you rest from all your enemies. Moreover the LORD declares to you that the LORD will make you a house. When your days are fulfilled and you lie down with your fathers, I will raise up your offspring after you, who shall come forth from your body, and I will establish his kingdom. He shall build a house for my name, and I will establish the throne of his kingdom for ever. I will be his father, and he shall be my son. When he commits iniquity, I will chasten him with the rod of men, with the stripes of the sons of men; but I will not take my steadfast love from him, as I took it from

Saul, whom I put away from before you. And your house and your kingdom
shall be made sure for ever before me; your throne shall be established for ever.
(2 SAMUEL 7:8–16)

David then initiated sweeping wars of liberation and expansion. In a series of swift battles he destroyed the power of the Philistines and defeated
the Ammonites, the Moabites, and the Edomites in Transjordan, concluding his campaigns with the subjugation of the Arameans far to the north.
Returning in triumph to Jerusalem, David now ruled over a vast territory,
far more extensive even than the tribal inheritances of Israel. But David did
not find peace even in this time of glory. Dynastic conflicts—including
the revolt of his son Absalom—led to great concern for the continuation
of his dynasty. Just before David's death, the priest Zadok anointed
Solomon to be the next king of Israel.

Solomon, to whom God gave "wisdom and understanding beyond
measure," consolidated the Davidic dynasty and organized its empire,
which now stretched from the Euphrates to the land of the Philistines and
to the border of Egypt (1 Kings 4:24). His immense wealth came from a sophisticated system of taxation and forced labor required of each of the
tribes of Israel and from trading expeditions to exotic countries in the
south. In recognition of his fame and wisdom, the fabled queen of Sheba
visited him in Jerusalem and brought him a caravan of dazzling gifts.

Solomon's greatest achievements were his building activities. In
Jerusalem he constructed a magnificent, richly decorated Temple to
YHWH, inaugurated it in great pomp, and built a beautiful palace nearby.
He fortified Jerusalem as well as the important provincial cities of Hazor,
Megiddo, and Gezer, and maintained stables with forty thousand stalls of
horses for his fourteen hundred chariots, and twelve thousand cavalrymen.
He concluded a treaty with Hiram, king of Tyre, who dispatched cedars of
Lebanon for the building of the Temple in Jerusalem and became
Solomon's partner in overseas trading ventures. The Bible summarizes
Solomon's reputation: "Thus king Solomon excelled all the kings of the
earth in riches and in wisdom. And the whole earth sought the presence of
Solomon to hear his wisdom, which God had put into his mind" (1 Kings
10:23–24).

Did David and Solomon Exist?

This question, put so baldly, may sound intentionally provocative. David
and Solomon are such central religious icons to both Judaism and Christianity that the recent assertions of radical biblical critics that King David
is "no more a historical figure than King Arthur," have been greeted in
many religious and scholarly circles with outrage and disdain. Biblical historians such as Thomas Thompson and Niels Peter Lemche of the University of Copenhagen and Philip Davies of the University of Sheffield,
dubbed "biblical minimalists" by their detractors, have argued that David
and Solomon, the united monarchy of Israel, and indeed the entire biblical
description of the history of Israel are no more than elaborate, skillful ideological constructs produced by priestly circles in Jerusalem in post-exilic
or even Hellenistic times.

Yet from a purely literary and archaeological standpoint, the minimalists have some points in their favor. A close reading of the biblical description of the days of Solomon clearly suggests that this was a portrayal of an
idealized past, a glorious Golden Age. The reports of Solomon's fabulous
wealth (making "silver as common in Jerusalem as stone," according to 1
Kings 10:27) and his legendary harem (housing seven hundred wives and
princesses and three-hundred concubines, according to 1 Kings 11:3) are details too exaggerated to be true. Moreover, for all their reported wealth and
power, neither David nor Solomon is mentioned in a single known Egyptian or Mesopotamian text. And the archaeological evidence in Jerusalem
for the famous building projects of Solomon is nonexistent. Nineteenth-
and early twentieth-century excavations around the Temple Mount in
Jerusalem failed to identify even a trace of Solomon's fabled Temple or
palace complex. And while certain levels and structures at sites in other regions of the country have indeed been linked to the era of the united
monarchy, their dating, as we shall see, is far from clear.

On the other hand, strong arguments have been marshaled to counter
some of the minimalists' objections. Many scholars argue that remains
from the Solomonic period in Jerusalem are missing because they were
completely eradicated by the massive Herodian constructions on the Temple Mount in the Early Roman period. Moreover, the absence of outside

references to David and Solomon in ancient inscriptions is completely understandable, since the era in which they were believed to have ruled (c. 1005–c. 930 BCE) was a period in which the great empires of Egypt and Mesopotamia were in decline. So it is not surprising that there are no references to either David or Solomon in the rather meager contemporary Egyptian or Mesopotamian texts.

Yet in the summer of 1993, at the biblical site of Tel Dan in northern Israel, a fragmentary artifact was discovered that would change forever the nature of the debate. It was the "House of David" inscription, part of a black basalt monument, found broken and reused in a later stratum as a building stone. Written in Aramaic, the language of the Aramean kingdoms of Syria, it related the details of an invasion of Israel by an Aramean king whose name is not mentioned on the fragments that have so far been discovered. But there is hardly a question that it tells the story of the assault of Hazael, king of Damascus, on the northern kingdom of Israel around 835 BCE. This war took place in the era when Israel and Judah were separate kingdoms, and the outcome was a bitter defeat for both.

The most important part of the inscription is Hazael's boasting description of his enemies:

> [I killed Jeho]ram son of [Ahab] king of Israel, and [I] killed [Ahaz]iahu son of [Jehoram kin]g of the House of David. And I set [their towns into ruins and turned] their land into [desolation].

This is dramatic evidence of the fame of the Davidic dynasty less than a hundred years after the reign of David's son Solomon. The fact that Judah (or perhaps its capital, Jerusalem) is referred to with only a mention of its ruling house is clear evidence that the reputation of David was not a literary invention of a much later period. Furthermore, the French scholar André Lemaire has recently suggested that a similar reference to the house of David can be found on the famous inscription of Mesha, king of Moab in the ninth century BCE, which was found in the nineteenth century east of the Dead Sea. Thus, the house of David was known throughout the region; this clearly validates the biblical description of a figure named David becoming the founder of the dynasty of Judahite kings in Jerusalem.

The question we must therefore face is no longer one of David and

Solomon's mere existence. We must now see if the Bible's sweeping description of David's great military victories and of Solomon's great building projects is consistent with the archaeological evidence.

A New Look at the Kingdom of David

We have already seen that the first stage of Israelite settlement in the highlands of Canaan was a gradual, regional phenomenon in which local pastoralist groups began to settle down in the sparsely populated highlands and form self-sufficient village communities. In time, with the growth of the highland population, new villages were founded in previously unoccupied areas, moving from the eastern steppe land and the interior valleys toward the western rocky and rugged niches of the highlands. At this stage, cultivation of olives and grapes began, especially in the northern highlands. With a growing diversity among the location and crops produced by the various villages throughout the hill country, the old regime of self-sufficiency could not be maintained. Villagers who concentrated on orchards and vines would necessarily have to exchange some of their surplus production of wine and olive oil for basic commodities like grain. With specialization came the rise of classes of administrators and traders, professional soldiers, and eventually kings.

Similar patterns of highland settlement and gradual social stratification have been uncovered by archaeologists working in Jordan in the ancient lands of Ammon and Moab. A fairly uniform process of social transformation may have happened in many highland regions of the Levant, once they were freed from the control of the great Bronze Age empires or the lowland city-state kings.

At a time when the entire world was coming to life again in the Iron Age, new kingdoms were emerging that were wary of their neighbors and apparently marked themselves off from one another by distinctive ethnic customs and the worship of national deities. Still, their process of specialization, organization, and group identity is a far cry from the formation of a vast empire. Extensive conquests of the kind ascribed to David take enormous organization, manpower, and armor. So, scholarly interest has begun to focus on the archaeological evidence of population, settlement patterns,

TABLE TWO
THE KINGS OF THE UNITED MONARCHY

KING	DATES*	BIBLICAL TESTIMONY	ARCHAEOLOGICAL FINDS
Saul	ca. 1025–1005	First king, appointed by the prophet Samuel	In the highlands continuation of Iron I settlement system
David	ca. 1005–970	Conquers Jerusalem and makes it his capital; establishes a vast empire covering most territories of the Land of Israel	No evidence for David's conquests or for his empire. In the valleys Canaanite culture continues uninterrupted. In the highlands continuation of Iron I settlement system
Solomon	ca. 970–931	Builds the Temple and the palace in Jerusalem. Also active at Megiddo, Hazor, and Gezer	No sign of monumental architecture, or important city in Jerusalem. No sign of grand-scale building activity at Megiddo, Hazor, and Gezer; in the north, Canaanite material culture continues

* According to Galil's *The Chronology of the Kings of Israel and Judah*

and economic and organizational resources in David's home region of Judah to see if the biblical description makes historical sense.

The recent archaeological surveys in the highlands have offered important new evidence of the unique character of Judah, which occupies the southern part of the highlands, roughly stretching southward from Jerusalem to the northern fringes of the Negev. It forms a homogenous environmental unit of rugged terrain, difficult communications, and meager and highly unpredictable rainfall. In contrast to the northern hill country with its broad valleys and natural overland routes to the neighboring regions, Judah has always been marginal agriculturally and isolated from the neighboring regions by topographical barriers that encircle it on all sides except the north.

On the east and south, Judah is bordered by the arid zones of the Judean desert and the Negev. And on the west—in the direction of the fertile and prosperous Shephelah foothills and the coastal plain—the central ridge drops abruptly. Traveling westward from Hebron, one is forced to descend more than thirteen hundred feet down steep, rocky slopes in a distance of just a little over three miles. Farther north, west of Jerusalem and Bethlehem, the slope is more moderate, but it is even more difficult to traverse since it comprises a set of narrow, long ridges separated by deep ravines. Today, the flat central plateau, from Jerusalem to Bethlehem and to Hebron, is crisscrossed by roads and extensively farmed. But it took millennia of concentrated labor to clear the rocky terrain enough to allow these activities. In the Bronze Age and in the beginning of the Iron Age the area was rocky and covered with dense scrub and forest, with very little open land available for agricultural fields. A mere handful of permanent villages were established there at the time of the Israelite settlement; Judah's environment was far better suited to pastoral groups.

Judah's settlement system of the twelfth–eleventh centuries BCE continued to develop in the tenth century. The number of villages and their size gradually grew, but the nature of the system did not change dramatically. North of Judah, extensive orchards and vineyards developed on the western slopes of the highlands; in Judah they did not, due to the forbidding nature of the terrain. As far as we can see on the basis of the archaeological surveys, Judah remained relatively empty of permanent population, quite isolated, and very marginal right up to and past the presumed time of David and Solomon, with no major urban centers and with no pronounced hierarchy of hamlets, villages, and towns.

Searching for Jerusalem

The image of Jerusalem in the time of David, and even more so in the time of his son Solomon, has for centuries been a subject of mythmaking and romance. Pilgrims, Crusaders, and visionaries of all kinds have spread fabulous stories about the grandeur of David's city and of Solomon's Temple.

It was therefore no accident that the quest for the remains of Solomon's Temple was among the first challenges taken up by biblical archaeology in the nineteenth century. The quest was hardly easy and very rarely fruitful, due to the nature of the site.

Lived in continuously and highly overbuilt, Jerusalem lies in a saddle to the east of the watershed of the Judean hills, very close to the fringe of the Judean desert. In the heart of its historical part is the Old City, which is surrounded by Ottoman walls. The Christian quarter lies in the northwest of the Old City, around the church of the Holy Sepulchre. The Jewish quarter lies in the southeast, overlooking the Wailing Wall and the Temple Mount. The latter covers the southeastern corner of the Ottoman city. To the south of the Temple Mount, outside of the walls of the Ottoman city, stretches the long, narrow, relatively low ridge of the city of David—the old mound of Bronze and Early Iron Age Jerusalem. It is separated from the surrounding hills by two ravines. The eastern one, the Kidron valley, separates it from the village of Siloam. The main water source of biblical Jerusalem—the spring of Gihon—is located in this ravine.

Jerusalem has been excavated time and again—and with a particularly intense period of investigation of Bronze and Iron Age remains in the 1970s and 1980s under the direction of Yigal Shiloh, of the Hebrew University, at the city of David, the original urban core of Jerusalem. Surprisingly, as Tel Aviv University archaeologist David Ussishkin pointed out, fieldwork there and in other parts of biblical Jerusalem failed to provide significant evidence for a tenth century occupation. Not only was any sign of monumental architecture missing, but so were even simple pottery sherds. The types that are so characteristic of the tenth century at other sites are rare in Jerusalem. Some scholars have argued that later, massive building activities in Jerusalem wiped out all signs of the earlier city. Yet excavations in the city of David revealed impressive finds from the Middle Bronze Age and from later centuries of the Iron Age—just not from the tenth century BCE. The most optimistic assessment of this negative evidence is that tenth century Jerusalem was rather limited in extent, perhaps not more than a typical hill country village.

This modest appraisal meshes well with the rather meager settlement pattern of the rest of Judah in the same period, which was composed of only about twenty small villages and a few thousand inhabitants, many of them wandering pastoralists. In fact, it is highly unlikely that this sparsely inhabited region of Judah and the small village of Jerusalem could have become the center of a great empire stretching from the Red Sea in the south to Syria in the north. Could even the most charismatic king have marshaled the men and arms needed to achieve and hold such vast territorial conquests? There is absolutely no archaeological indication of the wealth, manpower, and level of organization that would be required to support large armies—even for brief periods—in the field. Even if the relatively few inhabitants of Judah were able to mount swift attacks on neighboring regions, how would they have possibly been able to administer the vast and even more ambitious empire of David's son Solomon?

How Vast Were David's Conquests?

For decades, archaeologists believed that the evidence uncovered in many excavations outside Jerusalem supported the Bible's account of a vast united monarchy (Figure 16). The most prominent of David's victories, according to the Bible, were against the Philistine cities, a number of which have been extensively excavated. The first book of Samuel offers great detail on the encounters between Israelites and Philistines: how the Philistine armies captured the ark of God at the battle of Ebenezer; how Saul and his son Jonathan died during the wars against the Philistines; and of course, how the young David toppled Goliath. While some of the details of these stories are clearly legendary, the geographical descriptions are quite accurate. More important, the gradual spread of the Philistines' distinctive Aegean-inspired decorated pottery into the foothills and as far north as the Jezreel valley provides evidence for the progressive expansion of the Philistines' influence throughout the country. And when evidence of destruction—around 1000 BCE—of lowland cities was found, it seemed to confirm the extent of David's conquests.

One of the best examples of this line of reasoning is the case of Tel Qasile, a small site on the northern outskirts of modern Tel Aviv, first excavated by the Israeli biblical archaeologist and historian Benjamin Mazar in 1948–50. Mazar uncovered a prosperous Philistine town, otherwise unknown in the biblical accounts. The last layer there that contained characteristic Philistine pottery and bore other hallmarks of Philistine culture was destroyed by fire. And even though there was no specific reference in the Bible to David's conquest of this area, Mazar did not hesitate to conclude that David leveled the settlement in his wars against the Philistines.

And so it went throughout the country, with David's destructive handiwork seen in ash layers and tumbled stones at sites from Philistia to the Jezreel valley and beyond. In almost every case where a city with late Philistine or Canaanite culture was attacked, destroyed, or even remodeled, King David's sweeping conquests were seen as the cause.

Could the Israelites of the central hill country have established control not only over small sites like Tel Qasile, but over the large "Canaanite" centers like Gezer, Megiddo, and Beth-shean? Theoretically, yes; there are some examples in history of rural people exerting control over big cities— especially in cases where highland warlords or outlaw chieftains used both the threat of violence and the promise of godfatherly protection to secure tribute and professions of loyalty from the farmers and shopkeepers of lowland towns. But in most cases these were not outright military conquests and the establishment of a formalized, bureaucratic empire so much as a more subtle means of leadership in which a highland chieftain offered a kind of security to lowland communities.

The Stables, Cities, and Gates of King Solomon?

The heart of the debate took place not over evidence of David's conquests, but rather their aftermath. Did Solomon establish a glorious reign over the kingdom conquered by David? Even though no trace of the Solomonic Temple and palace in Jerusalem has ever been identified, there have been many other places for scholars to look. The biblical narrative describes Solomon's rebuilding of the northern cities of Megiddo, Hazor, and Gezer (1 Kings 9:15). When one of those sites—Megiddo—was excavated by an expedition of the Oriental Institute of the University of Chicago in the 1920s and 1930s, some of its most impressive Iron Age remains were attributed to Solomon.

Located in a strategic spot, where the international highway from Egypt in the south to Mesopotamia and Anatolia in the north descends from the hills into the Jezreel valley, Megiddo was one of the most important cities of biblical Israel. And apart from 1 Kings 9:15, it is mentioned also in 1 Kings

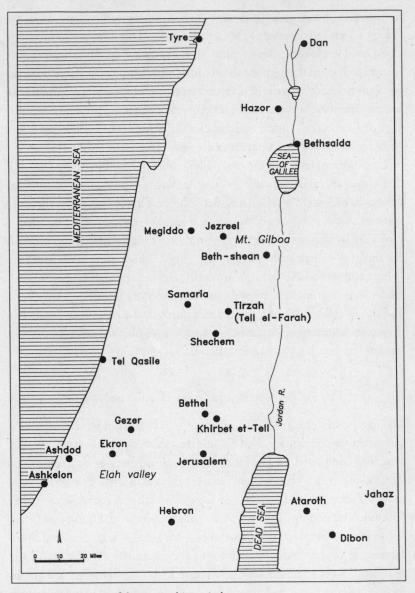

Figure 16: Main sites of the monarchic period.

4:12, in the list of districts of the Solomonic state. The city level called stratum IV—the last to be almost fully exposed over the entire area of the ancient mound—contained two sets of large public buildings, each composed of a series of long chambers attached to one another in a row. Each of the individual chambers was divided into three narrow aisles separated from one another by low partition walls of stone pillars and troughs (Figure 17).

One of the directors of the expedition, P.L.O. Guy, identified these buildings as stables dated to the time of Solomon. His interpretation was based on the biblical description of Solomonic building techniques in Jerusalem (1 Kings 7:12), on the specific reference to the building activity of Solomon at Megiddo in 1 Kings 9:15, and on the mention of Solomonic cities for chariots and horsemen in 1 Kings 9:19. Guy put it this way: "If we ask ourselves who, at Megiddo, shortly after the defeat of the Philistines by King David, built with the help of skilled foreign masons a city with many stables? I believe that we shall find our answer in the Bible . . . if one reads the history of Solomon, whether in Kings or in Chronicles, one is struck by the frequency with which chariots and horses crop up."

The apparent evidence of the grandeur of the Solomonic empire was significantly enhanced in the 1950s, with the excavations of Yigael Yadin at Hazor. Yadin and his team uncovered a large city gate dated to the Iron Age. It had a peculiar plan: there was a tower and three chambers on each side of the gateway—thus giving rise to the term "six-chambered" gate (Figure 18). Yadin was stunned. A similar gate—in both layout and size— was uncovered twenty years earlier by the Oriental Institute team at Megiddo! Perhaps this and not the stables was the telltale sign of Solomonic presence throughout the land.

So Yadin went to dig Gezer, the third city mentioned in 1 Kings 9:15 as being rebuilt by Solomon—not in the field but in the library. Gezer had been excavated at the beginning of the century by the British archaeologist R.A.S. Macalister. As Yadin paged through Macalister's reports he was astounded. In a plan of a building that Macalister had identified as a "Maccabean castle" dated to the second century BCE, Yadin could easily identify the outline of one side of exactly the same type of gate structure that had been found at Megiddo and Hazor. Yadin did not hesitate any longer. He argued that a royal architect from Jerusalem drew a master plan for the

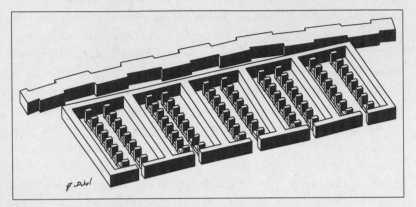

Figure 17: A set of pillared buildings at Megiddo, identified as stables.

Solomonic city gates and that this master plan was then dispatched to the provinces.

Yadin summed it up this way: "There is no example in the history of archaeology where a passage helped so much in identifying and dating structures in several of the most important tells in the Holy Land as has I Kings 9:15 . . . Our decision to attribute that layer [at Hazor] to Solomon was based primarily on the 1 Kings passage, the stratigraphy, and the pottery. But when in addition we found in that stratum a six-chambered, two-towered gate connected to a casemate wall identical in plan and measurement with the gate at Megiddo, we felt sure we had successfully identified Solomon's city."

Too Good to Be True?

Yadin's Solomonic discoveries were not over. In the early 1960s, he went to Megiddo with a small team of students to clarify the uniformity of the Solomonic gates, which at Gezer and Hazor were connected to a hollow casemate fortification but only at Megiddo linked to a solid wall. Yadin was sure that the Megiddo excavators had mistakenly attributed a solid wall to the gate, and that they missed an underlying casemate wall. Since the gate had been fully exposed by the University of Chicago team, Yadin chose to excavate east of the gate, where the American team had located an apparent set of stables that they attributed to Solomon.

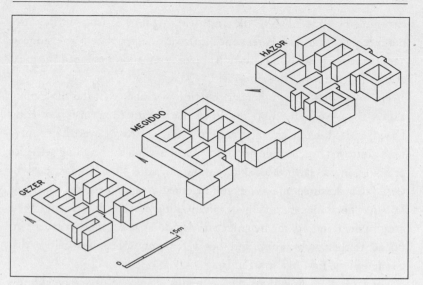

Figure 18: Six-chambered gates at Megiddo, Hazor, and Gezer.

What he found revolutionized biblical archaeology for a generation.
Under the stables Yadin found the remains of a beautiful palace measuring
about six thousand square feet and constructed of large ashlar blocks (Figure 24). It was built on the northern edge of the mound, and was connected to a row of rooms that Yadin interpreted as the missing casemate
wall that was attached to the six-chamber gate. A somewhat similar palace,
also built of beautiful dressed blocks, had been uncovered by the Oriental
Institute team on the southern side of the mound, and it also lay under the
city of the stables. The architectural style of both buildings was closely parallel to a common and distinctive type of north Syrian palace of the Iron
Age, known as the *bit hilani,* consisting of a monumental entrance and
rows of small chambers surrounding an official reception room. This style
would therefore have been appropriate for a resident official at Megiddo,
perhaps the regional governor Baana, the son of Ahilud (1 Kings 4:12).
Yadin's student David Ussishkin soon clinched the connection of these
buildings to Solomon by demonstrating that the biblical description of the
palace that Solomon built in Jerusalem perfectly fits the Megiddo palaces.
    The conclusion seemed unavoidable. The two palaces and the gate rep-
resented Solomonic Megiddo, while the stables actually belonged to a later

city, built by King Ahab of the northern kingdom of Israel in the early
ninth century BCE. This latter conclusion was an important cornerstone in
Yadin's theory, as a ninth century Assyrian inscription described the great
chariot force of King Ahab of Israel.

For Yadin and many others, archaeology seemed to fit the Bible more
closely than ever. The Bible described the territorial expansion of King
David; indeed, late Canaanite and Philistine towns all over the country
were destroyed by a terrible fire. The Bible describes the building activities
of Solomon at Hazor, Megiddo, and Gezer; surely the similar gates revealed that the three cities were built together, on a unified plan. The Bible
says that Solomon was an ally of Hiram, king of Tyre, and that he was a
great builder; indeed, the magnificent Megiddo palaces show northern influence in their architecture, and they were the most beautiful edifices discovered in the Iron Age strata in Israel.

For some years, Solomon's gates symbolized archaeology's most impressive support for the Bible. Yet basic questions of historical logic eventually
undermined their significance. Nowhere else in the region—from eastern
Turkey in the north through western Syria to Transjordan in the south—
was there any sign of similarly developed royal institutions or monumental
building in the tenth century BCE. As we have seen, David and Solomon's
homeland of Judah was conspicuously undeveloped—and there is no evidence whatever of the wealth of a great empire flowing back to it. And
there is an even more troubling chronological problem: the *bit hilani*
palaces of Iron Age Syria—which were supposed to be the prototypes for
the Solomonic palaces at Megiddo—appear for the first time in Syria in
the early ninth century BCE, at least half a century *after* the time of
Solomon. How would it have been possible for Solomon's architects to
adopt an architectural style that did not yet exist? Finally, there is the question of the contrast between Megiddo and Jerusalem: is it possible that a
king who constructed fabulous ashlar palaces in a provincial city ruled
from a small, remote, and underdeveloped village? As it turned out, we
now know that the archaeological evidence for the vast extent of Davidic
conquests and the grandeur of the Solomonic kingdom came as the result
of badly mistaken dates.

Questions of Dating

Identification of the remains from the period of David and Solomon—and indeed from the reigns of the kings that followed for the next century—was based on two classes of evidence. The end of distinctive Philistine pottery (dated c. 1000 BCE) was closely linked to David's conquests. And the construction of the monumental gates and palaces at Megiddo, Hazor, and Gezer were connected with the reign of Solomon. In the last few years, both supports have begun to crumble (see Appendix D for more details).

First, we can no longer be sure that the characteristic Philistine pottery styles did not continue well into the tenth century—long after the death of David—and would therefore be useless for dating (much less verifying) his supposed conquests. Second, renewed analysis of the architectural styles and pottery forms in the famous Solomonic levels at Megiddo, Gezer, and Hazor indicates that they actually date to the early ninth century BCE, decades after the death of Solomon!

A third class of evidence, the more precise laboratory techniques of carbon 14 dating, now seems to clinch the case. Until recently it was impossible to use radiocarbon dating for such relatively modern periods as the Iron Age because of its wide margin of probability, often extending over a century or more. But refinements of carbon 14 dating techniques have greatly reduced the margin of uncertainty. A number of samples from the major sites involved in the tenth century debate have been tested and seem to support the new chronology.

The site of Megiddo, in particular, has produced some stunning contradictions to the accepted interpretations. Fifteen wood samples were taken from large roof beams that had collapsed in the terrible fire and destruction attributed to David. Since some of the beams could have been used in earlier buildings, only the latest dates in the series can safely indicate when the structures were built. Indeed most of the samples fall well into the tenth century—long after the time of David. The palaces ascribed to Solomon, built two layers above this destruction, would have been much later.

These dates have been confirmed by tests of parallel strata at such prominent sites as Tel Dor on the Mediterranean coast and Tel Hadar on the shore of the Sea of Galilee. Sporadic readings from several other, less well known sites, such as Ein Hagit near Megiddo and Tel Kinneret on the northern coast of the Sea of Galilee, also support this dating. Finally, a series of samples from the destruction of a stratum at Tel Rehov near Bethshean, which is contemporary with Megiddo's supposed Solomonic city, gave mid-ninth century dates—long after its reported destruction by Pharaoh Shishak in 926 BCE.

Essentially, archaeology misdated both "Davidic" and "Solomonic" remains by a full century. The finds dated to the time just before David in the late eleventh century belonged in the mid-tenth century and those dated to the time of Solomon belonged in the early ninth century BCE. The new dates place the appearance of monumental structures, fortifications, and other signs of full statehood precisely at the time of their first appearance in the rest of the Levant. They rectify the disparity in dates between the *bit hilani* palace structures in Megiddo and their parallels in Syria. And they allow us finally to understand why Jerusalem and Judah are so poor in finds in the tenth century. The reason is that Judah was still a remote and undeveloped region at that time.

There is hardly a reason to doubt the historicity of David and Solomon. Yet there are plenty of reasons to question the extent and splendor of their realm. If there was no big empire, if there were no monuments, if there was no magnificent capital, what *was* the nature of David's realm?

The Davidic Legacy: From Iron Age Chiefdom to Dynastic Myth

The material culture of the highlands in the time of David remained simple. The land was overwhelmingly rural—with no trace of written documents, inscriptions, or even signs of the kind of widespread literacy that would be necessary for the functioning of a proper monarchy. From a demographic point of view, the area of the Israelite settlement was hardly homogeneous. It is hard to see any evidence of a unified culture or centrally administered state. The area from Jerusalem to the north was quite densely settled, while the area from Jerusalem to the south—the hub of the future kingdom of Judah—was still very sparsely settled. Jerusalem itself was, at best, no more than a typical highland village. We can say no more than that.

The population estimates for the later phases of the Israelite settlement period apply also to the tenth century BCE. They give an idea of the scale of historical possibilities. Out of a total of approximately forty-five thousand people living in the hill country, a full 90 percent would have inhabited the villages of the north. That would have left about five thousand people scattered among Jerusalem, Hebron, and about twenty small villages in Judah, with additional groups probably continuing as pastoralists. Such a small and isolated society like this would have been likely to cherish the memory of an extraordinary leader like David as his descendants continued to rule in Jerusalem over the next four hundred years. At first, in the tenth century, their rule extended over no empire, no palatial cities, no spectacular capital. Archeologically we can say no more about David and Solomon except that they existed—and that their legend endured.

Yet the fascination of the Deuteronomistic historian of the seventh century BCE with the memories of David and Solomon—and indeed the Judahites' apparent continuing veneration of these characters—may be the best if not the only evidence for the existence of some sort of an early Israelite unified state. The fact that the Deuteronomist employs the united monarchy as a powerful tool of political propaganda suggests that in his time the episode of David and Solomon as rulers over a relatively large territory in the central highlands was still vivid and widely believed.

Of course, by the seventh century BCE conditions in Judah had changed almost beyond reckoning. Jerusalem was now a relatively large city, dominated by a Temple to the God of Israel that served as the single national shrine. The institutions of monarchy, a professional army, and administration had reached a level of sophistication that met and even exceeded the complexity of the royal institutions of the neighboring states. And once again we can see the landscapes and costumes of seventh century Judah as the setting for an unforgettable biblical tale, this time of a mythical golden age. The lavish visit of Solomon's trading partner the queen of Sheba to Jerusalem (1 Kings 10:1–10) and the trade in rare commodities with distant markets such as the land of Ophir in the south (1 Kings 9:28; 10:11) no doubt reflect the participation of seventh century Judah in the lucrative Arabian trade. The same holds true for the description of the building of Tamar in the wilderness (1 Kings 9:18) and the trade expeditions to faraway lands setting out from Ezion-geber in the Gulf of Aqaba (1 Kings 9:26)—two sites that have been securely identified and that were not inhabited before late monarchic times. And David's royal guard of Cherethites and Pelethites (2 Samuel 8:18), long assumed by scholars to have been Aegean in origin, should be understood on the background of the service of Greek mercenaries, the most advanced fighting force of the day, in the Egyptian and possibly Judahite armies of the seventh century.

In late monarchic times, an elaborate theology had been developed in Judah and Jerusalem to validate the connection between the heir of David and the destiny of the entire people of Israel. According to the Deuteronomistic History, the pious David was the first to stop the cycle of idolatry (by the people of Israel) and divine retribution (by YHWH). Thanks to his devotion, faithfulness, and righteousness, YHWH helped him to complete the unfinished job of Joshua—namely to conquer the rest of the promised land and establish a glorious empire over all the vast territories that had been promised to Abraham. These were theological hopes, not accurate historical portraits. They were a central element in a powerful seventh century vision of national renaissance that sought to bring scattered, war-weary people together, to prove to them that they had experienced a stirring history under the direct intervention of God. The glorious epic of the united monarchy was—like the stories of the patriarchs and the sagas of the Exodus and conquest—a brilliant composition that wove together ancient heroic tales and legends into a coherent and persuasive prophecy for the people of Israel in the seventh century BCE.

To the people of Judah at the time when the biblical epic was first crafted, a new David had come to the throne, intent on restoring the glory of his distant ancestors. This was Josiah, described as the most devoted of all Judahite kings. And Josiah was able to roll history back from his own days to the time of the legendary united monarchy. By cleansing Judah of the abomination of idolatry—first introduced into Jerusalem by Solomon with his harem of foreign wives (1 Kings 11:1–8)—Josiah could nullify the transgressions that led to the breakdown of the Davidic "empire." What the Deuteronomistic historian wanted to say is simple and powerful: there is still a way to regain the glory of the past.

So Josiah embarked on establishing a united monarchy that would link Judah with the territories of the former northern kingdom through the royal institutions, military forces, and single-minded devotion to Jerusalem that are so central to the biblical narrative of David. As the monarch sitting on the throne of David in Jerusalem, Josiah was the only legitimate heir to the Davidic empire, that is, to the Davidic territories. He was about to "regain" the territories of the now destroyed northern kingdom, the kingdom that was born from the sins of Solomon. And the words of 1 Kings 4:25, that "Judah and Israel dwelt in safety from Dan even to Beersheba," summarize those hopes of territorial expansion and quest for peaceful, prosperous times, similar to the mythical past, when a king ruled from Jerusalem over the territories of Judah and Israel combined.

As we have seen, the historical reality of the kingdom of David and Solomon was quite different from the tale. It was part of a great demographic transformation that would lead to the emergence of the kingdoms of Judah and Israel—in a dramatically different historical sequence than the one the Bible describes. So far we have examined the biblical version of Israel's formative history written in the seventh century BCE, and we have provided glimpses at the archaeological reality that underlies it. Now it is time to tell a new story. In the chapters that follow, we will present the main outlines of the rise, fall, and rebirth of a very different Israel.

PART TWO

The Rise and Fall of Ancient Israel

[6]

One State, One Nation, One People?

(C. 930–720 BCE)

The course of Israel's history—the books of Kings gravely inform us—moves with almost tragic inevitability from unity to schism and from schism to national catastrophe. After the glorious reigns of David and Solomon, when all Israel was ruled from Jerusalem and experienced a period of unprecedented prosperity and power, the tribes of the northern hill country and Galilee—resisting the tax demands of Solomon's son Rehoboam—angrily break away. What follows is two hundred years of division and hatred between brothers, with the independent Israelite kingdoms of Israel in the north and of Judah in the south intermittently poised to strike at each other's throats. It is a tale of tragic division, and of violence and idolatry in the northern kingdom. There, according to the biblical accounts, new cult centers are founded to compete with the Jerusalem Temple. New northern Israelite dynasties, rivals of the house of David, bloodily come to power one after another. In time, the northerners pay for their sinfulness with the ultimate punishment—destruction of their state and the exile of the ten northern tribes.

This vision is central to the theology of the Bible—and to the biblical hope for an eventual reunion of Judah and Israel under the rule of the Davidic dynasty. But it is simply not an accurate representation of the historical reality. As we have seen, there is no compelling archaeological evidence for the historical existence of a vast united monarchy, centered in Jerusalem, that encompassed the entire land of Israel. On the contrary, the evidence reveals a complex demographic transformation in the highlands, in which a unified ethnic consciousness began only slowly to coalesce.

And here we reach perhaps the most unsettling clash between the archaeological finds and the Bible. If there was no Exodus, no conquest, no united monarchy, what are we to make of the biblical desire for unification? What are we to make of the long and difficult relationship between the kingdoms of Judah and Israel for almost two hundred years? There is good reason to suggest that there were *always* two distinct highland entities, of which the southern was always the poorer, weaker, more rural, and less influential—until it rose to sudden, spectacular prominence *after* the fall of the northern kingdom of Israel.

A Tale of Twelve Tribes and Two Kingdoms

In the Bible, the northern tribes are consistently depicted as weakhearted failures, with a pronounced tendency to sinfulness. This is particularly clear in the book of Judges, where the individual tribes struggle with the idolatrous peoples around them. Among the descendants of the twelve sons of Jacob, only the tribes of Judah and Simeon succeeded in conquering all the Canaanite enclaves in their God-given inheritance. As a result, in the south there were no Canaanites left, no Canaanite women to marry and to be influenced by. The tribes of the north are another story. Benjamin, Manasseh, Ephraim, Zebulun, Asher, Naphtali, and Dan did not accomplish what they had to; they did not finish off the Canaanites. As a result they would be tempted again and again.

There is no question in the text that the northern tribes were more numerous and occupied a vast territory, and it is certainly no accident that the first king of Israel, Saul, from the tribe of Benjamin, is said to have ruled over northern territories in the highlands. Yet Saul violated the laws of the cult and was driven to suicide after the defeat of his forces by the Philistines. God withdrew his blessing from this anointed northern leader, and the elders of the northern tribes duly turned to David, the outlaw-hero-king of Judah, and proclaimed him king over all of Israel. Despite their wealth and strength, however, the northern tribes are depicted in

1 Kings as being treated like little more than colonial subjects by David's son Solomon. Solomon's great regional capitals and store cities of Gezer, Megiddo, and Hazor were built in their midst and the people of the north were taxed and conscripted into public works projects by Solomonic appointees. Some northerners—like Jeroboam, son of Nebat, of the tribe of Ephraim—served under the Jerusalem court in positions of importance. But Judah is depicted as the stronger party, having the northern tribes as subjects.

Upon the death of Solomon and the accession of his son Rehoboam, the northerners appealed for a reduction in their burden. But the arrogant Rehoboam dismissed the advice of his moderate counselors and replied to the northerners with the now famous words "My father made your yoke heavy, but I will add to your yoke; my father chastised you with whips, but I will chastise you with scorpions" (1 Kings 12:14). The banner of rebellion was unfurled as the northerners rallied to the cry of secession: "And when all Israel saw that the king did not hearken to them, the people answered the king: 'What portion have we in David? We have no inheritance in the son of Jesse. Look to your tents, O Israel! Look to your own house, David.' So Israel departed to their tents" (1 Kings 12:16). The northerners proceeded to stone to death Rehoboam's chief taskmaster, and King Rehoboam fled in terror back to the safety of Jerusalem.

The northerners then gathered to proclaim for themselves a monarch and chose Jeroboam, son of Nebat, who had served in the court of Solomon. The united monarchy of David and Solomon was completely shattered. Two independent states were created: Judah, which was ruled by the Davidic dynasty from Jerusalem, with its territory limited to the southern part of the central hill country; and Israel, which controlled vast territories in the north. The first capital of the northern kingdom was set at Tirzah, located to the northeast of Shechem. The new king, Jeroboam, decided to set up rivals to the Temple in Jerusalem and ordered that two golden calves be fashioned and installed in shrines at the farthest corners of his kingdom—at Bethel in the far south and Dan in the north.

Thus began a turbulent and fateful period in the biblical history of Israel. From the family solidarity of the patriarchal period, from the spiritual solidarity of the Exodus, and from the political unity of the united monarchy, the people of Israel were now torn in two.

A Mistaken Scheme of Evolution?

Archaeologists and biblical historians alike have generally taken the biblical narrative of the rise and disintegration of the united monarchy at face value. The ethnic unity and distinctiveness of the people of Israel as a whole were taken for granted. And the historical sequence was believed by most biblical historians to have run approximately like this (minus, of course, the occasional biblical mythmaking and heroic hyperbole): Whether by conquest or peaceful infiltration, the Israelites settled in the empty highlands. At first they organized themselves as a sort of egalitarian society, with charismatic military heroes who saved them from their foes. Then, mainly because of the Philistine threat, which was far more dangerous than the other local menaces, they opted for a monarchy, built a strong army, and expanded to establish a formidable empire under David and Solomon. It was a tale of steady political evolution of a unified people, from tribes to unified statehood, an evolutionary process that was essentially completed by the time of Solomon in the tenth century BCE.

The breakup of the united monarchy was therefore seen as an unfortunate postscript to a story that had already run its course. It appeared as if only the arrogant and ill-advised tyranny of Solomon's son Rehoboam destroyed the expansive grandeur of the Solomonic empire. This vision of the united monarchy and its downfall seemed to be confirmed by the archaeological finds. Scholars believed that the construction of the great "Solomonic" cities with their gates and palaces was indisputable evidence of full-blown statehood by the tenth century BCE and of Jerusalem's iron-fisted control of the north. By the 1980s, even though the understanding of the initial period of Israelite history had become somewhat more nuanced, it was taken for granted that the united monarchy of David and Solomon—and its sudden breakup—were historical facts.

In tracing the subsequent history of the two sister states of Judah and Israel, scholars followed the biblical story almost word for word, with most assuming that the two successor states shared a nearly identical level of political organization and complexity. Since both Judah and Israel had their origins in the full-fledged monarchy of Solomon, both inherited fully developed state institutions of court, fiscal administration, and military force. As a result, the two independent kingdoms were believed to have competed with each other, fought each other, and helped each other, according to the changing political circumstances in the region, but always on more or less equal terms. Certain regional differences did, of course, become apparent. But most scholars concluded that the rest of the history of the Israelite kingdoms was one of population increase, intensive building, and warfare—but no further dramatic social development.

This widely accepted picture now appears to be wrong.

North Versus South Through the Millennia

The intensive archaeological surveys in the central hill country in the 1980s opened new vistas for understanding the character and origins of the two highland states of Judah and Israel. The new perspectives differed dramatically from the biblical accounts. The surveys showed that the emergence of the Israelites in the highlands of Canaan was not a unique event, but actually just one in a series of demographic oscillations that could be traced back for millennia.

In each of the two earlier settlement waves—in the Early Bronze Age (c. 3500–2200 BCE) and in the Middle Bronze Age (c. 2000–1550 BCE)—the indigenous highland population moved from pastoralism to seasonal agriculture, to permanent villages, to complex highland economies in a manner that was strikingly similar to the process of Israelite settlement in the Iron Age I (1150–900 BCE). But even more surprising, the surveys (and the fragmentary historical information) indicated that in each wave of highland settlement, there always seemed to have been *two* distinct societies in the highlands—northern and southern—roughly occupying the areas of the later kingdoms of Judah and Israel.

A map of Early Bronze Age highland sites, for example, clearly shows two different regional settlement systems, with a dividing line between them running roughly between Shechem and Jerusalem, a boundary that would later mark the frontier between Israel and Judah. Like the later kingdom of Israel, the northern settlement system was dense and possessed a complex hierarchy of large, medium, and small sites, all heavily dependent on settled agriculture. The southern region, like the later kingdom of Judah, was more sparsely settled, mostly in small sites, with no such variety of sizes. The south also had a relatively large number of archaeological sites with only scatters of pottery sherds, rather than permanent buildings; this suggested a significant population of migratory pastoral groups.

Northern and southern regions were each dominated by a single center that was apparently the focus of regional political and economic centralization—and perhaps of regional religious practices as well. In the south, in the Early Bronze Age, it was a large site named Khirbet et-Tell (the biblical Ai), located northeast of Jerusalem. It covered an area of about twenty-five acres, which represented a full *fifth* of all the built-up area in the southern hill country. Its impressive fortifications and monumental temple underline its paramount status in the largely rural and pastoral south. In the north there were a few central sites, but a dominating one, Tell el-Farah, situated near a large freshwater spring and guarding the main road down to the Jordan valley, seems to have controlled the rich agricultural lands of the region. It is not pure coincidence—as we will see—that this city, later known as biblical Tirzah, became the first capital of the northern kingdom of Israel.

In the succeeding Middle Bronze Age, the wave of settlement in the highlands possessed exactly the same characteristics. There were very few permanent settlement sites in the south, most of them tiny, and there were a large number of pastoral groups, evidenced by their isolated cemeteries not related to sedentary sites. The north was much more densely inhabited, with settled farmers in much greater proportion than pastoralists. The major urban site in the south was now Jerusalem, which was heavily fortified (as Ai had been in the Early Bronze Age), joined by a secondary center, Hebron, which was also fortified. The great center of the north was now Shechem. Excavations at the site of Tell Balatah on the eastern outskirts of the city revealed imposing fortifications and a massive temple.

In addition to the archaeological indications of the north-south split there is some important textual evidence from Egypt. One source is the so-called execration texts—curse inscriptions, written on pottery fragments on statuettes of prisoners of war that were meant to be broken and buried ceremonially to bring misfortune upon the enemies of Egypt. Like ancient versions of voodoo dolls covered with angry graffiti, these texts offer us a glimpse at the political geography of Canaan during that era, in particular those places and peoples whom the Egyptians found most threatening. The texts mention a large number of coastal and lowland cities, but only two highland centers: Shechem and (according to most scholars) Jerusalem.

Another Egyptian reference to the highlands adds to the picture. It is an inscription recording the exploits of an Egyptian general named Khu-Sebek, who led an Egyptian military campaign to the highlands of Canaan in the nineteenth century BCE. The inscription refers to the "land" (rather than "city") of Shechem, and mentions *Shechem* as a parallel to *Retenu*—one of the Egyptian names for all of the land of Canaan. This seems to indicate that as early as the beginning of the second millennium BCE, Shechem—one of the most important centers of the kingdom of Israel—was the hub of a large territorial entity.

We have no textual information about the southern territories in the Middle Bronze Age, but there is abundant information about their extent in the next period—the Late Bronze Age. The fourteenth century BCE Tell el-Amarna letters confirm the partition of the central hill country between two city-states, or actually early territorial states, Shechem and Jerusalem (Figure 19). A number of the letters refer by name to the rulers of these two city-states—a king named Abdi-Heba who reigned in Jerusalem and a king named Labayu who reigned in Shechem—each of whom controlled territories of about a thousand square miles. These were the largest areas held by a single local ruler, for at this time the Canaanite coastal plain and valleys were divided into many tiny city-states, each ruling a small territory with a relatively dense population. Although the political units in the highlands were much larger, their population was much smaller.

Shechem and Jerusalem, Israel and Judah, were always distinct and competing territories. And there was good reason for the differences between them: north and south occupied dramatically different environmental zones.

Two Worlds in the Highlands

At first glance, the highlands between the Jezreel and the Beersheba valleys seem to form a homogeneous geographical block. But the environmental and topographical details offer a very different picture. The north and south have distinct ecosystems that differ in almost every aspect: topography, rock formations, climate, vegetation cover, and potential economic

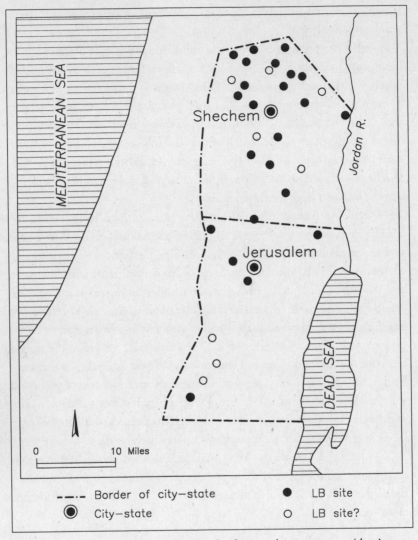

Figure 19: The two highland entities in the fourteenth century BCE (the Amarna period).

resources. Judah was always the most remote part of the hill country, isolated by topographical and climatic barriers. By contrast, the northern part
of the highlands consisted of a patchwork of fertile valleys nestled between
adjoining hilly slopes. Some of those valleys offered enough fertile farmland to support the inhabitants of several villages. It was thus a relatively
productive region, with the inner valleys and the eastern marginal land of
the desert fringe cultivated mainly for grain growing, while the hilly areas
were cultivated with olive and vine orchards. Though a casual traveler
through this region today may find it much hillier in appearance than the
south, communication and transport of agricultural produce are immeasurably easier. The slopes to the west are much more moderate and, in fact,
facilitate rather than obstruct passage down toward the cities of the
Mediterranean coastal plain. On the northern edge of this region lay the
broad expanse of the Jezreel valley, an extremely rich agricultural area that
also served as the major overland route of trade and communication between Egypt and Mesopotamia. In the east, the desert steppe area was less
arid and less rugged than farther south—enabling the relatively free movement of people and commodities between the central ridge, the Jordan valley, and the Transjordanian highlands to the east.

Any territorial unit that arose in the northern highlands had a far greater
economic potential than those of the south. Even though the basic process
of highland settlement in both regions was similar—shifting from herding
and seasonal farming to an ever greater dependence on specialized agriculture—the north had more resources and a richer climate to exploit. In the
early stages of each wave of settlement, when the bulk of the highland population was concentrated in the eastern fringes of the steppe and
eastern highlands valleys, they maintained a balanced, essentially self-
sufficient economy. Each village community provided its own supply of
both agricultural crops and animal products. But when population pressure and the temptation of economic opportunities forced expansion to
the western edge of the hill country, the northerners had a distinct advantage. They were able to develop a more specialized and sophisticated economy because the western slopes of the northern hill country were less
precipitous and rocky than those in the south—and far more suitable for
growing olive and vine orchards on small, terraced plots on the hillsides.
The initial specialization in olive and grape growing encouraged the devel-

opment of the technology to process these products efficiently into oil and wine. It also gave rise to the economic institutions of markets, transport, and exchange in order for the wine- and oil-producing villages to obtain vitally needed grain and animal products in return for their own produce.

The result was increasing complexity of the northern highland societies and, eventually, the crystallization of something like a state. Export trade to the people of the lowlands and, more important, to the markets in the great cities of Egypt and the ports of the Phoenician coast pushed things still further. Thus, in the beginning of the Iron Age, the northern highlands were poised to become richer and more populous than the highlands in the south.

State Formation in the Biblical World

The evolution of the highlands of Canaan into two distinct polities was a natural development. There is no archaeological evidence whatsoever that this situation of north and south grew out of an earlier political unity—particularly one centered in the south. In the tenth and ninth centuries BCE, Judah was still very thinly inhabited, with a limited number of small villages, in fact not much more than twenty or so. There is good reason to believe from both the distinctive clan structure and the archaeological finds in Judah that the pastoral segment of the population was still significant there. And we still have no hard archaeological evidence—despite the unparalleled biblical descriptions of its grandeur—that Jerusalem was anything more than a modest highland village in the time of David, Solomon, and Rehoboam. At the same time, the northern half of the highlands—essentially the territories that reportedly broke away from the united monarchy—was thickly occupied by dozens of sites, with a well-developed settlement system that included large regional centers, villages of all sizes, and tiny hamlets. Put simply, while Judah was still economically marginal and backward, Israel was booming.

In fact, Israel was well on the way to fully developed statehood within a few decades of the presumed end of the united monarchy, around 900 BCE. By *fully developed* we mean a territory governed by bureaucratic machinery, which is manifested in social stratification as seen in the distribution of luxury items, large building projects, prospering economic activity including trade with neighboring regions, and a fully developed settlement system.

In Israel, regional administrative centers developed in the early ninth century. They were fortified and provided with elaborate palaces built of ashlar blocks and decorated with stone capitals. The best examples are found at Megiddo, Jezreel, and Samaria. Yet in the south, ashlar masonry and stone capitals appear only in the seventh century BCE, in smaller sizes, showing less foreign influence, and with lesser quality of construction. There is also a great difference in the layout and development of the capital cities. Samaria, the capital of the northern kingdom, was established as a large, palatial government center as early as the ninth century. Jerusalem was fully urbanized only in the late eighth century.

In addition, the olive oil industry developed in Israel as early as the ninth century. But in Judah, olive oil production shifted from local, private households to state industry only in the seventh century BCE. Finally, we should look at the settlement history of the highlands, in which the north was settled earlier than Judah and reached much higher levels of population. In sum, it is safe to say that the northern kingdom of Israel emerged as a fully developed state no later than the beginning of the ninth century BCE—at a time when the society and economy of Judah had changed but little from its highland origins. All this is also supported by the historical record. In the next chapter we will see how the northern kingdom suddenly appeared on the ancient Near Eastern stage as a major regional power in the coalition that confronted the Assyrian king Shalmaneser III at the battle of Qarqar in the year 853 BCE.

There is no doubt that the two Iron Age states—Israel and Judah—had much in common. Both worshiped YHWH (among other deities). Their peoples shared many legends, heroes, and tales about events in the distant past. They also spoke similar languages, or dialects of Hebrew, and by the eighth century BCE, both wrote in the same script. But they were also very different from each other in their demographic composition, economic potential, material culture, and relationship with their neighbors. Put simply, Israel and Judah experienced quite different histories and developed distinctive cultures. In a sense, Judah was little more than Israel's rural hinterland.

The Age of Israel Begins

Throughout all the millennia of Canaan's human history, the northern highlands may have been richer than the southern highlands, but they were not nearly as prosperous and urbanized as the Canaanite city-states of the lowlands and the coastal plain. What made possible the initial independence of the highlands was the fact that, as we have seen, the city-state system of Canaan suffered a series of catastrophically destructive upheavals at the end of the Late Bronze Age. Whether caused by the depredations of the Sea Peoples, or intercity rivalries, or social unrest, the lowland economy was dealt a crushing blow.

In time, the Canaanite inhabitants of the lowlands again began to prosper. By the eleventh century BCE, the Philistines, who had previously settled along the southern coast, consolidated the power of their cities. The Phoenician successors of the coastal Canaanites occupied the maritime ports of the north. In the northern valleys, while major sites such as Megiddo suffered destruction in the course of the twelfth century BCE, life in the less urbanized countryside continued uninterrupted. After a few decades of abandonment even the major sites were reoccupied, apparently by the same population—the local Canaanite inhabitants of the lowlands—and some of the most important Canaanite centers were rejuvenated and continued well into the tenth century BCE.

Megiddo is a good example of the process. A few decades after the destruction of the Late Bronze Age city with its elaborate palace, settlement at the site was resumed in a modest way. After a few more decades there were significant signs of building and population growth, to the point that Megiddo once again became a substantial city (called stratum VIA), with almost all the features of its former Canaanite culture. The styles of pottery resembled those of the twelfth century BCE; the plan of the town resembled the size and plan of the last Late Bronze city at Megiddo; and most important, the Canaanite temple was still functioning. Excavations at other major sites in the valleys and the northern coastal plain, such as Tel Dor (on the coast to the west of Megiddo) and Tel Rehov (to the south of the Sea of Galilee), have revealed a similar picture of the continuation of the Canaanite city-state world, with large towns or cities dominating the prosperous countryside.

But this late blooming of Canaan was not to last long. The northern cities would be destroyed by violence and fire. The devastation was so overwhelming that they never recovered from the shock. This was Canaan's last gasp. What happened?

Egypt, which had gone through a long period of decline and withdrawal from the international stage, was at last ready to reassert its power over the lands to the north. Near the end of the tenth century BCE, the pharaoh Shishak, founder of the Twenty-second Dynasty (known as Sheshonq in Egyptian inscriptions), launched an aggressive raid northward. This Egyptian invasion is mentioned in the Bible, from a distinctly Judahite perspective, in a passage that offers the earliest correlation between external historical records and the biblical text: "In the fifth year of Rehoboam, Shishak king of Egypt came up against Jerusalem; he took away the treasures of the house of the LORD and the treasures of the king's house; he took away everything. He also took away the shields of gold that Solomon had made" (1 Kings 14:25–26). Yet we now know that Jerusalem was hardly the only or even the most important target. A triumphal inscription commissioned by Sheshonq for the walls of the great temple of Karnak in Upper Egypt lists about one-hundred fifty towns and villages devastated in the operation. They are located in the south, through the central hill country, and across the Jezreel valley and the coastal plain.

The once-great Canaanite cities of Rehov, Beth-shean, Taanach, and Megiddo are listed as targets of the Egyptian forces, and indeed a fragment of a victory stele bearing the name of Shishak was found at Megiddo—unfortunately in the dump of previous excavations, so its precise archaeological connection was unclear. Thick layers of conflagration and collapse uncovered in these and other major sites in the north provide dramatic evidence for the sudden and total demise of this late Canaanite system in the late tenth century BCE. And Shishak, who campaigned in the region in 926 BCE, is the likeliest candidate to have caused this wave of destruction.* The Karnak list and the results of recent excavations seem to indicate that

---

* The Shishak alternative raises a problem: Why would the Egyptian king destroy the cities in the Jezreel valley if he intended to continue dominating Canaan? And why would he erect an elaborate victory stele in a destroyed city like Megiddo? Another possible candidate for the agent of destruction of the Canaanite cities could be the northern kingdom of Israel in its early days.

Shishak struck at the developing network of early Israelite villages in the highlands as well.

But Shishak's campaign did not result in lasting Egyptian control of Canaan. When the dust settled, it was clear that the strike in the highlands was only glancing (with the only apparent effects being the abandonment of some villages north of Jerusalem). Yet the blow struck at the revived Canaanite cities in the Jezreel valley was terminal. This had enormous implications, since the destruction of the last vestiges of the Canaanite city-state system opened a window of opportunity for the people of the northern highlands, who were already experiencing a period of intense economic and demographic growth. It opened the way for the rise of a full-fledged kingdom to expand from the northern hill country to the adjoining lowlands in the very late tenth century, or more probably in the beginning of the ninth century BCE.

Far to the south, the southern highlands—the few villages around Jerusalem—continued the old regime of dispersed villages and pastoralism. Despite the later biblical narratives of the great empire of David and Solomon that would conquer and administer the country from northernmost Dan to southernmost Beersheba, true statehood would not arrive there for another two hundred years.

Four Self-Fulfilling Prophecies

Why does the Bible tell a story of schism and secession of Israel from Judah that is at such great odds with the historical evidence? If the age-old rhythms of life in the highlands of Canaan dictated two distinct regional cultures—and if the states of Israel and Judah were so different in their nature from the very beginning—why were they so systematically and convincingly portrayed in the Bible as twin states?

The answer is hinted at in four divinely inspired predictions of the future that are skillfully woven into the narrative of the breakdown of the united monarchy and the establishment of the independent kingdom of Israel. These oracles—written in the form of direct communication between God and a number of prophets—represent the efforts of a later generation of Judahite interpreters to explain the unexpected twists and turns of history.

The people of Judah believed that God had promised David that his dynasty would be secure forever, based in Jerusalem. Yet for centuries Judah found itself in the shadow of Israel, whose kings paid little heed to Jerusalem. How could this have happened? The biblical narrative puts the blame squarely on the religious infidelity of a *Judahite* king. And it promises that the division of Israel into two rival kingdoms will be only a temporary punishment for the sins of a senior member of the divinely blessed Davidic dynasty.

The first prophecy flatly blamed the personal transgressions of David's son Solomon for the breakup of Israel's unity. Though Solomon was portrayed as one of the greatest kings of all times, wise and wealthy, ruling from the Euphrates to the borders of Egypt, he was also a sinner, taking foreign women as wives in his royal harem, precisely the kind of liaisons that YHWH strictly prohibited for the Israelites, lest the marriages with idolatrous women turn their heart to the worship of other gods. And that is precisely what the Bible reports:

> For when Solomon was old his wives turned away his heart after other gods; and his heart was not wholly true to the LORD his God, as was the heart of David his father. For Solomon went after Ashtoreth the goddess of the Sidonians, and after Milcom the abomination of the Ammonites. So Solomon did what was evil in the sight of the LORD, and did not wholly follow the LORD, as David his father had done. Then Solomon built a high place for Chemosh the abomination of Moab, and for Molech the abomination of the Ammonites, on the mountain east of Jerusalem. And so he did for all his foreign wives, who burned incense and sacrificed to their gods. (1 KINGS 11:4–8)

Punishment was thus inevitable for a Davidic heir who "did not wholly follow the Lord, as David his father had done." Therefore YHWH said to Solomon:

> "Since this has been your mind and you have not kept my covenant and my statutes which I have commanded you, I will surely tear the kingdom from you and will give it to your servant. Yet for the sake of David your father I will not do it in your days, but I will tear it out of the hand of your son. However I will not tear away all the kingdom; but I will give one tribe to your son, for the sake of David my servant and for the sake of Jerusalem which I have chosen." (1 KINGS 11:11–13)

Thus the original promise to David was compromised—though not entirely suspended—by Solomon's sin.

The second prophecy dealt with the "servant of Solomon" who would rule in place of David. He was Jeroboam, the son of Nebat, an Ephraimite, who served in the Solomonic administration as officer in charge of recruiting forced labor among the tribes of the north. One day on his way out of Jerusalem he was confronted by the prophet Ahijah from Shiloh, who ripped up the garment he was wearing and tore it into twelve pieces, handing Jeroboam ten of the shreds. Ahijah's prophecy was dramatic and fateful:

"Take for yourself ten pieces; for thus says the LORD, the God of Israel, 'Behold, I am about to tear the kingdom from the hand of Solomon, and will give you ten tribes (but he shall have one tribe, for the sake of my servant David and for the sake of Jerusalem, the city which I have chosen out of all the tribes of Israel), because he has forsaken me, and worshiped Ashtoreth the goddess of the Sidonians, Chemosh the god of Moab, and Milcom the god of the Ammonites, and has not walked in my ways, doing what is right in my sight and keeping my statutes and my ordinances, as David his father did. Nevertheless I will not take the whole kingdom out of his hand; but I will make him ruler all the days of his life, for the sake of David my servant whom I chose, who kept my commandments and my statutes; but I will take the kingdom out of his son's hand, and will give it to you, ten tribes. Yet to his son I will give one tribe, that David my servant may always have a lamp before me in Jerusalem, the city where I have chosen to put my name. And I will take you, and you shall reign over all that your soul desires, and you shall be king over Israel. And if you will hearken to all that I command you, and will walk in my ways, and do what is right in my eyes by keeping my statutes and my commandments, as David my servant did, I will be with you, and will build you a sure house, as I built for David, and I will give Israel to you. And I will for this afflict the descendants of David, but not for ever.' " (1 KINGS 11:31–39)

Unlike the promise to David, God's promise to Jeroboam was conditional: YHWH would secure his state only as long as he did what was right in the eyes of God. But he did not:

Then Jeroboam built Shechem in the hill country of Ephraim, and dwelt there; and he went out from there and built Penuel. And Jeroboam said in his heart,

"Now the kingdom will turn back to the house of David; if this people go up to offer sacrifices in the house of the Lord at Jerusalem, then the heart of this people will turn again to their lord, to Rehoboam king of Judah, and they will kill me and return to Rehoboam king of Judah." So the king took counsel, and made two calves of gold. And he said to the people, "You have gone up to Jerusalem long enough. Behold your gods, O Israel, who brought you up out of the land of Egypt." And he set one in Bethel, and the other he put in Dan. And this thing became a sin, for the people went to the one at Bethel and to the other as far as Dan. (1 KINGS 12:25–30)

The newly installed King Jeroboam soon received a shocking vision of doom. In the midst of officiating at the golden calf shrine of Bethel, at an autumn festival probably meant to divert pilgrims from the celebrations at Jerusalem, Jeroboam was confronted at the altar by a prophet-like figure who is identified in the biblical text only as "a man of God."

And behold, a man of God came out of Judah by the word of the LORD to Bethel. Jeroboam was standing by the altar to burn incense. And the man cried against the altar by the word of the LORD, and said, "O altar, altar, thus says the LORD: 'Behold, a son shall be born to the house of David, Josiah by name; and he shall sacrifice upon you the priests of the high places who burn incense upon you, and men's bones shall be burned upon you.' " (1 KINGS 13:1–2)

This is an unparalleled prophecy, because the "man of God" revealed the name of a specific king of Judah who would, three centuries later, order the destruction of that very shrine, killing its priests and defiling its altar with their remains. It is something like reading a history of slavery written in seventeenth century colonial America in which there is a passage predicting the birth of Martin Luther King. And that is not all: Jeroboam was deeply shaken by the prophecy, and soon afterward his son Abijah fell ill. Jeroboam's wife proceeded immediately to the old cult center at Shiloh to confer with the prophet Ahijah—the very prophet who had predicted that Jeroboam would soon reign as king of the northern tribes. Ahijah had no words of reassurance for the worried mother. Instead he issued the fourth prophecy, one of the most chilling the Bible contains:

"Go, tell Jeroboam, 'Thus says the LORD, the God of Israel: "Because I exalted you from among the people, and made you leader over my people Israel, and tore the kingdom away from the house of David and gave it to you; and yet you have not been like my servant David, who kept my commandments, and followed me with all his heart, doing only that which was right in my eyes, but you have done evil above all that were before you and have gone and made for yourself other gods, and molten images, provoking me to anger, and have cast me behind your back; therefore behold, I will bring evil upon the house of Jeroboam, and will cut off from Jeroboam every male, both bond and free in Israel, and will utterly consume the house of Jeroboam, as a man burns up dung until it is all gone. Any one belonging to Jeroboam who dies in the city the dogs shall eat; and any one who dies in the open country the birds of the air shall eat; for the LORD has spoken it.' " Arise therefore, go to your house. When your feet enter the city, the child shall die. And all Israel shall mourn for him, and bury him; for he only of Jeroboam shall come to the grave, because in him there is found something pleasing to the LORD, the God of Israel, in the house of Jeroboam. Moreover the LORD will raise up for himself a king over Israel, who shall cut off the house of Jeroboam today. And henceforth the LORD will smite Israel, as a reed is shaken in the water, and root up Israel out of this good land which he gave to their fathers, and scatter them beyond the Euphrates, because they have made their Asherim, provoking the LORD to anger. And he will give Israel up because of the sins of Jeroboam, which he sinned and which he made Israel to sin." (1 KINGS 14:7–16)

The precision of the earlier prophecy of the "man of God" gives away the era when it was written. The Davidic king Josiah, who conquered and destroyed the altar at Bethel, lived at the end of the seventh century BCE. Why does a story that takes place in the late tenth century BCE need to bring in a figure from such a distant future? What is the reason for describing what a righteous king named Josiah will do? The answer is much the same as we suggested in explaining why the stories of the patriarchs, the Exodus, and the conquest of Canaan are overflowing with seventh century allusions. The inescapable fact is that the books of Kings are as much a passionate religious argument—written in the seventh century BCE—as they are works of history.

By that time the kingdom of Israel was already a fading memory, with its cities destroyed and large numbers of its inhabitants deported to far corners of the Assyrian empire. But Judah was, in the meantime, prospering and developing territorial ambitions, claiming to be the only legitimate heir to the extensive territories of Israel. The ideology and theology of the late monarchic historian was based on several pillars, one of the most important of which was the idea that the Israelite cult must be totally centralized in the Temple in Jerusalem. The rival northern cult center at Bethel, not so far from Jerusalem, must have been seen as a threat even before the destruction of the northern kingdom. And worse, it was still active in the early seventh century, probably attracting people living in the territories of the ex–northern kingdom, most of them Israelites who did not go into exile. It posed a dangerous competition to the political, territorial, and theological ambitions of Judah in the days of King Josiah. And the inevitability of Israel's fall—and Josiah's triumph—became a central theme in the biblical account.

A Most Cautionary Tale

These are the reasons why, throughout the description of the history of the northern kingdom, the Deuteronomistic historian transmits to the reader a dual, somewhat contradictory message. On the one hand he depicts Judah and Israel as sister states; on the other hand he develops strong antagonism between them. It was Josiah's ambition to expand to the north and take over the territories in the highlands that once belonged to the northern kingdom. Thus the Bible supports that ambition by explaining that the northern kingdom was established in the territories of the mythical united monarchy, which was ruled from Jerusalem; that it was a sister Israelite state; that its people were Israelites who should have worshiped in Jerusalem; that the Israelites still living in these territories must turn their eyes to Jerusalem; and that Josiah, the heir to the Davidic throne and to YHWH's eternal promise to David, is the only legitimate heir to the territories of vanquished Israel. On the other hand, the authors of the Bible needed to delegitimize the northern cult—especially the Bethel shrine—and to show that the distinctive religious traditions of the northern kingdom were all evil, that they should be wiped out and replaced by centralized worship at the Temple of Jerusalem.

The Deuteronomistic History accomplishes all of this. At the end of 2 Samuel, the pious David is shown establishing a great empire. At the beginning of 1 Kings, his son Solomon comes to the throne and continues to prosper. But wealth and prosperity were not enough. To the contrary, they brought about idolatry. The sin of Solomon led to the death of the golden age. YHWH then chose Jeroboam to lead the breakaway state of the northern kingdom, to be a second David. But Jeroboam sins even more than Solomon and the northern kingdom misses its once-in-history opportunity. The rest of the history of the north is a sad decline to destruction.

Under Josiah, however, the time comes for Judah to rise to greatness. But in order to revive the golden age, this new David needs first to undo the sins of Solomon and Jeroboam. The path to greatness must pass through the cleansing of Israel, mainly the destruction of the shrine of Bethel. This will lead to the reunification of all Israel—people and territory—under the Temple of YHWH and the throne of David in Jerusalem.

The important thing to remember, then, is that the biblical narrative does not see the partition of the united monarchy of David and Solomon as a final act, but as a temporary misfortune. There can still be a happy ending. If the people resolve to change their ways and live again as a holy people apart from foreign idols and seductions, YHWH will overcome all their enemies and give them eternal rest and satisfaction within their promised land.

[7]

Israel's Forgotten First Kingdom

(884–842 BCE)

Violence, idolatry, and greed were the hallmarks of the northern kingdom of Israel as it is depicted in gory detail in the first and second books of Kings. After Jeroboam, the main villains of the story are the Omrides, the great northern dynasty founded by a former Israelite general named Omri, whose successors grew so powerful that they eventually managed to put one of their princesses on the throne of the kingdom of Judah as well. The Bible accuses the most famous Omride couple—King Ahab and his notorious wife Jezebel, the Phoenician princess—of repeatedly committing some of the greatest biblical sins: introducing the cult of foreign gods into the land of Israel, murdering faithful priests and prophets of YHWH, unjustly confiscating the property of their subjects, and violating Israel's sacred traditions with arrogant impunity.

The Omrides are remembered as among the most despised characters of biblical history. Yet the new archaeological vision of the kingdom of Israel offers an entirely different perspective on their reigns. Indeed, had the biblical authors and editors been historians in the modern sense, they might have said that Ahab was a mighty king who first brought the kingdom of Israel to prominence on the world stage and that his marriage to the daughter of the Phoenician king Ethbaal was a brilliant stroke of international diplomacy. They might have said that the Omrides built magnificent cities to serve as administrative centers of their expanding kingdom. They might have said that Ahab and Omri, his father before him, succeeded in building one of the most powerful armies in the region—with which they conquered extensive territories in the far north and in Transjordan. Of course, they might also have noted that Omri and Ahab were not particularly pious and that they sometimes were capricious and acted brutally. But the same could be said of virtually every other monarch of the ancient Near East.

Indeed, Israel, as a state, enjoyed natural wealth and extensive trade connections that made it largely indistinguishable from other prosperous kingdoms of the region. As noted in the previous chapter, Israel had the necessary organization to undertake monumental building projects, to establish a professional army and bureaucracy, and to develop a complex settlement hierarchy of cities, towns, and villages—which made it the first full-fledged Israelite kingdom. Its character, goals, and achievements were dramatically different from those of the kingdom of Judah. Therefore, they have been almost totally obscured by the Bible's condemnation, which supports the later claims of the southern, Davidic dynasty for predominance by demeaning and misrepresenting nearly everything that the northern, Omride dynasty did.

The Rise and Fall of the House of Omri

The books of Kings offer only a sketchy description of the first turbulent decades in the independent kingdom of Israel. After the twenty-two-year reign of Jeroboam, his son and successor, Nadab, was overthrown by a military coup in which all the surviving members of the house of Jeroboam were killed (thus neatly fulfilling the words of the prophet Ahijah that none of Jeroboam's heirs would survive). The new king, Baasha, possibly a former military commander, immediately showed his bellicose nature by declaring war on the kingdom of Judah and advancing his forces toward Jerusalem. But he was quickly forced to lift his pressure on the southern kingdom when his own kingdom was invaded by the king of Damascus, Ben-hadad.

Soon after the death of Baasha, his son Elah was deposed in yet another army uprising, in which the house of Baasha was annihilated (1 Kings 16:8–11). But the rebel leader, Zimri, a chariot commander, reigned for

TABLE THREE

THE OMRIDE DYNASTY

KING	DATES*	BIBLICAL TESTIMONY	EXTRABIBLICAL EVIDENCE	ARCHAEOLOGICAL FINDS
Omri	884–873 BCE	Foundation of Samaria	Mentioned in the Mesha stele from Moab	Foundation of Samaria
Ahab	873–852	Marries the Phoenician princess Jezebel; builds a House for the Baal at Samaria; sacks the vineyard of Naboth; confronted by prophet Elijah; fights several wars against the Arameans and dies on battlefield	Shalmaneser III mentions great chariot force of Ahab at the battle of Qarqar in 853 BCE; was possibly mentioned in the Tel Dan inscription	Main building phase at Samaria; Jezreel compound; Megiddo palaces; Hazor wall and gate
Ahaziah	852–851	Short reign; falls sick and dies		
Jehoram	851–842	Defeats Moab; wounded in battle against Hazael of Aram-Damascus; prophecies of Elisha	Apparently mentioned in the Tel Dan inscription	Destruction of the Jezreel compound; destruction layers in other sites in the north

* According to the *Anchor Bible Dictionary* and Galil's *The Chronology of the Kings of Israel and Judah*

only seven days. The people of Israel rose up to declare Omri, the commander of the army, the next king of Israel. After a brief siege of the royal capital of Tirzah—and the suicide of the usurper Zimri in the flames of the palace—Omri consolidated his power and established a dynasty that would rule the northern kingdom for the next forty years.

In the twelve years of his reign, Omri built a new capital for himself at a place called Samaria and laid the foundations for the continued rule of his own dynasty. Omri's son Ahab then came to the throne, reigning over Israel for twenty-two years. The biblical evaluation of Ahab was even harsher than its usual treatment of northern monarchs, detailing the extent of his foreign liaisons and idolatry, with an emphasis on his famous foreign wife, who led her husband to apostasy:

> And Ahab the son of Omri did evil in the sight of the LORD more than all that
> were before him. And as if it had been a light thing for him to walk in the sins of
> Jeroboam the son of Nebat, he took for wife Jezebel the daughter of Ethbaal
> king of the Sidonians, and went and served Baal, and worshiped him. He
> erected an altar for Baal in the house of Baal, which he built in Samaria. And
> Ahab made an Asherah. Ahab did more to provoke the LORD, the God of Israel,
> to anger than all the kings of Israel who were before him. (1 KINGS 16:30–33)

Jezebel is reported to have supported the pagan priesthood in Samaria, hosting at her spacious royal table "four hundred and fifty prophets of Baal and four hundred prophets of Asherah." And she further ordered that all the prophets of YHWH in the kingdom of Israel be slain.

The biblical narrative then goes on to devote most of its description of the Omrides to their crimes and sins—and to their ongoing battle of wits with Elijah and his protégé, Elisha, two famous prophets of YHWH who roamed throughout the north. Elijah soon confronted Ahab and demanded that all the prophets of Baal and Asherah "who eat at Jezebel's table" gather at Mount Carmel for a contest of sacred wills. There, in front of "all the people," each of the two sides constructed an altar to their god and sacrificed a bull upon it, crying to the chosen deity to consume the offering by fire. While Baal did not respond to the cries of his prophets, YHWH immediately sent a great fire from the heavens to consume Elijah's offering. Seeing this, the assembled witnesses fell on their faces. "The Lord, he is God," they cried and seized the prophets of Baal, whom they slaughtered by the brook Kishon.

Queen Jezebel reacted in fury and Elijah quickly escaped into the desert. Reaching the desolate wilderness at Horeb, the mountain of God, he received a divine oracle. YHWH spoke directly to Elijah and pronounced a prophecy of doom on the entire house of Omri. YHWH instructed him to anoint Hazael as king of Israel's most dangerous rival, Aram-Damascus. Elijah was also ordered to anoint Ahab's military commander, Jehu, as the next king of Israel. Finally, Elijah was instructed to make Elisha prophet in his place. These three, YHWH had determined, would punish the house of Omri for its sins: "And him who escapes from the sword of Hazael shall Jehu slay; and him who escapes from the sword of Jehu shall Elisha slay" (1 Kings 19:17).

Yet YHWH gave the northern kingdom a second chance when he came to the rescue of Israel when Ben-hadad, king of Aram-Damascus, invaded the country and laid siege to Samaria. He gave it a third chance when he allowed Ahab to defeat Ben-hadad in a battle near the Sea of Galilee in the following year. But Ahab proved unworthy of this divine assistance. He decided to spare the life of his enemy in exchange for earthly rewards: the return of cities that had formerly belonged to the kingdom of Israel and the right to "establish bazaars" in Damascus. A prophet of YHWH told Ahab that he would pay with his life for not obeying YHWH's demand that Ben-hadad be put to the sword.

The Bible then narrates a story about the immoral conduct of the wicked couple toward their own people—another sin for which they would have to pay with their lives. It so happened that a man named Naboth owned a vineyard near the palace of Ahab at Jezreel, and that vineyard got in the way of Ahab's development plans. Seeking to take over the land for an expansion of his palace, Ahab made Naboth an offer he thought he could hardly refuse: he would take Naboth's vineyard and give him a much better one, or if Naboth preferred, Ahab would pay him off in cash. But Naboth was not interested in giving away his family inheritance for any reason and he stubbornly refused. Ahab's wife Jezebel had another solution: she fabricated evidence of blasphemy against Naboth and watched in satisfaction as the people of Jezreel stoned Naboth to death. No sooner

had Ahab taken possession of the vineyard than the prophet Elijah appeared once more on the scene. His prophecy was chilling:

> Thus says the Lord: "Have you killed, and also taken possession? . . . In the
> place where dogs licked up the blood of Naboth shall dogs lick your own
> blood. . . . Behold, I will bring evil upon you; I will utterly sweep you away, and
> will cut off from Ahab every male, bond or free, in Israel; and I will make your
> house like the house of Jeroboam the son of Nebat, and like the house of Baasha
> the son of Ahijah, for the anger to which you have provoked me, and because
> you have made Israel to sin. And of Jezebel the LORD also said, 'The dogs shall
> eat Jezebel within the bounds of Jezreel. Any one belonging to Ahab who dies in
> the city the dogs shall eat; and any one of his who dies in the open country the
> birds of the air shall eat." (1 KINGS 21: 19–24)

At that time the kingdoms of Israel and Judah had concluded an alliance
in which Jehoshaphat, king of Judah, joined forces with Ahab to wage war
against Aram-Damascus at Ramoth-gilead, across the Jordan. In the course
of the fighting Ahab was struck by an arrow and died on the battlefield. His
body was brought back to Samaria for a royal burial and when his chariot
was being washed, dogs licked his blood—a grim fulfillment of Elijah's
prophecy.

Ahab's son Ahaziah then came to the throne and he too gravely sinned.
Injured in a fall "through the lattice in his upper chamber in Samaria," he
dispatched messengers to consult Baal-zebub the god of the Philistine city
of Ekron, about his prospects for recovery. But Elijah, chastising him for
appealing to a foreign idol rather than YHWH, announced his imminent
death.

Finally Jehoram, Ahaziah's brother and the fourth and last king of the
Omride dynasty, ascended the throne. In response to a rebellion by Mesha,
king of Moab, who had long been Israel's vassal, Jehoram marched against
Moab, joined by Jehoshaphat, king of Judah, and an unnamed king of
Edom. The prophet Elisha predicted victory only because the just Judahite
king, Jehoshaphat, was with them. And indeed, the Moabites were vanquished by the Israelite-Judahite-Edomite alliance and their cities were destroyed.

Yet the Omride dynasty could not ultimately escape its destiny of utter
destruction. With the accession of Hazael as king of Damascus, the mili-

tary and political fortunes of the Omride dynasty declined. Hazael defeated the army of Israel at Ramoth-gilead east of the Jordan, and the Israelite king, Jehoram, was badly wounded on the battlefield. At that moment of crisis, Elisha dispatched one of the sons of the prophets of YHWH to anoint Jehu, the commander of the army, as king of Israel, so that he would finally smite the house of Ahab. And so it happened. Returning to the Omride palace at Jezreel to heal his wounds in the company of King Ahaziah of Judah, Jehoram was confronted by Jehu (symbolically, in the vineyard of Naboth), who killed him with an arrow shot into his heart. Ahaziah attempted to escape, but was wounded and died at the nearby city of Megiddo, to which he had fled.

The liquidation of the family of Ahab was nearing a climax. Jehu then entered the royal compound of Jezreel and ordered that Jezebel be thrown from an upper window of the palace. Jehu commanded his servants to take off her body for burial, but they discovered only her skull, her feet, and the palms of her hands in the courtyard—for stray dogs had eaten the flesh of Jezebel, just as Elijah's chilling prophecy had warned. In the meanwhile, the sons of the king of Israel living in Samaria—seventy altogether—were slaughtered and their heads were put in baskets and sent to Jehu in Jezreel. He ordered that those heads be piled up in full public view at the entrance to the city gate. Jehu then set off for Samaria, where he killed all that remained of the house of Ahab. The Omride dynasty was thus extinguished forever and the terrible prophecy of Elijah was fulfilled to its last word.

Distant Borders and Military Might

The court tragedy of the house of Omri is a literary classic, filled with vivid characters and theatrical scenes, in which a royal family's crimes against their own people are paid back with a bloody demise. The memory of the reigns of Ahab and Jezebel obviously remained vivid for centuries, as we can see from their inclusion in such a prominent way in the Deuteronomistic History—compiled over two hundred years after their deaths. Nonetheless, the biblical narrative is so thoroughly filled with inconsistencies and anachronisms, and so obviously influenced by the theology of the seventh century BCE writers, that it must be considered more of a historical novel than an accurate historical chronicle. Among other inconsistencies, the reported invasion of Samaria by Ben-hadad of Damascus did not take place during the reign of Ahab but later in the history of the northern kingdom. The mention of an alliance of Israel with an unnamed king of Edom is also an anachronism, for there is no evidence of monarchy in Edom until more than a century after the time of the Omrides. In fact, when one takes out the anachronisms and the stories of threats issued and prophecies fulfilled, there is very little verifiable historical material left in the biblical account, except for the sequence of Israelite kings, some of their most famous building projects, and the general areas of military activity.

Fortunately there are—for the first time in the history of Israel—some important external sources of historical information that allow us to see the Omrides from a different perspective: as the militarily powerful rulers of one of the strongest states in the Near East. The key to this new understanding is the sudden appearance of monumental inscriptions that directly refer to the kingdom of Israel. The first mention of the northern kingdom in the time of the Omrides is not accidental. The westward advance of the Assyrian empire from its Mesopotamian heartland—with its fully developed bureaucracy and long tradition of recording its rulers' acts in public declarations—profoundly influenced the culture of crystallizing states like Israel, Aram, and Moab. Beginning in the ninth century BCE, in the records of the Assyrians themselves and those of smaller powers of the Near East, we at last gain some firsthand testimony on events and personalities described in the biblical text.

In the time of David and Solomon, political organization in the region had not yet reached the stage where extensive bureaucracies and monumental inscriptions existed. By the time of the Omrides a century later, internal economic processes and external political pressures had brought about the rise of fully developed territorial, national states in the Levant. In an anthropological sense, *fully developed* implies a territory governed by a complex bureaucratic organization that is capable of organizing major building projects, maintaining a standing army, and developing organized trade connections with neighboring regions. It is capable of keeping records of its actions in archives and in monumental inscriptions open to public view. In the ninth century and after, major political events were recorded in monumental writing, from the perspective of each king. These inscriptions are crucial for establishing precise dates for events and personalities mentioned in the Bible. And for anyone who knows the Bible's version, they offer an unexpected picture of the extent and power of the kingdom of Israel.

One of the most important is the Mesha stele, found in 1868 on the surface of the remote mound of Dhiban in southern Jordan, east of the Dead Sea—the site of biblical Dibon, the capital of the kingdom of Moab. This monumental inscription was badly damaged in the wrangling between rival European explorers and the local bedouin, but its surviving fragments have been pieced together to offer what is still the longest extrabiblical text ever found in the Levant. It is written in the Moabite language, which is closely related to biblical Hebrew, and it records the achievements of King Mesha, who conquered the territories of northern Moab and established his capital in Dibon. The discovery of this inscription caused great excitement in the nineteenth century because Mesha is mentioned in 2 Kings 3 as a rebellious vassal of the northern kingdom of Israel.

Here for the first time was the other side of the story, the first nonbiblical description of the Omrides ever found. The events recorded in the inscription took place in the ninth century BCE, when, according to its fragmentary text, "Omri [was] king of Israel, and he oppressed Moab many days. . . . And his son succeeded him, and he too said: 'I will humble Moab.' In my days, he spoke thus. . . . And Omri had taken possession of the land of Medeba. And he dwelt in it his days and the sum of the days of his sons: forty years."

The inscription goes on to relate how Mesha gradually expanded his territory in rebellion against Israel, destroying the main settlements of the Israelites east of the Jordan, while fortifying and embellishing his own capital. Though Mesha barely disguises his contempt for Omri and his son Ahab, we nonetheless learn from his triumphal inscription that the kingdom of Israel reached far east and south of its earlier heartland in the central hill country.

Likewise we hear about the conflicts with Aram-Damascus from the "House of David" inscription discovered at the biblical city of Dan in 1993. Although the name of the monarch who erected it was not found on the fragments that have so far been recovered, there is little doubt, from the overall context, that this was the mighty Hazael, king of Aram-Damascus. He is mentioned several times in the Bible, in particular as God's instru-

ment to humble the House of Omri. From the inscription, it seems that
Hazael captured the city of Dan and erected a triumphal stele there around
835 BCE. The inscription records the words of the victorious Hazael in his
angry accusation that "the king of I[s]rael entered previously in my father's
land." Since the inscription apparently mentioned the name of Ahab's son
and successor, Jehoram, the implication is clear. The kingdom of Israel
under the Omrides stretched from the vicinity of Damascus throughout
the central highlands and valleys of Israel, all the way to the southern territory of Moab, ruling over considerable populations of non-Israelites.

   This Omride "empire," we also learn, possessed a mighty military force.
Though the biblical account of the Omride dynasty stresses repeated military disasters—and makes no mention whatsoever of a threat from Assyria—there is some dramatic evidence of the Omrides' power from
Assyria itself. Shalmaneser III, one of the greatest Assyrian kings, who
ruled in the years 858–824 BCE, offers perhaps the clearest (if entirely unin-
tentional) praise for the power of the Omride dynasty. In the year 853 BCE,
Shalmaneser led a major Assyrian invasion force westward to intimidate
and possibly conquer the smaller states of Syria, Phoenicia, and Israel. His
advancing armies were confronted by an anti-Assyrian coalition near Qarqar on the river Orontes in western Syria. Shalmaneser boasted of his great
victory in an important ancient text known as the Monolith Inscription,
found in the 1840s by the English explorer Austen Henry Layard at the ancient Assyrian site of Nimrud. The dark stone monument, thickly inscribed with cuneiform characters, proudly recorded the forces ranged
against Shalmaneser: "1,200 chariots, 1,200 cavalry men, 20,000 foot soldiers of Hadadezer of Damascus, 700 chariots, 700 cavalrymen, 10,000
foot soldiers of Irhuleni from Hamath, 2,000 chariots, 10,000 foot soldiers
of Ahab, the Israelite, 500 soldiers from Que, 1,000 soldiers from Musri, 10
chariots, 10,000 soldiers from Irqanata. . . ."

   Not only is this the earliest nonbiblical evidence of a king of Israel, it is
clear from the mention of the "heavy arms" (chariots) that Ahab was the
strongest member of the anti-Assyrian coalition. And although the great
Shalmaneser claimed victory, the practical outcome of this confrontation
spoke much louder than royal boasts. Shalmaneser quickly returned to Assyria, and at least for a while the Assyrian march to the west was blocked.

   Thus we learn from three ancient inscriptions (ironically from three of

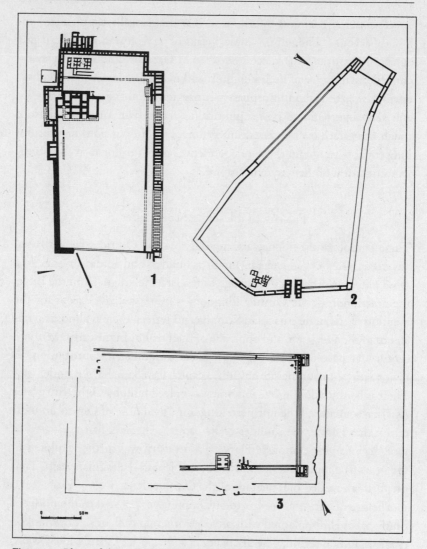

Figure 20: Plans of three Omride sites: 1) Samaria; 2) Hazor; 3) Jezreel. The plans are drawn to the same scale. *Numbers 1 and 2 courtesy of Professor Zeev Herzog, Tel Aviv University.*

Israel's bitterest enemies) information that dramatically supplements the
biblical account. Though the Bible speaks of an Aramean army besieging
Samaria, Omri and his successors were in fact powerful kings who expanded the territory of their kingdom and maintained what was certainly
one of the largest standing armies in the region. And they were deeply involved in international power politics (at a time when the kingdom of
Judah was passed over in silence in Shalmaneser's inscription) in a continuing effort to maintain their independence against regional rivals and the
looming threat of the Assyrian Empire.

Palaces, Stables, and Store Cities

The archaeological evidence also reveals that the Omrides far surpassed
any other monarchs in Israel or Judah as builders and administrators. In a
sense, theirs was the first golden age of the Israelite kings. Yet in the Bible,
the description of the Omride kingdom is quite sketchy. Except for the
mention of elaborate palaces in Samaria and Jezreel, there is almost no reference to the size, scale, and opulence of their realm. In the early twentieth
century, archaeology first began to make a significant contribution, as
major excavations at the site of Omri's capital city, Samaria, got under way.
There is hardly a doubt that Samaria was indeed built by Omri, since later
Assyrian sources call the northern kingdom "the house of Omri," an indication that he was the founder of its capital. The site, first excavated in
1908–10 by an expedition of Harvard University, was further explored in
the 1930s by a joint American, British, and Jewish–Palestinian team. That
site further revealed the splendor of the Omride dynasty.

The site of Samaria is, even today, impressive. Located in the midst of
gently rolling hills, planted with olive and almond orchards, it overlooks a
rich agricultural region. The discovery of some pottery sherds, a few walls,
and a group of rock-cut installations indicated that it was already inhabited
before the arrival of Omri; there seems to have been a small, poor Israelite
village or a farm there in the eleventh and tenth centuries BCE. This may
perhaps be the inheritance of Shemer, the original owner of the property
mentioned in 1 Kings 16:24. In any case, with the arrival of Omri and his
court around 880 BCE, the farm buildings were leveled and an opulent

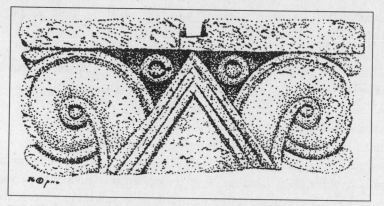

Figure 21: A Proto-Aeolic capital. *Courtesy of the Israel Exploration Society.*

palace with auxiliary buildings for servants and court personnel arose on the summit of the hill.

Samaria was apparently conceived from the start as the personal capital of the Omride dynasty. It was the most grandiose architectural manifestation of the rule of Omri and Ahab (Figure 20:1, p. 179). Located on a small hilltop, however, it was not the ideal place for a vast royal compound. The builders' solution to this problem—a daring innovation in Iron Age Israel—was to carry out massive earthmoving operations to create a huge, artificial platform on the summit of the hill. An enormous wall (constructed of linked rooms, or casemates) was build around the hill, framing the summit and the upper slopes in a large rectangular enclosure. When that retaining wall was completed, construction gangs filled its interior with thousands of tons of earth hauled from the vicinity.

The scale of this project was enormous. The earthen fill packed behind the supporting wall was, in some places, almost twenty feet deep. That was probably why the enclosure wall surrounding and supporting the palace complex was built in the casemate technique: the casemate chambers (which were also filled with earth) were designed to relieve the immense pressure of the fill. A royal acropolis of five acres was thus created. This huge stone and earth construction can be compared in audacity and extravagance (though perhaps not in size) only to the work that Herod the

Great carried out almost a millennium later on the Temple Mount in Jerusalem.

Rising on one side of this artificial platform was an exceptionally large and beautiful palace, which in scale and grandeur rivaled the contemporary palaces of the states in northern Syria. Although the Omride palace at Samaria has been only partially excavated, enough of its plan has been uncovered to recognize that the central building alone covered an area of approximately half an acre. With its outer walls built entirely of finely hewn and closely fitted ashlar stones, it is the largest and most beautiful Iron Age building ever excavated in Israel. Even the architectural ornamentation was exceptional. Stone capitals of a unique early style, called Proto-Aeolic (because of the resemblance to the later Greek Aeolic style), were found in the rubble of later centuries' accumulations (Figure 21). These ornate stone capitals probably adorned the monumental outer gate to the compound, or perhaps an elaborate entrance into the main palace itself. Of the interior

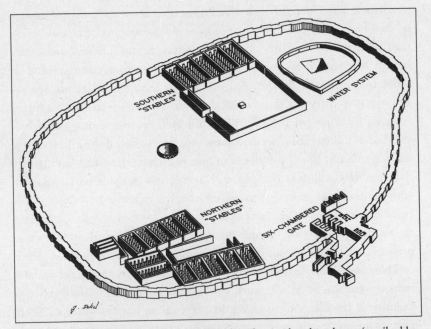

Figure 22: The eighth century BCE at Megiddo. The six-chambered gate (ascribed by Yadin to a "Solomonic" level) most probably belongs to this stratum. *Courtesy Prof. David Ussishkin, Tel Aviv University.*

furnishings little remained except for a number of intricately carved ivory plaques, probably dating from the eighth century BCE and bearing Syro-Phoenician and Egyptian motifs. These ivories, used as inlays on the palace furniture, might explain the allusion in 1 Kings 22:39 to the ivory house that Ahab reportedly built.

Several administrative buildings surrounded the palace, but most of the enclosure was left open. The simple houses of the people of Samaria apparently clustered on the slopes beneath the acropolis. For visitors, traders, and official emissaries arriving at Samaria, the visual impression of the Omrides' royal city must have been stunning. Its elevated platform and huge, elaborate palace bespoke wealth, power, and prestige.

Samaria was only the beginning of the discovery of Omride grandeur. Megiddo came next. In the mid-1920s, the University of Chicago team uncovered an Iron Age palace built of beautifully dressed ashlar blocks. The first director of the Oriental Institute excavations at Megiddo, Clarence S. Fisher, had also worked at Samaria and was immediately impressed by the similarity of construction. He was supported in this observation by John Crowfoot, the leader of the Joint Expedition to Samaria, who suggested that the similarity of building techniques and overall plan at Samaria and Megiddo indicated that both were built under Omride patronage. But this matter of architectural similarity was not fully pursued for many decades. The members of the University of Chicago team were more interested in the glory of Solomon than in the wicked Omrides. They ignored the similarity of the Megiddo and Samaria building styles and dated the complexes of pillared buildings (presumably stables) in the succeeding stratum to the days of the united monarchy. In the early 1960s, when Yigael Yadin of the Hebrew University came to Megiddo, he dated the Megiddo palaces—the one excavated in the 1920s and one he himself uncovered—to the time of Solomon and linked the later level containing the stables and other structures to the era of the Omrides.

That city was certainly impressive (Figure 22). It was surrounded by a massive fortification and, according to Yadin, furnished with a large four-chambered city gate (built directly on top of the earlier "Solomonic" gate). The most dominant features inside the city were the two sets of pillared buildings that had long before been identified as stables. Yet Yadin did not link them to the biblical descriptions of Solomon's great chariot army but to that of Ahab, noted in the Shalmaneser inscription. Yet as we will see, Yadin had not correctly identified Ahab's city; those stables probably belonged to another, even later Israelite king.

The northern city of Hazor, which Yadin excavated in the 1950s and 1960s, provided additional apparent evidence of Omride splendor. Hazor was also surrounded by a massive fortification. In the center of that city Yadin uncovered a pillared building somewhat similar in form to the Megiddo stables, divided into three long aisles by rows of stone pillars. But this structure contained no stone troughs for feeding, so it was accordingly interpreted as a royal storehouse. An imposing citadel was uncovered on the eastern, narrow tip of the mound, enclosed by the massive city wall.

Another important site connected with the Omrides is the city of Dan in the far north at the headwaters of the Jordan River. We have already cited the opening lines of the stele erected at Dan by Hazael, king of Aram-Damascus, noting that the Omrides had previously taken that area from the Arameans. The excavations at Dan, directed by Abraham Biran, of the Hebrew Union College, uncovered massive Iron Age fortifications, a huge, elaborate city gate, and a sanctuary with a high place. This large podium, measuring about sixty feet on a side, and built of beautifully dressed ashlar stones, has been dated with the city's other monumental structures to the time of the Omrides.

Yet perhaps the most impressive engineering achievements initially linked to the Omrides are the enormous underground water tunnels cut through the bedrock beneath the cities of Megiddo and Hazor. These tunnels provided the city's inhabitants with secure access to drinking water even in times of siege. In the ancient Near East this was a critical challenge, for while important cities were surrounded by elaborate fortifications to allow them to withstand an attack or siege by even the most determined enemy, they seldom had a source of freshwater within their city walls. The inhabitants could always collect rainwater in cisterns, but this would not be sufficient when a siege extended through the hot, rainless months of summer—especially if the population of the city had swelled with refugees.

Since most ancient cities were located near springs, the challenge was to devise safe access to them. The rock-cut water tunnels at Hazor and Megiddo are among the most elaborate solutions to this problem. At

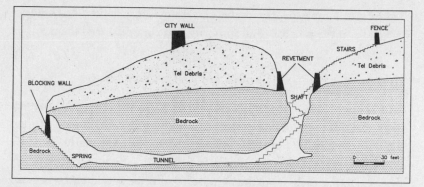

Figure 23: A cross-section of the Megiddo water system

Hazor, a large vertical shaft was cut through the remains of earlier cities into the solid rock below. Because of its enormous depth, of almost a hundred feet, support walls had to be constructed to prevent collapse. Broad steps led to the bottom, where a sloping tunnel, some eighty feet long, led into a pool-like rock-cut chamber into which groundwater seeped. One can only imagine a procession of water bearers threading their way single-file down the stairs and the length of the subterranean tunnel to fill their jars in the dark cavern and returning up to the streets of the besieged city with water to keep its people alive.

The Megiddo water system (Figure 23) consisted of a somewhat simpler shaft, over a hundred feet in depth, cut through the earlier remains to bedrock. From there it led to a horizontal tunnel, more than two hundred feet long, wide and high enough for a few people to walk at the same time, which led to a natural spring cave on the edge of the mound. The entrance to the cave from outside was blocked and camouflaged. Yadin dated both the Megiddo and Hazor water systems to the time of the Omrides. He proposed to connect the Israelite skill of hewing water systems to a section in the Mesha stele where the Moabite king recounted how he dug a water reservoir in his own capital city with the help of Israelite prisoners of war. It was obvious that the construction of such monumental installations required an enormous investment and efficient state organization—and a high level of technical skill. From a functional point of view, Iron Age engineers could perhaps have reached a similar result with a much smaller investment by simply digging a well into the water table under the mound.

But the visual impressiveness of these great water installations certainly enhanced the prestige of the royal authority that commissioned them.

A Forgotten Turning Point in Israelite History

Even though early and mid-twentieth century archaeologists assigned many magnificent building projects to the Omrides, the period of their rule over the kingdom of Israel was never seen as a particularly formative moment in biblical history. Colorful, yes. Vivid, to be sure. But in purely historical terms, the story of the Omrides—of Ahab and Jezebel—seemed to be spelled out in quite adequate detail in the Bible, with supporting information from Assyrian, Moabite, and Aramean texts. There seemed to be so many more intriguing historical questions to be answered by excavation and further research: the precise process of the Israelite settlement; the political crystallization of the monarchy under David and Solomon; or even the underlying causes of the eventual Assyrian and Babylonian conquests in the land of Israel. Omride archaeology was usually considered just a sidelight on the main agenda of biblical archaeology, given less attention than the Solomonic period.

But there was something seriously wrong with this initial correlation between biblical history and archaeological finds. The new questions that began to be asked about the nature, extent, or even historical existence of Solomon's vast kingdom—and the redating of the archaeological layers—inevitably affected the scholarly understanding of the Omrides as well. For if Solomon had not actually built the "Solomonic" gates and palaces, who did? The Omrides were the obvious candidates. The earliest architectural parallels to the distinctive palaces dug at Megiddo (and initially attributed to Solomon) came from northern Syria—the supposed place of origin of this type—in the ninth century BCE, a full century after the time of Solomon! This was precisely the time of the Omrides' rule.

The clinching clue to a redating of the "Solomonic" gates and palaces came from the biblical site of Jezreel, located less than ten miles to the east of Megiddo in the heart of the Jezreel valley. The site is located in a beautiful elevated spot, enjoying a mild climate in the winter and a cool breeze in the summer and commanding a sweeping panorama of the entire Jezreel valley and the hills surrounding it, from Megiddo in the west through

Galilee in the north, to Beth-shean and the Gilead in the east. Jezreel is famous largely due to the biblical story of Naboth's vineyard, and Ahab and Jezebel's plans for palace expansion, and as the scene of the bloody, final liquidation of the Omride dynasty. In the 1990s the site was excavated by David Ussishkin of Tel Aviv University and John Woodhead of the British School of Archaeology in Jerusalem. They uncovered a large royal enclosure, very similar to that of Samaria (Figure 20:3, p. 179). This impressive compound was occupied for only a brief period in the ninth century BCE—presumably only during the reign of the Omride Dynasty—and was destroyed shortly after its construction, perhaps in connection with the fall of the Omrides or the subsequent invasions of northern Israel by the armies of Aram-Damascus.

As in Samaria, an enormous casemate wall built around the original hill at Jezreel formed a "box" to be filled with many tons of earth. As a result of large-scale filling and leveling operations, a level podium was created on which the inner structures of the royal compound were built. At Jezreel the archaeologists discovered other striking elements of a hitherto unrecognized Omride architectural style. A sloping earthen rampart supported the casemate wall on the outside to prevent it from collapsing. As an additional defensive element, the compound was surrounded by a formidable moat dug in the bedrock, at least twenty-five feet wide and more than fifteen feet deep. The entrance to the Omride royal enclosure at Jezreel was provided by a gate, probably of the six-chamber type.

Because Jezreel was chronologically restricted to a brief occupation in the ninth century BCE, it offered a unique case where the distinctive styles of pottery found within it could be used as a clear dating indicator for the Omride period at other sites. Significantly, the pottery styles uncovered in the Jezreel enclosure were almost identical to those found in the level of the "Solomonic" palaces of Megiddo. It was thus becoming quite evident, from both architectural and ceramic standpoints, that the Omrides—not Solomon—had constructed the ashlar buildings at Megiddo, in addition to the Jezreel and Samaria compounds.

The hypothesis that the Omrides, not Solomon, established the first fully developed monarchy in Israel grew more convincing with a new look at the evidence from the other major cities of the kingdom of Israel. At Hazor, Yadin had identified a triangular compound on the acropolis—surrounded by a casemate wall and entered through a six-chambered gate—as the city established by Solomon in the tenth century BCE. The redating of the pottery on the basis of the Jezreel discoveries would place this city level in the early ninth century BCE. Indeed, there was an unmistakable structural resemblance to the palace compounds in Samaria and Jezreel (Figure 20:2, p. 179). Although the triangular shape of the Hazor compound was dictated by the topography of the site, its construction involved a massive leveling and filling operation that raised the level of the gate area in relation to the outside area to its east. A colossal moat, estimated to be 150 feet wide and over thirty feet deep, was dug outside the casemate wall. The overall similarity to Jezreel and Samaria is clear. Thus, another city long believed to be Solomonic is likely Omride.

Evidence of the extent of Omride building projects emerges from a closer analysis of the remains at Megiddo and Gezer. Although Megiddo has no casemate compound, the two beautiful palaces on its summit that were built of distinctive ashlar masonry recall the building techniques used at Samaria (Figure 24). The resemblance is particularly strong in the case of

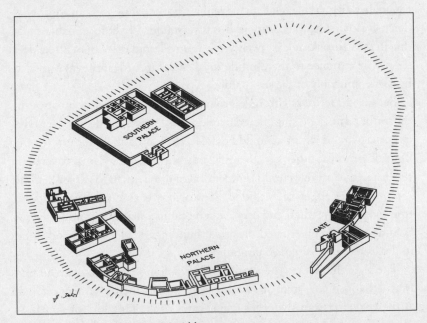

Figure 24: The Omride city at Megiddo

the southernmost palace at Megiddo, which was built at the edge of a large courtyard, in the style of a north Syrian *bit hilani* palace, covering an area of about sixty-five by a hundred feet. Two exceptionally large Proto-Aeolic capitals (like those used in Samaria) were found in the vicinity of the gate leading into the palace's compound, and they may have decorated the entrance to the palace itself. Norma Franklin of the current Megiddo expedition identified another similarity: the southern palace at Megiddo and the palace at Samaria are the only Iron Age buildings in Israel whose ashlar blocks share a specific type of masons' marks. A second palace, which was partially uncovered by Yadin on the northern edge of the mound—and is now being fully unearthed by the new expedition to Megiddo—is also built of ashlar in the north Syrian palace style.

The evidence at Gezer is perhaps the most fragmentary of all the supposed Solomonic cities, but enough has been found to indicate a similarity to the other Omride sites. A six-chambered gate built of fine masonry, with ashlars at the jambs and connected to a casemate wall, was discovered on the southern edge of the site. The construction of the gate and the casemate wall involved the leveling of a terrace on the hillside and the import of a massive fill. In addition, fragmentary walls indicate that a large building, possibly an ashlar palace, was built on the northwestern side of the mound. It too may have been decorated with distinctive Proto-Aeolic capitals that were found at Gezer in the beginning of the twentieth century.

These five sites offer a glimpse at the royal architecture of Israel's Omride golden age. In addition to the artificial platforms for palace compounds of varying sizes and scale, the compounds—at least at Samaria, Jezreel, and Hazor—seem to have been largely empty, except for the specialized administrative buildings and royal palaces. Fine ashlar stones and Proto-Aeolic capitals were distinctive decorative elements in these sites. The main entrances to the royal compounds seem to have been guarded by six-chambered gates, and in some cases the compounds were surrounded by a moat and a glacis.*

Archaeologically and historically, the redating of these cities from Solomon's era to the time of the Omrides has enormous implications. It re-

---

* The dates of the water systems have now been called into question and may relate to a later period in the history of the kingdom of Israel. Yet their absence does not diminish the grandeur of the network of royal cities that was apparently centrally planned and constructed in the course of the ninth century BCE.

moves the only archaeological evidence that there was ever a united monarchy based in Jerusalem and suggests that David and Solomon were, in political terms, little more than hill country chieftains, whose administrative reach remained on a fairly local level, restricted to the hill country. More important, it shows that despite the biblical emphasis on the uniqueness of Israel, a highland kingdom of a thoroughly conventional Near Eastern type arose in the north in the early ninth century BCE.

A Forgotten Monument of Omride Rule?

It is now possible to search for additional examples of Omride cities in more distant places, far beyond the traditional tribal inheritances of Israel. The Mesha stele reported that Omri built two cities in Moab, Ataroth and Jahaz, probably as his southern border strongholds in Transjordan (Figure 16, p. 136). Both are also mentioned in various geographical lists in the Bible, with Ataroth identified with the still unexcavated site of Khirbet Atarus southwest of the modern Jordanian town of Madaba. Jahaz is more difficult to identify. It is mentioned a few times in the Bible as being located on the desert fringe near the Arnon, the deep, winding canyon that runs through the heartland of Moab—from the eastern desert to its outlet in the Dead Sea. The Omrides seem to have extended their rule to this region. And on the northern bank of the Arnon is a remote Iron Age ruin called Khirbet el-Mudayna that contains all the features we have described as being typical of Omride architecture.

The site, now being excavated by P.M. Michèle Daviau, of the Wilfrid Laurier University in Canada, consists of a large fortress built on an elongated hill. A casemate wall encloses an area of about two and a half acres and is entered through a six-chambered gate. Defensive features include a sloping earthen rampart and a moat. Inside the compound are remains of a monumental building, including collapsed ashlars. Aerial photographs of the site hint that the entire complex was based on an artificial podium fill. The pioneering explorer of Jordan, Nelson Glueck, who visited the site in the 1930s, was so impressed with the compound's features that he compared it to the immense and famous Maiden Castle Iron Age hill fort in England.

Is it possible that this remote ruin is the ancient Omride outpost of Jahaz mentioned in the Mesha stele? Could it be that in the building of this remote border fort the Omride engineers and architects utilized the typical characteristics of their great construction projects in the northern kingdom west of the Jordan? Is it possible that as in the case of Samaria and Jezreel, they employed sophisticated earthmoving operations and huge retaining walls to turn a small hilltop settlement into an imposing stronghold? Perhaps the Omrides were even more powerful—and their cultural influence even more far-reaching—than is currently recognized.*

The Power of Diversity

Where did the power and wealth to establish and maintain this full-fledged kingdom come from? What development in the northern hill country led to the emergence of the Omride state? We have already mentioned how the relatively limited resources and sparse population of Judah would have made it quite unlikely that David could have achieved vast territorial conquests or that his son Solomon would have been able to administer large territories. But as we have also mentioned, the resources of the northern hill country were much richer and its population was relatively large. With the destruction of the Canaanite centers in the lowlands, possibly during the raid of Shishak at the end of the tenth century BCE, any potential northern strongman would have been able to gain control of the fertile valleys of the north as well. That fits with what we see in the pattern of the most prominent Omride archaeological remains. In expanding from the original hill country domain of the northern kingdom of Israel to the heart of former Canaanite territory at Megiddo, Hazor, and Gezer, and into the territories of southern Syria and Transjordan, the Omrides fulfilled the centuries-old dream of the rulers of the hill country of establishing a vast and diverse territorial state controlling rich agricultural lands and bustling international trade routes. It was also—of necessity—a multiethnic society.

The northern kingdom of Israel joined the Samarian highlands with the northern valleys, integrating several different ecosystems and a heterogeneous population into its state. The highlands of Samaria—the core terri-

---

* A C14 sample from the gate area was dated to the late 9th century BCE (personal communication from the excavator, Michèle Daviau). The possible chronological range of this reading does not exclude a mid-ninth century BCE construction. Nonetheless, we cannot dismiss the possibility that the "Omride" features at the site represent a Moabite version of the building activity in the northern Kingdom.

tory of the state and the seat of the capital—were inhabited by village communities that would have identified themselves culturally and religiously as Israelites. In the northern lowlands—the Jezreel and the Jordan valleys—the rural population was comprised mainly of settled peasant villages that had been for centuries closely linked to the Canaanite city-states. Farther north were villages more closely aligned to the Aramean culture of Syria and to the Phoenicians of the coast.

In particular, the large and vibrant Canaanite population that endured in the north had to be integrated into the administrative machinery of any full-fledged state. Even before the recent archaeological discoveries, the unique demographic mix of the population of the northern kingdom, especially the relationship between Israelites and Canaanites, did not escape the attention of biblical scholars. On the basis of the biblical accounts of religious turmoil within the Omride kingdom, the German scholar Albrecht Alt suggested that the Omrides had developed a system of dual rule from their two main capitals, with Samaria functioning as a center for the Canaanite population and Jezreel serving as the capital for the northern Israelites. The recent archaeological and historical findings indicate exactly the opposite. The Israelite population was actually concentrated in the hill country around Samaria, while Jezreel, in the heart of the fertile valley, was situated in a region of clear Canaanite cultural continuity. Indeed, the remarkable stability in settlement patterns and the unchanging layout of small villages in the Jezreel Valley are clear indications that the Omrides did not shake the Canaanite rural system in the northern lowlands.

For the Omrides, the task of political integration was especially pressing since competing states were emerging at the same time in neighboring Damascus, Phoenicia, and Moab—each with powerful cultural claims on population groups on the borders with Israel. The early ninth century was therefore the time when national and even some sort of territorial boundaries had to be defined. Thus the Omrides' construction of impressive fortified compounds, some of them with palatial quarters, in the Israelite heartland, in the Jezreel valley, on the border with Aram-Damascus, and even further afield should be seen as serving both administrative necessities and royal propaganda. The British biblical scholar Hugh Williamson characterized them as visual displays of the power and prestige of the Omride state, aimed to impress, awe, and even intimidate the population both at home and along new frontiers.

Of all the resources that the Omrides had at their disposal, heterogeneous population was perhaps the most important of all—for agriculture, building activities, and war. Although it is difficult to estimate the ninth century population of the kingdom of Israel with great precision, large-scale surveys in the region indicate that by the eighth century BCE—a century after the Omrides—the population of the northern kingdom may have reached about 350,000. At that time, Israel was surely the most densely populated state in the Levant, with far more inhabitants than Judah, Moab, or Ammon. Its only possible rival was the kingdom of Aram-Damascus in southern Syria, which—as we will see in greater detail in the next chapter—bitterly competed with Israel for regional hegemony.

Other positive developments from outside the region greatly benefited the fortunes of the Omride kingdom. Its rise to power coincided with the revival of the eastern Mediterranean trade, and the harbor cities of Greece, Cyprus, and the Phoenician coast were once again strongly involved in maritime commerce. The strong Phoenician artistic influence on Israelite culture, the sudden appearance of large quantities of Cypro-Phoenician-style vessels in the cities of the kingdom of Israel, and—not coincidentally—the biblical testimony that Ahab married a Phoenician princess all seem to indicate that Israel was an active participant in this economic revival as a supplier of valuable agricultural products and a master over some of the most important overland trade routes of the Levant.

Thus the Omride idea of a state covering large territories of both highlands and lowlands in certain ways revived ideas, practices, and material culture of Bronze Age Canaan, in the centuries before the rise of Israel. In fact, from the conceptual and functional points of view, the great Omride citadels resembled the capitals of the great Canaanite city-states of the Late Bronze Age, which ruled over a patchwork of peoples and lands. Thus from the point of view of both form and function, the layout of Megiddo in the ninth century BCE was not very different from its layout in the Late Bronze Age. Large parts of the mound were devoted to public buildings and open areas, while only limited areas were occupied by domestic quarters. As was the case in Canaanite Megiddo, the urban population constituted mainly the ruling elite, which controlled the rural hinterland. And a similar cultural continuity is exquisitely manifested in the nearby city of Taanach, where a magnificent decorated cult stand from the ninth century BCE bears elaborate motifs drawn from the Canaanite traditions of the Late Bronze Age.

That is why it is difficult to insist, from a strictly archaeological perspective, that the kingdom of Israel as a whole was ever particularly Israelite in either the ethnic, cultural, or religious connotations of that name as we understand it from the perspective of the later biblical writers. The Israeliteness of the northern kingdom was in many ways a late monarchic Judahite idea.

The Ultimate Villains?

The writer of the books of Kings was concerned to show only that the Omrides were evil and that they received the divine punishment that their sinful arrogant behavior had so richly earned. Of course, he had to recount details and events about the Omrides that were well known through folktales and earlier traditions, but in all of them he wanted to highlight the Omrides' dark side. Thus he diminished their military might with the story of the Aramean siege of Samaria, which was taken from events of later days, and with the accusation that in a moment of victory Ahab disobeyed a divine command to utterly annihilate his enemy. The biblical author closely linked the grandeur of the palace at Samaria and the majestic royal compound in Jezreel with idolatry and social injustice. He linked the images of the awesome might of Israelite chariots in full battle order with the Omride family's horrible end. He wanted to delegitimize the Omrides and to show that the entire history of the northern kingdom had been one of sin that led to misery and inevitable destruction. The more Israel had prospered in the past, the more scornful and negative he became about its kings.

The true character of Israel under the Omrides involves an extraordinary story of military might, architectural achievement, and (as far as can be determined) administrative sophistication. Omri and his successors earned the hatred of the Bible precisely because they were so strong, precisely because they succeeded in transforming the northern kingdom into an important regional power that completely overshadowed the poor, marginal, rural-pastoral kingdom of Judah to the south. The possibility that the Israelite kings who consorted with the nations, married foreign women, and built Canaanite-type shrines and palaces would prosper was both unbearable and unthinkable.

Moreover, from the perspective of late monarchic Judah, the internationalism and openness of the Omrides was sinful. To become entangled with the ways of the neighboring peoples was, according to the seventh century Deuteronomistic ideology, a direct violation of divine command. But a lesson could still be learned from that experience. By the time of the compilation of the books of Kings, history's verdict had already been returned. The Omrides had been overthrown and the kingdom of Israel was no more. Yet with the help of archaeological evidence and the testimony of outside sources, we can now see how the vivid scriptural portraits that doomed Omri, Ahab, and Jezebel to ridicule and scorn over the centuries skillfully concealed the real character of the first true kingdom of Israel.

[8]

In the Shadow of Empire

(c. 842–720 BCE)

A dark sense of foreboding hovers over the kingdom of Israel as the biblical narrative of its history moves toward its tragic climax. Suffering, dispossession, and exile seem to be the inescapable destiny of the people of the breakaway kingdom in punishment for their impious acts. Instead of remaining faithful to the Temple in Jerusalem and to the worship of YHWH to the exclusion of all other gods, the people of northern Israel— and particularly its sinful monarchs—provoked a series of catastrophes that would end in their destruction. Faithful prophets of YHWH arose to call Israel to account and demand a return to righteousness and justice, but their calls went unheeded. The invasions of foreign armies and the devastation of the kingdom of Israel were an essential part of a divine plan.

The Bible's interpretation of the fate of the northern kingdom is purely theological. By contrast, archaeology offers a different perspective on the events in the century that followed the fall of the Omrides. While Judah continued to be poor and isolated, the natural richness and relatively dense population of the kingdom of Israel made it a tempting target for the increasingly complex regional politics of the Assyrian period. The Omrides' prosperity and power brought jealousies and military rivalries with neighbors—and the covetous ambition of the great Assyrian empire. The wealth of the kingdom of Israel also brought growing social tensions and pro-phetic condemnations from within. We can now see that Israel's greatest misfortune—and the cause of its destruction and the exile of many of its people—was that as an independent kingdom living in the shadow of a great empire, it succeeded too well.

Faithlessness, God's Mercy, and Israel's Final Fall

The books of Kings show how all of Elijah's grim prophecies of doom on the house of Omri were fulfilled to the letter. Yet the biblical narra-tive goes on to show that the extermination of the old royal family did not end Israel's pursuit of idolatry. After the fall of the Omrides, the newly anointed king, Jehu, son of Nimshi (who reigned from 842 to 814 BCE), followed in the footsteps of Jeroboam, Omri, and Ahab in his lack of regard for Jerusalem. For even though he massacred all the prophets, priests, and worshipers of Baal in Samaria and made the house of Baal it-self a public latrine (2 Kings 10:18–28), the Bible informs us that Jehu "did not turn aside from the sins of Jeroboam the son of Nebat, which he made Israel to sin, the golden calves that were in Bethel and in Dan" (2 Kings 10:29). In other words, though he eliminated the Baal cult, Jehu failed to abolish the rival northern cult centers that challenged the re-ligious supremacy of Jerusalem. Nor did any of the kings of Israel who came after him abolish them.

Punishment was not long in coming, as the prophet Elijah had de-creed. This time, God's agent of destruction was Hazael, king of Aram-Damascus, who defeated Israel both in Transjordan and in a campaign of destruction down the Mediterranean coastal plain (2 Kings 10:32–33; 12:17–18; 13:3,7,22). This is a period of decline for the northern king-dom, for throughout the days of both Jehu and his son Jehoahaz, Israel was pressed by Aram-Damascus. Israel's army was defeated and its ter-ritories reduced. But the time of chastisement for the common people of the Kingdom of Israel soon ended, since "the Lord was gracious to them and had compassion on them and he turned toward them, because of his covenant with Abraham, Isaac, and Jacob, and would not de-stroy them; nor has he cast them from his presence until now" (2 Kings 13:23).

Thus the next Israelite king, Joash,* was blessed with at least temporary divine favor and took back the cities that Israel lost to Aram (2 Kings 13:25). And the fortunes of Israel seemed to take a decided turn for the better—even after a punitive raid by Joash on Judah—with the accession of his son to the throne of Israel. This, too, was a matter of divine compassion, for Joash's son, named Jeroboam—after the greatest of all the royal northern sinners—reigned peacefully in Samaria for the next forty-one years (788–747 BCE). Even though this king did not depart from any of the sins of the original Jeroboam in maintaining the idolatrous northern sanctuaries, and though voices of prophetic protests by Amos and Hosea echoed throughout the land, Jeroboam

> restored the border of Israel from the entrance of Hamath as far as the Sea of the Arabah, according to the word of the LORD, the God of Israel, which he spoke by his servant Jonah the son of Amittai, the prophet, who was from Gath-hepher. For the LORD saw that the affliction of Israel was very bitter, for there was none left, bond or free, and there was none to help Israel. But the LORD had not said that he would blot out the name of Israel from under heaven, so he saved them by the hand of Jeroboam the son of Joash. (2 KINGS 14:25–27)

Yet this period of divine blessing did not last long, for as 2 Kings 10:30 explains, God had promised to Jehu that only four generations of his family would reign. Thus Jeroboam II's son Zechariah was assassinated after only six months of his reign, and Israel entered another period of civil strife and external pressures. The murderer, Shallum, was soon killed by another, even more brutal pretender, Menahem, son of Gadi, who ruled in Samaria for ten years (747–737 BCE). At this point God prepared a new agent of chastisement for the northern kingdom and a chain of events that would lead to its final destruction. It was the mighty Assyrian empire, whose armies came and demanded a massive tribute, for which Menahem was forced to levy a tax of fifty silver shekels of every wealthy man in Israel (2 Kings: 15:19–20).

The outside and internal pressures were building. Menahem's son and

---

* The Bible mentions two kings from roughly the same era—one from Israel and one from Judah—who are *both* referred to by the alternative Hebrew names Jehoash and Joash. For the sake of clarity, we will refer to the northern king (who ruled 800–784 BCE) as "Joash" and to the southern king (who ruled 836–798 BCE) as "Jehoash."

successor, Pekahiah, was murdered by a military officer, Pekah, son of Remaliah. But by that time the Assyrians were no longer content with tribute.
They sought to take the rich land of Israel for themselves: "In the days of
Pekah king of Israel, Tiglath-pileser king of Assyria came and captured
Ijon, Abel-beth-maacah, Janoah, Kedesh, Hazor, Gilead, and Galilee, all
the land of Naphtali; and he carried the people captives to Assyria" (2 Kings
15:29). The northern valleys and Galilee were thus conquered (732 BCE)
and its inhabitants were deported, reversing the divine promises of the secure inheritance given at the time of the original conquest of Canaan by
the Israelites. The kingdom of Israel lost some of its richest lands and was
reduced to the highlands around the capital of Samaria. With this disastrous turn of events, the usurper Pekah was assassinated—the fourth Israelite king to be murdered in just fifteen years. Pekah's assassin and
successor, Hoshea, would be the last king of the kingdom of Israel.

The Assyrian noose was tightening with the accession of Shalmaneser V,
an aggressive new Assyrian king. Hoshea proclaimed himself to be a loyal
vassal and offered Shalmaneser tribute, but he secretly sought an alliance
with the king of Egypt for an open revolt. When Shalmaneser learned of
the conspiracy he took Hoshea captive and invaded what was left of the
kingdom of Israel. For three years the Assyrian king laid siege to the Israelite capital of Samaria, eventually capturing it in 720 BCE, "and he carried the Israelites away to Assyria, and placed them in Halah, and on the
Habor, the river of Gozan, and in the cities of Medes" (2 Kings 17:6).

Conquest and deportation were not the end of the story. After exiling
the Israelites from their land to Mesopotamia, the Assyrians brought in
new settlers to Israel: "And the king of Assyria brought people from Babylon, Cuthah, Avva, Hamath, and Sepharvaim, and placed them in the
cities of Samaria instead of the people of Israel; and they took possession
of Samaria, and dwelt in its cities" (2 Kings 17:24). The ten northern tribes
of Israel were now lost among the distant nations. Only the kingdom of
Judah, with its Temple and Davidic kings, now survived to carry on God's
commandments and to redeem the land of Israel.

A Closer Look at Israel's Later History

Archaeologists often speak of long periods of time in which little is changed—but only because the nature of their finds makes it hard to identify chronological divisions. There is, after all, no human society that can remain substantially unchanged for as much as two hundred years. Yet that was the traditional archaeological understanding of the northern kingdom, for since the 1920s archaeologists have excavated some of the most important sites of the kingdom of Israel taking note of no significant change except for its ultimate destruction. As was the case with the archaeological study of the Omrides, the post-Omride era of Israel's independent history was not considered formative or particularly interesting from an archaeological point of view. In an unconscious echoing of the Bible's theological interpretations, archaeologists depicted a rather monotonous continuity followed by inevitable destruction. Very little attention was given to the inner dynamics of the kingdom and its economic history (except for some speculation on a single collection of crop receipts from Samaria). As we will see, these are crucial areas of research if we are ever to move beyond the Bible's exclusively theological interpretation of Israel's history—that its demise was a direct and inevitable punishment for its sins. The 120 years of Israelite history that followed the fall of the Omrides was, in fact, an era of dramatic social change in the kingdom, of economic ups and downs and constantly shifting strategies to survive the threat of empire.

One of the main reasons for this misunderstanding was the conventional dating system, according to which the entire history of the northern kingdom—from rise to fall—tended to be lumped into a single chronological block. Many important centers in the Jezreel valley and on the nearby Mediterranean coast, such as Megiddo, Jokneam, and Dor, were believed to contain only a *single* stratum spanning the entire history of the kingdom of Israel, from Jeroboam I (in fact, from the Shishak campaign in 926 BCE) to the fall of Samaria in 722 BCE. This despite the evidence of major changes and military defeats that took place during this long period—among the most important of which was the invasion of Israel by King Hazael of Damascus, as recorded in the Bible and on the Dan stele by the scribes of Hazael himself.

Something was wrong in the conventional archaeological understand-

TABLE FOUR

ASSYRIAN KINGS INVOLVED IN THE
HISTORY OF ISRAEL AND JUDAH*

Shalmaneser III	859–824 BCE
Adad-nirari III	811–783
Tiglath-pileser III	745–727
Shalmaneser V	727–722
Sargon II	722–705
Sennacherib	705–681
Esarhaddon	681–669
Ashurbanipal	669–627

* According to Cogan and Tadmor, *II Kings*.

ing: how could it be possible that Hazael captured Dan and spread havoc in the territories of the northern kingdom but left no perceptible archaeological trace of destruction?

Aram in Israel

Hazael's incursion into the territory formerly controlled by Israel was clearly devastating and did much to weaken the power of the northern kingdom. In the famous stele from Moab, King Mesha boasts that he succeeded in taking Moabite territories from Israel and even managed to expand into Israelite territories farther to the north. The Bible reports that the formerly Israelite-controlled areas of Transjordan to the north of Moab were taken by Hazael (2 Kings 10:32–33). Yet the most striking evidence for Hazael's offensive is the Tel Dan inscription. While the biblical narrative of the fall of the Omrides connects the massacre of the royal family at their palace at Jezreel with the revolt of Jehu—the reigning king of Israel, Jehoram, being felled by Jehu's arrow—the reconstructed text of the Dan inscription links the death of Jehoram with an Aramean victory. Hazael boasts: "[I killed Jeho]ram son of [Ahab] king of Israel, and [I] killed [Ahaz]iahu son of [Jehoram kin]g of the House of David. And I set [their towns into ruins and turned] their land into [desolation]."

So was it Hazael, or Jehu? It is difficult to know for sure. Hazael's pressure and Jehu's coup are connected in the biblical text. Hazael may have seen Jehu as his instrument, or perhaps memories of the two events became blurred together during the two hundred years that passed until the first compilation of the Deuteronomistic History. Certainly an all-out offensive by the Syrian leader played a major role in the serious decline of Israel. Hazael's prime target was control of the fertile and strategic borderland between the two kingdoms, and he apparently not only conquered the Aramean lands formerly taken by the Omrides but also devastated some of Israel's most fertile agricultural regions and disrupted their trade routes.

The Bible mentions no significant long-term territorial conquests by foreign powers in the lands lying west of the Jordan between the time of the conquest of Canaan by Joshua and the Assyrian conquest. The biblical borders of the land of Israel as outlined in the book of Joshua had seemingly assumed a sacred inviolability. Except for the small area reportedly given by Solomon to King Hiram of Tyre in return for his help in building the Temple, the Bible pictures a stormy but basically continuous Israelite occupation of the land of Israel all the way to the Assyrian conquest. But a reexamination of the archaeological evidence supported by new, more precise dating techniques points to a period of a few decades, between around 835 and 800 BCE, when the kingdom of Aram-Damascus controlled the upper Jordan valley and significant areas in northeastern Israel—and devastated major Israelite administrative centers in the fertile Jezreel valley as well.

Important new evidence for this has emerged from the excavation of the Omride palace compound at Jezreel, which was occupied for only a relatively brief period in the ninth century BCE as it was destroyed a relatively short while after it was built. There was a small settlement at Jezreel in the later days of the Iron Age, but the site never regained its former importance. There is therefore good reason to associate Jezreel's destruction with the Jehu revolt or with the invasion of Hazael, which both occurred a few years after the middle of the ninth century.

Because Jezreel was occupied for such a relatively short period, the pottery forms found in its destruction level offer a valuable sample of the styles current in the mid–ninth century BCE, and indeed are found in the levels of the "Solomonic" palaces of Megiddo and at parallel strata in sites throughout the north. Readers who were not convinced earlier that the Omrides built these "Solomonic" cities must now consider (in addition to the ceramic evidence, the architectural parallels, and the carbon 14 dates) the likelihood that the violent destruction of those sites—long ascribed to the Egyptian raid led by Pharaoh Shishak in the late tenth century BCE—took place around 835, at the time of Hazael.

Across the fertile expanses of the rich northern valleys, cities went up in flames, from Tel Rehov, to Beth-shean, to Taanach, to Megiddo. On the basis of this new evidence, the Israeli biblical historian Nadav Naaman concluded that these destruction layers represent a devastation of the northern kingdom by Hazael so severe that some of the sites never recovered. The military pressure of Damascus on Israel perhaps culminated in a siege of the capital, Samaria, probably by Bar-hadad III (known in the Bible as Ben-hadad), the son of Hazael. The two sieges of Samaria described in the Bible in the days of Ahab and Jehoram most probably refer to this period.

Archaeology has thus discovered something that the Bible neglected to mention: The very heartland of Israel was occupied for an extended period. None of the earlier archaeologists seem to have found evidence of this event. At Hazor, the period between the Omrides and the destruction of Israel was divided by Yigael Yadin into four strata, none of which was specifically connected with Hazael's invasion. Yet once the city of the six-chambered gate and casemate wall—long associated with Solomon—is placed at the time of the Omrides, its destruction can be associated with the campaign of Hazael. In Dan, the very city taken by Hazael—in which he erected a victory stele proclaiming his recapture of territory for his kingdom—the conventional dating failed to identify a mid-ninth century destruction, much less a period of Aramean occupation. But at Dan too, the alternative dating allows the identification of a destruction layer for the conquest of Hazael that is commemorated in the Dan stele.

But Hazael was not strong enough to annex the devastated Israelite centers farther south in the Jezreel and Beth-shean valleys, which were far away from the core area of his rule. He apparently left them in ruins, bringing about the desertion of many sites and the decline of the whole region for a few decades. Some of the centers of this region never recovered; Jezreel and Taanach, for example, never regained their former importance. An analysis of the pottery of Megiddo seems to indicate that this pivotal city for the Is-raelite administration of the north was deserted for almost half a century.

The Israelite kingdom thus lost effective control of some of its most fer-tile agricultural regions, and even more important, its rival gained a more permanent foothold at the strategic sites of Hazor and Dan in the north-east. Those sites were located closer to Damascus than to Samaria and were situated in territories that Hazael claimed were originally Aramean. To quote again from Hazael's own inscription, describing the situation follow-ing the death of his predecessor: "And my father lay down, he went to his [ancestors]. And the king of I[s]rael entered previously in my father's land." It is inconceivable that Hazael conquered the upper Jordan valley, erected a victory stele at Dan, and then withdrew. Here the victories in the battle-field were translated into long-term territorial dominance.

It is therefore likely that the new city built at Hazor immediately after Hazael's conquest was actually an important link in a chain of *Aramean* cities and fortresses that guarded Aram-Damascus's southeastern border against Israel. The city built on top of the destruction layer expanded to in-clude the entire upper Bronze Age acropolis and was surrounded by a new, massive wall. A citadel or a palace was built at its western end, apparently on top of the now destroyed Omride citadel. Even the magnificent rock-cut water system may have been built in this phase of the city's history.

At Dan, the famous stele was no doubt erected in a new city that Hazael rebuilt. The late ninth century city there is characterized by the construc-tion of a formidable stone city wall, similar to the one uncovered at Hazor, and an exceptionally elaborate city gate. The gate features a special ele-ment, unknown in the Israelite and Judahite territories of the time: re-mains of a canopy, or an elevated platform, were found outside of the right-hand tower as one enters the city. They include two carved round stone bases with typical northern (that is, Syrian) features. The commem-orative stele itself, which presumably also mentioned Hazael's building ac-tivities, could have been placed either at the gate of the city or at the elaborately rebuilt ashlar cult place, probably rededicated to Aram's god Hadad.

Another formidable stronghold built at the same time—and possibly related to Hazael's occupation of northern Israel—is a site known as et-Tell on the northern shore of the Sea of Galilee. It has been tentatively

identified by the excavators as the location of the much later settlement of
Bethsaida in Roman times. In the ninth century a massive stone wall surrounded the site, similar to the walls built at Hazor and Dan. A huge city
gate is similar in shape and size to the one uncovered at Dan. In the front of
the city gate the excavators recovered an extraordinary find, which seems to
disclose the ethnic, or perhaps more accurately the cultural and political
identity of the inhabitants. A basalt stele was found near the right-hand
tower as one enters the gate. Its depiction of a horned deity is characteristically Aramean. And its location in front of the gate offers the possibility
that a similar stele may have been erected near the Dan gate, under the
elaborate canopy.

Thus we have hints that Hazael's invasion of Israel in the mid-ninth century BCE was followed up by prolonged occupation and the establishment
of at least three fortresses—at Dan, Hazor, and Bethsaida—that display
common features, some of them characteristically Aramean. And there is
further reason to believe that the population in this part of the Israelite
kingdom was at least partially, if not mostly, Aramean. This is indicated by
the fact that in almost every major Iron Age II site in the region, excavations yielded ostraca written in Aramaic.

Assyria Returns

The Syrian occupation of Israel did not last long. From Assyrian sources we
know that Hazael was able to push to the west and south into Israel because
for a few decades in the second half of the ninth century the reigning Assyrian kings were preoccupied with disorders in other parts of the empire.
But with the accession of a powerful new Assyrian monarch, Adad-nirari
III, in 811 BCE, the balance of power between Aram and Israel changed dramatically. Adad-nirari immediately renewed the military pressure in the
west and besieged Damascus, now the strongest regional power. Damascus
may have been able to overcome Israel, but it was no match for the armies
of the Mesopotamian superpower of the time. Bar-hadad III, the son of
Hazael, surrendered and paid massive tribute to Assyria. These events
brought the hegemony of Aram-Damascus to an end and terminated the
military pressure on Israel.

In this light we can begin to understand the enormous impact that Assyrian imperialism had on the course of events in the kingdom of Israel and how so much of the history that is described in the Bible as a function of the impiety or greed of the kings of Israel had far more to do with the winds of international power politics. Although the books of Kings depict Ahab primarily as an idolatrous tyrant, we know from the monolith inscription of Shalmaneser III that he was one of the most energetic opponents of Assyrian domination—sending his massive chariot force to confront the Assyrians at Qarqar. And while Jehu, the rebel, is pictured in the Bible as God's instrument to destroy idolatry in Israel, the famous "black obelisk" of Shalmaneser shows him bowing low to the ground at the feet of the great Assyrian king. Shalmaneser also notes: "The tribute of Jehu, son of Omri; I received from him silver, gold, a golden saplu-bowl, a golden vase with pointed bottom, golden tumblers, golden buckets, tin, a staff for a king." (The fact that Jehu is named "son of Omri"—in essence son of the family he is reported to have exterminated—implies only that he ruled a vassal kingdom whose capital city was founded by Omri.)

The resurgence of Israel under Jehu's grandson Joash (2 Kings 13:22–25) had more directly to do with the Assyrian humbling of Damascus than God's reported change of heart. The end of the regional hegemony of Aram-Damascus gave the northern kingdom of Israel—which had pledged its loyalty to Assyria as early as the time of Shalmaneser III—a splendid opportunity to be recognized as Assyria's most-favored vassal. Under the leadership of King Joash the northern kingdom quickly recovered and started regaining its territories that had been lost to Damascus (2 Kings 13:25). And the expansion of Israel apparently continued under Jeroboam II (2 Kings 14:25,28), who is reported to have extended Israel's boundaries well into the former territories of Aram. When we look at the archaeological record, there is clear confirmation that Joash's son Jeroboam II, whose term was the longest in the history of the northern kingdom, presided over a period of unparalleled prosperity in Israel.

Rewards of a New World Order

The new phase of prosperity that began around 800 BCE was apparently long remembered as a golden age for the northern kingdom—even in the memory of the people of Judah. The biblical author of the books of Kings was forced to find an explanation for this otherwise puzzling good fortune enjoyed by the sinful northerners. He explained the turn of events by the sudden compassion of the God of Israel (2 Kings 14:26–27), but we can now see that a more likely reason was the Assyrian aggression against Damascus and Israel's eager participation in the growing Assyrian world economy. At Dan, the victory stele of Hazael was apparently smashed and the fragments reused in later construction (where they would be found by archaeologists some twenty-eight hundred years later), when Israelite builders established a new city there. At Bethsaida, the stele bearing the Aramean-style deity was likewise intentionally upended and laid upside down. And at about the same time, Hazor was taken, destroyed, and rebuilt anew; it may not be complete coincidence that Hebrew inscriptions appear at Hazor for the first time in this building phase.

The strength of the Israelite economy during the reign of Jeroboam II may best be demonstrated by Israel's developments in agriculture and its impressive population growth. For millennia, the highlands around Samaria had formed the best region in the country for the cultivation of vineyards and olive groves. Intensive archaeological surveys in the hilly regions to the south of Samaria have yielded evidence for unprecedented expansion of olive oil production in the Iron Age. In the eighth century, we see for the first time settlements built on rocky spurs in the heart of the best orchard-growing regions, whose inhabitants apparently specialized in this branch of agriculture (Figure 25). Scores of olive presses and other processing installations were cut in the bedrock around these villages, some of which may have been royal estates or at least built specifically for this purpose. There was no lack of potential markets: the olive oil from the highlands of Israel could have been profitably exported to Assyria and shipped to Egypt, since both Egypt and Assyria lacked prime olive-growing regions. Indeed the famous Samaria ostraca—a collection of sixty-three ink-inscribed pottery sherds written in Hebrew and plausibly dated to the time of Jeroboam II—record shipments of oil and wine from outlying villages to the capital city, Samaria.

That agricultural hinterland was, in the meantime, becoming more thickly populated than ever before. Tied to a world economy and facing no significant military threat, the population of the northern kingdom expanded dramatically. The large-scale surveys undertaken in the last few

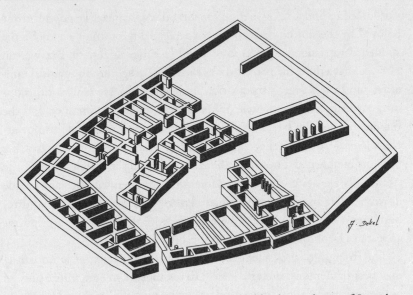

Figure 25: Plan of an oil-producing site in the highlands, northwest of Jerusalem. *After a plan published in* Atiqot.

decades throw light on the dramatic demographic growth from the tenth to the eighth centuries BCE. By the late eighth century the northern kingdom—the highlands of Samaria and the northern valleys alike—was the most densely settled region in the entire Levant.*

Though the numbers are admittedly sketchy, they provide a general estimation that the population of the northern kingdom in the eighth century, including its territory in Transjordan, was about 350,000. By the same procedure scholars estimate that in the Bronze Age, the population of the *entire* territory of western Palestine did not even reach 250,000. The demographic growth is particularly dramatic when we consider that the highlands population in the Early Iron Age numbered hardly more than 45,000. Even in the eighth century, the population of the kingdom of Judah did not count much more than 100,000 souls. The population of the

* We base this assumption on a rough population estimate, arrived at by using a combination of archaeological and ethnographic data. In this technique of estimating ancient populations, the built-up area of all sites occupied during the eighth century BCE (determined by the presence of distinctive eighth century pottery types) is multiplied by a density coefficient, that is, the average density of population observed in traditional, premodern societies of the nineteenth or the beginning of the twentieth century.

Transjordanian states of Ammon and Moab together hardly reached a third of the population of northern Israel.

These comparative numbers explain the military might and economic power of the northern kingdom. They also hint at the human resources of Israel, which enabled both a military buildup and impressive building activities. It appears that Joash, or more likely Jeroboam II, undertook major building operations not only at Megiddo (including the great water system and the two huge sets of stables) but also in the rebuilding of Hazor as a stronghold in the territories taken back from the Arameans and in the reconstruction of the city of Gezer, a strategic outpost of the northern kingdom on the borders of Judah and Philistia. A massive new city wall and gate at Gezer may date to this time.

The grandeur of the reborn kingdom of Israel is clear from the evidence. It is significant that Jeroboam II is the earliest Israelite monarch for whom we have an official seal. This exceptionally large and beautiful artifact was found in the beginning of the twentieth century at Megiddo. It depicts a powerful, roaring lion and a Hebrew inscription reading: "Belonging to Shema the servant [i.e., high official] of Jeroboam." The design of the lion on the seal is typical of the eighth century BCE, so it cannot be ascribed to the earlier Jeroboam, who founded the northern kingdom almost two centuries earlier. By the standards of its prosperity, international connections, and expansive building projects, Jeroboam II's realm may have remained alive in the memory of both Israelites and Judahites as the model for a glorious monarchy. Recall the famous passage of 1 Kings 9:15, which describes the building activities of Solomon at Hazor, Megiddo, and Gezer. Is it possible that the later Judahite author, composing his history almost a hundred years later, romantically (and patriotically) ascribed the ruins of the great structures built by Jeroboam to the golden age of Solomon?

The Riddle of the Megiddo Stables—Again

Horses, it seems, were one of the northern kingdom's most prized and most valuable products. Some tantalizing clues to the extent of horse breeding and training in Israel may come from the rebuilding of Megiddo in the time of Jeroboam II (Figure 22, p. 182).

The most prominent element in the last Israelite city of Megiddo is the two large complexes of pillared buildings that the University of Chicago team suggested in the 1920s were stables built by Solomon—and later re-dated by Yadin as stables built by Ahab, who had marshaled such an enor-mous chariot force against the Assyrians at the battle of Qarqar. Whether arguing for an association with Solomon or with Ahab, the supporters of the stables theory argued that the horses were kept in long, narrow side aisles of the buildings, where they were tied to stone pillars and fed in the mangers placed between the pillars (Figure 17, p. 138). The central aisle, whose floor was covered with smooth plaster, supposedly served as a service area, where the grooms could groom the horses and distribute feed. The ar-chaeologists also suggested that the large courtyard in front of the southern set of stables served as a training and exercise yard.

There was only one problem with this attractive theory: no items related to horses, chariotry, or cavalry were found in any of the buildings. And the side aisles of similar structures uncovered at other sites were filled with pot-tery vessels, which suggested to many scholars that *all* such three-aisled buildings were used as storehouses. Some theorized that the mangers found in the Megiddo buildings were used to feed beasts of burden, prob-ably donkeys, who brought goods to the storehouses in caravans. Other scholars proposed that the pillared buildings at Megiddo, as well as at other places in the region, served as army barracks or even as public bazaars.

In the ongoing excavations at Megiddo, attempts are being made to re-solve the problem by the systematic chemical testing of earth recently exca-vated from the floors of the pillared buildings—to identify traces of feed or animal excrement. So far the results are inconclusive. But one thing has al-ready been clarified in the renewed excavations. We should not expect to find any significant horse-related items in the buildings, since after the As-syrian takeover of the city they were thoroughly cleaned and at least par-tially reused, and later dismantled at the time of their abandonment. They were intentionally destroyed by having their walls pulled down.

Due to the redating of the Megiddo strata—and the reassessment of the archaeological history of the northern kingdom—we can now reject the earlier theories and say with confidence that the stable-like structures at Megiddo belong to the time of Jeroboam II. Ahab, though clearly main-taining a great chariot force, constructed the great palaces at Megiddo that *precede* the level of the "stables" (even though some scholars suggest that this city too, which was only partially excavated, had stables). But linking the "stables" to Jeroboam II does not definitively settle the problem of their function. Are there any other clues for highlighting the importance of horses in the kingdom of Israel—and perhaps understanding Israel's military role in the larger Assyrian imperial society?

Critical evidence comes from the Assyrian sources, which reveal that the kingdom of Israel was famous for its chariot forces long after King Ahab faced Shalmaneser III with two thousand chariots at the battle of Qarqar in Syria in 853 BCE. The Assyriologist Stephanie Dalley has found convincing evidence in Assyrian records that some of the empire's vassal states specialized in the breeding and export of horses used in chariot and cavalry warfare. We know that Jeroboam's Israel prospered through its specialization in certain commodities. Could it be that what we see at Megiddo is the architectural remains of an important horse breeding center for the famous chariot corps of the kingdom of Israel? And is it possible that in the days of Jeroboam II Israel bred horses not only for its own military requirements but for chariot units throughout the Assyrian empire? A clue in this direction comes from another Assyrian vassal state, the kingdom of Urartu in eastern Anatolia, which was considered to possess the best cavalry in the world. We know from an explicit mention in Assyrian sources that horses were bred there for export. And interestingly, buildings have been uncovered in Iron II sites in Urartu that are strikingly similar in plan to the Megiddo "stables."

But perhaps the most indicative association of Israelites with military horsemanship comes from a period immediately after the conquest of the northern kingdom by Assyria—when a special Israelite chariot unit was incorporated into the Assyrian army. In fact, the research of Stephanie Dalley on Assyrian tablets called the "horse lists" provides information on officials, officers, and units in the Assyrian army in the days of Sargon II. These records indicate that while other specialized troops from conquered regions were incorporated into the Assyrian army as individuals, the Israelite chariot brigade was the only foreign unit permitted to retain its national identity. The Assyrian king Sargon II says it best: "I formed a unit with two hundred of their chariots for my royal force."

It would seem, therefore, that because Israelite charioteers were so famous for their skill, they were allowed a special status. Among other details in the horse lists was mention of an Israelite commander named Shema, probably from the chariot corps, who served in a high post in the Assyrian army and was a member of the king's entourage.

The First Voices of Protest

The prosperity and prominence that the kingdom of Israel attained during the reign of Jeroboam II offered great wealth to the Israelite aristocracy. Although the rather chaotic digging methods of the early twentieth century excavations of Samaria do not permit a detailed analysis of the buildings and renovations of the royal city in the early eighth century, two extremely interesting sets of small finds offer at least a glimpse of the opulence and wealth of Israel's ruling class. Over two hundred delicate ivory plaques carved in Phoenician style with Egyptian motifs and stylistically dated to the eighth century BCE probably decorated the walls of the palace or the fine furniture of Israelite royalty. They attest to the wealth and cosmopolitan tastes of the Israelite monarchs and the noble families of their kingdom. The famous Samaria ostraca, receipts for shipments of oil and wine delivered from the countryside to the capital city, represent a sophisticated system of credit and record keeping in which the produce of the hinterland was claimed by large landowners or by government tax officials who supervised the collection of the crop.

It is at the height of prosperity of the northern kingdom under the rule of Jeroboam II that we can finally identify the full complement of the criteria of statehood: literacy, bureaucratic administration, specialized economic production, and a professional army. It is also the period when we have the first record of prophetic protest. The oracles of the prophets Amos and Hosea are the earliest preserved prophetic books, containing material that reflects the heyday of Jeroboam II. Their scathing denunciations of the corrupt and impious aristocracy of the north serve both to document the opulence of this era and to express for the first time ideas that would exert a profound effect on the crystallization of the Deuteronomistic ideology.

Amos is described as a shepherd who wandered north from the rural Judahite village of Tekoa. But whatever his precise social status or reason for preaching in the kingdom of Israel, the oracles recorded in his name provide a searing condemnation of the lavish lifestyles and material reality of Israel's aristocracy in the eighth century BCE:

> Woe to those who lie upon beds of ivory, and stretch themselves upon their couches, and eat lambs from the flock, and calves from the midst of the stall; who sing idle songs to the sound of the harp, and like David invent for themselves instruments of music; who drink wine in bowls, and anoint themselves with the finest oils . . . (AMOS 6:4–6)

Amos goes on to condemn those who "have built houses of hewn stone" (5:11), and his contemporary, the prophet Hosea, speaks out against those who "multiply falsehood and violence; they make a bargain with Assyria, and oil is carried to Egypt" (Hosea 12:1). In these and many other allusions, the two prophets outline the economic connections and material culture that have been so abundantly illustrated by the archaeology of the kingdom of Israel.

Beyond the condemnation of the rich and the powerful, Amos and Hosea both offer searing critiques of the social injustices, idolatry, and domestic tensions that international trade and the dependence on Assyria have brought. According to Hosea, "Assyria shall not save us, we will not ride upon horses; and we will say no more, 'Our God,' to the work of our hands" (Hosea 14:3). Amos condemns the wickedness of those who merely pay lip service to the dictates of religion while gathering riches for themselves and abusing the poor:

> Hear this, you who trample upon the needy, and bring the poor of the land to an end, saying, "When will the new moon be over, that we may sell grain? And the sabbath, that we may offer wheat for sale, and that we may make the ephah small and the shekel great, and deal deceitfully with false balances, that we may buy the poor for silver and the needy for a pair of sandals, and sell the refuse of the wheat?" (AMOS 8:4–6)

These prophetic condemnations were preserved by the followers of Amos and Hosea and took on a new meaning after the fall of the kingdom of Israel. For in their critique of the wealthy and in their revulsion at the effect of foreign ways on the life of the people of Israel, they heralded the spiritual and social movement that would leave an indelible impression on the crystallizing biblical text.

The Death Throes of Israel

With the death of Jeroboam II in 747 BCE, the structure of Israelite society—despite its material prosperity and achievements in architecture and military arts—proved hollow. Factions probably arose among regional administrators, army officers, and special interest groups. King followed king in relatively quick and usually bloody succession. The delicate balance of economic independence and political alliance with, or subservience to, Assyria gradually broke down. The narrative presented in the second book of Kings, supplemented by occasional confirmations in the records of Assyria, is all we have to go on in documenting the fall of Israel.

The series of violent dynastic upheavals at Samaria could not have come at a more dangerous time. Great changes were taking place in Mesopotamia. In 745—precisely after two kings were assassinated in Samaria—the ambitious governor of the great Assyrian city of Calah in the Tigris valley revolted against his own overlords and began the process of transforming Assyria into a brutal and predatory state.

This new king, Tiglath-pileser III (also known by his Babylonian name, Pul, in the Bible), began nothing less than a thorough revamping of the Assyrian empire—primarily in its relations to its former vassals, which would now be much more directly controlled. In 738 BCE, he led his army on a great threatening campaign westward, in which he succeeded in cowering Assyria's formerly semi-independent vassals with unprecedented economic demands. But that was only the beginning. In the era of Assyrian imperialism that Tiglath-pileser had inaugurated, vassaldom would soon give way to conquest and annexation—with local populations being subject to deportation wherever the Assyrian authorities wished.

In Samaria, the Israelite capital—with the death of King Menahem in 737 BCE and the almost immediate assassination of his son and successor by a military officer named Pekah, son of Remaliah—the foreign policy of the kingdom of Israel changed. We have no information on the political and personal motives of Pekah, this latest usurper, but he suddenly ended Israel's obsequious vassaldom to Assyria. Perhaps in a desperate reaction to the change of Assyrian policies and the inability to meet Assyrian demands, Pekah joined a coalition of other local powers—including King Rezin of Damascus and some Philistine cities—in a desperate gamble for independence.

What followed was a tragic series of miscalculations that spelled the end of independent Israel—and indeed the possibility that any of the states in the Levant would ever be free to act independently as long as the Assyrian empire survived. Pekah and Rezin hoped to organize a broad, committed front of resistance to Assyria by all the states of the region. The coalition failed to materialize and Tiglath-pileser reacted in fury. After capturing Damascus, executing Rezin, and making his way down the Mediterranean coast, destroying potentially rebellious cities and ensuring that no help for the insurgents would be coming from Egypt, Tiglath-pileser set his sights with full force on the kingdom of Israel. Conquering most of its territories, destroying its main cities, and deporting part of its population, Tiglath-pileser brought Israel to its knees.

By the time of Tiglath-pileser's death in 727 BCE, most of the territory of the northern kingdom had been annexed directly to the Assyrian empire. They were then administratively divided into the provinces of Dor (along the northern coast), Megiddo (in the Jezreel valley and Galilee), and Gilead (in the Transjordanian highlands). A relief from the time of Tiglath-pileser III depicting the siege of a city named Gaazru—probably Gezer—indicates that the southern coastal plain of Israel did not escape the bitter fate of the northern provinces. All that was left of the northern kingdom was merely the hill country around the capital, Samaria. And so Tiglath-pileser could boast in a monumental inscription: "The land of Bit-Humria [i.e., the House of Omri], all of whose cities I leveled to the ground in my former campaigns . . . I plundered its livestock, and I spared only isolated Samaria."

The Assyrianization of the North

The new-style Assyrian empire under Tiglath-pileser was not content with mere territorial conquest. The Assyrians viewed all the lands, animals, resources, and peoples of the areas they had conquered as objects—as chattel—that could and should be moved or exploited to serve the best interests of the Assyrian state. Thus the Assyrians deployed a policy of deportation and repopulation on a grand scale. This policy had many objectives, which all served the goals of continuing imperial development. From a military point of view, the capture and removal of native villages had the effect of terrorizing and demoralizing the population and splitting them up to prevent further organized resistance. From an economic point of view, large-scale conscription into the imperial army brought new manpower and military technologies into a framework where the new recruits could be carefully watched. The forced resettlement of artisans in the centers of the Assyrian heartland boosted the trained human resources at the disposal of the Assyrian economy. And finally, the systematic resettling of new populations in empty or recently conquered territory was intended to expand the overall agricultural output of the empire.

Tiglath-pileser III initiated these processes almost immediately in the regions of the kingdom of Israel his armies had overrun. The number of deportees given by his annals amounts to 13,500 people. If it is not an exaggeration—as archaeological surveys in lower Galilee, indicating widespread depopulation, suggest—then the Assyrians deported a significant component of the rural population of these areas to Assyria.

The disastrous results of Tiglath-Pileser's initial assault can be seen at many sites. At Hazor, which is specifically mentioned in the Bible in relation to his campaign (2 Kings 15:29), the last Israelite city was destroyed and burned to ashes. There is clear archaeological evidence that in the days before the final Assyrian assault, the city's fortifications were reinforced—in vain, as events transpired. Wholesale destruction has also been traced at Dan and Beth-shean. But at Megiddo, the Assyrian intentions were somewhat different since it would become a new center of imperial administration. The domestic quarters were set on fire; collapsed, burnt buildings and crushed vessels tell the story of the last hours of the Israelite city. But the pillared buildings—the famous Megiddo stables—were left untouched and probably reused for a while. The Assyrians intended to rebuild the site for their own ends, and the fine stones in the stable structures proved to be an excellent source of building materials.

Megiddo provides the best evidence for the early stages of the Assyrian occupation. After the partial destruction of the last Israelite city, a short period of abandonment was followed by extensive rebuilding. The Assyrians made Megiddo the capital of their new province, covering former territories of the northern kingdom in the northern valleys and the hills of Galilee. Within a few decades, official documents refer to Megiddo as the seat of the governor. The focus of the new city, which was rebuilt in a totally new plan, was near the gate, where two palaces were built in typical Assyrian style. The rest of the city was laid out in a precise grid of parallel east-west and north-south streets forming rectangular blocks for domestic buildings—a method of city planning hitherto unknown in the Levant. In light of the radical changes, it is possible that new people, deported from other conquered areas of the Assyrian empire, were now settled there.

The End of the Kingdom

Hemmed into the immediate vicinity of Samaria, the rump kingdom of Israel proved to be little more than a tidbit to be gobbled up at the first opportunity by the ascendant Assyrian state. Yet Hoshea, the assassin of Pekah and the last king of Israel, having quickly offered tribute to Assyria, just as quickly began a disastrously dangerous plot. In the brief period of uncertainty about succession between the death of Tiglath-pileser III and the accession of Shalmaneser V, Hoshea reportedly sent secret word to one of the regional lords of the Egyptian delta, hoping that Egypt would now be ready to enter the anti-Assyrian fray. Taking the ultimate gamble, Hoshea ended his tribute payments to the new Assyrian king forthwith.

Who could have been surprised at what happened? Shalmaneser V immediately embarked on a campaign of liquidation. He reduced the countryside around Samaria and laid siege to the city itself. After a long siege, the city was stormed and at least part of its surviving population was marshaled off to concentration points from which they were eventually resettled in distant Assyrian domains. There is considerable debate among scholars whether Shalmaneser V survived to see the capture of Samaria or whether his successor, Sargon II, who came to the throne in 722 BCE, was responsible for the coup de grâce. In any event, it is from Sargon's chronicles that we have the fullest Assyrian account of what transpired:

> The inhabitants of Samaria, who agreed and plotted with a king hostile to me
> not to endure servitude and not to bring tribute to Assur and who did battle, I

TABLE FIVE

ISRAELITE KINGS FROM JEHU TO HOSHEA

KING	DATES*	BIBLICAL TESTIMONY	ASSYRIAN RECORDS	ARCHAEOLOGICAL FINDS
Jehu	842–814	Leads a coup against the Omrides and eliminates their family; demolishes the House of Baal at Samaria; confrontation with Aram-Damascus continues; prophet Elisha	Pays tribute to Shalmaneser III	Hazor and the north in the hands of Aram-Damascus; Megiddo deserted?
Jehoahaz	817–800**	Israel is defeated and Samaria besieged by Aram; prophet Elisha		
Joash	800–784	Defeats the Arameans and Israel recovers; attacks Jerusalem	Pays tribute to Adad-nirari III	Hazor in Israelite hands again?
Jeroboam II	788–747**	Defeats Damascus and extends the borders of the northern kingdom to their greatest extent; prophecies of Hosea and Amos		Unprecedented prosperity in the northern kingdom; large scale building activities at Hazor, Gezer, and Megiddo (stables and water system); Samaria ostraca and ivories; a seal carrying his name found at Megiddo

Zechariah	747	Reigns for six months, then killed in a coup		
Shallum	747	Reigns one month and killed in a coup		
Menahem	747–737	Pays tribute to the king of Assyria	Pays tribute to Tiglath-pilester III	
Pekahiah	737–735	Killed in a coup		
Pekah	735–732	Fights with Damascus against Ahaz of Judah; Tiglath-pileser III conquers the Galilee and the Jezreel Valley	Deposed by Tiglath-pileser III; Tiglath-pileser conquers the Galilee	Destruction of Israelite cities in the north
Hoshea	732–724***	Last king of Israel; Shalmaneser V king of Assyria besieges Samaria, takes it, and deports Israelites to Assyria	Installed by Tiglath-pileser III and pays tribute to him	

* According to the *Anchor Bible Dictionary*
** Includes years of coregency
*** Or 722 BCE

fought against them with the power of the great gods, my lords. I counted as spoil 27,280 people, together with their chariots, and gods, in which they trusted. I formed a unit with 200 of their chariots for my royal force. I settled the rest of them in the midst of Assyria. I repopulated Samaria more than before. I brought into it people from countries conquered by my hands. I appointed my commissioner as governor over them. And I counted them as Assyrians.

Sargon's account provides us with the number of the deportees from Samaria—though it is unclear whether it refers to the population of the capital and its immediate surroundings or to the total number taken from the kingdom over the preceding years. The Bible mentions some of the destinations—"Halah, on the Habor, the river of Gozan, and in the cities of Medes" (2 Kings 17:6). But the ultimate fate of most of them—the ten tribes of northern Israel—would never be known. In the beginning the deportees might have tried to preserve their identity, for instance by continuing Israelite forms of worship or giving Israelite names to their children. But they were soon Assyrianized and assimilated into the empire.

It was all over. Two stormy centuries had come to a catastrophic end. The proud northern kingdom and a significant part of its population were lost to history.

Deportees and Survivors

As they had probably done in resettling key sites in the north such as Megiddo with dependable subjects, the Assyrian authorities brought in new population groups to settle in the heartland of the Israelite highlands in place of deported Israelites: "And the king of Assyria brought people from Babylon, Cuthah, Avva, Hamath, and Sepharvaim, and placed them in the cities of Samaria instead of the people of Israel; and they took possession of Samaria, and dwelt in its cities" (2 Kings 17:24). A few historical and archaeological clues suggest that these new groups, from rebellious areas of southern Mesopotamia, were settled not only in Samaria but also in the particularly strategic area around Bethel—the old Israelite cult center—on the northern border of the still-independent kingdom of Judah. The biblical historian provides circumstantial testimony about this in the inclusion of Avvim as one of the towns of seventh century Judah in the area of Bethel (Joshua 18:23). This name probably relates to Avva, which is mentioned as one of the places of origin of the deportees. An Aramaic text mentions deportees who were settled in Bethel itself. In addition, a few seventh century cuneiform texts bearing Babylonian names that have been found in Gezer and its vicinity provide tangible evidence of the presence of these deportees in the southwestern territory of vanquished Israel, also near the border of Judah. Finally, Adam Zertal of Haifa University suggested that a special type of pottery carrying cuneiform-like signs, which is found at some sites in the highlands of Samaria, may also be related to these newly arrived groups.

But the population exchange was far from total. The gross number given in the Assyrian sources for both deportations—by Tiglath-pileser III from Galilee and by Sargon II from Samaria—is about forty thousand people. This comprises no more than a fifth of the estimated population of the northern kingdom west of the Jordan in the eighth century BCE. Tiglath-pileser III seems to have deported mainly the troublesome villagers of the hills of Galilee and the population of the main centers, such as Megiddo, and it seems that Sargon II deported mainly the aristocracy of Samaria, and possibly soldiers and artisans with skills that were needed in Assyria. As a result, most of the surviving Israelites were left on the land. In the hill country around the city of Samaria, which was destined to serve as the hub of the new Assyrian province of Samerina, the deportation was apparently minimal. The Assyrians had good economic reasons not to devastate the rich, oil-producing area. In the northern valleys, the Assyrians destroyed the Israelite administrative centers but left the rural population (which was basically Canaanite, Phoenician, and Aramean in tradition) unhurt—as long as they remained docile and contributed their share to the Assyrian tribute demands. Even the brutal Assyrian conquerors recognized that wholesale destruction and deportation of the rural population of Israel could have devastated the agricultural output of their new province, so when possible they opted for stability and continuity.

Indeed, surveys and excavations in the Jezreel valley confirm the surprising demographic continuity. And about half of the rural sites near Samaria continued to be occupied in subsequent centuries. We may even have a biblical reference to this demographic situation. A few years after the destruction of the northern kingdom, the Judahite king Hezekiah celebrated the Passover in Jerusalem. He reportedly "sent to all Israel and Judah, and wrote letters also to Ephraim and Manasseh, that they should come to the house of the Lord at Jerusalem, to keep the passover to the Lord the God of Israel" (2 Chronicles 30:1). Ephraim and Manasseh refer to the highlands of Samaria to the north of Judah. While the historicity of Chronicles may be questioned, Jeremiah also reports, about 150 years after the fall of the northern kingdom, that Israelites from Shechem, Shiloh, and Samaria came with offerings to the Temple in Jerusalem (Jeremiah 41:5).

The fact that a significant number of Israelites were still living in the hill country of Samaria, including the southern area of Bethel, alongside the new populations brought by the Assyrians would play a major role in the foreign policy of Judah and in the development of the biblical ideology of the seventh century BCE.

The Grim Lesson of the Kingdom of Israel

We can never know how reliable were the traditions, texts, or archives used by the biblical authors to compile their history of the kingdom of Israel. Their aims were not to produce an objective history of the northern kingdom but rather to provide a *theological explanation* for a history that was probably already well known, at least in its broad details. No matter what popular legends might have said about individual kings of Israel, the biblical authors judge each and every one of them negatively. The reigns of most merited only a few words of summation: such-and-such a king "did what was evil in the sight of the Lord; he did not depart from all the sins of Jeroboam son of Nebat." A noteworthy few—like Jeroboam I and the Omrides—were condemned in harsher words and stories. But even the best of the northern kings are still considered sinners: Jehoram, son of Ahab, is credited with removing the *massebah,* or cult monument, of Baal, and Jehu is praised for wiping out its worship, but at the same time, both are condemned for walking in the footsteps of "Jeroboam son of Nebat." Even Hoshea, the last king of Israel, who belatedly tried to break Israel away from the iron grip of Assyria, is judged in only a marginally milder way: "He did what was evil in the sight of the Lord yet not as the kings of Israel who were before him" (2 Kings 17:2). Hence, starting with the sins of Jeroboam, the Bible offers a story of doom foreseen.

The periods of prosperity that the kingdom of Israel enjoyed, and that were probably remembered for centuries through the monumental remains still visible in many of the north's cities, posed a serious theological problem for the later Judahite observers who compiled the books of Kings. If the northern kingdom was so evil, why didn't YHWH wipe it out while Jeroboam I was still in power, or immediately after his reign, still in the days of his own dynasty? Or at the latest, in the days of the Omrides, the lovers of Baal? If they were so evil, why did YHWH allow them to prosper? The Deuteronomistic historian found an elegant way of rationalizing the almost-two-century life of northern Israel by suggesting that its doom was postponed because YHWH found some merits even in the sinful monarchs of the northern kingdom. Seeing "the affliction of Israel," he could not resist saving it on a few occasions of great calamities.

There were undoubtedly competing, elaborate explanations of the rising and falling fortunes of the northern kingdom from the official priesthoods of the northern shrines of Dan and Bethel. It is only natural to assume that there were northern prophets—"who prophesy falsely," as the Bible might have put it—who were closer to the royal institutions in Samaria. This kind of material could not possibly have entered the Bible as we know it today. Had Israel survived, we might have received a parallel, competing, and very different history. But with the Assyrian destruction of Samaria and the dismantling of its institutions of royal power, any such competing histories were silenced. Though prophets and priests from the north very likely joined the flow of refugees to find shelter in the cities and towns of Judah, biblical history would henceforth be written by the winners—or at least the survivors—and it would be fashioned exclusively according to the late Judahite Deuteronomistic beliefs.

From the point of view of seventh century Judah, in full awareness of the terrible destruction that had been visited on the northern kingdom, the meaning of Israel's history was clear. It is described succinctly and eloquently in the eulogy for Israel after the description of the fall of Samaria. From the point of view of the Deuteronomistic historian the climax of the story of the northern kingdom is not in the days of Ahab or Jeroboam II, not even in the tragic end, but in the summary that tells the story of Israel's sins and God's retribution. This theological climax is inserted in the middle of the great drama, between the two calamities—immediately following the description of the capture of Samaria and the deportation of the Israelites and before the mention of the repopulation of Israel's land by foreign people:

> And this was so, because the people of Israel had sinned against the LORD their God, who had brought them up out of the land of Egypt from under the hand of Pharaoh king of Egypt, and had feared other gods and walked in the customs of the nations whom the LORD drove out before the people of Israel, and in the customs which the kings of Israel had introduced. And the people of Israel . . . built for themselves high places at all their towns, from watchtower to fortified city; they set up for themselves pillars and Asherim on every high hill and under every green tree; and there they burned incense on all the high places, as the nations did whom the LORD carried away before them. . . . They went after false idols, and became false, and they followed the nations that were round about them, concerning whom the LORD commanded them that they should not do like them. And they forsook all the commandments of the LORD their God, and made for themselves molten images of two calves; and they made an Asherah, and worshiped all the host of heaven, and served Baal. And they burned their sons and their daughters as offerings, and used divination and sorcery, and sold themselves to do evil in the sight of the LORD, provoking him to anger. Therefore the LORD was very angry with Israel, and removed them out of his sight; none was left but the tribe of Judah only. . . . When he had torn Israel from the house of David they made Jeroboam the son of Nebat king. And Jeroboam drove Israel from following the LORD and made them commit great sin. The people of Israel walked in all the sins which Jeroboam did; they did not depart from them, until the LORD removed Israel out of his sight, as he had spoken by all his servants the prophets. So Israel was exiled from their own land to Assyria until this day. (2 KINGS 17:7–23)

Of course, today, through the help of archaeological work and ecological studies, we can see that the end was inevitable. Israel was destroyed and Judah survived because in the grand scheme of Assyria's imperial designs, Israel—with its rich resources and productive population—was an incomparably more attractive target than poor and inaccessible Judah. Yet to an audience in Judah in the grim years after the Assyrian conquest of Israel, facing the threat of empire and foreign entanglements, the biblical story of Israel served as a hint, a warning of what could happen to *them*. The older and once powerful kingdom of Israel, though blessed with fertile lands and productive people, had lost its inheritance. Now, the surviving kingdom of Judah would soon act the part of a divinely favored younger brother—like Isaac, Jacob, or their own ancestral king David—eager to snatch up a lost birthright and redeem the land and the people of Israel.

PART THREE

Judah and the Making of Biblical History

[9]

The Transformation of Judah

(c. 930–705 BCE)

The key to understanding the passion and power of the Bible's great historical saga is a recognition of the unique time and place in which it was initially composed. Our story now approaches that great moment in religious and literary history, because it was only after the fall of Israel that Judah grew into a fully developed state with the necessary complement of professional priests and trained scribes able to undertake such a task. When Judah suddenly faced the non-Israelite world on its own, it needed a defining and motivating text. That text was the historical core of the Bible, composed in Jerusalem in the course of the seventh century BCE. And because Judah was the birthplace of ancient Israel's central scripture, it is hardly surprising that the biblical text repeatedly stresses Judah's special status from the very beginnings of Israel's history.

It was in the ancient Judahite capital of Hebron—in the cave of Machpelah—that the revered patriarchs and matriarchs were buried, as we read in the book of Genesis. It was Judah, among all of Jacob's sons, whose destiny was to rule over all the other tribes of Israel (Genesis 49:8). The Judahites' fidelity to God's commands was unmatched among other Israelite warriors; at the time of the invasion of Canaan, only they were said to have fully eradicated the idolatrous Canaanite presence from their tribal inheritance. It was from the rural Judahite village of Bethlehem that David,

Israel's greatest king and military leader, emerged onto the stage of biblical history. His reported heroic exploits and intimate relationship with God became important scriptural themes. Indeed, David's conquest of Jerusalem represented the final act of the drama of the conquest of Canaan. Jerusalem, now transformed into a royal city, became the site of the Temple, a political capital for the Davidic dynasty, and a sacred focus for the people of Israel through all eternity.

Despite Judah's prominence in the Bible, however, there is no archaeological indication until the eighth century BCE that this small and rather isolated highland area, surrounded by arid steppe land on both east and south, possessed any particular importance. As we have seen, its population was meager; its towns—even Jerusalem—were small and few. It was Israel, not Judah, that initiated wars in the region. It was Israel, not Judah, that conducted wide-ranging diplomacy and trade. When the two kingdoms came into conflict, Judah was usually on the defensive, forced to call in neighboring powers to come to its aid. Until the late eighth century, there is no indication that Judah was anything more than a marginal factor in regional affairs. In a candid moment the biblical historian quotes a fable in which he diminishes Judah to the status of the "thistle of Lebanon," as compared to Israel, the "cedar of Lebanon" (2 Kings 14:9). On the international scene, Judah seems to have been just a rather small and isolated kingdom that, as the great conquering Assyrian king Sargon II derisively put it, "lies far away."

But beginning in the late eighth century BCE, something extraordinary happened. A series of epoch-making changes, beginning with Israel's fall, suddenly altered the political and religious landscape. Judah's population swelled to unprecedented levels. Its capital city became a national religious center and a bustling metropolis for the first time. Intensive trade began with surrounding nations. Finally, a major religious reform movement—focused on the exclusive worship of YHWH in the Jerusalem Temple—started cultivating a revolutionary new understanding of the God of Israel. An analysis of the historical and social developments of the ninth and eighth centuries BCE in the Near East explains some of these changes. The archaeology of late monarchic Judah offers even more important clues.

Good Kings and Bad

There is no reason to doubt seriously the reliability of the biblical list of Davidic kings who ruled in Jerusalem over the two centuries that followed the time of David and Solomon. The books of Kings intricately interweave the histories of the northern and southern kingdoms into a single, composite national history, frequently referring to now-lost royal annals called "the Book of the Chronicles of the Kings of Judah" and "the Book of the Chronicles of the Kings of Israel." The accession dates of the kings of Judah are precisely correlated with those of the kings of Israel—as in a typical passage, from 1 Kings 15:9, that states, "In the twentieth year of Jeroboam king of Israel Asa began to reign over Judah." This system of cross-dating, which can be checked by external datable references to individual Israelite and Judean kings, has proved to be generally reliable and consistent—with a few slight chronological revisions for certain reigns and the addition of possible coregencies (see Figure 3, p. 20).

Thus we learn that eleven kings (all but one heirs of the Davidic dynasty) ruled in Jerusalem between the late tenth and mid–eighth century BCE. The reports of each reign are laconic. In no case is there the kind of dramatic, damning character portrayal seen in the biblical presentation of the northern king Jeroboam or the idolatrous house of Omri. But that is not to say that theology plays no role in the biblical description of the history of Judah. God's retribution was swift and crystal clear. When sinful kings ruled in Jerusalem and idolatry was rampant, we learn, they were punished and Judah experienced military setbacks. When righteous kings reigned over Judah and the people were faithful to the God of Israel, the kingdom prospered and expanded its territory. Unlike the northern kingdom, which is described in negative terms throughout the biblical text, Judah is basically good. Though the number of Judah's good and bad kings is almost equal, the length of their reigns is not. Good kings cover most of the history of the southern kingdom.

Thus as early as the days of Rehoboam, Solomon's son and successor, "Judah did what was evil in the sight of the Lord"; its people worshiped at high places "on every high hill" and imitated the practices of the nations (1 Kings 14:22–24). The punishment for this apostasy was quick and painful. The Egyptian pharaoh Shishak marched on Jerusalem in the fifth year of Rehoboam (926 BCE) and took away a heavy tribute from the treasures of the Temple and the palace of the Davidic kings (1 Kings 14:25–26). The lesson was not learned by Rehoboam's son Abijam, who "walked in all the sins which his father did before him; and his heart was not wholly true to the LORD his God" (1 Kings 15:3). The misfortunes of Judah continued with intermittent conflicts with the armies of the kingdom of Israel.

Matters took a turn for the better during the reign of Asa, who ruled in Jerusalem for forty-one years beginning in the late tenth century. Asa reportedly "did what was right in the eyes of the LORD, as David his father had done" (1 Kings 15:11). It is not surprising, therefore, that in his time Jerusalem was saved from the assault of Baasha, king of Israel. Asa appealed for help from the king of Aram-Damascus, who attacked Israel's far northern borders, thus forcing Baasha to withdraw his invasion force from the northern outskirts of Jerusalem.

The next king, Jehoshaphat (the first Hebrew monarch to bear a name compounded with a variant of the divine name YHWH: *Yeho + shaphat* = "YHWH has judged"), was praised for walking in the way of his righteous father, Asa. He ruled in Jerusalem for twenty-five years in the first half of the ninth century BCE, concluded peace with the kingdom of Israel, and joined it in successful offensive operations against Aram and Moab.

The kingdom of Judah experienced ups and downs through the following centuries, reaching a low point when Jehoshaphat's son Jehoram married into the sinful family of Ahab and Jezebel. Predictable misfortune resulted: Edom (long a dependency of Judah) rose up in revolt, and Judah lost rich agricultural territories to the Philistines in the western Shephelah. Even more serious were the bloody repercussions of the fall of the Omrides that rocked the royal palace in Jerusalem. Ahaziah—the son of Jehoram and the Omride princess Athaliah—was killed in the course of Jehu's coup. Back in Jerusalem, Athaliah, on hearing news of the death of her son and all her relatives at the hands of Jehu, ordered the liquidation of all the royal heirs of the house of David and took the throne herself. For six years a priest of the Temple named Jehoiada waited. When the time was ripe he publicly announced that a Davidic heir had been saved from Athaliah's carnage, and produced the boy Jehoash, son of Ahaziah from another wife. With the anointing of Jehoash as the rightful Davidic king, Athaliah was slain. The period of northern, Omride influence in the southern kingdom, in the course of which the cult of Baal was introduced to Jerusalem (2 Kings 11:18), came to a bloody end.

Jehoash reigned in Jerusalem for forty years and "did what was right in the eyes of the Lord all his days" (2 Kings 12:2). His most important act was the renovation of the Temple. In his time Hazael, king of Aram-Damascus, threatened Jerusalem. He left the city in peace only after demanding—and collecting—a crippling tribute from the Judahite king (2 Kings 12:18–19); but this was not as terrible as the destruction that Hazael spread in the northern kingdom.

The Judahite pendulum of good and bad kings—and sometime both mixed together—would continue. Amaziah, a moderately righteous king who "did what was right in the eyes of the Lord, yet not like David his father" (2 Kings 14:3), launched a successful war against Edom, only to be defeated and captured by the armies of the kingdom of Israel, which invaded the territory of Judah and broke down the wall of Jerusalem. And so the story continued, through the reigns of the righteous Azariah (also known as Uzziah), who expanded the borders of Judah in the south, and his son Jotham.

A dramatic turn for the worse came with the death of Jotham and the coronation of Ahaz (743–727 BCE). Ahaz is judged exceptionally harshly by the Bible, going far beyond the usual measure of apostasy:

> And he did not do what was right in the eyes of the LORD his God, as his father David had done, but he walked in the way of the kings of Israel. He even burned his son as an offering, according to the abominable practices of the nations whom the LORD drove out before the people of Israel. And he sacrificed and burned incense on the high places, and on the hills, and under every green tree. (2 KINGS 16:2–4)

The result was disastrous. The restive Edomites took Elath on the Gulf of Aqaba, and Rezin, the powerful king of Damascus, and his ally Pekah, king of Israel, went to war against Judah and laid siege to Jerusalem. With his back to the wall, King Ahaz appealed to Tiglath-pileser III, king of Assyria, for help, with gifts from the Temple: "And the king of Assyria hearkened to him; the king of Assyria marched up against Damascus, and took it, carrying its people captive to Kir, and he killed Rezin" (2 Kings 16:9). Judah was at least temporarily saved by the clever stratagem of a wicked king appealing to the mighty Assyrian empire.

But the time for a far-reaching religious change had come. The unending cycle of apostasy, punishment, and repentance was about to be broken. For Ahaz's son Hezekiah, who ruled in Jerusalem for twenty-nine years, embarked on a sweeping religious reform, restoring the purity and fidelity to YHWH that had been lacking since the days of King David. One of the strongest manifestations of the cult that was practiced in the countryside of Judah was the popularity of the high places—or open-air altars—which were rarely disturbed, even by the most righteous of kings. Like a mantra, the Bible recites a formula in the summary of the acts of every just king, that "the high places were not taken away"; the people of Judah continued to sacrifice and to burn incense on the high places. Hezekiah was the first to remove the high places as well as other objects of idolatrous worship:

> And he did what was right in the eyes of the LORD, according to all that David his father had done. He removed the high places, and broke the pillars, and cut down the Asherah. And he broke in pieces the bronze serpent that Moses had made, for until those days the people of Israel had burned incense to it; it was called Nehushtan. He trusted in the LORD the God of Israel; so that there was none like him among all the kings of Judah after him, nor among those who were before him. For he held fast to the LORD; he did not depart from following him, but kept the commandments which the LORD commanded Moses. And the LORD was with him; wherever he went forth, he prospered. (2 KINGS 18:3–7)

The biblical picture of Judah's history is therefore unambiguous in its belief that the kingdom had once been exceptionally holy but had sometimes abandoned the faith. Only the accession of Hezekiah was able to restore Judah's holiness.

Yet archaeology suggests quite a different situation—one in which the golden age of tribal and Davidic fidelity to YHWH was a late religious ideal, not a historical reality. Instead of a restoration, the evidence suggests that a centralized monarchy and national religion focused in Jerusalem took centuries to develop and was *new* in Hezekiah's day. The idolatry of the people of Judah was not a departure from their earlier monotheism. It was, instead, the way the people of Judah had worshiped for hundreds of years.

The Hidden Face of Ancient Judah

Until a few years ago, virtually all biblical archaeologists accepted the scriptural description of the sister states of Judah and Israel at face value. They portrayed Judah as a fully developed state as early as the time of Solomon and tried their best to produce archaeological proof of the building activities and effective regional administration of the early Judahite kings. Yet as we have shown, the supposed archaeological evidence of the united monarchy was no more than wishful thinking. And so it was also with the monuments attributed to the successors of Solomon. The identification of forts reportedly built by Solomon's son Rehoboam throughout Judah (according to 2 Chronicles 11:5–12) and the linking of the massive fortifications at the site of Tell en-Nasbeh north of Jerusalem with the defense works undertaken by the Judahite king Asa at the biblical city of Mizpah (1 Kings 15:22) proved to be illusory. Like the Solomonic gates and palaces, these royal building operations are now known to have taken place almost two hundred years after the reigns of those particular kings.

Archaeology shows that the early kings of Judah were not the equals of their northern counterparts in power or administrative ability despite the fact that their reigns and even accession dates are intertwined in the books of Kings. Israel and Judah were two different worlds. With the possible exception of the city of Lachish in the foothills of the Shephelah, there are *no* signs of elaborate regional centers within Judah on the scale of the northern sites of Gezer, Megiddo, and Hazor. Likewise, Judahite urban planning and architecture was far more rustic. Monumental building techniques— such as the use of ashlar masonry and Proto-Aeolic capitals that typified the elaborate Omride building style in the northern kingdom—did not appear in the south before the seventh century BCE. Even if royal structures of the house of David in Jerusalem (supposedly obliterated by later buildings) achieved some measure of impressiveness, if not grandeur, there is no evidence for monumental construction in the few towns and villages anywhere else in the southern hills.

Despite the long-standing contention that the opulent Solomonic court was the scene of a flourishing of belles lettres, religious thought, and history writing, evidence for widespread literacy is utterly lacking in Judah during the time of the divided monarchy. Not a single trace of supposed

TABLE SIX

JUDAHITE KINGS FROM REHOBOAM TO AHAZ

KING	DATES*	BIBLICAL EVALUATION	BIBLICAL TESTIMONY	EXTRABIBLICAL EVIDENCE
Rehoboam	931–914	Bad	First king of Judah; fortifies cities	Shishak's campaign
Abijam	914–911	Bad	Fights Jeroboam of Israel	
Asa	911–870	Good	Cleans Judah from foreign cults; fights Baasha of Israel with the assistance of the king of Damascus; builds two forts on the northern border of Judah	
Jehoshaphat	870–846**	Good	Fights the Arameans with Ahab and Moab with Jehoram; marries his son to an Omride princess	
Jehoram	851–843**	Bad	Edom revolts against Judah	Mentioned in the Tel Dan inscription?
Ahaziah	843–842	Bad	An Omride offspring; killed in the course of the Jehu coup in Israel	Mentioned in the Tel Dan inscription?
Athaliah	842–836	Bad	Murders many of the House of David; killed in a bloody coup	
Jehoash	836–798	Good	Renovates the temple; saves Jerusalem from Hazael; killed in a coup	

Amaziah	798–769	Good	Defeats Edom; attacked by Joash king of Israel	
Azariah (also known as Uzziah)	785–733**	Good	Secluded in leper's house; days of the prophet Isaiah	Two seals carry his name
Jotham	759–743**	Good	Pressed by the kings of Israel and Aram; days of Isaiah	
Ahaz	743–727**	Bad	Attacked by the kings of Israel and Aram; calls Tiglath-pileser III for help; days of Isaiah	Pays tribute to Tiglath-pileser III; prosperity in the Judahite hill country begins

* According to the *Anchor Bible Dictionary* and Galil's *The Chronology of the Kings of Israel and Judah*
** Includes years as co-regent

tenth century Judahite literary activity has been found. Indeed, monumental inscriptions and personal seals—essential signs of a fully developed
state—appear in Judah only *two hundred years after Solomon,* in the late
eighth century BCE. Most of the known ostraca and inscribed weight
stones—further evidence of bureaucratic record keeping and regularized
trade standards—appear only in the seventh century. Nor is there any evidence for mass production of pottery in centralized workshops or industrial production of oil for export until the same late period. The estimated
population figures show precisely how unequal Judah and Israel were. As
mentioned, archaeological surveys indicate that until the eighth century
the population of the Judahite highlands was about one-tenth that of the
highlands of the northern kingdom of Israel.

In light of these findings, it is now clear that Iron Age Judah enjoyed no
precocious golden age. David and his son Solomon and the subsequent
members of the Davidic dynasty ruled over a marginal, isolated, rural region, with no signs of great wealth or centralized administration. It did not
suddenly decline into weakness and misfortune from an era of unparalleled
prosperity. Instead it underwent a long and gradual development over
hundreds of years. David and Solomon's Jerusalem was only one of a number of religious centers within the land of Israel; it was surely not acknowl-
edged as the spiritual center of the entire people of Israel initially.

So far we have produced only negative evidence of what Judah was not.
Yet we do have a picture of what Jerusalem and its vicinity must have been
like at the time of David and Solomon and their early successors. That picture does not come from the Bible. It comes from the Tell el-Amarna
archive of Egypt in the Late Bronze Age.

The Faraway City-State in the Hills

Among the more than 350 cuneiform tablets from the fourteenth century
BCE discovered at the ancient Egyptian capital of Akhetaten, the modern
Tell el-Amarna, containing correspondence between the pharaoh of Egypt
and the kings of Asiatic states and petty rulers of Canaan, a group of six
tablets offers a unique insight on the royal rule and economic possibilities
in the southern highlands—precisely where the kingdom of Judah would
later arise. Written by Abdi-Heba, the king of Urusalim (the Late Bronze

Age name for Jerusalem), the letters reveal the character of his kingdom as a thinly settled highland region, loosely supervised from the royal citadel in Jerusalem.

As we now know from surveys and the recognition of repeated cycles of occupation throughout the millennia, Judah's distinctive society was determined in large measure by its remote geographical position, unpredictable rainfall, and rugged terrain. In contrast to the northern hill country with its broad valleys and natural overland routes to the neighboring regions, Judah was always marginal agriculturally and isolated from the main trade routes, offering any would-be ruler only meager opportunities for wealth. Its economy was concentrated around the self-sufficient production of the individual farming community or pastoral group.

A similar picture emerges from Abdi-Heba's correspondence. He controlled the highlands from the region of Bethel in the north to the region of Hebron in the south—an area of about nine hundred square miles, in conflict with neighboring rulers in the northern highlands (Shechem) and the Shephelah. His land was very sparsely populated, with only eight small settlements detected so far. The sedentary population of Abdi-Heba's territory, including those living in Jerusalem, probably did not exceed fifteen hundred people; it was the most thinly populated area of Canaan. But there were many pastoral groups in this remote highland frontier zone—possibly outnumbering the settled village population. We may assume that the main authority in the remote parts of Abdi-Heba's territory was in the hands of the outlaws known as Apiru, the bedouin-like Shosu, and the independent clans.

Abdi-Heba's capital, Urusalim, was a small highlands stronghold, located in the southeastern ridge of ancient Jerusalem, which would later be known as the city of David. No monumental buildings or fortifications from the fourteenth century BCE have been found there, and as suggested by the historian Nadav Naaman Abdi-Heba's capital was a modest settlement for the elite who ruled over the surrounding region's few agricultural villages and large number of pastoral groups.

We do not know the fate of the dynasty of Abdi-Heba and we do not have sufficient archaeological evidence to understand the changes that took place in Jerusalem in the transition from the Late Bronze to Early Iron Age. Yet from the larger perspective of environment, settlement patterns, and economy, nothing seems to have changed dramatically over the succeeding centuries. A few agricultural villages (admittedly increasing slightly in number) existed on the central plateau, pastoral groups continued to follow seasonal cycles with their flocks, and a tiny elite exerted nominal rule over all of them from Jerusalem. Of the historical David we can say almost nothing, except to note the uncanny similarity between the ragtag Apiru bands that threatened Abdi-Heba and the biblical tales of the outlaw chief David and his band of mighty men roaming in the Hebron hills and the Judean desert. But whether or not David conquered Jerusalem in the daring Apiru-like raid described in the books of Samuel, it seems clear that the dynasty he established represented a change in rulers but hardly altered the basic way that the southern highlands were ruled.

All this suggests that the institutions of Jerusalem—Temple and palace—did not dominate the lives of the rural population of Judah in anything close to the extent suggested by the biblical texts. Continuity with the past, not sudden political or religious innovations, was Judah's most obvious characteristic in the early centuries of the Iron Age. In fact, this is to be seen clearly even in the matter of religious practices, about which the later historians of the kingdom of Judah seem to be so singularly obsessed.

The Traditional Religion of Judah

The books of Kings are explicit in their description of the apostasy that brought so much misfortune to the kingdom of Judah. It is set out in typical detail in the report of Rehoboam's reign:

> And Judah did what was evil in the sight of the LORD, and they provoked him to jealousy with their sins which they committed, more than all that their fathers had done. For they also built for themselves high places, and pillars, and Asherim on every high hill and under every green tree; and there were also male cult prostitutes in the land. They did according to the abominations of the nations which the LORD drove out before the people of Israel. (1 KINGS 14:22–24)

Likewise at the time of King Ahaz, some two hundred years later, the nature of the sins seems to be substantially the same. Ahaz was a notorious apostate who walked in the way of the kings of Israel and even burned his son as an offering (2 Kings 16:2–4).

Biblical scholars have demonstrated that these are not arbitrary isolated pagan practices, but part of a complex of rituals to appeal to heavenly powers for the fertility and well-being of the people and the land. In their outward form they resembled the practices used by neighboring peoples to honor and gain the blessings of other gods. Indeed, the archaeological finds of clay figurines, incense altars, libation vessels, and offerings stands throughout Judah merely suggest that the practice of religion was highly varied, geographically decentralized, and certainly not restricted to worship of YHWH only in the Temple of Jerusalem.

Indeed, for Judah, with its relatively underdeveloped state bureaucracy and national institutions, religious rituals were carried out in two distinct arenas—sometimes working in concert, sometimes in open conflict. The first was the Temple in Jerusalem, about which there is abundant biblical description from various periods but (since its site was obliterated in later building operations) virtually no archaeological evidence. The second focus of religious practice was among the clans scattered throughout the countryside. There, complex networks of kinship relations dominated all phases of life, including religion. Rituals for the fertility of the land and the blessings of the ancestors gave people hope for the well-being of their families and sanctified their possession of their village fields and grazing lands.

Biblical historian Baruch Halpern and archaeologist Lawrence Stager have compared the biblical descriptions of clan structure with the remains of Iron Age settlements in the hill country and have identified a distinctive architectural pattern of extended family compounds, whose inhabitants probably performed rituals that were sometimes quite different from those in the Temple of Jerusalem. Local customs and traditions insisted that the Judahites inherited their houses, their land, and even their tombs from their God and their ancestors. Sacrifices were offered at shrines within domestic compounds, at family tombs, and at open altars throughout the countryside. These places of worship were rarely disturbed, even by the most "pious" and aggressive of kings. Thus it is no wonder that the Bible repeatedly notes that "the high places were not taken away."

The existence of high places and other forms of ancestral and household god worship was not—as the books of Kings imply—apostasy from an earlier, purer faith. It was part of the timeless tradition of the hill country settlers of Judah, who worshiped YHWH along with a variety of gods and goddesses known or adapted from the cults of neighboring peoples. YHWH, in short, was worshiped in a wide variety of ways—and sometimes pictured as having a heavenly entourage. From the indirect (and pointedly negative) evidence of the books of Kings, we learn that priests in the countryside also regularly burned incense on the high places to the sun, the moon, and the stars.

Since the high places were presumably open areas or natural hilltops, no definite archaeological traces of them have as yet been identified. So the clearest archaeological evidence of the popularity of this type of worship throughout the kingdom is the discovery of hundreds of figurines of naked fertility goddesses at every late monarchic site in Judah. More suggestive are the inscriptions found in the early eighth century site of Kuntillet Ajrud in northeastern Sinai—a site that shows cultural links with the northern kingdom. They apparently refer to the goddess Asherah as being the consort of YHWH. And lest it be assumed that YHWH's married status was just a sinful northern hallucination, a somewhat similar formula, speaking of YHWH and his Asherah, appears in a late-monarchic inscription from the Shephelah of Judah.

This deep-rooted cult was not restricted to the rural districts. There is ample biblical and archaeological information that the syncretistic cult of YHWH flourished in Jerusalem even in late monarchic times. The condemnations of various Judahite prophets make it abundantly clear that YHWH was worshiped in Jerusalem *together* with other deities, such as Baal, Asherah, the hosts of heaven, and even the national deities of the neighboring lands. From the biblical critique of Solomon (probably reflecting late monarchic realities), we learn of worship in Judah of Milcom of Ammon, Chemosh of Moab, and Ashtoreth of Sidon (1 Kings 11:5; 2 Kings 23:13). Jeremiah tells us that the number of deities worshiped in Judah equaled the number of its cities and that the number of altars to Baal in Jerusalem equaled the number of bazaar stalls in the capital (Jeremiah 11:13). Moreover, cult objects dedicated to Baal, Asherah, and the host of heaven were installed in the Temple of YHWH in Jerusalem. Ezekiel 8 describes in detail all the abominations practiced in the Temple in Jerusalem, including the worship of the Mesopotamian god Tammuz.

Thus the great sins of Ahaz and the other evil kings of Judah should not be seen as exceptional in any way. These rulers merely allowed the rural traditions to go on unhampered. They and many of their subjects expressed their devotion to YHWH in rites performed at countless tombs, shrines, and high places throughout the kingdom, with the occasional and subsidiary worship of other gods.

A Sudden Coming of Age

Through most of the two hundred years of the era of the divided monarchy, Judah remained in the shadows. Its limited economic potential, its relative geographical isolation, and the tradition-bound conservatism of its clans made it far less attractive for imperial exploitation by the Assyrians than the larger, richer kingdom of Israel. But with the rise of the Assyrian king Tiglath-pileser III (745–727 BCE) and Ahaz's decision to become his vassal, Judah entered a game with enormous stakes. After 720, with the conquest of Samaria and the fall of Israel, Judah was surrounded by Assyrian provinces and Assyrian vassals. And that new situation would have implications for the future almost too vast to contemplate. The royal citadel of Jerusalem was transformed in a single generation from the seat of a rather insignificant local dynasty into the political and religious nerve center of a regional power—both because of dramatic internal developments and because thousands of refugees from the conquered kingdom of Israel fled to the south.

Here archaeology has been invaluable in charting the pace and scale of Jerusalem's sudden expansion. As first suggested by Israeli archaeologist Magen Broshi, excavations conducted there in recent decades have shown that suddenly, at the end of the eighth century BCE, Jerusalem underwent an unprecedented population explosion, with its residential areas expanding from its former narrow ridge—the city of David—to cover the entire western hill (Figure 26). A formidable defensive wall was constructed to include the new suburbs. In a matter of a few decades—surely within a single generation—Jerusalem was transformed from a modest highland town of about ten or twelve acres to a huge urban area of 150 acres of closely packed houses, workshops, and public buildings. In demographic terms, the city's population may have increased as much as fifteen times, from about one thousand to fifteen thousand inhabitants.

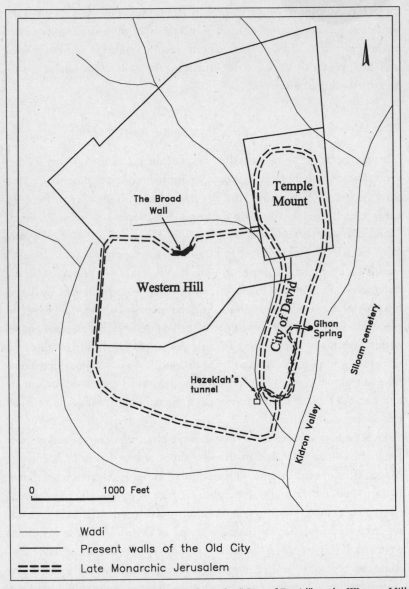

Figure 26: The expansion of Jerusalem from the "City of David" to the Western Hill

A similar picture of tremendous population growth emerges from the archaeological surveys in Jerusalem's agricultural hinterland. Not only were many farmsteads built at this time in the immediate environs of the city, but in the districts south of the capital, the formerly relatively empty countryside was flooded with new farming settlements, both large and small. Sleepy old villages grew in size and became, for the first time, real towns. In the Shephelah too, the great leap forward came in the eighth century, with a dramatic growth in the number and size of sites. Lachish—the most important city in the region—provides a good example. Until the eighth century it was a modest town; it was then surrounded by a formidable wall and transformed into a major administrative center. Likewise, the Beersheba valley in the far south witnessed the establishment of a number of new towns in the late eighth century. All in all, the expansion was astounding; by the late eighth century there were about three hundred settlements of all sizes in Judah, from the metropolis of Jerusalem to small farmsteads, where once there were only a few villages and modest towns. The population, which had long hovered at a few tens of thousands, now grew to around 120,000.

In the wake of Assyria's campaigns in the north, Judah experienced not only sudden demographic growth but also real social evolution. In a word, it became a full-fledged state. Starting in the late eighth century, the archaeological indications of mature state formation appear in the southern kingdom: monumental inscriptions, seals and seal impressions, and ostraca for royal administration; the sporadic use of ashlar masonry and stone capitals in public buildings; the mass production of pottery vessels and other crafts in central workshops, and their distribution throughout the countryside. No less important was the appearance of middle-sized towns serving as regional capitals and the development of large-scale industries of oil and wine pressing, which shifted from local, private production to state industry.

The evidence of new burial customs—mainly but not exclusively in Jerusalem—suggests that a national elite emerged at this time. In the eighth century some of the inhabitants of Jerusalem began to cut elaborate tombs in the rock of the ridges surrounding the city. Many are extremely elaborate, with gabled ceilings and architectural elements such as cornices and surmounting pyramids skillfully carved from the bedrock. There is no doubt that these tombs were used for the burial of nobility and high public officials, as indicated by a fragmentary inscription on one of the tombs in the village of Siloam in Jerusalem (to the east of the city of David), dedicated to "[. . .]yahu who is in charge of the House." It is not out of the realm of possibility that this was the tomb of Shebna (whose name may have been compounded with the divine name to become Shebnayahu), the royal steward whom Isaiah (22:15–16) condemns for his arrogance in hewing a tomb in the rock. Elaborate tombs are also found in a few places in the Shephelah, indicating a sudden accumulation of wealth and differentiation of social status in Jerusalem and in the countryside in the eighth century.

The question is, where did this wealth and apparent movement toward full state formation come from? The inescapable conclusion is that Judah suddenly cooperated with and even integrated itself into the economy of the Assyrian empire. Although King Ahaz of Judah started cooperating with Assyria even before the fall of Samaria, the most dramatic changes undoubtedly came after the collapse of Israel. The sudden growth of settlement far to the south in the Beersheba valley may hint that the kingdom of Judah took part in the intensification of the Arabian trade in the late eighth century under Assyrian domination. There is good reason to believe that new markets were opened to Judahite goods, stimulating intensified production of oil and wine. As a result, Judah went through an economic revolution, from a traditional system based on the village and clan to cash-cropping and industrialization under state centralization. Wealth began accumulating in Judah, especially in Jerusalem, where the kingdom's diplomatic and economic policies were determined and where the institutions of the nation were controlled.

The Birth of a New National Religion

Along with the extraordinary social transformation in the late eighth century BCE came an intense religious struggle that had a direct connection to the emergence of the Bible as we know it today. Before the crystallization of the kingdom of Judah as a fully bureaucratic state, religious ideas were diverse and dispersed. Thus, as we have mentioned, there was the royal cult in the Jerusalem Temple, there were the countless fertility and ancestor cults in the countryside, and there was the widespread mixing of the worship of YHWH with that of other gods. As far as we are able to tell from the archaeological evidence of the northern kingdom, there was a similar diversity of religious practice in Israel. Aside from memories of the strident preaching of figures like Elijah and Elisha, the anti-Omride puritanism of Jehu, and the harsh words of prophets like Amos and Hosea, there was never any concerted or long-lasting effort by the Israelite government to sanction the worship of YHWH alone.

But after the fall of Samaria, with the increasing centralization of the kingdom of Judah, a new, more focused attitude toward religious law and practice began to catch hold. Jerusalem's influence—demographic, economic, and political—was now enormous and it was linked to a new political and territorial agenda: the unification of all Israel. And the determination of its priestly and prophetic establishment to define the "proper" methods of worship for all the people of Judah—and indeed for those Israelites living under Assyrian rule in the north—rose accordingly. These dramatic changes in religious leadership have prompted biblical scholars such as Baruch Halpern to suggest that in a period of no more than a few decades in the late eighth and early seventh century BCE, the monotheistic tradition of Judeo-Christian civilization was born.

That is a big claim—to be able to pinpoint the birth of the modern religious consciousness, especially when its central scripture, the Bible, places the birth of monotheism hundreds of years earlier. But in this case too the Bible offers a retrospective interpretation rather than an accurate description of the past. Indeed, the social developments going on in Judah in the decades after the fall of Samaria offer a new perspective on how the traditional tales of wandering patriarchs and of a great national liberation from Egypt served the cause of religious innovation—the emergence of monotheistic ideas—within the newly crystallized Judahite state.

Sometime in the late eighth century BCE there arose an increasingly vocal school of thought that insisted that the cults of the countryside were sinful—and that YHWH alone should be worshiped. We cannot be sure where the idea originated. It is expressed in the cycle of stories of Elijah and Elisha (set down in writing long after the fall of the Omrides) and, more important, in the works of the prophets Amos and Hosea, both of whom were active in the eighth century in the north. As a result, some biblical scholars have suggested that this movement originated among dissident priests and prophets in the last days of the northern kingdom who were aghast at the idolatry and social injustice of the Assyrian period. After the destruction of the kingdom of Israel, they fled southward to promulgate their ideas. Other scholars have pointed to circles connected with the Temple of Jerusalem intent on exercising religious and economic control over the increasingly developed countryside. Perhaps both factors played a part in the close-packed atmosphere of Jerusalem after the fall of Samaria, when refugees from the north and Judahite priests and royal officials worked together.

Whatever its makeup, the new religious movement (dubbed the "YHWH-alone movement" by the iconoclastic historian Morton Smith) waged a bitter and continuing conflict with the supporters of the older, more traditional Judahite religious customs and rituals. It is difficult to assess their relative strength within the kingdom of Judah. Even though they seem to have been initially a small minority, they were the ones who later produced or influenced much of the biblical historiography that has survived. The moment was fortuitous for this; with the expansion of bureaucratic administration came a spread in literacy. For the first time the authority of written texts, rather than recited epics or ballads, had an enormous effect.

As should be abundantly clear by now, the passages in the books of Kings about the righteousness and sinfulness of the earlier kings of Judah reflects the ideology of the YHWH-alone movement. Had the supporters of the traditional modes of syncretistic worship won out in the end, we might have possessed an entirely different scripture—or perhaps none at all. For it was the intention of the YHWH-alone movement to create an unquestioned orthodoxy of worship—and a single, Jerusalem-centered national history. And it succeeded brilliantly in the crafting of what would become the laws of Deuteronomy and the Deuteronomistic History.*

Biblical scholars have usually emphasized the strictly religious aspects of

---

* It is important to stress that while some of the basic ideas that would later characterize Deuteronomy (and perhaps even an early version of a "national" history) may have been formulated in the late eighth century BCE, those ideas reached maturity only in the late seventh century BCE, when the texts of Deuteronomy and the Deuteronomistic History were compiled in their recognizable forms.

the struggle between the Jerusalem factions, but there is no doubt that their positions encompassed strong views on domestic and foreign policy as well. In the ancient world, as today, the sphere of religion could never be separated from the spheres of economics, politics, and culture. The ideas of the "YHWH-alone" groups had a territorial aspect—the quest for the "restoration" of the Davidic dynasty over all Israel, including the territories of the vanquished northern kingdom, where, as we have seen, many Israelites continued to live after the fall of Samaria. This would bring about the unification of all Israel under one king ruling from Jerusalem, the destruction of the cult centers in the north, and the centralization of the Israelite cult in Jerusalem.

It is easy to see why the biblical authors were so upset by idolatry. It was a symbol of chaotic social diversity; the leaders of the clans in the outlying areas conducted their own systems of economics, politics, and social relations—without administration or control by the court in Jerusalem. That countryside independence, however time-honored by the people of Judah, came to be condemned as a "reversion" to the barbarity of the pre-Israelite period. Thus, ironically, what was most genuinely Judahite was labeled as Canaanite heresy. In the arena of religious debate and polemic, what was old was suddenly seen as foreign and what was new was suddenly seen as true. And in what can only be called an extraordinary outpouring of retrospective theology, the new, centralized kingdom of Judah and the Jerusalem-centered worship of YHWH was read back into Israelite history as the way things should always have been.

King Hezekiah's Reforms?

It is difficult to know when the new, exclusivist theology first had a practical impact on the conduct of affairs in Judah; various reforms in the direction of YHWH-alone worship are mentioned in the books of Kings as early as the time of King Asa in the early ninth century BCE. But their historical reliability is questionable. One thing seems to be fairly clear: the accession of King Hezekiah to the throne of Judah in the late eighth century BCE was remembered by the authors of the books of Kings as an event without precedent.

As described in 2 Kings 18:3–7, the ultimate goal of Hezekiah's reform was the establishment of the exclusive worship of YHWH, in the only legitimate place for that worship—the Temple of Jerusalem. But Hezekiah's religious reforms are difficult to detect in the archaeological record. The evidence found for them, especially at two sites in the south—Arad and Beersheba—is disputed.* Baruch Halpern has therefore proposed that Hezekiah banned countryside worship but did not close the state temples in the kingdom's administrative centers. Yet there is no question that by the reign of King Hezekiah, a profound change had come over the land of Judah. Judah was now the center of the people of Israel. Jerusalem was the center of the worship of YHWH. And the members of the Davidic dynasty were the only legitimate representatives and agents of YHWH's rule on earth. The unpredictable course of history had elected Judah to a special status at a particularly crucial moment.

The most dramatic events were yet to come. In 705 BCE, the venerable Assyrian king Sargon II died, leaving his largely untested son Sennacherib to inherit his throne. Troubles in the east of the empire ensued, and the once invincible façade of Assyria seemed in danger of toppling. For many in Jerusalem, it must have seemed that YHWH had miraculously readied Judah—just in the nick of time—to fulfill its historic destiny.

---

* The excavator of both sites, the Israeli archaeologist Yohanan Aharoni, identified a small temple at Arad, which he believed was erected in the ninth century BCE, and suggested that its altar—if not the temple itself—was dismantled in the late eighth century. He linked this change to Hezekiah's reform. But other scholars have argued that Aharoni misdated the Arad temple. They contend that it was built only in the seventh century; in other words, it is post-Hezekiah in date. At Beersheba, some smoothly carved stone blocks of a large sacrificial altar were found dismantled and reused in late-eighth century storehouses, while others were tossed into the fill of the earthen fortification rampart of that city. Aharoni proposed that the dismantled altar had originally stood in a temple in the city, and that it was removed and dismantled in the course of Hezekiah's reform. Just to complicate things we should note that the famous Assyrian relief of the conquest of Lachish by Sennacherib in 701 BCE casts some doubt on the success of Hezekiah's policy of religious centralization. The relief depicts what seem to be cult items removed by Assyrian troops from the vanquished city, possibly indicating the continuing existence of a cult place there until late in the days of Hezekiah.

[10]

Between War and Survival

(705–639 BCE)

King Hezekiah's decision to rebel against the Assyrian empire was surely one of the most fateful decisions taken in the kingdom of Judah. To declare independence from the region's brutal imperial overlord—which had just two decades before violently dismantled the kingdom of Israel—required the political power and state organization to make far-reaching economic and military preparations. It also required a clear religious reassurance that despite the awesome might of the Assyrian empire, YHWH would ensure Judah's eventual military success. According to the Bible all of the terrible misfortunes of the kingdom of Israel were ascribed to the idolatrous ways of its people. Now, a purification of the cult of YHWH was the only way to ensure the victory of Judah and save its people from the fate of destruction and exile that had befallen the people of the sinful north.

And so, after the death of Sargon in 705 BCE, when the ability of the empire to control its faraway territories looked questionable, Judah entered an anti-Assyrian coalition, which was backed by Egypt (2 Kings 18:21; 19:9), and raised the banner of rebellion—with far-reaching, unantici- pated effects. Four years later, in 701 BCE, the new Assyrian king, Sen- nacherib, came to Judah with a formidable army. The books of Kings put a brave face on the outcome: Hezekiah was a great hero, an ideal king comparable only to David. He followed in the footsteps of Moses and cleansed Judah from all the transgressions of the past. Thanks to his piety, the Assyrians retreated from Judah without being able to conquer Jerusalem. As we will see, that is not the whole story, nor is the entire story provided in the Bible's subsequent account of the fifty-five-year reign of Manasseh, Hezekiah's son. In contrast to the ideal King Hezekiah, the books of Kings make Manasseh out to be the ultimate apostate, who spends his long career on the throne bringing back all the terrible abominations of the past.

Had we only the biblical materials to depend on, we would have no reason to question this black-and-white picture of Hezekiah's righteousness and Manasseh's apostasy. However, contemporary Assyrian sources and modern archaeology show that the Bible's theological interpretation of Judah's rebellion against Assyria hides quite a different historical reality.

A Great Miracle and Its Betrayal

The second book of Kings narrates the story of Hezekiah's great gamble in a set-piece drama in which a small cast of characters declaims formalized speeches on readily recognizable theological themes. This style of soliloquies performed for the benefit of the biblical reader is one of the hallmarks of the Deuteronomistic history. The use of religious rhetoric is transparent: the point of the biblical story is to show how the mere force of arms or balance of power has no effect on the outcome of nations at war. Behind it all is the guiding force of YHWH, who uses armies and battles to reward those who jealously and exclusively worship him—and to punish those who do not.

After the description of Hezekiah's religious behavior, the second book of Kings inserts a brief digression, in fact a repetition, on the fall of the northern kingdom and the deportation of its people because of their sins. It is meant to remind the reader of the contrast between the fates of sinful Israel and of righteous Judah. The situations are similar, the results are the opposite: Israel rebelled, Shalmaneser V laid siege to Samaria, the northern kingdom was destroyed, and its people deported; because of their sins, YHWH was not there to help them. Judah also rebelled, Sennacherib laid siege to Jerusalem, but Hezekiah was a righteous king, so Jerusalem was delivered and Sennacherib's army destroyed. The moral is clear even when the fearsome Assyrian forces invade the kingdom and conquer all its outlying fortified cities. Reliance on the power of YHWH is the only key to salvation.

The Assyrian commanders laying siege to Jerusalem challenged the bewildered defenders on the walls of the city, taunting the citizens and trying to break their spirit by questioning the wisdom of King Hezekiah and ridiculing his faith:

> "Hear the word of the great king, king of Assyria! Thus says the king: 'Do not let Hezekiah deceive you, for he will not be able to deliver you out of my hand. Do not let Hezekiah make you to rely on the LORD by saying, The LORD will surely deliver us, and this city will not be given into the hand of the king of Assyria.' Do not listen to Hezekiah; for thus says the king of Assyria: 'Make your peace with me and come out to me; then every one of you will eat of his own vine, and every one of his own fig tree, and every one of you will drink the water of his own cistern; until I come and take you away to a land like your own land, a land of grain and wine, a land of bread and vineyards, a land of olive trees and honey, that you may live, and not die. And do not listen to Hezekiah when he misleads you by saying, The LORD will deliver us. Has any of the gods of the nations ever delivered his land out of the hand of the king of Assyria? Where are the gods of Hamath and Arpad? Where are the gods of Sepharvaim, Hena, and Ivvah? Have they delivered Samaria out of my hand? Who among all the gods of the countries have delivered their countries out of my hand, that the LORD should deliver Jerusalem out of my hand?' " (2 KINGS 18:28–35)

Hezekiah is deeply shaken but the prophet Isaiah reassures him with a divine oracle:

> "Thus says the LORD: Do not be afraid because of the words that you have heard, with which the servants of the king of Assyria have reviled me. Behold, I will put a spirit in him, so that he shall hear a rumor and return to his own land; and I will cause him to fall by the sword in his own land. . . . Therefore thus says the LORD concerning the king of Assyria. He shall not come into this city or shoot an arrow there, or come before it with a shield or cast up a siege mound against it. By the way that he came, by the same he shall return. . . . For I will defend this city to save it, for my own sake and for the sake of my servant David." (2 KINGS 19:6–7,32–34)

And indeed, a miraculous deliverance comes that very night:

> And that night the angel of the LORD went forth, and slew a hundred and
> eighty-five thousand in the camp of the Assyrians; and when men arose early in
> the morning, behold, these were all dead bodies. Then Sennacherib king of As-
> syria departed, and went home, and dwelt at Nineveh. And as he was worship-
> ing in the house of Nisroch his god, Adrammelech and Sharezer, his sons, slew
> him with the sword. (2 KINGS 19:35–37)

The independence of Judah—and its fervent belief in the saving power of
YHWH against all enemies—was thus miraculously preserved.

But soon afterward, the story takes a bizarre turn with the assumption of
Hezekiah's son Manasseh to the Davidic throne. At a time when the power
of YHWH should have been evident to the people of Judah, the new king
Manasseh makes a sharp theological about-face:

> And he did what was evil in the sight of the LORD, according to the abominable
> practices of the nations whom the LORD drove out before the people of Israel.
> For he rebuilt the high places which Hezekiah his father had destroyed; and he
> erected altars for Baal, and made an Asherah, as Ahab king of Israel had done,
> and worshiped all the host of heaven, and served them. And he built altars in the
> house of the LORD, of which the LORD had said, "In Jerusalem will I put my
> name." And he built altars for all the host of heaven in the two courts of the
> house of the LORD. And he burned his son as an offering, and practiced sooth-
> saying and augury, and dealt with mediums and with wizards. He did much evil
> in the sight of the LORD, provoking him to anger. (2 KINGS 21:2–6)

Despite the belief that a sanctified Jerusalem now was—and had always
implicitly been—YHWH's seat on earth and that its purity guaranteed the
well-being of the people of Israel, Manasseh reportedly seduced his subjects "to do more evil than the nations had done whom the LORD destroyed before the people of Israel" (2 Kings 21:9).

What was going on here? What caused these dramatic reversals? Was
Hezekiah really so righteous and Manasseh so bad?

Preparing to Defy a World Empire

The books of Kings offer only the briefest background to the rebellion of Hezekiah, reporting that he "rebelled against the king of Assyria and would not serve him" (2 Kings 18:7). The books of Chronicles, written several centuries later and generally considered to be a less reliable historical source than the books of Kings, nevertheless offer more detailed information on the preparations that Hezekiah ordered in the months and weeks before the Assyrian attack. In this case, as we will see later, archaeology suggests that Chronicles may preserve reliable historical information that was not included in the books of Kings. In addition to creating storehouses for grain, oil, and wine, and stalls for flocks and cattle throughout the kingdom (2 Chronicles 32:27–29), Hezekiah expended great effort to ensure Jerusalem's water supply during a time of siege:

> When Hezekiah saw that Sennacherib had come and intended to fight against Jerusalem, he planned with his officers and his mighty men to stop the water of the springs that were outside the city; and they helped him. A great many people were gathered, and they stopped all the springs and the brook that flowed through the land, saying, "Why should the kings of Assyria come and find much water?" He set to work resolutely and built up all the wall that was broken down, and raised towers upon it, and outside it he built another wall; and he strengthened the Millo in the city of David. He also made weapons and shields in abundance. And he set combat commanders over the people, and gathered them together to him in the square at the gate of the city and spoke encouragingly to them, saying, "Be strong and of good courage. Do not be afraid or dismayed before the king of Assyria and all the horde that is with him; for there is one greater with us than with him. With him is an arm of flesh; but with us is the LORD our God, to help us and to fight our battles." And the people took confidence from the words of Hezekiah king of Judah. (2 CHRONICLES 32:2–8)

While there are only meager and disputed archaeological indications for Hezekiah's religious reforms throughout his kingdom, there is abundant evidence for both the planning and the ghastly outcome of his revolt against Assyria. Jerusalem was naturally a focus of operations. Defensive preparations are most clearly seen in excavations in the Jewish quarter of Jerusalem, where a fortification wall, more than twenty feet thick, was built to protect the recently established neighborhoods on the western hill. This defensive wall was apparently built at a time of national emergency; the western hill was already thickly settled and the private houses that lay along the planned course of the city fortifications had to be razed. The construction of this wall is apparently mentioned in the Bible, in Isaiah's remonstrance to the king that he coldheartedly "broke down the houses to fortify the wall" (Isaiah 22:10).

Another important mission was to provide the city with a secure supply of water in the case of a siege. The only perennial spring in Jerusalem—the Gihon—was located at the bottom of the Kidron valley, apparently outside the line of the city wall (Figure 26, p. 244). This was an old problem in Jerusalem, and there were earlier attempts to solve it by cutting a tunnel in the rock to give access to the spring from within the fortified town. Hezekiah had a much more ambitious idea: instead of providing means to go down to the water, he planned to bring the water inside. Indeed, we have a precious contemporary description of this extraordinary engineering project—originally hewn on the walls of the water tunnel itself. First discovered in the late nineteenth century near the southern end of the tunnel, this unique monumental inscription in Hebrew relates how a long subterranean tunnel was cut through bedrock to bring water from the Gihon spring to a protected pool within the city walls.

Almost a third of a mile in length, and wide and high enough for a person to walk through, it was cut in such a precise way that the difference in elevation between the spring and the pool is just over one foot in height. Indeed, the ancient text commemorating the work, now known as the Siloam inscription, captures the drama of the project as it neared completion, describing how the tunnel was cut by two teams hewing their way toward each other from opposite ends of the tunnel:

> . . . when the tunnel was driven through. And this was the way in which it was
> cut through: While [. . .] were still [. . .] axe[s], each man toward his fellow,
> and while there were still three cubits to be cut through, [there was heard] the
> voice of a man calling to his fellow, for there was an overlap in the rock on the
> right [and on the left]. And when the tunnel was driven through, the quarry-
> men hewed [the rock], each man toward his fellow, axe against axe; and the

water flowed from the spring toward the reservoir for 1,200 cubits, and the height of the rock above the head[s] of the quarrymen was 100 cubits.

How they managed to meet despite the fact that the tunnel is curved is a matter of debate. It was probably a combination of technical skills and intimate knowledge of the geology of the hill. Such an extraordinary achievement did not escape the attention of the biblical historians and represents one of the rare instances when a specific project of a Hebrew king can safely be identified archaeologically: "The rest of the deeds of Hezekiah, and all his might, and how he made the pool and the conduit and brought water into the city, are they not written in the Book of the Chronicles of the kings of Judah?" (2 Kings 20:20).

Outside Jerusalem, Hezekiah apparently took full advantage of the institutions of the state to make sure that his entire kingdom was prepared for war (Figure 27). The city of Lachish in the Shephelah was surrounded by a formidable fortification system consisting of a sloping stone revetment halfway down the slope of the mound and a massive brick wall at its crest. A huge bastion protected a six-chambered gate to the city and a large elevated podium inside the walls probably supported a palace, or a residency, for the royal commander of the city. In addition, a complex of buildings, similar to the Megiddo stables, was built near the palace to serve as stables or storehouses. A large shaft cut in the rock may have served as the upper part of a water system. Though some of these elements may have been built before Hezekiah, they were all there and reinforced by his time, ready to face the army of Sennacherib.

Never before had a Judahite king devoted so much energy and expertise and so many resources in preparations for war.* Archaeological finds suggest that the organization of provisions in Judah was centralized for the first time. The clearest evidence of this is a well-known class of large store jars found throughout the territory of Hezekiah's kingdom, mass produced in similar shape and size. Their most important and unique feature is the seal impressions stamped into the still wet clay of their handles before they

---

* If the list of the fortresses built by Rehoboam (2 Chronicles 11:5–12) has any historical basis, it may rather date to the time of Hezekiah, as some historians argue, attesting to the preparations in other centers in the countryside.

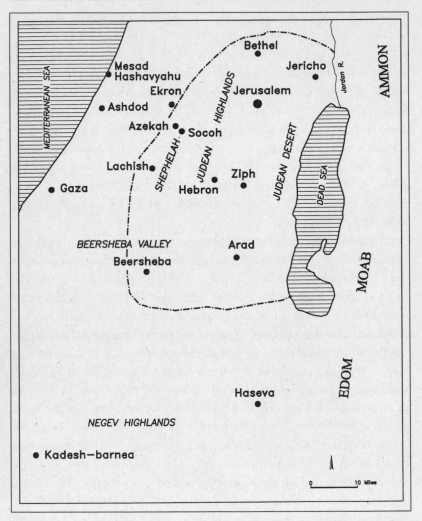

Figure 27: Main sites of late-monarchic Judah. The line marks the heartland of the kingdom in the late seventh century—the days of Josiah.

were fired. The impressions bear an emblem in the shape of a winged sun disc or scarab beetle, which is believed to be a royal Judahite insignia, and a short Hebrew inscription reading *lmlk* ("belonging to the king"). The royal reference is combined with the name of one of four cities: Hebron, Socoh, Ziph, and a still unidentified place designated by the letters *MMST*. The first three are known from other sources, while the last, enigmatic site may have been a title for Jerusalem or an unknown Judahite town.

Scholars have suggested several alternative explanations for the function of these jars: that they contained the products of royal estates; that they were used as official containers for tax collection and distribution of commodities; or that the seal impressions were merely the identifying marks of pottery workshops where official royal storage jars were manufactured. In any event, it is quite clear that they were associated with the organization of Judah before the rebellion against Assyria.

We cannot be sure of the geographical extent of Hezekiah's preparations for rebellion. The second book of Chronicles notes that he sent emissaries to Ephraim and Manasseh, that is, to the highland territory of the vanquished northern kingdom, to call the Israelites there to join him in Jerusalem for the celebration of the Passover (2 Chronicles 30:1,10,18). Most of this account is hardly historical; it was written from the point of view of an anonymous fifth or fourth century BCE writer, who presented Hezekiah as a second Solomon, uniting all Israel around the Temple in Jerusalem. But the hint of Hezekiah's interest in the territories of the former kingdom of Israel may not be a total invention, for Judah could now claim its leadership over the entire land of Israel. Even if so, however, claims are one thing and achievable goals are quite another. In the event, Hezekiah's revolt against Assyria proved to be a disastrous decision. Though untested, Sennacherib, at the head of a massive Assyrian invasion force, more than adequately proved his battlefield talents. King Hezekiah of Judah was no match for him.

What Really Happened? Sennacherib's Violent Revenge

Despite the biblical report of the miraculous deliverance of Jerusalem, contemporary Assyrian records provide a very different picture of the outcome of Hezekiah's revolt. The Assyrian account of Sennacherib's devastation of the Judahite countryside is presented concisely and coldly:

As to Hezekiah, the Judahite, he did not submit to my yoke. I laid siege to 46 of his strong cities, walled forts and to the countless small villages in their vicinity, and conquered them by means of well-stamped earth ramps, and battering rams brought thus near to the walls combined with the attack by foot soldiers, using mines, breeches as well as sapper work. I drove out of them 200,150 people, young and old, male and female, horses, mules, donkeys, camels, big and small cattle beyond counting, and considered them booty. Himself, I made prisoner in Jerusalem, his royal residence, like a bird in a cage. I surrounded him with earthwork in order to molest those who were leaving his city's gate. His towns which I had plundered, I took away from his country and gave them over to Mitinti, king of Ashdod, Padi, king of Ekron, and Sillibel, king of Gaza. Thus I reduced his country, but I still increased the tribute.

Though the stated number of captives may be a major exaggeration, the combined information from the Assyrian records and archaeological excavations in Judah adequately confirm the intensity of the systematic campaign of siege and pillage—first through Judah's richest agricultural areas in the Shephelah foothills and then up toward the highland capital. The devastation of the Judahite cities can be seen in almost every mound excavated in the Judean hinterland. The grim archaeological remains mesh perfectly with Assyrian texts recounting, for example, the conquest of the prominent Judahite city of Azekah, which was described as being "located on a mountain ridge, like pointed iron daggers without number reaching high to heaven." It was taken by storm, pillaged, and then ravaged.

This was not haphazard violence, meant only to terrify the Judahites into submission. It was also a calculated campaign of economic destruction, in which the sources of wealth of the rebellious kingdom would be taken away. The city of Lachish, located in Judah's most fertile agricultural area, was the single most important regional center of royal Judahite rule. It was the second most important city in the kingdom after Jerusalem. The pivotal role it played in the events of 701 BCE is hinted at in the biblical text (2 Kings 18:14,17; 19:8). Sennacherib's attack was meant to bring about its utter destruction. A vivid illustration of the Assyrian siege of this city is preserved in extraordinary detail on a large wall relief that once decorated the palace of Sennacherib at Nineveh, in northern Iraq (Figure 28). This re-

Figure 28: An Assyrian relief from the palace of Sennacherib at Nineveh, depicting the Conquest of the City of Lachish. *Drawn by Judith Dekel; courtesy of Professor David Ussishkin, Tel Aviv University.*

lief, about sixty feet long and nine feet high, was discovered in the 1840s by the British explorer Austen Henry Layard and was subsequently shipped to London, where it remains on display in the British Museum. Its original location on the wall of an inner chamber of Sennacherib's palace indicates the importance of the events it depicts. A short inscription reveals its subject: "Sennacherib, king of all, king of Assyria, sitting on his throne while the spoil from the city of Lachish passed before him."

This impressive Lachish relief narrates the whole horrible course of events in a single frame. It shows Lachish as an extremely well fortified city. A ferocious battle is being fought near the walls. The Assyrians constructed a siege ramp, on which they advance their heavily armored battering rams toward the fortification walls. The defenders of Lachish fight back desperately, trying to prevent the battering rams from approaching the wall. They hurl torches in an attempt to set the war machines on fire, while the Assyrians pour water on the battering rams. Assyrian archers standing behind the battering rams barrage the walls with arrows while the Judahite defenders shoot back. But all of the city's defensive preparations—and all the defenders' heroic fighting—are in vain. Captives are taken out of the gate, some of them dead, their lifeless bodies hoisted on spears. Booty is taken from the city, including the sacred vessels of its religious rituals. All the while Sennacherib sits with impassive majesty on a throne in front of his royal tent, not far from the Assyrian camp, overseeing the procession of captives and plunder taken from the houses and public buildings of the rebellious community.

Some scholars have questioned the accuracy of the details of this relief and have argued that this is self-serving imperial propaganda, not a reliable record of what happened in Lachish. But there is hardly a doubt that the relief deals with the specific city of Lachish and with the specific events of 701 BCE. Not only are the topography of the city and the local vegetation represented accurately; it is even possible to identify the precise vantage point of the artist who made the sketch for the relief. Furthermore, the archaeological excavations at Lachish have provided details about the location of the gate and the nature of the fortifications and the siege system that confirm the accuracy of the relief.

The British excavations at Lachish in the 1930s and the renewed dig of David Ussishkin on behalf of Tel Aviv University in the 1970s revealed independent dramatic evidence for the last hours of this great Judahite fortress. The Assyrian siege ramp, which is depicted in the relief, was identified and excavated. It is the only surviving example of such a siege structure from anywhere in the former lands of the Assyrian empire. It is not surprising that it was built on the most vulnerable side of the mound, where it is connected to a ridge; on all other sides the slopes are too steep to allow the construction of a ramp and the deployment of battering rams.

The archaeological finds from inside the city offer evidence for the desperate actions of the defenders. They erected a huge counter-ramp directly opposite the Assyrian ramp, but this last attempt by the defenders to prevent the Assyrians from breaching the wall was a failure. The city was burnt to the ground. Other finds provide evidence for the fierceness of the battle.

Hundreds of arrowheads were found at the foot of the city wall. Perforated boulders, some of them with remains of burnt ropes in the holes—apparently flung from the ramparts by the defenders in an attempt to destroy the siege machines—were retrieved near the point of the assault on the wall. A mass burial of about fifteen hundred people—men, women, and children—was uncovered in the caves on the western slopes of the mound, mixed with late eighth century pottery.

Another Biblical Perspective

Though the second book of Kings concentrates on the saving power of YHWH over Jerusalem and only laconically mentions the capture of "all the fortified cities of Judah" (2 Kings 18:13), other biblical texts disclose the horrors of the Assyrian campaign for those Judahites unfortunate enough to have been victims of Sennacherib's rampage in the countryside. These passages are to be found not in the Deuteronomistic History but in the prophetic works. Two contemporary witnesses—the prophets Isaiah and Micah—speak of the fear and grief that paralyzed Judah in the wake of the Assyrian advance. Isaiah, who was in Jerusalem at the time of the siege, vividly describes a military campaign that hit the area north of Jerusalem (10:28–32). And Micah, who was a native of the Shephelah from a town not far from Lachish, describes the numbed shock of the homeless survivors, blaming their misfortune on their own idolatry:

> Tell it not in Gath, weep not at all; in Beth-le-aphrah roll yourselves in the dust. Pass on your way, inhabitants of Shaphir, in nakedness and shame; the inhabitants of Zaanan do not come forth; the wailing of Beth-ezel shall take away from you its standing place. For the inhabitants of Maroth wait anxiously for good, because evil has come down from the LORD to the gate of Jerusalem. Harness the steeds to the chariots, inhabitants of Lachish; you were the beginning of sin to the daughter of Zion, for in you were found the transgressions of Israel. (MICAH 1:10–13)

The blow suffered by the Shephelah is also made abundantly clear in the results of archaeological surveys, which show that the region never recovered from Sennacherib's campaign. Even in the following decades, after the partial revival of Judah, the Shephelah was still sparsely inhabited. Both the

number of sites and the built-up area—on which all population estimates
are based—shrank to about a third of what they were in the late eighth
century. Some of the main towns were rebuilt, but many small towns, villages, and farmhouses were left in ruins. This fact is particularly significant
when we remember that in the eighth century, prior to the Assyrian assault,
the population of the Shephelah numbered about fifty thousand, almost
half the population of the entire kingdom.

Faith in YHWH alone did not save Hezekiah's territory against the
wrath of the Assyrians. Large parts of Judah were devastated and valuable
agricultural land in the Shephelah was given by the Assyrian victors to the
city-states of Philistia. Judah's territory shrank dramatically, Hezekiah was
forced to pay a heavy tribute to Assyria, and a significant number of Judahites were deported to Assyria. Only Jerusalem and the Judean hills immediately to the south of the capital were spared. For all the Bible's talk of
Hezekiah's piety and YHWH's saving intervention, Assyria was the only
victor. Sennacherib fully achieved his goals: he broke the resistance of
Judah and subjugated it. Hezekiah had inherited a prosperous state, and
Sennacherib destroyed it.

Picking Up the Pieces

In the aftermath of the failed rebellion against Assyria, Hezekiah's policy of
religious purification and confrontation with Assyria must have seemed to
many to have been a terrible, reckless mistake. Some of the rural priesthood may even have argued that it was, in fact, Hezekiah's blasphemous
destruction of the venerated high places and his prohibition against worshiping Asherah, the stars, moon, and other deities along with YHWH
that had brought such misfortune on the land. Having mainly the literature of the YHWH-alone camp, we do not know what their opponents
might have claimed. What we know is that in 698 BCE, three years after
Sennacherib's invasion, when Hezekiah died and his twelve-year-old son
Manasseh came to the throne, the religious pluralism in the (now considerably shrunken) countryside of Judah was restored. The second book of
Kings reports it in great denunciatory outrage. For the Deuteronomistic
historian, Manasseh was more than a run-of-the-mill apostate. He was described as the most sinful monarch that the kingdom of Judah had ever

seen (2 Kings 21:3–7). In fact, the book of Kings puts the blame for the "future" destruction of Jerusalem on his head (2 Kings 21:11–15).

There was obviously something more than theological considerations behind this switch in official religious policy. The kingdom's survival was in the hands of Manasseh and his closest advisers, and they were determined to revive Judah. That necessitated restoring a certain measure of economic autonomy to the countryside—still the greatest potential source of the kingdom's wealth. The revival of the once devastated rural areas could not be achieved without the cooperation of the networks of village elders and clans—and that meant allowing the worship at long-venerated local high places to resume. In a word, the cults of Baal, Asherah, and the host of heaven returned.

Even as he was compelled to be an obedient vassal, Manasseh apparently calculated correctly that the economic recuperation of Judah could be seen to be in the interest of Assyria. A prosperous Judah would be loyal to the empire and serve as an effective buffer against Egypt—Assyria's archenemy in the south. And the Assyrians may even have granted a contrite Judah most-favored-vassal status: a seventh century text reporting tribute given by south Levantine states to the Assyrian king indicates that Judah's tribute was considerably smaller than that paid by the neighboring, poorer Assyrian vassals Ammon and Moab.

Manasseh seems to have justified his Assyrian overlords' faith in him. A document from the time of Esarhaddon, who replaced Sennacherib on the throne in Assyria, mentions Manasseh among a group of twenty-two kings who were ordered to send building materials for a royal project at Nineveh. The next Assyrian king, Ashurbanipal, listed Manasseh among the kings who gave him gifts and helped him to conquer Egypt. Though the second book of Chronicles informs us that at a certain moment in his reign Manasseh was imprisoned by the Assyrians in Babylon (2 Chronicles 33:11), the circumstances and even historical reliability of that reported imprisonment are the subject of continuing debate. What is clear is that his long reign—fifty-five years—was a peaceful time for Judah. The cities and settlements established during his reign survived until the final destruction of Judah in the following century.

Archaeologically, it is not easy to distinguish the finds of the early seventh century from those of the second half of that century (see Appendix

E). Yet we know enough to argue that with the widespread devastation in the Shephelah (and the annexation of large tracts by the Philistine cities), the population of the Judean highlands grew. This was almost certainly due to the arrival of displaced Judahite refugees who fled from the desolated regions of the Shephelah. Agricultural production intensified around the capital. A dense system of farmsteads was built around Jerusalem and south of it, near Bethlehem, in the seventh century BCE. They were probably aimed at feeding the growing population of the metropolis.

But the most fascinating development in Judah during the seventh century is the demographic expansion of Judahite settlements into the arid zones to the east and south (Figure 27, p. 258). In the Judean desert, which was empty of permanent settlement during the eighth century, something extraordinary happened in the following decades. In the seventh century, groups of small sites were established in every ecological niche that was slightly better suited for cultivation than the rest of the desert: in the Buqeah valley halfway between Jerusalem and the Dead Sea, near Jericho, and along the western coast of the Dead Sea. In the Beersheba valley the number of sites grew far beyond that of the previous period. Between the eighth and the seventh centuries the built-up area and thus the population in this region grew by ten times. Could this development be related to Manasseh's policies?

That seems very likely. It is clear that until Sennacherib's campaign, the economy of the Judahite kingdom was well balanced by the different ecological niches of its territory: olive and vine orchards were grown mainly in the hill country, grain was grown primarily in the Shephelah, and animal husbandry was practiced mostly in the desert fringe in the south and east. When the Shephelah was handed over to the Philistine city-states, Judah lost its rich grain-producing lands in the west. At the same time the population that had to be fed in the remaining parts of the kingdom grew significantly. These pressures probably drove part of the population of Judah to the marginal areas of the kingdom, in a desperate attempt to compensate for the loss of the rich farmland of the Shephelah. Indeed, the exploitation of the arid zones could solve the problem. Estimates of the agricultural potential of the Beersheba valley in antiquity suggest that if production there was well organized, it alone could have supplied up to one quarter of the overall grain needs of Judah. But this could not have been done on such a large scale without the assistance of the state. It is therefore reasonable to assume that the expansion into the arid zones was inspired if not actually directed by Manasseh's new political and economic policies.

Arabian Caravans and Olive Oil

Manasseh's program went far beyond subsistence. He was intent on integrating Judah into the Assyrian world economy. The two main economic activities of Assyria in and around the region of Judah were trade in exotic luxury goods and incense from Arabia and the mass production and distribution of olive oil.

The Arabian trade was one of the main economic interests of Assyria and there is hardly a doubt that from the late eighth century it provided the empire with significant revenues. Assyria accordingly had a strong interest in the security of the desert roads leading northward from the Arabian peninsula to their termini on the Mediterranean coast. The Assyrian king Tiglath-pileser III counted Gaza, the traditional terminus of the desert roads, in one of his triumphal inscriptions "as the custom-house of Assyria" and he set his officials there to collect duties from the harbor, which served as an outlet for the overland caravan routes. Sargon II declared that he opened the border of Egypt to trade and mingled Assyrians and Egyptians. A number of Assyrian forts and administrative centers have indeed been uncovered in different places in the southern coastal plain, and a large fortified site, with remains of storehouses, has been excavated on the coast south of Gaza. The assemblage of animal bones excavated from Tell Jemmeh, another site near Gaza, shows a dramatic increase in the number of camels in the seventh century. A study of the bones by archaeozoologist Paula Wapnish suggests that these camels—all of mature age and therefore not part of a natural, locally raised flock—were probably used in the caravan trade.

The southernmost territories still controlled by the kingdom of Judah in the Beersheba valley, the Edomite highlands, and the southern coastal plain contained some of the most important caravan routes. They were areas that experienced unprecedented demographic growth in the seventh century. The first widespread occupation of the Edomite plateau took place at this time, under Assyrian domination. In fact, Edom emerged only then as a fully developed state, as a result of these developments.

The rich and varied archaeological finds from the vast area between Edom and Philistia indicate that Assyrians, Arabs, Phoenicians, and Edomites were involved in this thriving commercial activity. Judah under Manasseh was also a prominent participant. The wave of settlement in the Beersheba valley should be understood on this background. Judah may have been expanded even farther south along the trade routes. Two large seventh century forts have been excavated in the deep desert. The first is Kadesh-barnea on the western margin of the Negev highlands, about fifty miles to the southwest of Beersheba. The site commands the largest oasis on the important trade road from southern Palestine to the head of the Gulf of Aqaba and onward to Arabia. The second fort has recently been excavated in Haseva, a site located about twenty miles to the south of the Dead Sea on another route to the south. The finds at the two forts led the biblical historian Nadav Naaman to suggest that both were built in the early seventh century BCE under Assyrian auspices with the assistance of the local vassal states—and were manned by troops from Judah and Edom.

South Arabian inscriptions found in several sites in Judah supply conclusive evidence for the strong connections with Arabia at that time. This kind of evidence also comes from Jerusalem. Three ostraca with south Arabian script were uncovered in the city of David. Since they were carved on typical Judahite vessels—rather than on imported types—they probably attest to a resident Arabian population in Judah. And an otherwise typical seventh century Hebrew seal seems to carry a south Arabian name. In this connection several scholars have argued that Manasseh's wife Meshullemeth was an Arabian woman. Could this have been a diplomatic marriage aimed at strengthening Judah's commercial interests in the south? Could the Deuteronomistic tale of the queen of Sheba visiting Solomon in Jerusalem be inspired by the cultural contacts and economic ambitions of another Davidic king in the seventh century?

Arabian contact was not the only widened economic horizon. The Assyrians also monopolized and developed Levantine olive oil production.

Evidence for this comes from Tel Miqne, a site in the western Shephelah that is the location of ancient Ekron, one of the main cities of Philistia. A modest site in the centuries before the Assyrian takeover of the region, Ekron grew to be a huge olive oil production center in the early seventh century. Over a hundred olive oil presses were found there—more than in any other site in the history of the country. In fact, this is the most impressive olive oil production center known anywhere in the ancient Near East. The industrial zone covered about one-fifth of the area of the city. The annual capacity has been estimated at about a thousand tons.

The Ekron oil was apparently transported to both Assyria and Egypt—the two lands lacking the environment to grow olive orchards and to produce their own oil. But Ekron itself is not located in the classical olive-growing country in the hills. In fact, it is situated in typical, flat grain-growing land. It was apparently chosen as the center of production because of its location on the main road network of the southern coastal plain, halfway between the olive regions of the hill country and the main distribution centers on the coast to the west.

The groves that supplied the olives to the Ekron industry must have been located in the hill country of Judah and possibly also in the Assyrian province of Samaria to the north. As we have already mentioned, the seventh century marked the real industrialization of olive production in Judah and it was probably the major supplier of olives to the Ekron industry. The excavators of the site of Ekron—Trude Dothan, of the Hebrew University of Jerusalem, and Seymour Gitin of the Albright Institute—noting the significant numbers of typical Israelite horned incense altars in the buildings of the oil presses, have suggested that large numbers of Judahites might have been resettled in Philistia by Sennacherib as forced laborers. Thus another barrier—in however cruel and coldhearted a fashion—was broken between Judah and the outside world.

All these active, centrally planned economic initiatives required a further centralization of the Judahite state. Large-scale cultivation of olives and grapes and their industrial products required facilities for storage, transport, and efficient distribution. Moreover, extensive settlement and cultivation in arid areas required long-range planning. It was necessary to store large quantities of surplus grain in good years and to distribute them from the centers in years of severe drought. The archaeological evidence supports the assumption of heightened government involvement in all phases of life in Judah—to the extent that the number of seals, seal impressions, administrative ostraca, and official weights in seventh century Judahite levels far exceed the quantities found before.

Changing Fortunes

The Assyrian century—from the last years of the rule of Ahaz to the days of Hezekiah and Manasseh—is a fascinating case of dramatic policy swings in Judah. The three kings—grandfather, father, and son—flip-flopped between defiance and engagement with the Assyrian authorities and between syncretistic and puritan religious policies. Their treatment by the biblical historian also reflects these changes, but from an entirely different perspective. Ahaz was described as an idolater who cooperated with the Assyrians. Hezekiah is the complete reverse. There were no mistakes in his reign, only merits. He was an ideal king, who cleansed Judah from all the transgressions of the past. And unlike his sinful father, who willingly subjected Judah to Assyria, Hezekiah fought bravely and threw off the yoke of Assyria. The Assyrians threatened Jerusalem, but YHWH delivered the city miraculously. The story ends with no hint of future subjugation to Assyria, and except for one verse, there is no word on the catastrophic results of the Assyrian campaign in the Judahite countryside. Manasseh is also a mirror image of his father, but this time a negative one. He is the ultimate apostate, who wiped out the reforms and brought back all the abominations of the past.

What we get from the external sources and from archaeology is very different. The collapse of the northern kingdom raised dreams in Jerusalem of uniting the entire Israelite population under one capital, one Temple, and one dynasty. But in the face of the mighty Assyrians, there were only two options: forget the dream and cooperate with Assyria, or push for nationalistic policy and wait for the right moment to throw off the yoke of Assyria. High stakes call for extreme measures; the Assyrian century witnessed dramatic shifts between these two options.

Ahaz was a cautious and pragmatic king who saved Judah from the terrible fate of Israel and led it to prosperity. He understood that the only way to survive was to ally with Assyria, and as a loyal vassal he gained economic concessions from his overlords, and incorporated Judah into the Assyrian regional economy. Ahaz reigned over a period of unprecedented prosperity in Judah, when it first reached the stage of fully developed statehood. But by allowing traditional religious practices to flourish, he gained the wrath of the Deuteronomistic historian.

In his first years in power, Hezekiah had no choice but to follow in the footsteps of his father. But when the great Sargon died on the battlefield and Sennacherib came to power, Assyria faced rebellion in various parts of the empire. All of a sudden, the "restoration" of a Pan-Israelite state looked realistic, especially with the expected assistance from Egypt. Hezekiah launched a religious reform that served to justify the uprising and rouse the population to support it. But the revolt against Assyria proved to be a reckless decision that resulted in disaster.

When Manasseh came to the throne, power in Jerusalem returned to the moderate camp. Since he was only twelve years old at that time, there can hardly be a doubt that the coup in Jerusalem was preplanned. Manasseh turned the wheel back to the days of Ahaz. His long rule marks a complete triumph of the pragmatic, syncretistic camp. He opted for cooperation with Assyria and reintegrated Judah into the Assyrian regional economy. Like a phoenix rising from the ashes, Judah started to recover from the trauma of Sennacherib's campaign.

The prophets and sages of the YHWH-alone movement must have been terribly frustrated at this turn of events. All the former achievements of their hero Hezekiah in destroying the sin of idolatry and challenging the foreign empire were wiped out—first by Sennacherib's brutal armies and then by Hezekiah's own son. If Hezekiah might have been considered Israel's potential savior, his son Manasseh was the devil for them. There are indications in the biblical narrative that civil unrest occasionally flared up in Judah. The specific incidents behind the report that Manasseh "shed very much innocent blood, till he had filled Jerusalem from one end to another" (2 Kings 21:16), are unknown, but we can imagine that the king's opponents might have tried to seize power. Little wonder, then, that when the Deuteronomists won over the power in Judah a short while after Man-

TABLE SEVEN
JUDAHITE KINGS FROM HEZEKIAH TO JOSIAH

KING	DATES*	BIBLICAL EVALUATION	BIBLICAL TESTIMONY	EXTRABIBLICAL EVIDENCE	ARCHAEOLOGICAL EVIDENCE
Hezekiah	727–698	Righteous	Religious reform; rebels against Assyria; Jerusalem delivered	Sennacherib devastates Judah—annals and the Lachish relief in Nineveh	Jerusalem grows dramatically; a new wall in Jerusalem; the Siloam Tunnel; the Siloam cemetery; fortifications at Lachish; prosperity in the Beersheba valley; destruction in Lachish and other sites; evidence for literacy
Manasseh	698–642	Most wicked	Great apostate; sheds lots of innocent blood	Pays tribute to Assyria	Demographic growth in the Beer-sheba valley and Judean desert; construction of the Kadesh-barnea fort? Judah takes part in olive oil production at Ekron; growing evidence of literacy
Amon	641–640	Bad	Killed in a coup		
Josiah	639–609	Most righteous	Great religious reform; takes Bethel; killed by Pharaoh Necho		Continuous prosperity in Beer-sheba valley; recovery in the Shephelah; aniconism in seals and seal impressions

* According to the *Anchor Bible Dictionary*

asseh's death and set out to write the history of the kingdom, they settled the account. They portrayed Manasseh as the wickedest of all kings and the father of all apostates.

Nearing the Climax

Manasseh's success in transforming Judah from the wasteland left by Sennacherib into a highly developed state in the Assyrian empire brought great wealth to some and social dislocation and uncertainty to many. As Baruch Halpern first pointed out, with the influx of refugees from the north after the fall of Samaria, the reorganization of the countryside under Hezekiah, and the second torrent of refugees from the desolation of the Shephelah by Sennacherib, many of the traditional clan attachments to particular territories had been forever destroyed. In the countryside, economies of scale— needed to produce the enormous quantities of olives for pressing and grain for distribution—benefited those who could organize the machinery of trade and agricultural production far more than those who labored in the fields. To whatever extent the surviving clans could claim an unbroken chain of inheritance on their fields, villages, and hilltops, the effects of war, population change, and intensified royal economic planning may have encouraged many to dream of a past golden age—real or imagined—when their ancestors were settled securely in well-defined territories and enjoyed the divine promise of eternal peace and prosperity on their land.

Soon will come the climax of the story. Manasseh died in the year 642 BCE and was succeeded by his son Amon. According to the second book of Kings, Amon "did what was evil in the sight of the Lord, as Manasseh his father had done" (2 Kings 21:20). Within two years a coup d'état broke out in Jerusalem, during which Amon was assassinated. In horror, the "people of the land"—apparently the social and economic elite of Judah—slew the conspirators and placed Amon's eight-year-old son Josiah on the throne. Josiah would reign in Jerusalem for thirty-one years and be praised as the most righteous king in the history of Judah, rivaling the reputation of even David himself. And during his reign the "YHWH-alone" camp would once more come into power.

This time, too, their passionate religious convictions and single-minded vision of the power of YHWH to protect Judah and the Davidic dynasty against all earthly opponents would founder on the hard realities of history. But this time they would leave behind them a brilliant testament that would keep their ideas alive. Their great monument would be a timeless collection of Hebrew texts expressing their view of history and their hopes for the future. That collective saga would be the unshakable foundation for the Hebrew Bible we know today.

A Great Reformation

(639–586 BCE)

The reign of King Josiah of Judah marks the climax of Israel's monarchic history—or at least it must have appeared that way at the time. For the author of the Deuteronomistic History, Josiah's reign marked a metaphysical moment hardly less important than those of God's covenant with Abraham, the Exodus from Egypt, or the divine promise to King David. It is not just that King Josiah is seen in the Bible as a noble successor to Moses, Joshua, and David: the very outlines of those great characters—as they appear in the biblical narrative—seem to be drawn with Josiah in mind. Josiah is the ideal toward which all of Israel's history seemed to be heading. "Before him there was no king like him, who turned to the LORD with all his heart and with all his soul and with all his might, according to all the law of Moses; nor did any like him arise after him," reports 2 Kings 23:25 in a level of praise shown for no other biblical king.

A sixteenth-generation lineal descendant of King David, Josiah came to the throne at age eight in the violent aftermath of his father's assassination in Jerusalem. Of his early life, we know very little. Stories of his teenage religious awakening reported in 2 Chronicles 34:3 are almost certainly biographical idealizations after-the-fact. But during his thirty-one-year reign over the Kingdom of Judah, Josiah was recognized by many as the greatest hope for national redemption, a genuine messiah who was destined to restore the fallen glories of the house of Israel. Because of—or in accordance with—the tenets of a law book miraculously "discovered" in the Temple in Jerusalem, he embarked on a campaign to root out every trace of foreign or syncretistic worship, including the age-old high places in the countryside. He and his puritan forces did not even stop at the traditional northern border of his kingdom but continued northward to Bethel, where the hated Jeroboam had established a rival temple to that of Jerusalem—and where (so the prophecy of 1 Kings 13:2 related) a Davidic heir named Josiah would someday burn the bones of the north's idolatrous priests.

Josiah's messianic role arose from the theology of a new religious movement that dramatically changed what it meant to be an Israelite and laid the foundations for future Judaism and for Christianity. That movement ultimately produced the core documents of the Bible—chief among them, a book of the Law, discovered during renovations to the Jerusalem Temple in 622 BCE, the eighteenth year of Josiah's reign. That book, identified by most scholars as an original form of the book of Deuteronomy, sparked a revolution in ritual and a complete reformulation of Israelite identity. It contained the central features of biblical monotheism: the exclusive worship of one God in one place; centralized, national observance of the main festivals of the Jewish Year (Passover, Tabernacles); and a range of legislation dealing with social welfare, justice, and personal morality.

This was the formative moment in the crystallization of the biblical tradition as we now know it. Yet the narrative of Josiah's reign concentrates almost entirely on the nature of his religious reform and its reported geographical extent. Little is recorded of the larger historical events that were unfolding in the areas around Judah and how they may have influenced the rise of the Deuteronomistic ideology. An examination of the contemporary historical sources and archaeological finds may help us to understand how Josiah, this otherwise forgotten king, who ruled over a tiny kingdom under the shadow of the world's great powers, would—consciously or unwittingly—become the patron of the intellectual and spiritual movement that produced some of the Bible's major ethical teachings and its unique vision of Israel's history.

An Unexpected Discovery in the Temple

This momentous chapter in the political and spiritual life of Judah began with the accession of the young prince Josiah as king in 639 BCE. It seemed to mark a turning point in the Bible's view of the ups-and-downs of "evil" and "righteous" kings in the history of Judah. For Josiah was a faithful successor of David, who "did what was right in the eyes of the LORD, and walked in all the way of David his father, and he did not turn aside to the right hand or to the left" (2 Kings 22: 2).

According to the Bible, that righteousness led Josiah to decisive action. In his eighteenth year of rule—622 BCE—Josiah commanded the high priest Hilkiah to use public funds to renovate the House of the God of Israel. The renovations led to the dramatic surfacing of a text, found by the high priest in the Temple and read to the King by his secretary Shaphan. Its impact was enormous, for it suddenly and shockingly revealed that the traditional practice of the cult of YHWH in Judah had been wrong.

Josiah soon gathered all the people of Judah to conclude a solemn oath to devote themselves entirely to the divine commandments detailed in the newly discovered book.

> And the king went up to the house of the LORD, and with him all the men of Judah and all the inhabitants of Jerusalem, and the priests and the prophets, all the people, both small and great; and he read in their hearing all the words of the book of the covenant which had been found in the house of the LORD. And the king stood by the pillar and made a covenant before the LORD, to walk after the LORD and to keep his commandments and his testimonies and his statutes, with all his heart and all his soul, to perform the words of this covenant that were written in this book; and all the people joined in the covenant." (2 KINGS 23:2–3).

Then, in order to effect a thorough cleansing of the cult of YHWH, Josiah launched the most intense puritan reform in the history of Judah. His first targets were the idolatrous rites being practiced in Jerusalem, even within the Temple itself:

> And the king commanded Hilkiah, the high priest, and the priests of the second order, and the keepers of the threshold, to bring out of the temple of the LORD

all the vessels made for Baal, for Asherah, and for all the host of heaven; he burned them outside Jerusalem in the fields of the Kidron and carried their ashes to Bethel. And he deposed the idolatrous priests whom the kings of Judah had ordained to burn incense in the high places at the cities of Judah and round about Jerusalem; those also who burned incense to Baal, to the sun, and the moon, and the constellations, and all the host of the heavens. And he brought out the Asherah from the house of the LORD, outside Jerusalem, to the brook Kidron, and burned it at the brook Kidron, and beat it to dust and cast the dust of it upon the graves of the common people. And he broke down the houses of the male cult prostitutes, which were in the house of the LORD, where women wove hangings for the Asherah. (2 KINGS 23: 4–7)

He eradicated the shrines of foreign cults, notably the shrines that had reportedly been established under royal patronage in Jerusalem as early as the time of Solomon:

And he defiled Topheth, which is in the valley of the sons of Hinnom, that no one might burn his son or his daughter as an offering to Molech. And he removed the horses that the kings of Judah had dedicated to the sun, at the entrance to the house of the LORD, by the chamber of Nathan-melech the chamberlain, which was in the precincts; and he burned the chariots of the sun with fire. And the altars on the roof of the upper chamber of Ahaz, which the kings of Judah had made, and the altars which Manasseh had made in the two courts of the house of the LORD, he pulled down and broke in pieces, and cast the dust of them into the brook of Kidron. And the king defiled the high places that were east of Jerusalem, to the south of the mount of corruption, which Solomon the king of Israel had built for Ashtoreth the abomination of the Sidonians, and for Chemosh the abomination of Moab, and for Milcom the abomination of the Ammonites. And he broke in pieces the pillars, and cut down the Asherim, and filled their place with the bones of men. (2 KINGS 23: 10–14)

Josiah also put an end to the sacrificial rituals conducted by the rural priesthood who conducted their rites at the scattered high places and shrines throughout the countryside. "And he brought all the priests out of the cities of Judah, and defiled the high places where the priests had burned incense, from Geba to Beersheba" (2 Kings 23:8).

The old scores were being settled one by one. Next was the great "sin of

Jeroboam" at the idolatrous altar at Bethel, where he fulfilled the biblical prophecy that one day a righteous king named Josiah would see that it was destroyed:

> Moreover the altar at Bethel, the high place erected by Jeroboam the son of Nebat, who made Israel to sin, that altar with the high place he pulled down and he broke in pieces its stones, crushing them to dust; also he burned the Asherah. And as Josiah turned, he saw the tombs there on the mount; and he sent and took the bones out of the tombs, and burned them upon the altar, and defiled it, according to the word of the LORD which the man of God proclaimed, who had predicted these things. Then he said, "What is yonder monument that I see?" And the men of the city told him, "It is the tomb of the man of God who came from Judah and predicted these things which you have done against the altar at Bethel." And he said, "Let him be; let no man move his bones." So they let his bones alone, with the bones of the prophet who came out of Samaria. (2 KINGS 23:15–18)

Josiah did not stop at Bethel, and the purge continued farther north:

> And all the shrines also of the high places that were in the cities of Samaria, which kings of Israel had made, provoking the LORD to anger, Josiah removed; he did to them according to all that he had done at Bethel. And he slew all the priests of the high places who were there, upon the altars, and burned the bones of men upon them. Then he returned to Jerusalem. (2 KINGS 23:19–20)

Even as he battled idolatry, Josiah instituted national religious celebrations:

> And the king commanded all the people, "Keep the passover to the LORD your God, as it is written in this book of the covenant." For no such passover had been kept since the days of the judges who judged Israel, or during all the days of the kings of Israel or of the kings of Judah; but in the eighteenth year of King Josiah this passsover was kept to the LORD in Jerusalem. (2 KINGS 23:21–23)

In retrospect, the biblical description of the religious reform of Josiah in 2 Kings 23 is not a simple record of events. It is a carefully crafted narrative that contains allusions to all the great personalities and events of Israel's history. Josiah is implicitly compared to Moses, the great liberator and leader of the first Passover. He is also modeled after Joshua and David the great conquerors—and he follows the example of Solomon, the patron of the Temple in Jerusalem. The story of Josiah's reformation also redresses the evils of the past. The sins of the northern kingdom are also called to mind as Josiah succeeds in destroying Jeroboam's altar at Bethel, the cult center of the kingdom of Israel, which had competed with Jerusalem for so long. Samaria is there, with its high places, and the bitter memories of its destruction are evoked. The entire history of Israel had now reached a turning point. After centuries of wrongdoing, Josiah had arisen to overturn the sins of the past and lead the people of Israel to redemption through a proper observance of the Law.

What Was the "Book of the Law"?

The discovery of the book of the Law was an event of paramount significance to the subsequent history of the people of Israel. It was regarded as the definitive law code given by God to Moses at Sinai, whose observance would ensure the survival of the people of Israel.

As early as the eighteenth century, biblical scholars noted the clear similarities between the description of the book of the Law found in the Temple and the book of Deuteronomy. The specific and direct parallels between the contents of Deuteronomy and the ideas expressed in the biblical account of Josiah's reform clearly suggest that both shared the same ideology. Deuteronomy is the only book of the Pentateuch that asserts it contains the "words of the covenant" that all Israel must follow (29:9). It is the only book that prohibits sacrifice outside "the place which the Lord your God will choose" (12:5), while the other books of the Pentateuch repeatedly refer, without objection, to worship at altars set up throughout the land. Deuteronomy is the only book to describe the national Passover sacrifice in a national shrine (16:1–8). And while it is evident that there are later additions included in the present text of the book of Deuteronomy, its main outlines are precisely those that are observed by Josiah in 622 BCE in Jerusalem *for the first time.*

The very fact that a written law code suddenly appeared at this time meshes well with the archaeological record of the spread of literacy in Judah. Although the prophet Hosea and King Hezekiah were associated with ideas that are similar to those contained in Deuteronomy, the report of the appearance of a definitive written text and its public reading by the king accords with the evidence for the sudden, dramatic spread of literacy in seventh-century Judah. The discovery of hundreds of personal signet seals and seal impressions inscribed in Hebrew from this era attests to the extensive use of writing and written documents. As we have mentioned, such relatively widespread evidence of literacy is an important indication that Judah reached the level of a fully developed state in this period. It hardly had the capability of producing extensive biblical texts before.

In addition, scholars have pointed out that the literary form of the covenant between YHWH and the people of Israel in Deuteronomy is strikingly similar to that of early seventh-century Assyrian vassal treaties that outline the rights and obligations of a subject people to their sovereign (in this case, Israel and YHWH). Furthermore, as the biblical historian Moshe Weinfeld has suggested, Deuteronomy shows similarities to early Greek literature, in expressions of ideology within programmatic speeches, in the genre of blessing and cursing, and in the ceremonies for the foundation of new settlements. To sum up, there is little doubt that an original version of Deuteronomy is the book of the Law mentioned in 2 Kings. Rather than being an old book that was suddenly discovered, it seems safe to conclude that it was written in the seventh century BCE, just before or during Josiah's reign.

A Rising Pharaoh and a Dying Empire

In order to understand why the book of Deuteronomy took the form it did—and why it had such obvious emotional power—we need first to look at the international scene of the last decades in the history of Judah. A review of the historical and archaeological sources will show how major changes in the balance of power throughout the entire region were central factors in the shaping of biblical history.

By the time the eight-year-old prince Josiah ascended to the throne of Judah in 639 BCE, Egypt was experiencing a great political renaissance in which images of its remote past—and of the great conquering founders— were used as powerful symbols to enhance Egyptian power and prestige throughout the region. Starting in 656 BCE, Psammetichus I, the founder of the Twenty-sixth Dynasty, had thrown off the imperial overlordship of the Assyrian empire and later expanded his rule over much of the area in the Levant that the great pharaoh Ramesses II had controlled in the thirteenth century BCE.

The key to this Egyptian renaissance was, first of all, the sudden and precipitous decline of Assyria in the closing decades of the seventh century BCE. The precise date and cause of the collapse of Assyrian power, after more than a hundred years of unquestioned world dominance, are still debated by scholars. Yet Assyrian power clearly began to decline near the end of the reign of the last great Assyrian king, Ashurbanipal (669–627 BCE), due to the pressure of the mounted nomadic Scythian tribes on the northern borders of the empire and from continuous conflicts with the subject peoples of Babylonia and Elam on the east. After the death of Ashurbanipal, Assyrian rule was further challenged by a revolt in Babylonia in 626 and by the eruption of a civil war in Assyria itself three years later, in 623 BCE.

Egypt was an immediate beneficiary of Assyrian weakness. Pharaoh Psammetichus I, founder of the Twenty-sixth Dynasty, ruling from the Nile Delta city of Sais, succeeded in uniting the local Egyptian aristocracy under his leadership. During his reign from 664 to 610 BCE, the Assyrian forces withdrew from Egypt and left much of the Levant to be controlled by the Egyptians. The Greek historian Herodotus, who is an important source for the events of this period, recounts (in a story embellished with many legendary details) how Psammetichus marched north and laid a twenty-nine-year-long siege to the city of Ashdod on the Mediterranean coast. Whatever the truth of that report, archaeological finds at sites along the coastal plain indeed seem to indicate a growing Egyptian influence in the late seventh century. In addition, Psammetichus boasts in a contemporary inscription that he controlled the Mediterranean coast as far north as Phoenicia.

The Assyrians' retreat from their former possessions in the coastal plain and in the territory of the former northern kingdom of Israel appears to have been peaceful. It is even possible that Egypt and Assyria reached some sort of an understanding, according to which Egypt inherited the Assyrian provinces to the west of the Euphrates in exchange for a commitment to provide Assyria with military support. In any case, the five-centuries-long Egyptian dream to reestablish their Canaanite empire was fulfilled. The Egyptians regained control of agricultural wealth and international routes of trade in the rich lowlands. Yet as in the time of the great conquering pharaohs of the New Kingdom, the relatively isolated inhabitants of the highlands—now organized as the kingdom of Judah—were relatively unimportant to the Egyptians. And so, at least in the beginning, they were largely left to themselves.

A New Conquest of the Promised Land

The withdrawal of the Assyrians from the northern regions of the land of Israel created a situation that must have seemed, in Judahite eyes, like a long-expected miracle. A century of Assyrian domination had come to an end; Egypt was interested mainly in the coast; and the wicked northern kingdom of Israel was no more. The path seemed open for a final fulfillment of Judahite ambitions. Finally it seemed possible for Judah to expand to the north, take over the territories of the vanquished northern kingdom in the highlands, centralize the Israelite cult and establish a great, Pan-Israelite state.

Such an ambitious plan would require active and powerful propaganda. The book of Deuteronomy established the unity of the people of Israel and the centrality of their national cult place, but it was the Deuteronomistic History and parts of the Pentateuch that would create an epic saga to express the power and passion of a resurgent Judah's dreams. This is presumably the reason why the authors and editors of the Deuteronomistic History and parts of the Pentateuch gathered and reworked the most precious traditions of the people of Israel: to gird the nation for the great national struggle that lay ahead.

Embellishing and elaborating the stories contained in the first four books of the Torah, they wove together regional variations of the stories of the patriarchs, placing the adventures of Abraham, Isaac, and Jacob in a world strangely reminiscent of the seventh century BCE and emphasizing the dominance of Judah over all Israel. They fashioned a great national epic of liberation for all the tribes of Israel, against a great and dominating pharaoh, whose realm was uncannily similar in its geographical details to that of Psammetichus.

In the Deuteronomistic History, they created a single epic of the conquest of Canaan, with the scenes of the fiercest battles—in the Jordan val-

ley, the area of Bethel, the Shephelah foothills, and the centers of former Israelite (and lately Assyrian) administration in the north—precisely where
their new conquest of Canaan would have to be waged. The powerful and
prosperous northern kingdom, in whose shadow Judah had lived for more
than two centuries, was condemned as an historical aberration—a sinful
breakaway from the true Israelite heritage. The only rightful rulers of all Israelite territories were kings from the lineage of David, especially the pious
Josiah. Bethel, the great cult center of the northern kingdom, which Josiah
took over, was strongly condemned. "Canaanites," that is, all non-Israelite
inhabitants, were also disparaged, with a strict prohibition against intermarriage of Israelites with foreign women, which, according to the
Deuteronomistic History and the Pentateuch, would only lure the people
into idolatry. Both those policies were probably related to the practical
challenge of expanding into parts of the Land of Israel where large numbers
of non-Israelites had been settled by the Assyrians, especially the southern
regions of the former northern kingdom, around Bethel.

It is impossible to know if earlier versions of the history of Israel were
composed in the time of Hezekiah or by dissident factions during the long
reign of Manasseh, or if the great epic was composed entirely during
Josiah's reign. Yet it is clear that many of the characters described in the
Deuteronomistic History—such as the pious Joshua, David, and
Hezekiah and the apostate Ahaz and Manasseh—are portrayed as mirror
images, positive and negative, of Josiah. The Deuteronomistic History was
not history writing in the modern sense. It was a composition simultane-
ously ideological and theological.

In the seventh century BCE, for the first time in the history of ancient
Israel, there was a popular audience for such works. Judah had become a
highly centralized state in which literacy was spreading from the capital
and the main towns to the countryside. It was a process that had apparently
started in the eighth century, but reached a culmination only in the time of
Josiah. Writing joined preaching as a medium for advancing a set of quite
revolutionary political, religious, and social ideas. Despite its tales of apostasy and the disloyalty of Israel and its monarchs, despite its cycles of sin,
retribution, and redemption, with all its calamities of the past, the Bible offers a profoundly optimistic history. It promised its readers and listeners
they would be participants in the story's happy ending—when their own

King Josiah would purge Israel from the abominations of its neighbors, redeem its sins, institute general observance of the true laws of YHWH, and take the first steps to make the legendary kingdom of David a reality.

Revolution in the Countryside

Josiah's were clearly messianic times. The Deuteronomistic camp was winning and the atmosphere in Jerusalem must have been one of exceptional exhilaration. But the lesson of the transition from the righteous Hezekiah to the sinful Manasseh had not been forgotten. Josiah's reformers surely faced opposition. So the time would also have been one for education and social reform. In that connection, it is important to note that the book of Deuteronomy contains ethical laws and provisions for social welfare that have no parallel anywhere else in the Bible. Deuteronomy calls for the protection of the individual, for the defense of what we would call today human rights and human dignity. Its laws offer an unprecedented concern for the weak and helpless within Judahite society:

> If there is among you a poor man, one of your brethren, in any of your towns within your land which the LORD your God gives you, you shall not harden your heart or shut your hand against your poor brother, but you shall open your hand to him, and lend him sufficient for his need, whatever it may be. (DEUTERONOMY 15: 7–8)

> You shall not pervert the justice due to the sojourner or to the fatherless, or take a widow's garment in pledge; but you shall remember that you were a slave in Egypt and the LORD your God redeemed you from there; therefore I command you to do this. (DEUTERONOMY 24: 17–18)

This was not to be a matter of mere charity, but a consciousness that grew out of the shared perception of nationhood, now strongly reinforced by the historical saga of Israel, codified in text. The rights of family land were to be protected by prohibition against the moving of ancient boundary stones (19:14) and the inheritance rights of wives rejected by their husbands were secured (21:15–17). Farmers were instructed to give the tithe to the poor every third year (14:28–29); resident aliens were protected from discrimination (24:14–15). Slaves were to be freed after six years of servitude (15:12–15).

These are only a few examples of the wide range of personal legislation that was meant to override the traditional injustices and inequalities of everyday life.

The functioning of government was also addressed, with a clear intention to limit the power of the leaders of Judahite society to exploit their positions for their own interest or oppress the population at large:

> You shall appoint judges and officers in all your towns which the LORD your God gives you, according to your tribes; and they shall judge the people with righteous judgment. You shall not pervert justice; you shall not show partiality; and you shall not take a bribe, for a bribe blinds the eyes of the wise and subverts the cause of the righteous. (16:18–19)

Even the king was to be subject to the laws of the covenant and it is clear that the authors of Deuteronomy had both the sins of the kings of Israel and the righteousness of Josiah in mind:

> One from among your brethren you shall set as king over you; you may not put a foreigner over you, who is not your brother. Only he must not multiply horses for himself, or cause the people to return to Egypt in order to multiply horses, since the LORD has said to you, "You shall never return that way again." And he shall not multiply wives for himself, lest his heart turn away; nor shall he greatly multiply for himself silver and gold. And when he sits on the throne of his kingdom, he shall write for himself in a book a copy of this law, from that which is in the charge of the Levitical priests; and it shall be with him, and he shall read in it all the days of his life, that he may learn to fear the LORD his God, by keeping all the words of this law and these statutes, and doing them; that his heart may not be lifted up above his brethren, and that he may not turn aside from the commandment, either to the right hand or to the left; so that he may continue long in his kingdom, he and his children, in Israel. (17:15–20)

Perhaps the single most evocative archaeological artifact seemingly exemplifying this new consciousness of individual rights was discovered in 1960 at a fortress of the late seventh century BCE known to archaeologists as Mesad Hashavyahu, located on the Mediterranean coast south of modern Tel Aviv (Figure 27, p. 258). Inside the ruins of this fortress were fragments of imported Greek pottery that testify to the probable presence of Greek mercenary soldiers there. To judge from the Yahwistic names that appear on ostraca found at the site, there were also Judahites at the fortress, some of them working in the surrounding fields and some serving as soldiers and officers. One of the workers composed an outraged appeal to the commander of the garrison, written in ink on a broken pottery sherd. This precious Hebrew inscription is perhaps the earliest archaeological evidence that we possess of the new attitude and the new rights offered by the Deuteronomic law:

> May the official, my lord, hear the plea of his servant. Your servant is working at the harvest. Your servant was in Hasar-asam. Your servant did his reaping, finished and stored [the grain] a few days ago before stopping. When your servant had finished his reaping and had stored it a few days ago, Hoshayahu son of Shabay came and took your servant's garment. When I had finished my reaping, at that time, a few days ago, he took your servant's garment. All my companions will testify for me, all who were reaping with me in the heat of the sun—they will testify for me that this is true. I am guiltless of an infraction. (So) please return my garment. If the official does not consider it an obligation to return your servant's garment, then have pity upon him and return your servant's garment. You must not remain silent when your servant is without his garment.

Here was a personal demand that the law be observed, despite the difference in social rank between the addressee and the petitioner. A demand of rights by one individual against another is a revolutionary step away from the traditional Near Eastern reliance solely on the power of the clan to ensure its members' communal rights.

This is a single example, preserved by chance, in the ruins of a site far from the center of Judah. Yet its significance is clear. The laws of Deuteronomy stand as a new code of individual rights and obligations for the people of Israel. They also served as the foundation for a universal social code and system of community values that endure—even today.

Archaeology and the Josianic Reforms

Although archaeology has proved invaluable in uncovering the long-term social developments that underlie the historical evolution of Judah and the birth of the Deuteronomistic movement, it has been far less successful in providing evidence for Josiah's specific accomplishments. The temple of

Bethel—Josiah's primary target in his campaign against idolatry—has not yet been located and only one contemporary Judahite temple outside Jerusalem has so far been discovered. Its fate during Josiah's program of religious centralization is unclear.*

Likewise, seals and seal impressions of late-monarchic Judahite officials and dignitaries provide only *possible* evidence for Josiah's reforms. Though earlier Judahite seals had featured icons related to astral cult—images of stars and the moon that appear to be sacred symbols—in the late seventh century most of the seals include only names (and sometimes floral decoration), conspicuously lacking iconic decorations. Artistic styles in other regions such as Ammon and Moab evidence a similar shift, which may be related to the general spread of literacy throughout the region, but none is as pronounced as Judah's, which may possibly reflect the influence of Josiah's reform in insisting that the imageless YHWH was the only legitimate focus of veneration and in discouraging the worship of the heavenly powers in visible form.

Other evidence, however, seems to suggest that Josiah failed to stop the veneration of graven images, since figurines of a standing woman supporting her breast with her hands (generally identified with the goddess Asherah) have been found in abundance within private dwelling compounds at all major late-seventh century sites in Judah. Thus, at least on a household level, this popular cult seems to have continued despite the religious policy emanating from Jerusalem.

How Far Did Josiah's Revolution Go?

The extent of Josiah's territorial conquests has so far been only roughly determined by archaeological and historical criteria (see Appendix F). Although the sanctuary at Bethel has not been discovered, typical seventh-century Judahite artifacts have been found in the surrounding re-

---

* This temple was excavated at the fortress of Arad in the south. According to the excavator Yohanan Aharoni, the temple went out of use in the late seventh/early sixth century, when a new fortification wall was built over it. This apparently signified the temple's closure or abandonment, close to the time of Josiah's reforms. However, other scholars question this dating and are not so certain that the Arad temple ceased to function in this period, as Josiah apparently would have wished.

gion. It is possible that Josiah expanded farther north in the direction of Samaria (as suggested in 2 Kings 23:19), but as yet no clear archaeological evidence has been found.

In the west, the fact that Lachish was re-fortified and that it again served as a major Judahite fort is probably the best evidence that Josiah continued to control the areas of the Shephelah revived by his grandfather Manasseh. But Josiah could hardly expand farther west, into areas that were important for Egyptian interests. In the south, continuous Judahite occupation suggests that Josiah controlled the Beersheba valley and possibly the forts farther south, which had been established a few decades earlier by Manasseh, under Assyrian domination.

Basically, the kingdom under Josiah was a direct continuation of Judah under Manasseh's rule. Its population probably did not exceed seventy-five thousand, with relatively dense occupation of the rural areas in the Judean hill country, a network of settlements in the arid zones of the east and south, and a relatively sparse population in the Shephelah. It was in many ways a densely settled city-state, as the capital held about 20 percent of the population. Urban life in Jerusalem reached a peak that would be equaled only in Roman times. The state was well organized and highly centralized as in the time of Manasseh. But in terms of its religious development and literary expression of national identity, the era of Josiah marked a dramatic new stage in Judah's history.

Showdown at Megiddo

Josiah's life was cut short unexpectedly. In 610 BCE, Psammetichus I, the founder of the Egyptian Twenty-sixth Dynasty, died and was succeeded on the throne by his son Necho II. In the course of a military expedition northward, to help the crumbling Assyrian empire fight the Babylonians, a fateful confrontation occurred. The second book of Kings describes the event in laconic, almost telegraphic terms: "In his days Pharaoh Necho king of Egypt went up to the king of Assyria to the river Euphrates. King Josiah went to meet him; and Pharaoh Necho slew him at Megiddo, when he saw him" (2 Kings 23:29). The second book of Chronicles adds some detail, transforming the account of the death of Josiah into a battlefield tragedy:

Necho king of Egypt went up to fight at Carchemish on the Euphrates and Josiah went out against him. But he [Necho] sent envoys to him, saying, 'What have we to do with each other, king of Judah? I am not coming against you this day' . . . Nevertheless Josiah would not turn away from him . . . but joined battle in the plain of Megiddo. And the archers shot King Josiah; and the king said to his servants, "Take me away, for I am badly wounded." So his servants took him out of the chariot and carried him in his second chariot and brought him to Jerusalem. And he died, and was buried in the tombs of his fathers." (2 CHRONICLES 35:20–24)

Which of these accounts is more accurate? What do they say about the success or failure of Josiah's reforms? And what significance do the events at Megiddo have for the evolution of the biblical faith? The answer lies, once again, in the unfolding political situation in the region. Assyria's power continued to dwindle, and the ongoing Babylonian pressure on the heartland of the dying empire threatened to unbalance the ancient world and to endanger Egyptian interests in Asia. Egypt decided to intervene on the side of the Assyrians, and in 616 its army marched to the north. But this move did not stop the Assyrian collapse. The great Assyrian capital of Nineveh fell in 612, and the Assyrian court escaped to Haran in the west, an event that was recorded by the prophet Zephaniah (2:13–15). Two years later, in 610, when Psammetichus died and his son Necho came to the throne, the Egyptian forces in the north were forced to withdraw, and the Babylonians took Haran. In the following year, Necho decided to move and set off for the north.

Many biblical historians have preferred the version of 2 Chronicles, which describe a real battle between Necho and Josiah at Megiddo in 609. According to their view, Josiah had expanded over the entire hill country territories of the ex-northern kingdom, that is, he annexed the former Assyrian province of Samaria. He then extended his rule farther north to Megiddo, where he built a great fort on the east of the mound. He made Megiddo a northern, strategic outpost of the growing Judahite state. Some scholars proposed that his goal was to side with the Babylonians against Assyria by blocking the advance of Necho in the narrow pass that leads to Megiddo. Some even argued that the passage in 2 Chronicles 34:6 was reliable, and that Josiah managed to expand farther to the north, into the ex-Israelite territories in Galilee.

Yet the idea that Josiah arrived at Megiddo with an effective military force to try to stop Necho and prevent him from marching to the north is a bit far-fetched. It is highly unlikely that Josiah had a large enough army to risk a battle with the Egyptians. Until about 630 BCE, his kingdom was still under Assyrian domination, and later, it is inconceivable that Psammetichus, who was strong enough to control the entire eastern Mediterranean coast up to Phoenicia, would have let Judah develop a strong military force. In any case, it would have been a great gamble for Josiah to risk his army against the Egyptians so far from the heartland of his realm. So the version of Kings is probably more reliable.

Nadav Naaman has offered a very different explanation. He has suggested that one of the reasons for Necho to march through Palestine in 609, a year after the death of Psammetichus and his accession to the throne of Egypt, was to obtain a renewed oath of loyalty from his vassals. According to custom, their previous oath to Psammetichus would have become invalid with his death. Josiah, accordingly, would have been summoned to the Egyptian stronghold at Megiddo to meet Necho and to swear a new oath of loyalty. Yet for some reason, Necho decided to execute him.

What did Josiah do that infuriated the Egyptian monarch? Josiah's drive to the north, into the Samaria hill country, could have threatened the Egyptian interests in the Jezreel valley. Or perhaps an attempt by Josiah to expand in the west, beyond his territories in the Shephelah, could have endangered Egyptian interests in Philistia. No less plausible is Baruch Halpern's suggestion that Necho could have been angered by independent policies of Josiah in the south, along the sensitive routes of the Arabian trade.

One thing is clear. The Deuteronomistic historian, who saw Josiah as a divinely anointed messiah destined to redeem Judah and lead it to glory was clearly at a loss to explain how such a historical catastrophe could occur and left only a curt, enigmatic reference to Josiah's death. The dreams of this king and would-be messiah were brutally silenced at the hill of Megiddo. Decades of spiritual revival and visionary hopes seemingly collapsed overnight. Josiah was dead and the people of Israel were again enslaved by Egypt.

The Last of the Davidic Kings

If this was not devastating enough, the following years brought even greater calamities. After the death of Josiah, the great reform movement apparently crumbled. The last four kings of Judah—three of them sons of Josiah—are negatively judged in the Bible, as apostates. Indeed, the last two decades in the history of Judah are described by the Deuteronomistic History as a period of continuous decline, leading to the destruction of the Judahite state.

Josiah's successor Jehoahaz, seemingly anti-Egyptian, ruled for only three months and reverted to the idolatrous ways of the earlier kings of Judah. Deposed and exiled by Pharaoh Necho, he was replaced by his brother Jehoiakim, who also "did what was evil in the sight of the Lord," adding insult to impiety by exacting tribute from the people of the land in order to hand it over to Pharaoh Necho, his overlord.

There is clear documentation in the Bible (including the prophetic works of the time), confirmed by extrabiblical sources, that describes the tumultuous struggle between the rival great powers that took place in the years that followed the death of Josiah. Egypt apparently maintained control of the western territories of the former Assyrian empire for several more years, bringing to a new height the dreams of resurrecting the pharaonic glory of old. But in Mesopotamia, the power of the Babylonians steadily grew. In 605 BCE, the Babylonian crown prince later known as Nebuchadnezzar crushed the Egyptian army at Carchemish in Syria (an event recorded in Jeremiah 46:2), causing the Egyptian forces to flee in panic back toward the Nile. With that defeat, the Assyrian empire was finally and irrevocably dismembered, and Nebuchadnezzar, now king of Babylon, sought to gain complete control over all the lands to the west.

The Babylonian forces soon marched down the Mediterranean coastal plain, laying waste to the rich Philistine cities. In Judah, the pro-Egyptian faction that had taken over the Jerusalem court a few months after the death of Josiah was thrown into a panic—and their desperate appeals to

Necho for military assistance against the Babylonians merely heightened their political vulnerability in the terrible days that lay ahead.

And so the Babylonian noose around Jerusalem tightened. The Babylonians were now intent on the plunder and complete devastation of the Judahite state. After the sudden death of Jehoiakim, his son Jehoiachin faced the might of the terrifying Babylonian army:

> At that time the servants of Nebuchadnezzar king of Babylon came up to Jerusalem, and the city was besieged. And Nebuchadnezzar king of Babylon came to the city, while his servants were besieging it; and Jehoiachin the king of Judah gave himself up to the king of Babylon, himself, and his mother, and his servants, and his princes, and his palace officials. The king of Babylon took him prisoner in the eighth year of his reign, and carried off all the treasures of the house of the LORD, and the treasures of the king's house, and cut in pieces all the vessels of gold in the temple of the LORD, which Solomon king of Israel had made, as the LORD had foretold. He carried away all Jerusalem, and all the princes, and all the mighty men of valor, ten thousand captives, and all the craftsmen and the smiths; none remained, except the poorest people of the land. And he carried away Jehoiachin to Babylon; the king's mother, the king's wives, his officials, and the chief men of the land, he took into captivity from Jerusalem to Babylon. And the king of Babylon brought captive to Babylon all the men of valor, seven thousand, and the craftsmen and the smiths, one thousand, all of them strong and fit for war. (2 KINGS 24:10–16)

These events that took place in 597 BCE are also documented by the Babylonian Chronicle:

> In the seventh year, the month of Kislev, the king of Akkad mustered his troops, marched to the Hatti-land, and encamped against the City of Judah and on the second day of the month of Adar he seized the city and captured the king. He appointed there a king of his own choice and taking heavy tribute brought it back into Babylon.

The Jerusalem aristocracy and priesthood—among whom the Deuteronomistic ideology burned most passionately—were taken off into exile, to leave increasing conflict among those remaining factions of the Davidic royal house and court who had no clear idea what to do.

But that was only the first step in the forcible dismantling of Judah. Nebuchadnezzar immediately replaced the exiled Jehoiachin with his uncle Zedekiah, apparently a more docile vassal. It was a mistake; a few years later Zedekiah plotted with neighboring kings to rise up again, and like a character in a Greek tragedy, he doomed himself and his city. In 587 BCE Nebuchadnezzar arrived with his formidable army and laid siege to Jerusalem. It was the beginning of the end.

With the Babylonian forces rampaging through the countryside, the outlying cities of Judah fell one by one. Clear archaeological evidence for the last years of the southern kingdom has come from almost every late-monarchic site excavated in Judah: in the Beersheba valley, in the Shephelah, and in the Judahite highlands. At the fortress of Arad, a center of Judahite control and military operations in the south, a group of ostraca, or inscribed potsherds, were found in the rubble of the destruction containing the frantic orders for the movements of troops and transportation of food supplies. At Lachish in the Shephelah, ostraca found in the ruins of the last city gate offer a poignant glimpse of the last moments of the independence of Judah as the signal fires from the neighboring towns are snuffed out, one by one. Presumably written to the commander of Lachish from an outpost in the vicinity, it reveals an impending sense of doom:

> And may my lord know that we are watching for the signals of Lachish according to all the signs that my lord gave. For we do not see Azekah . . .

This grim report is confirmed by a description in the book of Jeremiah (34:7), that notes that Lachish and Azekah were indeed the last cities in Judah to withstand the Babylonian assault.

Finally, all that was left was Jerusalem. The biblical description of its last hours is nothing less than horrifying:

> . . . the famine was so severe in the city that there was no food for the people of the land. Then a breach was made in the city; the king with all the men of war fled by night . . . And they went in the direction of the Arabah. But the army of the Chaldeans pursued the king, and overtook him in the plains of Jericho; and all his army was scattered from him. Then they captured the king, and brought him up to the king of Babylon at Riblah, who passed sentence upon him. They

slew the sons of Zedekiah before his eyes, and put out the eyes of Zedekiah, and bound him in fetters, and took him to Babylon. (2 KINGS 25:3–7)

The last act in the tragedy took place about a month later:

> Nebuzaradan, the captain of the bodyguards, a servant of the king of Babylon, came to Jerusalem. And he burned the house of the LORD and the king's house and all the houses of Jerusalem . . . And all the army of the Chaldeans . . . broke down the walls around Jerusalem. And the rest of the people who were left in the city . . . Nebuzaradan the captain of the guard carried into exile. (2 KINGS 25:8–11)

The archaeological finds convey only the last horrible moments of violence. Signs of a great conflagration have been traced almost everywhere within the city walls. Arrowheads found in the houses and near the northern fortifications attest to the intensity of the last battle for Jerusalem. The private houses, which were set alight and collapsed, burying all that was in them, created the charred heaps of rubble that stood as a testament to the thoroughness of Jerusalem's destruction by the Babylonians for the next century and a half (Nehemiah 2:13).

And so it was all over. Four hundred years of Judah's history came to an end in fire and blood. The proud kingdom of Judah was utterly devastated, its economy ruined, its society ripped apart. The last king in a dynasty that had ruled for centuries was tortured and imprisoned in Babylon. His sons were all killed. The Temple of Jerusalem—the only legitimate place for the worship of YHWH—was destroyed.

The religion and national existence of the people of Israel could have ended in this great disaster. Miraculously, both survived.

[12]

Exile and Return

(586–c. 440 BCE)

In order to understand the full story of ancient Israel and the making of biblical history, we cannot stop at Josiah's death, nor can we halt at the destruction of Jerusalem and the Temple and the fall of the Davidic dynasty. It is crucial to examine what happened in Judah in the decades that followed the Babylonian conquest, to survey the developments that occurred among the exiles in Babylon, and to recount the events that took place in post-exilic Jerusalem. In these times and places, the texts of both the Pentateuch and the Deuteronomistic History underwent far-reaching additions and revisions, arriving at what was substantially their final form. Meanwhile the people of Israel developed new modes of communal organization and worship in Babylon and Jerusalem during the sixth and fifth centuries BCE that formed the foundations of Second Temple Judaism and thus of early Christianity. The events and processes that took place in the century and half after the conquest of the kingdom of Judah—as we can reconstruct them from the historical sources and archaeological evidence—are therefore crucial for understanding how the Judeo-Christian tradition emerged.

Before continuing with the biblical story we must take note of the meaningful change in the biblical sources at our disposal. The Deuteronomistic History, which narrated the history of Israel from the end of the wandering in the wilderness to the Babylonian conquest of Jerusalem, ends abruptly. Other biblical authors take over. The situation in Judah after the destruction is described in the book of Jeremiah, while the book of Ezekiel (written by one of the exiles) provides information on the life and expectations of the Judahite deportees in Babylonia. Events that took place when the successive waves of exiles returned to Jerusalem are reported in the books of Ezra and Nehemiah and by the prophets Haggai and Zechariah. This is also the moment in our story when we must change our terminology: the kingdom of Judah becomes Yehud—the Aramaic name of the province in the Persian empire—and the people of Judah, the Judahites, will henceforth be known as *Yehudim,* or Jews.

From Destruction to Restoration

This climactic phase of the history of Israel begins with a scene of utter disaster and hopelessness. Jerusalem is destroyed, the Temple is in ruins, the last reigning Davidic king, Zedekiah, is blinded and exiled, his sons slaughtered. Many members of the Judahite elite are deported. The situation has reached a low point and it seems as if the history of the people of Israel has reached a bitter and irreversible end.

Not quite so. From the concluding chapter of 2 Kings and from the book of Jeremiah, we learn that part of the population of Judah had survived and was not deported. The Babylonian authorities even allowed them a measure of autonomy, appointing an official named Gedaliah, the son of Ahikam, to rule over the people who remained in Judah, admittedly "the poorest of the land." Mizpah, a modest town north of Jerusalem, became the center of Gedaliah's administration and a haven for other Judahites, like the prophet Jeremiah, who had opposed the ill-fated uprising against Babylonia. Gedaliah tried to persuade the people of Judah to cooperate with the Babylonians and rebuild their lives and future, despite the destruction of the Temple and the city of Jerusalem. But soon Gedaliah was assassinated by Ishmael, the son of Nethaniah, "of the royal family"—possibly because Gedaliah's cooperation with the Babylonians was viewed as posing a threat to the future hopes of the Davidic house. Other Judahite officials and Babylonian imperial representatives present at Mizpah were also killed. The surviving members of the local population decided to flee for their lives, leaving Judah virtually uninhabited. The people "both small and great" went to Egypt, "for they were afraid of the Chaldeans" (as the Babylonians were also known). The prophet Jeremiah fled with them, bringing to an apparent end centuries of Israelite occupation of the Promised Land (2 Kings 25:22–26; Jeremiah 40:7–43:7).

The Bible provides few details about the life of the exiles during the next fifty years. Our only sources are the indirect and often obscure allusions in various prophetic works. Ezekiel and Second Isaiah (chapters 40–55 in the book of Isaiah) tell us that the Judahite exiles lived both in the capital city of Babylon and in the countryside. The priestly and royal deportees established new lives for themselves, with the exiled Davidic king Jehoiachin— rather than the disgraced and blinded Zedekiah—possibly maintaining some sort of authority over the community. From scattered references in the book of Ezekiel, it seems that the Judahite settlements were placed in undeveloped areas of the Babylonian kingdom, near newly dug canals. Ezekiel, himself an exiled priest of the Jerusalem Temple, lived for a while in a settlement on an ancient mound named Tel-abib (in Hebrew, Tel Aviv; Ezekiel 3:15).

Of the nature of their life, the biblical texts reveal little except to note that the exiles settled in for a long stay, following the advice of Jeremiah: "Build houses and live in them; plant gardens and eat their produce. Take wives and have sons and daughters; take wives for your sons, and give your daughters in marriage, that they may bear sons and daughters; multiply there, and do not decrease" (Jeremiah 29:5–6). But history would soon take a sudden and dramatic turn that would bring many of the exiles back to Jerusalem.

The mighty Neo-Babylonian empire crumbled and was conquered by the Persians in 539 BCE. In the first year of his reign, Cyrus, the founder of the Persian empire, issued a royal decree for the restoration of Judah and the Temple:

> Thus says Cyrus king of Persia: The LORD, the God of heaven, has given me all the kingdoms of the earth, and he has charged me to build him a house at Jerusalem, which is in Judah. Whoever is among you of all his people, may his God be with him, and let him go up to Jerusalem, which is in Judah, and re-build the house of the LORD, the God of Israel—he is the God who is in Jerusalem. (EZRA 1:2–3)

A leader of the exiles named Sheshbazzar, described in Ezra 1:8 as "the prince of Judah" (probably indicating that he was a son of the exiled Davidic king Jehoiachin), led the first group of returnees to Zion. They reportedly carried with them the Temple treasures that Nebuchadnezzar had taken from Jerusalem half a century earlier. A list of returnees by town of origin, family, and number follows, about fifty thousand altogether. They settled in their old homeland and laid the foundations for a new Temple. A few years later another wave of returnees gathered in Jerusalem. Led by Jeshua the son of Jozadak and an apparent grandson of Jehoiachin named Zerubbabel, they built an altar and celebrated the Feast of Tabernacles. In a moving scene they began to rebuild the Temple:

> And all the people shouted with a great shout, when they praised the LORD, because the foundation of the house of the LORD was laid. But many of the priests and Levites and heads of fathers' houses, old men who had seen the first house, wept with a loud voice when they saw the foundation of this house being laid, though many shouted aloud for joy; so that the people could not distinguish the sound of the joyful shout from the sound of the people's weeping, for the people shouted with a great shout, and the sound was heard afar. (EZRA 3:11–13)

The people of Samaria—the ex-citizens of the northern kingdom and the deportees who were brought there by the Assyrians—heard about the beginning of the construction of the second Temple, came to Zerubbabel, and asked to join the work. But Jeshua the priest and Zerubbabel sent the northerners away, bluntly saying that "you have nothing to do with us in building a house to our God" (Ezra 4:3). The faction that had preserved itself in exile now believed that it had the divine right to determine the character of Judahite orthodoxy.

In resentment, "the people of the land" hindered the work, and even wrote to the Persian king, accusing the Jews of "rebuilding that rebellious and wicked city" and predicting that "if this city is rebuilt and the walls finished, they will not pay tribute, custom, or toll, and the royal revenue will be impaired. . . . you will then have no possession in the province Beyond the River." (Ezra 4:12–16). Receiving this letter, the Persian king ordered a halt to the construction work in Jerusalem.

But Zerubbabel and Jeshua nevertheless continued the work. And when the Persian governor of the province learned about it and came to inspect the site, he demanded to know who gave the permission to start rebuilding. He was referred to the original decree of Cyrus. According to the book of Ezra, the governor then wrote to the new king, Darius, for a royal decision. Darius instructed him not only to let the work continue, but also to defray all expenses from the revenue of the state, to supply the Temple with animals for sacrifice, and to punish whoever tries to prevent the implementation of the royal edict. The construction of the Temple was then finished in the year 516 BCE. Thus began the era of Second Temple Judaism.

Another dark period of over half a century passed until Ezra the scribe, from the family of the chief priest Aaron, came to Jerusalem from Babylonia (probably in 458 BCE). "He was a scribe skilled in the law of Moses which the LORD the God of Israel had given . . . For Ezra had set his heart to study the law of the Lord" (Ezra 7:6,10). Ezra was sent to make inquiries "about Judah and Jerusalem" by Artaxerxes king of Persia, who authorized him to take with him an additional group of Jewish exiles from Babylon who wanted to go there. The Persian king provided Ezra with funds and judicial authority. Arriving in Jerusalem with the latest wave of returnees, Ezra was shocked to find out that the people of Israel, including priests and Levites, did not separate themselves from the abominations of their neighbors. They intermarried and freely mixed with the people of the land.

Ezra immediately ordered all the returnees to gather in Jerusalem:

> Then all the men of Judah and Benjamin assembled at Jerusalem. . . . And all the people sat in the open square before the house of God. . . . And Ezra the priest stood up and said to them, "You have trespassed and married foreign women, and so increased the guilt of Israel. Now then make confession to the LORD the God of your fathers, and do his will; separate yourselves from the peoples of the land and from the foreign wives." Then all the assembly answered with a loud voice, 'It is so; we must do as you have said. . . . "Then the returned exiles did so" (EZRA 10:9–16).

Ezra—one of the most influential figures of biblical times—then disappeared from the scene.

The other hero of that time was Nehemiah, the cupbearer, or high court official, of the Persian king. Nehemiah heard about the poor state of the inhabitants of Judah and about Jerusalem's terrible condition of disrepair. Deeply affected at this news, he asked the Persian king Artaxerxes to go to

Jerusalem to rebuilt the city of his fathers. The king granted Nehemiah permission and appointed him to the post of governor. Soon after arriving in Jerusalem (around 445 BCE), Nehemiah set out on a nighttime inspection tour of the city and then summoned the people to join in a great, communal effort to rebuild the walls of Jerusalem, so that "we may no longer suffer disgrace." But when the neighbors of Judah—the leaders of Samaria and Ammon, and the Arabs of the south—heard about Nehemiah's plans to fortify Jerusalem, they accused the Jews of planning an uprising against the Persian authorities and plotted to attack the city. Work on the wall continued to completion nonetheless. Nehemiah was also active in implementing social legislation, condemning those who extracted interest, and urging restitution of land to the poor. At the same time, he too prohibited Jewish intermarriage with foreign wives.

These rulings by Ezra and Nehemiah in Jerusalem in the fifth century BCE laid the foundations for Second Temple Judaism in the establishment of clear boundaries between the Jewish people and their neighbors and in the strict enforcement of the Deuteronomic Law. Their efforts—and the efforts of other Judean priests and scribes which took place over the one hundred and fifty years of exile, suffering, soul-searching, and political rehabilitation—led to the birth of the Hebrew Bible in its substantially final form.

From Catastrophe to Historical Revisionism

The great scriptural saga woven together during the reign of Josiah, which told the story of Israel from God's promise to the patriarchs, through Exodus, conquest, united monarchy, the divided states—ultimately to the discovery of the book of the Law in the Jerusalem Temple—was a brilliant and passionate composition. It aimed at explaining why past events suggested future triumphs, at justifying the need for the religious reforms of Deuteronomy, and most practically, at backing the territorial ambitions of the Davidic dynasty. But at the very moment when Josiah was about to redeem Judah, he was struck down by the pharaoh. His successors backslid into idolatry and small-minded scheming. Egypt reclaimed possession of the coast, and the Babylonians soon arrived to put an end to the national existence of Judah. Where was the God who promised redemption? While most other nations of the ancient Near East would have been content to accept the verdict of history, shrug their collective shoulders, and transfer their reverence to the god of the victor, the later editors of the Deuteronomistic History went back to the drawing board.

Jehoiachin, the king exiled from Jerusalem in 597 BCE and the leader of the Judahite community in Babylon, could have represented the last best hope for the eventual restoration of the Davidic dynasty. But the previously unchallenged belief that a Davidic heir would fulfill the divine promises could no longer be taken for granted in light of the catastrophe that had just occurred. Indeed, the desperate need to reinterpret the historical events of the preceding decades led to a reworking of the original Deuteronomistic History—in order to explain how the long-awaited moment of redemption, so perfectly keyed to the reign of Jehoiachin's grandfather Josiah, had failed to materialize.

The American biblical scholar Frank Moore Cross long ago identified what he believed to be two distinct redactions, or editions, of the Deuteronomistic History, reflecting the difference in historical awareness before and after the exile. The earlier version, which is known in biblical scholarship as Dtr[1], was presumably written during the reign of Josiah and was, as we have argued, entirely devoted to furthering that monarch's religious and political aims. According to Cross and the many scholars who have followed him, the first Deuteronomistic History, Dtr[1], ended with the passages describing the great destruction of idolatrous high places throughout the country and the celebration of the first national Passover in Jerusalem. That celebration was a symbolic replay of the great Passover of Moses, a feast commemorating deliverance from slavery to freedom under YHWH and anticipating Judah's liberation from the new yoke of Egypt under Pharaoh Necho. Indeed, the original Deuteronomistic History recounts the story of Israel from the last speech of Moses to the conquest of Canaan led by Joshua to the giving of a new Law and a renewed conquest of the Promised Land by Josiah. It was a story with an ending of divine redemption and eternal bliss.

But catastrophe struck. Centuries of efforts and hopes proved to be in vain. Judah was again enslaved by Egypt—the same Egypt from which the Israelites had been liberated. Then came the destruction of Jerusalem, and with it a terrible theological blow: the unconditional promise of

YHWH to David of the eternal rule of his dynasty in Jerusalem—the basis
for the Deuteronomistic faith—was broken. The death of Josiah and the
destruction of Jerusalem must have thrown the authors of the Deuteronomistic History into despair. How could the sacred history be maintained in
this time of darkness? What could its meaning possibly be?

With time, new explanations emerged. The aristocracy of Judah—
including perhaps the very people who had composed the original
Deuteronomistic History—were resettled in far-off Babylon. As the shock
of displacement began to wear off, there was still a need for a history; in
fact, the urgency for a history of Israel was even greater. The Judahites in
exile lost everything, including everything that was dear to the Deuteronomistic ideas. They had lost their homes, their villages, their land, their
ancestral tombs, their capital, their Temple, and even the political independence of their four-centuries old Davidic dynasty. A rewritten history
of Israel was the best way for the exiles to reassert their identity. It could
provide them with a link to the land of their forefathers, to their ruined
capital, to their burned Temple, to the great history of their dynasty.

So the Deuteronomistic History had to be updated. This second version
was based substantially on the first, but with two new goals in mind. First,
it had briefly to tell the end of the story, from the death of Josiah to destruction and exile. Second, it had to make *sense* of the whole story, to explain how it was possible to reconcile God's unconditional, eternal promise
to David with the destruction of Jerusalem and the Temple and the ouster
of the Davidic kings. And there was an even more specific theological question: how was it possible that the great righteousness and piety of Josiah
had been powerless to avert Jerusalem's violent and bloody conquest?

Thus arose the distinctive edition known to scholars as Dtr[2], whose closing verses (2 Kings 25:27–30) report the release of Jehoiachin from prison
in Babylon in 560 BCE (that means, of course that 560 BCE is the earliest
possible date for the composition of Dtr[2]). Its treatment of the death
of Josiah, the reigns of the four last Davidic kings, the destruction of
Jerusalem, and the exile displays almost telegraphic brevity (2 Kings
23:26–25:21). The most conspicuous changes are those that explain why
Jerusalem's destruction was inevitable, despite the great hopes invested
in King Josiah. In insertions into Dtr[1], a second Deuteronomistic historian added a condition to the previously unconditional promise to David

(1 Kings 2:4, 8:25, 9:4–9) and inserted ominous references to the inevitability of destruction and the exile throughout the earlier text (for example, 2 Kings 20:17–18). More important, he placed the blame on Manasseh, the archenemy of the Deuteronomistic movement, who ruled between the righteous kings Hezekiah and Josiah and who came to be portrayed as the wickedest of all Judahite kings:

> And the LORD said by his servants the prophets, "Because Manasseh king of Judah has committed these abominations, and has done things more wicked than all that the Amorites did, who were before him, and has made Judah also to sin with his idols; therefore thus says the LORD, the God of Israel, Behold, I am bringing upon Jerusalem and Judah such evil that the ears of every one who hears of it will tingle. And I will stretch over Jerusalem the measuring line of Samaria, and the plummet of the house of Ahab; and I will wipe Jerusalem as one wipes a dish, wiping it and turning it upside down. And I will cast off the remnant of my heritage, and give them into the hand of their enemies, and they shall become a prey and a spoil to all their enemies, because they have done what is evil in my sight and have provoked me to anger, since the day their fathers came out of Egypt, even to this day." (2 KINGS 21:10–15)

In addition, Dtr² presents a theological twist. Josiah's righteousness was now described as only *delaying* the inevitable destruction of Jerusalem, rather than bringing about the final redemption of Israel. A chilling oracle was placed in the mouth of Huldah the prophetess, to whom Josiah dispatched some of his courtiers to inquire:

> ". . . as to the king of Judah, who sent you to inquire of the LORD, thus shall you say to him, Thus says the LORD, the God of Israel: Regarding the words which you have heard, because your heart was penitent, and you humbled yourself before the LORD, when you heard how I spoke against this place, and against its inhabitants, that they should become a desolation and a curse, and you have rent your clothes and wept before me, I also have heard you, says the LORD. Therefore, behold, I will gather you to your fathers, and you shall be gathered to your grave in peace, and your eyes shall not see all the evil which I will bring upon this place." (2 KINGS 22: 18–20)

The righteousness of a single Davidic monarch was no longer enough to secure Israel's destiny. Josiah was pious and so was spared seeing Jerusalem's fall. But the righteousness of all the people—given their individual rights and obligations in the book of Deuteronomy—was now the determining factor in the future of the people of Israel. Thus the rewritten Deuteronomistic History brilliantly subordinated the covenant with David to the fulfillment of the covenant between God and the people of Israel at Sinai. Israel would henceforth have a purpose and an identity, even in the absence of a king.

But even with all his twists and explanations, the second Deuteronomist could not end the story with a hopeless future. So he ended the seven-book compilation of the history of Israel with a laconic chronicle of the release of Jehoiachin from prison in Babylon:

> And in the thirty-seventh year of the exile of Jehoiachin king of Judah . . . Evilmerodach king of Babylon, in the year that he began to reign, graciously freed Jehoiachin king of Judah from prison; and he spoke kindly to him, and gave him a seat above the seats of the kings who were with him in Babylon. So Jehoiachin put off his prison garments. And every day of his life he dined regularly at the king's table; and for his allowance, a regular allowance was given him by the king, every day a portion, as long as he lived. (2 KINGS 25:27–30).

The last king from the lineage of David, from the dynasty that made the connection to the land, the capital and the Temple, was still alive. If the people of Israel adhered to YHWH, the promise to David could still be revived.

Those Who Remained

In the early days of archaeological research there was a notion that the Babylonian exile was nearly total and that much of the population of Judah was carried away. It was thought that Judah was emptied of its population and the countryside was left devastated. Many scholars accepted the biblical report that the entire aristocracy of Judah—the royal family, Temple priests, ministers, and prominent merchants—was carried away, and that the people who remained in Judah were only the poorest peasantry.

Now that we know more about Judah's population, this historical reconstruction has proved to be mistaken. Let us first consider the numbers involved. Second Kings 24:14 gives the number of exiles in the first Babylonian campaign (in 597 BCE in the days of Jehoiachin) at ten thousand, while verse 16 in the same chapter counts eight thousand exiles. Although the account in Kings does not provide a precise number of exiles taken away from Judah at the time of the destruction of Jerusalem in 586 BCE, it does state that after the murder of Gedaliah and the massacre of the Babylonian garrison at Mizpah "all the people" fled to Egypt (2 Kings 25:26), presumably leaving the countryside of Judah virtually deserted.

A sharply different estimate of the number of exiles is ascribed to the prophet Jeremiah—who reportedly remained with Gedaliah in Mizpah until fleeing to Egypt and would therefore have been an eyewitness to the events. The book of Jeremiah 52:28–30 reports that the total of the Babylonian deportations amounted to forty-six hundred. Though this figure is also quite round, most scholars believe it to be basically plausible, because its subtotals are quite specific and are probably more precise than the rounded numbers in 2 Kings. Yet in neither Kings nor Jeremiah do we know whether the figures represent the *total* number of deportees or just male heads of households (a system of counting quite common in the ancient world). Given these compounded uncertainties, the most that can reasonably be said is that we are dealing with a total number of exiles ranging between a few thousand and perhaps fifteen or twenty thousand at most.

When we compare this number to the total population of Judah in the late seventh century, *before* the destruction of Jerusalem, we can gain an idea of the scale of the deportations. Judah's population can be quite accurately estimated from data collected during intensive surveys and excavations at about seventy-five thousand (with Jerusalem comprising at least 20 percent of this number—fifteen thousand—with another fifteen thousand probably inhabiting its nearby agricultural hinterland). Thus even if we accept the highest possible figures for exiles (twenty thousand), it would seem that they comprised *at most* a quarter of the population of the Judahite state. That would mean that at least seventy five percent of the population remained on the land.

What do we know about this vast majority of the Judahites, who did not go into exile? Scattered references in prophetic texts suggest that they continued their agricultural way of life much as before. Mizpah, north of Jerusalem, was one of several towns that remained. The ruins of the Temple in Jerusalem were also frequented, and some sort of cultic activity continued to take place there (Jeremiah 41:5). And it should be noted that this community included not only poor villagers but also artisans, scribes, priests, and prophets. An important part of the prophetic work of the time, particularly the books of Haggai and Zechariah, was compiled in Judah.

Intensive excavations throughout Jerusalem have shown that the city was indeed systematically destroyed by the Babylonians. The conflagration seems to have been general. When activity on the ridge of the City of David resumed in the Persian period, the new suburbs on the western hill that had flourished since at least the time of Hezekiah were not reoccupied. A single sixth-century BCE burial cave found to the west of the city may represent a family who moved to a nearby settlement but continued to bury its dead in its ancestral tomb.

Yet there is evidence of continued occupation both to the north and to the south of Jerusalem. Some measure of self-government seems to have continued at Mizpah on the plateau of Benjamin, about eight miles to the north of Jerusalem. The soon-to-be-assassinated governor who served there, Gedaliah, was probably a high official in the Judahite administration before the destruction. There are several indications (Jeremiah 37:12–13; 38:19) that the area to the north of Jerusalem surrendered to the Babylonians without a fight, and archaeological evidence supports this hypothesis.

The most thorough research on the settlement of Judah in the Babylonian period, conducted by Oded Lipschits of Tel Aviv University, has shown that the site of Tell en-Nasbeh near modern Ramallah—identified as the location of biblical Mizpah—was not destroyed in the Babylonian campaign, and that it was indeed the most important settlement in the region in the sixth century BCE. Other sites north of Jerusalem such as Bethel and Gibeon continued to be inhabited in the same era. In the area to the south of Jerusalem, around Bethlehem, there seems to have been significant continuity from the late monarchic to the Babylonian period. Thus, to both the north and south of Jerusalem, life continued almost uninterrupted.

Both text and archaeology contradict the idea that between the destruction of Jerusalem in 586 BCE and the return of the exiles after the proclamation of Cyrus in 538 BCE Judah was in total ruin and uninhabited. The Persian takeover and the return of a certain number of exiles who were supported by the Persian government changed the settlement situation there.

Urban life in Jerusalem began to revive and many returnees settled in the Judean hills. The lists of repatriates in Ezra 2 and Nehemiah 7 amount to almost fifty thousand people. It is unclear whether this significant number represents the cumulative figure of the successive waves of exiles who came back over more than a hundred years, or the total population of the province of Yehud, including those who remained. In either case, archaeological research has shown that this figure is wildly exaggerated. Survey data from all the settlements in Yehud in the fifth–fourth centuries BCE yields a population of approximately thirty thousand people (on the boundaries of Yehud, see Appendix G and Figure 29). This small number constituted the post-exilic community of the time of Ezra and Nehemiah so formative in shaping later Judaism.

From Kings to Priests

The edict of Cyrus the Great allowing a group of Judahite exiles to return to Jerusalem could hardly have been prompted by sympathy for the people remaining in Judah or for the suffering of the exiles. Rather, it should be seen as a well-calculated policy that aimed to serve the interests of the Persian empire. The Persians tolerated and even promoted local cults as a way to ensure the loyalty of local groups to the wider empire; both Cyrus and his son Cambyses supported the building of temples and encouraged the return of displaced populations elsewhere in their vast empire. Their policy was to grant autonomy to loyal local elites.

Many scholars agree that the Persian kings encouraged the rise of a loyal elite in Yehud, because of the province's strategic and sensitive location on the border of Egypt. This loyal elite was recruited from the Jewish exile community in Babylonia and was led by dignitaries who were closely connected to the Persian administration. They were mainly individuals of high social and economic status, families who had resisted assimilation and who were most probably close to the Deuteronomistic ideas. Though the returnees were a minority in Yehud, their religious, socioeconomic, and political status, and their concentration in and around Jerusalem, gave them power far beyond their number. They were probably also supported by the local people who were sympathetic to the Deuteronomic law code promulgated a century before. With the help of a rich collection of literature—

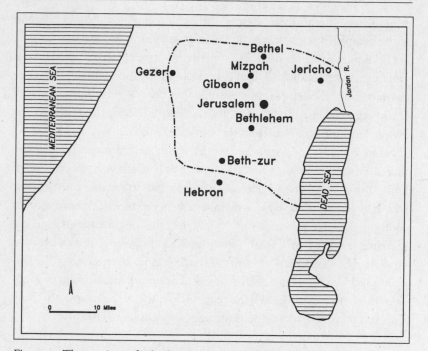

Figure 29: The province of Yehud in the Persian period.

historical compositions and prophetic works—and with the popularity of the Temple, which they controlled, the returnees were able to establish their authority over the population of the province of Yehud. What saved the day for them and made possible the future development of Judaism was the fact that (unlike the Assyrians' policy in the northern kingdom a century before) the Babylonians had not resettled vanquished Judah with foreign deportees.

But how is it that the Davidic dynasty suddenly disappeared from the scene? Why wasn't the monarchy reestablished, with a figure from the royal family as a king? According to the book of Ezra, the first two figures who led the repatriates were Sheshbazzar and Zerubbabel—both are described as "governor" of Yehud (Ezra 5:14; Haggai 1:1). Sheshbazzar, the one who brought back the treasures of the old Temple and who laid the foundations of the new Temple, is an enigmatic figure. He is called "the prince of Judah" (Ezra 1:8), hence many scholars identified him with Shenazzar of 1 Chronicles 3:18, who was one of the heirs to the Davidic throne, maybe even the son of Jehoiachin. Zerubbabel, who completed the construction of the Temple in 516 BCE, also apparently came from the Davidic lineage. Yet he did not function alone, but together with the priest Jeshua. And it is significant that Zerubbabel disappears from the biblical accounts after the completion of the Temple. It is possible that his origin from the house of David stirred messianic hopes in Judah (Haggai 2:20–23), which led the Persian authorities to recall him on political grounds.

From this point onward, the Davidic family played no role in the history of Yehud. At the same time, the priesthood, which rose to a position of leadership in exile, and which also played an important role among those who had remained in Yehud, maintained its prominence because of its ability to preserve group identity. So in the following decades the people of Yehud were led by a dual system: politically, by governors who were appointed by the Persian authority and who had no connection to the Davidic royal family; religiously, by priests. Lacking the institution of kingship, the Temple now became the center of identify of the people of Yehud. This was one of the most crucial turning points in Jewish history.

Refashioning Israel's History

One of the main functions of the priestly elite in post-exilic Jerusalem—beyond the conduct of the renewed sacrifices and purification rituals—was the continuing production of literature and scripture to bind the community together and determine its norms against the peoples all around. Scholars have long noted that the Priestly source (P) in the Pentateuch is, in the main, post-exilic—it is related to the rise of the priests to prominence in the Temple community in Jerusalem. No less important, the final redaction of the Pentateuch also dates to this period. The biblical scholar Richard Friedman went one step further and suggested that the redactor who gave the final shape to the "Law of Moses" was Ezra, who is specifically described as "the scribe of the law of the God of heaven" (Ezra 7:12).

The post-exilic writers, back in Jerusalem, needed not only to explain the Babylonian destruction of Jerusalem, but also to reunite the community of Yehud around the new Temple. They needed to give the people hope for a better, more prosperous future; to address the problem of the relationship with the neighboring groups, especially in the north and south; and to deal with questions related to domestic problems in the community. In those respects the needs of the post-exilic Yehud community were similar to the necessities of the late-monarchic Judahite state. Both were small communities, inhabiting a limited territory that was only a small part of the Promised Land, but of great importance as the spiritual and political center of the Israelites.

Both were surrounded by alien, hostile neighbors. Both claimed nearby territories that were outside their realm. Both faced problems with foreigners from within and without and were concerned with the questions of the purity of the community and assimilation. Hence, many of the teachings of Judah in the late monarchic period were not alien to the ears of the people in Jerusalem in post-exilic times. The idea of the centrality of Judah and its superiority to its neighbors certainly resonated in the consciousness of the Jerusalem community in the late sixth and fifth centuries BCE. But other circumstances—such as the decline of the house of David and life under an empire—forced the early post-exilic writers to reshape the old ideas.

The Exodus story took on pointed significance in Exilic and post-exilic times. The story of the great liberation must have had a strong appeal to the exiles in Babylon. As the biblical scholar David Clines pointed out, "the bondage in Egypt is their own bondage in Babylon, and the exodus past becomes the exodus that is yet to be." Indeed, the striking similarity of themes in the story of the Exodus from Egypt and the memories of the return from exile may have influenced the shaping of *both* narratives. Reading the saga of the Exodus, the returnees found a mirror of their own plight. According to Yair Hoffman, a biblical scholar from Tel Aviv University, both stories tell us how the Israelites left their land for a foreign country; how the land of Israel was considered as belonging to those who left and were expected to come back because of a divine promise; how after a difficult period in exile the people who left came back to their homeland; how on the way back the returnees had to cross a dangerous desert; how the return to the homeland evoked conflicts with the local population; how the returnees managed to settle only part of their promised homeland; and how measures were taken by the leaders of the returnees to avoid assimilation between the Israelites and the population of the land.

Likewise, the story of Abraham migrating from Mesopotamia to the promised land of Canaan, to become a great man and establish a prosperous nation there, no doubt appealed to the people of exilic and post-exilic times. The strong message about the separation of Israelites from Canaanites in the patriarchal narratives also fit the attitudes of the people of post-exilic Yehud.

Yet, from both the political and the ethnic points of view, the most severe problem of the post-exilic community lay in the south. After the destruction of Judah, Edomites settled in the southern parts of the vanquished kingdom, in the Beersheba valley and in the Hebron hills, a region that would soon be known as Idumea—the land of the Edomites. Drawing a boundary between "us" (the post-exilic community in the province of Yehud) and "them" (the Edomites in the southern hill country) was of utmost importance. Demonstrating, as in the story of Jacob and Esau, that Judah was the superior center and that Edom was secondary and uncivilized was therefore essential.

The tradition of the tombs of the patriarchs in the cave at Hebron, which belongs to the Priestly source, should also be understood on this background. The Yehud community controlled only part of the territories of the destroyed Judahite kingdom, and now the southern border of Yehud ran between the towns of Beth-zur and Hebron, the latter remaining outside its boundaries. Remembering the importance of Hebron in the time of the monarchy, the people of Yehud must have bitterly regretted the fact that in their own days it did not belong to them. A tradition placing the tombs of the patriarchs, the founders of the nation, at Hebron, would deepen their strong attachment to the southern hill country. Whether or not the story was old, and the tradition real, it was highly appealing to the authors of the Priestly source and was emphasized by them in the patriarchal narratives.

The latest editors of Genesis were not content with mere metaphors, however. They wanted to show how the origins of the people of Israel lay at the very heart of the civilized world. Thus unlike the lesser peoples that arose in undeveloped, uncultured regions around them, they hint that the great father of the people of Israel came from the cosmopolitan, famed city of Ur. Abraham's origins in Ur are mentioned only in two isolated verses (Genesis 11:28 and 31, a P document) while his story seems much more centered on the north Syrian—Aramean—city of Haran. But even that brief mention was enough. Ur as Abraham's birthplace would have bestowed enormous prestige as the homeland of a putative national ancestor. Not only was Ur renowned as a place of extreme antiquity and learning, it gained great prestige throughout the entire region during the period of its reestablishment as a religious center by the Babylonian, or Chaldean, king Nabonidus in the mid-sixth century BCE. Thus, the reference to Abraham's origin in "Ur of the Chaldeans" would have offered the Jews a distinguished and ancient cultural pedigree.

In short, the post-exilic stage of the editing of the Bible recapitulated many of the key themes of the earlier seventh-century stage that we have discussed in much of this book. This was due to the similar realities and needs of the two eras. Once again the Israelites were centered in Jerusalem, amid great uncertainty, without controlling most of the land that they considered theirs by divine promise. Once again a central authority needed to unite the population. And once again they did it by brilliantly reshaping the historical core of the Bible in such a way that it was able to serve as the main source of identity and spiritual anchor for the people of Israel as they faced the many disasters, religious challenges, and political twists of fate that lay ahead.

EPILOGUE

The Future of Biblical Israel

Yehud remained in the hands of the Persians for two centuries, until the conquest of Alexander the Great in 332 BCE. It then was incorporated into the empires established by Alexander's successors, first that of the Ptolemies of Egypt, then that of the Seleucids of Syria. For more than 150 years after Alexander's conquest the priestly leaders of the province now known as Judea maintained the customs and observed the laws that had first been formulated in the time of King Josiah and that had been further codified and refined in the exilic and post-exilic periods. Indeed, it is from the Hellenistic period, around 300 BCE, that we gain the first extensive description of biblical laws and customs from an outside observer. The Greek writer Hecataeus of Abdera, who traveled to the Near East not long after the death of Alexander, provides a glimpse of a stage of the Jewish tradition in which the prestige of the priesthood and the power of Deuteronomy's social legislation had completely overshadowed the tradition of the monarchy. Speaking of the laws established by "a man named Moses, outstanding for both his wisdom and his courage," Hecataeus noted:

> He picked out men of most refinement and with the greatest ability to head the entire nation, and appointed them priests; and he ordained that they should occupy themselves with the temple and the honors and sacrifices offered to their

God. These same men he appointed to be judges in all major disputes, and entrusted them to the guardianship of the laws and customs. For this reason, the Jews never have a king.

The Judeans, or Jews, became known throughout the Mediterranean as a community with a unique devotion to their God. At its heart were not only the shared law codes and rules of sacrifice, but the saga of national history that began with the call of Abraham in distant Ur and ended with the restoration of the Temple community by Ezra and Nehemiah in the postexilic period. With the abandonment of the monarchy and the scattering of Jews throughout the Greco-Roman world, the sacred text of the Hebrew Bible was gradually translated into Greek in the third and second centuries BCE and became the chief source of community identity and guidance for all those members of the house of Israel who lived beyond the immediate vicinity of the Temple of Jerusalem. Its saga of the Exodus and the conquest of the Promised Land offered a shared vision of solidarity and hope for every individual in the community—in a way that royal or heroic mythologies could not.

Dramatic changes would occur in the confrontation of the priestly leadership of Judea with Hellenistic culture and religion in the second century BCE. The Maccabees' radical movement of resistance—in many ways reminiscent in ideology of the Deuteronomistic movement of the days of Josiah—succeeded in conquering a great part of the traditional land of Israel and enforcing the Law on its inhabitants. Yet the greatest power of the Bible would not be as a guide to military conquest or political triumphs, intended only to boost the fortunes of a particular ruler or dynasty.

In the first century BCE, as the Hasmonean kings, of the Maccabean lineage, eventually declined into dynastic squabbling and the Roman client-king Herod took power in Judea, the Bible emerged as the uniting force and scriptural heart of a hard-pressed community. The stories of liberation and Joshua's conquest gave special emotional power to the popular movements of resistance against local tyrants and Roman overlords throughout the first century BCE and the first and second centuries CE. Nowhere else in the ancient world had such a powerful, shared saga been crafted: the Greek epics and myths spoke only by metaphor and example; Mesopotamian and Persian religious epics offered cosmic secrets but neither earthly history nor a practical guide to life. The Hebrew Bible offered both, providing a narrative framework in which every Jew could identify both family and national history. In short, the saga of Israel that had first crystallized in the time of Josiah became the world's first fully articulated national and social compact, encompassing the men, women, and children, the rich, the poor, and the destitute of an entire community.

With the destruction of the Second Temple in 70 CE and the rise of Christianity, the independent power of the Bible as a formative constitution—not just a brilliant work of literature or a collection of ancient law and wisdom—proved itself. It was the basis for ever-expanding elaboration in the Mishnah and Talmud of Rabbinic Judaism and was recognized as the "Old Testament" of formative Christianity. The consciousness of spiritual descent from Abraham and the common experience of the Exodus from bondage became a shared mindset for ever-growing networks of communities throughout the Roman empire and the Mediterranean world. The hope of future redemption, though no longer attached to the extinguished earthly dynasty of David, was kept alive in Judaism's prophetic and messianic expectations, and in Christianity's belief that Jesus belonged to the Davidic line. The poignant death of the would-be messiah Josiah so many centuries before had set the pattern that would survive throughout history.

The Hebrew Bible would offer an unparalleled source of solidarity and identity to countless communities in the centuries that followed. The details of its stories, drawn from a treasury of ancient memories, fragmentary histories, and rewritten legends, possessed power not as an objective chronicle of events in a tiny land on the eastern shore of the Mediterranean but as a timeless expression of what a people's divine destiny might be. Just as the subjects of Charlemagne paid homage to him as a new, conquering David—and the followers of the Ottoman sultan Suleiman saw in him the wisdom of Solomon—other communities in very different cultural contexts would identify their own struggles with the struggles of biblical Israel. Medieval European peasant communities rose up in apocalyptic rebellions with the images and heroes of the Hebrew Bible as their battle banners. The Puritan settlers of New England went so far in imagining themselves as Israelites wandering in the wilderness that they recreated the Promised Land—with its Salem, Hebron, Goshen, and New Canaan—in their newfound meadows and woods. And none of them doubted that the biblical epic was true.

It was only when the Hebrew Bible began to be dissected and studied in isolation from its powerful function in community life that theologians and biblical scholars began to demand of it something that it was not. From the eighteenth century, in the Enlightenment quest for thoroughly accurate, verifiable history, the historical factuality of the Bible became—as it remains—a matter of bitter debate. Realizing that a seven-day creation and spontaneous miracles could not be satisfactorily explained by science and reason, the scholars began to pick and choose what they found to be "historical" in the Bible and what they did not. Theories arose about the various sources contained in the text of the Bible, and archaeologists argued over the evidence that proved or disproved the historical reliability of a given biblical passage.

Yet the Bible's integrity and, in fact, its historicity, do not depend on dutiful historical "proof" of any of its particular events or personalities, such as the parting of the Red Sea, the trumpet blasts that toppled the walls of Jericho, or David's slaying of Goliath with a single shot of his sling. The power of the biblical saga stems from its being a compelling and coherent narrative expression of the timeless themes of a people's liberation, continuing resistance to oppression, and quest for social equality. It eloquently expresses the deeply rooted sense of shared origins, experiences, and destiny that every human community needs in order to survive.

In specific historical terms, we now know that the Bible's epic saga first emerged as a response to the pressures, difficulties, challenges, and hopes faced by the people of the tiny kingdom of Judah in the decades before its destruction and by the even tinier Temple community in Jerusalem in the post-exilic period. Indeed, archaeology's greatest contribution to our understanding of the Bible may be the realization that such small, relatively poor, and remote societies as late monarchic Judah and post-exilic Yehud could have produced the main outlines of this enduring epic in such a short period of time. Such a realization is crucial, for it is only when we recognize when and why the ideas, images, and events described in the Bible came to be so skillfully woven together that we can at last begin to appreciate the true genius and continuing power of this single most influential literary and spiritual creation in the history of humanity.

Theories of the Historicity of the Patriarchal Age

The Amorite Hypothesis

With the development of modern archaeology in the land of the Bible, it became clear that Canaan of the third millennium BCE—the Early Bronze Age—was characterized by fully developed urban life. This was obviously inappropriate as an historical background to the stories of the wanderings of the patriarchs, who had few urban encounters. In this first urban period of the Bronze Age, large cities, some of them reaching an area of fifty acres and accommodating several thousand people, developed in the lowlands. They were surrounded by formidable fortifications and contained palaces and temples. Though there are no texts from this period, a comparison of the situation in the third millennium BCE to that of the second urban period (in the second millennium BCE, when we do have texts) suggests that the major cities served as capitals of city-states, and that the rural population was subordinate to these centers. The material culture was that of highly organized sedentary people. But in the late third millennium BCE, this flourishing urban system collapsed. The cities were destroyed, and many of them became ruins, never to recover from the shock. And many of the rural settlements around them were abandoned. What followed was a period of a few centuries, in the late third millennium and possibly in the early second millennium, of a very different culture, with no big cities, that is, with no urban life. Most of the population of Palestine—as archaeologists believed in the 1950s and 1960s—was practicing a pastoral nomadic mode of subsistence before urban life gradually recovered and Canaan entered a second urban period, that of the Middle Bronze Age, in the early second millennium BCE.

The American scholar William F. Albright believed that he had identified the historical background of the patriarchs in this nomadic interlude between two periods of developed urban life in Canaan, an interlude that fell during the period 2100–1800 BCE, close to the time of the patriarchs, as indicated by biblical chronology. Albright called this period the Middle Bronze I (other scholars called it, more properly, the Intermediate Bronze Age, because it was an interval between two urban eras). Albright and other scholars of the time argued that the collapse of the Early Bronze urban culture was sudden and that it was the outcome of an invasion, or migration, of pastoral nomads from the northeast. He identified the invaders with the people called Amurru—the Amorites (literally, "westerners") of the Mesopotamian texts. Albright and his followers went a step further and identified the patriarchs as Amorites, and dated the Abraham episode in the Genesis stories to this phase in the history of Canaan. According to this reconstruction, Abraham was an Amorite, a merchant, who migrated from the north and wandered throughout the central highlands of Canaan as well as in the Negev.

And what was the historical cause of Abraham's migration? Albright suggested that Abraham, "a caravaneer of high repute," took part in the great trade network of the nineteenth century BCE. Texts of that time found near Kayseri in central Turkey attest to a prosperous trade relation between Mesopotamia and north Syria (thus paralleling the Ur-to-Haran movement of Abraham in Genesis), and a tomb painting from Egypt at the same period provides evidence for caravan trade between Transjordan and Egypt (as described in the Joseph story in Genesis). In both cases, donkeys were used as the beasts of burden. Thus Albright made a link between the two phenomena—the pastoral nature of the age of the patriarchs and the donkey caravan trade of the nineteenth century—by arguing that the Middle Bronze Age I continued until around 1800 BCE. The American archaeologist Nelson Glueck supplied apparent substantiation for this theory. His surveys in southern Transjordan and the Negev desert revealed hundreds of sites from the same period. Albright believed that these sites provided the historical background for the stories about Abraham's activity in the Negev and the destruction of the cities of the Dead Sea.

Yet the Amorite hypothesis did not last long. With additional excavations of sites throughout the country, most scholars came to the conclusion that the Early Bronze urban system did not collapse overnight but declined gradually over many decades, due more to local economic and social upheavals within Canaan than to a wave of outside invaders. In the meantime, the Amorite hypothesis took a blow from another direction, for it became clear that the term *Amorite* was not restricted to pastoral people. Village communities in northern Syria in the early second millennium were also termed Amorite. Thus it was unlikely that Abraham came into the country as part of a wave of invasion from outside.

Moreover, the apparent similarity between the pastoral way of life in the next phase in the history of the country and the descriptions of Abraham's nomadic lifestyle also proved to be an illusion. It is now clear that the Intermediate Bronze Age was not a completely nomadic period. True, there were no large cities at that time, and the ratio of the pastoral nomads to the general population grew significantly. But much of the population remained sedentary, living in villages and hamlets. In sharp contradiction to the theory of a great migration of nomads from the north, the continuity of architecture, pottery styles, and settlement patterns suggests that the population of Canaan in this interurban phase was predominantly indigenous. The population was descended from the people who had lived in the big cities a few generations before. And the same people would reestablish urban life in Canaan in the cities of the Middle Bronze Age.

No less important was the fact that some of the main sites mentioned in the patriarchal stories—such as Shechem, Beersheba, and Hebron—did not yield finds from the Intermediate Bronze Age; these sites were simply not inhabited at that time.

The Patriarchs in the Middle Bronze Age

Another theory linked the age of the patriarchs with the Middle Bronze II, the peak of urban life in the first half of the second millennium BCE. Schol-

ars advocating this view, such as the French biblical scholar Roland de
Vaux, argued that the nature of the Middle Bronze Age, as it emerges from
both text and archaeology, better fits the biblical description, mainly be-
cause the patriarchs are sometimes depicted as living in tents next to cities.
Archaeologically, all the major sites mentioned in Genesis—Shechem,
Bethel, Hebron, and Gerar—were fortified strongholds in the Middle
Bronze Age. Textually, this tent-city relationship is strongly attested in the
archive found in the ruins of the famous early second millennium city of
Mari on the Euphrates in Syria. In addition, the supporters of a Middle
Bronze date for the patriarchal period argued that the personal names of
the patriarchs resemble Amorite names of the early second millennium
BCE, while they are distinct from the names commonly used in the later
eras, when the biblical material was put in writing. The best example put
forward was that of Jacob, a name that occurs several times in the early second millennium BCE.

The American scholars Cyrus Gordon and Ephraim Speiser also referred to similarities between social and legal practices in the biblical description of the patriarchal period and social and legal practices in second
millennium BCE Near Eastern texts. Parallels like this, they argued, cannot
be found in later periods in the history of the ancient Near East. The
most important of these texts are the Nuzi tablets from northern Iraq,
which date to the fifteenth century BCE. The Nuzi tablets—most of them
come from family archives—portray the customs of the Hurrians, a non-
Semitic people who established the powerful state of Mitanni in northern
Mesopotamia in the mid-second millennium BCE. To cite a few examples,
in Nuzi a barren wife was required to provide a slave woman for her husband to bear his children—a clear parallel to the biblical story of Sarai and
Hagar in Genesis 16. At Nuzi, slaves were adopted by childless couples; this
is similar to the adoption of Eliezer by Abraham as his heir (Genesis
15:2–3). Jacob's arrangements with Laban in return for his marriage with
Rachel and Leah also find parallels in the Nuzi tablets. The similarities
between the Nuzi texts and the biblical material on the age of the patriarchs were understood on the background of the strong cultural influence
of the Hurrians, who spread as far south as Canaan. In order to bridge the
gap between Nuzi and the Middle Bronze Age, the Nuzi customs were

interpreted as reflecting older Hurrian practices of the early second millennium.

But soon the Middle Bronze II/Nuzi solution also disintegrated. From the point of view of the archaeology of Palestine, the difficulty came mainly from what we do not see or hear about in the biblical text. The Middle Bronze was a period of advanced urban life. Canaan was dominated by a group of powerful city-states, ruled from such capitals as Hazor and Megiddo. These cities were strongly fortified by huge earthen ramparts with massive gates. They had great palaces and towering temples. But in the biblical text we do not see this at all. True, a few cities are mentioned, but not necessarily the most important ones. Shechem (as a city) is not there, nor are Bethel and Jerusalem—all three were massive Middle Bronze strongholds. And in the plains we should have heard about Hazor, Megiddo, and Gezer, not Gerar. The biblical story of the patriarchs is clearly not the story of Middle Bronze Canaan. And the phenomenon of nomads living near city dwellers was not restricted to this era. And as for the names of the patriarchs, they have subsequently been found in later periods as well, in the Late Bronze and in the Iron Age. The name Jacob, for instance, which is indeed common in the Middle Bronze, is also found in the Late Bronze, in the fifth century BCE, and later.

As for the Nuzi texts, later studies have proven that the social and legal practices that show similarities to the biblical narratives cannot be restricted to a single period. They were common in the ancient Near East throughout the second and first millennia BCE. In fact, in some cases first millennium materials may offer better parallels. For instance, the responsibility of a barren wife to provide her husband with a servant to bear him children appeared in later periods, such as in a seventh century marriage contract from Assyria.

The Patriarchs in the Early Iron Age

Just when a second millennium solution seemed to be a lost case, the Israeli biblical scholar Benjamin Mazar took a different path, utilizing archaeological data to suggest that the description of the age of the patriarchs should be studied on the background of the early Iron Age. Mazar pointed mainly to the anachronisms in the text, such as the mention of a Philistine king (of Gerar) and of the Arameans. Needless to say, there were no Philistines in Canaan in either the Middle or Late Bronze Ages. Both Egyptian texts and archaeology have proved beyond doubt that they settled on the southern coast of Palestine in the twelfth century BCE. Instead of seeing their appearance here as a late insertion (in the time of the compilation) into an earlier tradition, Mazar argued that the text reflects an intimate knowledge of the Philistine kingdoms in a period just prior to the establishment of the monarchy in Israel. The Arameans also figure prominently in the patriarchal stories, but they too did not appear on the ancient Near Eastern stage before the early Iron Age, and their kingdoms emerged even later, mainly in the ninth century BCE. Mazar thought that the description of the Arameans as pastoral people reflects an early phase in their history, before they organized their first states. Thus he concluded that the wandering of the patriarchs in the central hill country between Shechem and Hebron fits the geographical framework of the early Israelite settlement in the Iron Age I. Some of these traditions, such as the one about Jacob building an altar at Bethel, can be understood on the background of the period of the judges, while other traditions, such as the centrality of Hebron, fit the early days of the monarchy, under David. The American biblical scholar Kyle McCarter took a somewhat similar view, though he was a bit more cautious. He saw in the patriarchal narratives different strata of composition and argued that some of them may go back to the Bronze Age. But on themes related to the special place given to Judah in the stories of the patriarchs—the prominence given to the figure of Abraham and to the tombs of the patriarchs at Hebron—McCarter took a point of view similar to the one suggested by Mazar. He argued that the prominence of Hebron in the patriarchal stories can best be understood against the background of the establishment of the monarchy under David.

Mazar was right in his claim that the reality behind the stories in the book of Genesis cannot be understood on the background of the Middle Bronze Age but should rather be tracked along the realities of the Iron Age. Yet he was wrong because his preferred date in the Iron Age was much too early. Modern archaeological research has shown that Judah, where the important J source was apparently written, was very sparsely inhabited until the late eighth century BCE. Likewise, a century of archaeological excavations in Jerusalem has indicated that the capital of Judah grew to become a significant city at about the same time; in the tenth century BCE, Jerusalem was no more than a small village. And the results of decades of excavations have shown that Judah did not reach a significant level of literacy before the late eight century BCE. Finally, and no less important, the patriarchal narratives are filled with references to late monarchic realities, mainly from the seventh century BCE.

APPENDIX B

Searching for Sinai

At least on the basis of modern tourist maps of the Sinai peninsula, there seems to be no special difficulty in identifying the most important places mentioned in the biblical stories of the wandering and the giving of the Law. Mount Sinai and other biblical places have been readily identified and visited since medieval times and even earlier, in the Byzantine period. In fact, the first full-fledged archaeological theory on the route of the wandering in the desert and the location of Mount Sinai is about fifteen hundred years old. It goes back to early Christian traditions related to the monastic movement, and to pilgrimage to the holy sites in the desert, in the fourth–sixth centuries CE. These traditions are still venerated today by tourists and pilgrims to Mount Sinai and the site of the burning bush.

In the heart of the mountainous region of southern Sinai, surrounded by awe-inspiring granite peaks, stands the Saint Catherine Monastery. Built in the sixth century CE by the Byzantine emperor Justinian to memorialize the supposed site of the burning bush (which is still shown today to visitors), the monastery acquired its present name in medieval times. Surrounded by high walls to protect it from marauders, the monastery evokes images of bygone ages. Its magnificent church and much of its fortifications belong to the original sixth century construction. Towering over the monastery is the peak of Jebel Musa ("the Mountain of Moses" in Arabic), which was identified, as early as the Byzantine period, with Mount Sinai. On this peak, which commands one of the most spectacular views of the desert, one can still identify the ruins of a sixth century chapel. And in the mountains around Jebel Musa and the Saint Catherine monastery there are other remains, of ancient, isolated monasteries with churches, hermit cells, and water installations.

References to some of these sites can be found in contemporary texts. A relatively large number of Byzantine sources describe the life of the Sinai monks and the construction of the monastery of the burning bush. No less interesting are texts related to the pilgrimage to the mount of God. The most detailed of these is the description of a late fourth century pilgrim named Egeria, who relates how she and her companions climbed the mount of God and how the monks living there showed her each of the places mentioned in the biblical accounts of Mount Sinai.

The historical reliability of these traditions, however, is open to question. While it is possible that the Byzantine monks preserved even more ancient traditions, there is no way to verify them, since there are absolutely no early remains from biblical times in this region. The most plausible explanation for the origins of the early Christian traditions in southern Sinai is their general location and environmental characteristics. The monastery of the burning bush and Mount Sinai of the Byzantine monks are located in a region of exceptional beauty, in the midst of great mountain scenery that could easily trigger veneration by monks and pilgrims. Moreover, continuous occupation of these sites was possible. The area around the monastery presented the monks with unique advantages, due to the particular combination of microclimate and geological formations. The high mountains of southern Sinai receive substantially more precipitation than the surrounding areas, and the red granite of the region is impermeable. The runoff of rainwater can therefore be collected in pools and cisterns. In addition, the wadis contain a large quantity of water in their subsoil, which can be reached in shallow wells. As a result, the Byzantine monks were able to cultivate fields and orchards in the small wadis between the mountains (as bedouin groups have continued to do up to present times).

It seems, therefore, that this combination of awe-inspiring scenery and relatively friendly environmental conditions encouraged pilgrimage and continuous veneration of sites in this part of the Sinai Peninsula. The power of the biblical story of Mount Sinai has always encouraged attempts to identify particular localities. Yet these remain in the realm of folklore and geographical speculation—not archaeology.

APPENDIX C

Alternative Theories of the Israelite Conquest

Peaceful Infiltration

In the 1920s and the 1930s, while Albright and his students were becoming increasingly convinced that they had found archaeological evidence for Joshua's conquest, a German biblical scholar named Albrecht Alt developed a very different hypothesis. Alt, a professor at the University of Leipzig, was highly skeptical that the book of Joshua could be read as history; like many of his German academic colleagues, he was a strong supporter of a critical approach to the Bible. He was convinced that the biblical account was compiled centuries after the alleged events took place and must be regarded as a heroic national myth. Yet Alt was not ready to conclude that an historical explanation of the origins of the Israelites was utterly beyond reach. While he discounted the narrative in Joshua, he was ready to accept the possibility of historical realities in the competing source—the first chapter of the book of Judges. In the course of his travels through Palestine in the early years of the twentieth century, Alt became fascinated with the lifeways and settlement patterns of the bedouin in the steppe regions of the Negev and in the Judean desert. And on the basis of his knowledge of ancient texts and his extensive ethnographic observations of bedouin life, especially their relationship with rural communities, he formulated a dramatic new theory of Israelite origins.

At the core of this new theory was the understanding that Middle Eastern pastoral nomads do not wander aimlessly but move with their herds in a fixed seasonal routine. Their complex movements are based on a precise understanding of seasonal climatic change. Since rain comes only in the winter and green pasture is a scarce resource through the long, dry summer, bedouin shepherds are forced to manage their flocks in a very careful way.

Alt observed that during the rainy winter seasons, when there was extensive pastureland even in relatively arid areas of steppe and desert, the bedouin moved far from the settled areas, establishing camps on desert fringe. When the dry season arrived and the winter pasturelands vanished, the bedouin groups moved their flocks closer to the greener, settled agricultural regions of the country, where grazing land could be found. The bedouin were hardly strangers to this region. Over the centuries they had established a customary and mutually beneficial arrangement with the inhabitants of the farming communities. They were allowed to let their animals roam in the recently harvested fields of the permanent villages, to graze in the stubble and manure the land. Yet at the height of summer, even this source of pasture was exhausted, with several months remaining until the arrival of the first winter rain. This was the most crucial time for the survival of the herds. And at this point the bedouin turned to the green pasture of the highlands, moving with their flocks between and among settled villages until the rainy season finally came and they moved out to the desert fringe again.

This annual routine was dependent on fluctuations in the timing and quantity of winter rainfall, and Alt also noted how drastic changes in climate or political conditions could influence the bedouin to give up their old way of life and settle down. This was a change in lifestyle that took a long time to accomplish; the pastoral way of life, with its customs, rhythms, and enormous flexibility, is in many ways a safer strategy for survival than farming a single plot of land. But the process was nevertheless observable as small seasonal plots began to appear in certain specific areas of summer pasture where bedouin groups had become accustomed to return year after year. After sowing wheat or barley in the small plots, they left with their flocks, to return late the following spring, in time to harvest the crop.

At first, small groups cultivated isolated plots, while they still continued to herd their flocks. Part of the family could stay behind near the fields, while the rest continued to move with the animals. These seasonal plots gradually grew larger and the bedouin cultivators became more dependent on them for grain, which they would otherwise have to obtain in trade from villagers. And as the time and effort devoted to farming gradually increased, the size of their flocks decreased, since they were compelled to stay near their fields and could no longer engage in long-range migration. The last stage in the process was permanent settlement, with the construction of permanent houses and the abandonment of herding except in the immediate vicinity of the fields. Alt noted that this was a gradual and largely peaceful process—at least in the beginning—since the bedouin initially settled in sparsely inhabited regions, where land and water were in relative abundance and ownership of the land was not carefully controlled. It was only at a later stage, when the newly settled bedouin began to compete for land and water with the inhabitants of nearby villages, that conflict—sometimes violent conflict—began.

In his observations of this process of settling down, or sedentarization, of pastoral nomads, Alt believed that he understood the situation described in the book of Judges. In time, he formulated what came to be known as the peaceful-infiltration theory of Israelite origins. According to Alt, the Israelites were originally pastoral nomads who routinely wandered with their flocks between the steppe regions in the east in the winter and, in the summer, in the highlands of western Canaan. Both areas were described by ancient Egyptian sources as sparsely settled. Even though the heavily wooded land was difficult to clear and the topography rugged, there was much free land for cultivation. Hence Alt believed that at the end of the Late Bronze Age, certain groups of pastoral nomads began to practice seasonal farming near their summer pasturelands in the highlands of Canaan. And the process of permanent settlement began.

As in modern times, this process was gradual and peaceful at the beginning. Yet Alt suggested that when the new settlers' numbers grew and their need of ever more land and water increased, they started having problems with their Canaanite neighbors, especially those who lived in the remote and isolated towns in the highlands, such as Jerusalem and Luz (Bethel). These conflicts over land and water rights—Alt hypothesized—eventually led to the local skirmishes and prolonged conflict that were the background to the struggles between Israelites and their Canaanite and Philistine neighbors in the book of Judges.

Though the peaceful-infiltration hypothesis was completely theoretical, it was a tempting proposal. It was logical, it fit the demographic and economic background of the country, and it fit the stories in Judges, which in any case looked more historical than the epic battle accounts of the book of Joshua. It had one more big advantage: it seemed to be backed by the ancient Egyptian texts. An Egyptian papyrus from the days of Ramesses II in the thirteenth century BCE, which recorded a contest between two scribes on the geography of Canaan, described the hill country as a rugged, wooded, almost empty region, inhabited by Shosu bedouin. Thus Alt believed that the Israelites could indeed be identified with these Shosu. Their initial stages of sedentarization in the highlands did not attract Egyptian hostility, because Egypt was concerned mainly with the fertile areas along the coast and in the northern valleys, close to the strategic international overland routes of trade.

In the early 1950s, Yohanan Aharoni, one of the most fervent supporters of Alt among Israeli archaeologists, believed that he had found conclusive evidence in upper Galilee. Aharoni explored this hilly and heavily wooded region in the north of the country to find that in the Late Bronze Age the area was almost empty of Canaanite settlements. In the succeeding period—Iron Age I—a relatively large number of small, isolated, poor settlements were established there. Aharoni identified the settlers with the early Israelites, more precisely with the people of the tribes of Naphtali and Asher, who were reported in the geographic chapters of the book of Joshua to have settled in mountainous Galilee.

Not unexpectedly, Aharoni's conclusions were bitterly contested by Yigael Yadin, who believed that the evidence of a massive conflagration of the Late Bronze city at Hazor—the city described by the book of Joshua as "the head of all those kingdoms"—precluded any theory of peaceful infiltration of any kind. Yadin, who adhered to the unified conquest theory, argued that as long as the city of Hazor was still powerful, the Israelites could not have settled in Galilee. In his view, the first act in this story must have been the destruction of Hazor by the Israelites in the late thirteenth century BCE. Only when Hazor lay in ruins did the door open for the Israelites to settle in upper Galilee and, in fact, also on the ruins of Hazor itself.

Aharoni's reconstruction of the events was less heroic, though no less romantic. In his opinion, the Israelites appeared in the region when Hazor was still a powerful city. But they did not opt for confrontation. Rather than settle in the vicinity of Hazor and attract the hostility of its inhabitants, the arriving Israelites gradually and peacefully settled in isolated, empty, wooded upper Galilee. There they chose a struggle with the harsh environment and the risks of highland farming rather than a conflict with mighty Hazor. The final showdown came later, according to Aharoni, when the Israelites gained enough strength to mount an attack on Hazor. Only after the city was destroyed did the Israelites expand into the richer and more fertile areas of the north, including the northern tip of the Jordan valley.

The peaceful-infiltration theory started gaining the upper hand two decades later, as a result of Aharoni's explorations in the Beersheba valley, an arid zone south of the Judean hill country. In the 1960s and 1970s Aharoni excavated some of the most important sites in the valley: the fortress of Arad, the ancient town of Beersheba, and the exceptionally large Early Iron Age site of Tel Masos, located near freshwater wells in the middle of the valley. Aharoni discovered that the settlement history of the Beersheba valley was similar to that of upper Galilee. While there were no permanent settlements in the valley in the Late Bronze Age, a number of small settlements were established there in the Iron Age I. Aharoni identified these Iron Age I settlers with the people of the tribe of Simeon. And though the tribe was different, Aharoni was convinced that the story was the same: peaceful settlement by Israelites in frontier territories that were empty of Canaanite cities.

Peasant Revolt

Despite their divergent backgrounds, religious faiths, and conflicting opinions, there was one fervent belief that Albright, Alt, Yadin, and Aharoni all shared. Both the military-conquest and peaceful-infiltration theories presumed that the Israelites were a new group that had entered the country at the end of the Late Bronze Age. And regardless of their differences regarding the understanding of the biblical text, all believed that this ethnic group lived at a far lower level of civilization than the native Canaanites. Both Yadin and Aharoni characterized these early Israelites as seminomads and both believed that the conquest of Canaan, whether by invasion or by infiltration, was a chapter in the timeless conflict between Middle Eastern farmers and nomads—between the desert and the sown.

This implicit belief was profoundly shaken in the 1960s and 1970s, when anthropologists and archaeologists working in other parts of the Middle East realized that the timeworn assumptions about clear distinctions between the worlds of wandering shepherds and settled villagers were simplistic, romantic, naive, and wrong. The first and most important of these assumptions was the nineteenth century belief that throughout antiquity the Syrian and Arabian deserts contained vast numbers of turbulent nomads who periodically invaded the settled land. This assumption was overturned by a growing consensus among anthropologists in the 1960s that the great deserts had not been able to support more than a handful of "pure" nomads before the widespread domestication of the camel as a herd animal in the late second millennium BCE, if not later. Since this development took place after the Israelites had already emerged in Canaan, it was extremely unlikely that the example of a bedouin invasion could be applied to them. Accordingly, certain scholars concluded that the Israelites were not pure camel nomads but primarily sheep and goat herders, of a type known to roam with their flocks not in the desert but on the fringes of the arable land.

As Albrecht Alt had noted, the summer grain harvest coincides with the drying up of the grazing lands on the edges of the desert, and the natural movement of pastoralists and their flocks back toward the well-watered agricultural regions encourages and even necessitates cooperation between the two groups. At the least, the pastoralists may be hired as seasonal agricultural workers and their flocks may be allowed to graze in the stubble of the harvested fields. But in many cases the pastoralists and the farmers may be members of a single community, whose nomadic members wander off to the desert steppe in the winter, while the sedentary members stay behind to prepare and plant the village fields.

Research into the nature of pastoral nomadism suggested that the old assumptions about the ancient Israelites' gradual transformation from nomads to farmers should be turned upside down. From an anthropological standpoint, Israelite pastoralists and Canaanite farmers belonged to the same economic system. If there had been any significant movements of population, its source could only have been in the settled regions, and it would have been, in the words of the historian John Luke, "*toward* the steppe and desert, not out of the desert toward the sown."

Then came George Mendenhall, a feisty biblical scholar at the University of Michigan, who rejected both the immigration and conquest theories of Israelite settlement with equal disdain. For years, Mendenhall had been a voice in the wilderness of biblical scholarship, claiming that the rise of the Israelite religion and tribal confederacy could be explained solely on the basis of internal social developments in Canaan during the Late Bronze Age. As early as 1947, he reviewed the evidence of the Tell el-Amarna letters and was one of the first to conclude that the Apiru, identified by some scholars as Hebrews, were not an ethnic group at all, but a well-defined social class.

Mendenhall argued that the city-states of Late Bronze Age Canaan were organized as highly stratified societies, with the king or mayor at the top of the pyramid, the princes, court officials, and chariot warriors right below him, and the rural peasants at the base. The Apiru were apparently outside this scheme of organization, and they seem to have threatened the social order in a number of ways. Mendenhall and others pointed out that the Apiru, though originally sedentary, withdrew from the urban–rural system, sometimes to serve as mercenaries for the highest bidder, and when that work was not forthcoming, some Apiru actively encouraged the peasants to rebel.

The context for this social unrest, Mendenhall asserted, was a conflict not between nomads and a settled population, but between the rural population and the rulers of the city-states. The Tell el-Amarna letters provide evidence of hardship and the increasingly onerous exactions, by the kings and by their Egyptian overlords, of agricultural and pastoral produce. It was no wonder that the Apiru had great success in stirring up the peasants and that many Canaanite cities were destroyed at that time. The Late Bronze Age cities of Canaan were little more than administrative centers of regional feudal regimes. Their destruction was not a military victory alone.

It was also the effective termination of the economic system that the city had maintained.

"Both the Amarna materials and the biblical events represent the same political process," Mendenhall wrote in 1970,

> namely, the withdrawal, not physically and geographically, but politically and subjectively, of large population groups from any obligation to existing political regimes, and therefore the renunciation of any protection from these sources. In other words, there was no statistically important invasion of Palestine at the beginning of the twelve-tribe system of Israel. There was no radical displacement of population, there was no genocide, there was no large scale driving out of population, only of royal administrators (of necessity!). In summary, there was no real conquest of Palestine in the sense that has usually been understood; what happened instead may be termed, from the point of view of the secular historian interested only in socio-political processes, a peasants' revolt against the network of interlocking Canaanite city-states.

At the heart of the peasant revolt theory was a novel explanation of how the Israelite religion began. Mendenhall maintained that the Apiru and their peasant supporters could never have united and overcome Canaanite feudal domination without a compelling ideology. And he believed that their ideology—the worship of a single, transcendent God, YHWH—was a brilliant response to the religion of the Canaanite kings. Instead of relying on a pantheon of divinities and elaborate fertility rituals (which could be performed only by the king and his official priesthood), the new religious movement placed its faith in a single God who established egalitarian laws of social conduct and who communicated them directly to each member of the community. The hold of the kings over the people was therefore effectively broken by the spread of this new faith. And for the supporters of the peasant revolt theory, the true Israelite conquest was accomplished— without invasion or immigration—when large numbers of Canaanite peasants overthrew their masters and became "Israelites."

In 1979, Norman K. Gottwald, another American biblical scholar, accepted and expanded Mendenhall's theories in his book *The Tribes of Yahweh*. But he also went a step further; he attacked the archaeological evidence head-on. While Mendenhall had merely dismissed all the talk of the settlement of seminomads in the hill country and on the fringes of the desert, Gottwald believed that those sites were, in fact, Israelite. But he made this identification for completely different reasons. He theorized that the remote frontier and forest regions were naturally attractive to the members of an independence movement who had fled from the more heavily populated (and more closely controlled) plains and valleys to establish a new way of life. Gottwald suggested that their settlement in this rocky and poorly watered region was possible primarily because of technological developments: iron tools for hewing cisterns in the bedrock, and waterproof plaster for sealing the cistern walls and terracing hilly slopes.

On the social front, Gottwald added that in their new homes the Israelites established a more equal society, with access to the means of production open to all. And on the cognitive level, he suggested that the new ideas of equality were imported to Canaan by a small group of people who came from Egypt and settled in the highlands. This group may have been influenced by unorthodox Egyptian ideas on religion, such as the ones that stimulated the revolution of Akhenaten in the fourteenth century, ideas that were closer to the much later concept of monotheism. So this new group was the nucleus around which the new settlers in the highlands crystallized.

The American archaeologist William Dever provided an explicitly archaeological context for the peasant revolt theory. Proposing a new interpretation of finds from earlier excavations, he argued that the pottery and architecture of the new settlements in the highlands in Iron Age I resembled the ceramic and building traditions of the inhabitants of the lowlands in the Late Bronze Age—thus suggesting that the early Israelites came from the sedentary communities of Canaan. Agreeing with Gottwald, Dever suggested that the Iron Age I was the first time that the hill country was densely settled, due in large measure to two technological innovations. These were the knowledge of hewing and plastering water storage cisterns in the bedrock (which enabled the new population to establish settlements away from perennial springs and wells) and the techniques of constructing agricultural terraces on steep hillsides (which opened the way for a more intense exploitation of the hill country, including specialization in vines and olive groves, which in turn led to the mass production of wine and olive oil). According to Dever both "inventions" must have originated in a technically sophisticated, complex society—namely that of the sedentary population of Canaan.

The peasant revolt or "social revolution" hypothesis was very attractive and gained the support of a large number of biblical scholars and archaeologists. It seemed to fit the social realities of Late Bronze Age Canaan, it seemed to explain the decline of the Late Bronze settlement system in the lowlands and the rise of the Iron Age I system in the highlands, and it was very much in tune with the radical political orientation of American and European academic life at the time. It also meshed with the mounting skepticism in biblical research regarding the historical value of both Joshua and Judges. But it was wrong. Indeed, it was abandoned with almost the same speed that it had emerged. The reason? It was highly speculative and theoretical, and had little real support from archaeology. In fact, archaeology testified against it.

It also came at the wrong time. By the 1980s, anthropologists and archaeologists were becoming more and more skeptical about the possibility that pottery and architectural styles could reveal the ethnicity or geographical origin of ancient people. Such elements of material culture could easily be imitated or borrowed by one society from another. In fact, most of the finds mentioned by Dever were uncovered in villages representing the second phase of settlement in the highlands. Therefore, the similarities to Late Bronze Age finds might indicate trade or economic connections of the Iron Age I settlers with the people of the lowlands rather than *origin*, since there was clear cultural continuity in the lowlands from the Late Bronze Age to the Iron Age I. More important, in the 1970s and early 1980s, hard data on the Iron I villages of the highlands started pouring in from the field, and the new evidence clearly contradicted the social revolution theory.

First and foremost, the new data showed that the Iron Age I was not the first period of intensive settlement activity in the highlands, and that the two "technological innovations" were known—and used—centuries before the rise of early Israel. In other words, the use of rock-cut, plastered cisterns and the construction of hillside terraces were characteristic outcomes of strong settlement activity in the hill country, not the prime movers behind it. The archaeological evidence from the lowlands also does not support the social revolution theory. It has become clear in recent years that by the Late Bronze Age, the rural sector of the Canaanite society had already been depleted and could not have supplied either the energy or the manpower behind the new wave of highland settlement. Moreover, the archaeological work in the highlands in the 1980s and 1990s produced some striking indications that most of the settlers there in Iron Age I came from a pastoral—rather than sedentary—background.

All three theories of the Israelite conquest—unified invasion, peaceful infiltration, and social revolution—endorsed the pivotal biblical notion that the rise of early Israel was a unique, singular phenomenon in the history of the country. New discoveries of recent decades have shattered that idea.

APPENDIX D

Why the Traditional Archaeology of the Davidic and Solomonic Period Is Wrong

The Davidic Conquests: A Ceramic Mirage

The most important archaeological evidence used to link destruction levels with the Davidic conquests was the decorated Philistine pottery, which was dated by scholars from the beginning of the twelfth century BCE until about 1000 BCE. The first strata that did not contain this distinctive style were dated to the tenth century, that is, to the time of the united monarchy. But this dating was based entirely on biblical chronology and was thus a circular argument because the lower date for the levels with this pottery was fixed according to the presumed era of the Davidic conquests around 1000 BCE. In fact, there was no clear evidence for the precise date of the transition from the Philistine style to later types.

Moreover, recent studies have revolutionized the dating of Philistine pottery. In recent decades, many major sites have been excavated in the southern coastal plain of Israel, the area of strong Egyptian presence in the twelfth century BCE, and the region where the Philistines settled. These sites included three of the cities mentioned in the Bible as the hub of Philistine life—Ashdod, Ashkelon, and Ekron (Tel Miqne) as well as several sites that served as Egyptian forts. The latter disclosed information about the Egypto-Canaanite material culture in the last decades of Egyptian hegemony in Canaan. Their finds included Egyptian inscriptions related to the imperial administration of Canaan as well as large quantities of locally made Egyptian vessels. Some of the inscriptions date from the reign of Ramesses III—the pharaoh who fought the Philistines and supposedly settled them in his forts in southern Canaan.

The surprise was that the strata that represent the last phases of Egyptian domination in Canaan under Ramesses III did not reveal the early types of the decorated Philistine vessels, and the earliest Philistine levels did not reveal any sign of Egyptian presence, not even a single Egyptian vessel. Instead, they were completely separated. Moreover, in a few sites, Egyptian forts of the time of Ramesses III were *succeeded* by the first Philistine settlements. In chronological terms this could not have happened before the collapse of Egyptian domination in Canaan in the mid–twelfth century BCE. The implications of this revelation for the archaeology of the united monarchy create a sort of domino effect: the whole set of pottery styles is pushed forward by about half a century, and that includes the transition from Philistine to the post-Philistine styles.

Another kind of evidence comes from stratum VIA at Megiddo, which represents the last phase of Canaanite material culture in the north. This stratum has always been dated to the eleventh century BCE and was believed to have been destroyed by King David. This assumption fitted the biblical ideology perfectly: the pious King David annihilated the last remaining stronghold of Canaanite culture. Since this stratum was violently destroyed by fire, hundreds of complete pottery vessels were crushed by the collapse of the walls and roofs. Indeed, a large number of vessels were uncovered by the Oriental Institute excavations and more recent Tel Aviv University dig at Megiddo. Yet no examples of the decorated Philistine style were found. It is therefore impossible to date this city to the eleventh century, a period of time in which the decorated Philistine pottery is common all over the country, including neighboring sites in the Jezreel valley. Indeed, there are Philistine vessels at Megiddo itself, but they all come from the previous stratum. This means that the last city at Megiddo featuring remnants of Canaanite material culture cannot have been destroyed by King David around 1000 BCE. Both the ceramic and carbon-14 evidence suggests it was still in existence several decades later—well into the tenth century BCE.

Rethinking Megiddo: Dates, Pottery, and Architectural Styles

Yigael Yadin argued that the identification of the Solomonic cities was based on stratigraphy, pottery, and the Bible. But stratigraphy and pottery provide only relative chronology. It is clear, therefore, that the whole idea of the archaeology of the united monarchy, of the blueprint city planning of Solomon's architects, and of the grandeur of the Solomonic palaces, rests on one verse in the Bible—1 Kings 9:15. We must repeat this again: the entire traditional reconstruction of the nature of the united monarchy of Israel—its territorial expansion, its material culture, its relationship with the neighboring countries—depends on the interpretation of a single biblical verse! And this verse is quite problematic, because we do not know if it is based on authentic sources from the time of Solomon or later realities. We do not even understand its exact meaning: Does "built" mean that Solomon founded new cities? Did he only fortify existing ones? Do the three cities mentioned—Megiddo, Gezer, and Hazor—merely symbolize, for the author of Kings, the three main administrative cities of northern Israel? Did the author of Kings project the great construction in these cities in later years back to the days of Solomon?

Let us start with the six-chambered gates. First, the idea that the Megiddo gate dates to the time of the ashlar palaces has been challenged, mainly because the gate is connected to the massive wall that runs *over* the two palaces. In other words, since the wall is later than the palaces and since it connects to the gate, there is good reason to believe that the gate is also later than the palaces. Moreover, recent excavations have shown that this type of gate was used outside the borders of the united monarchy and that similar gates were built in later phases of the Iron Age, until the seventh century BCE. So the single peg on which the whole structure hangs has also proved to be shaky. But this is not all.

The next clue comes from the nearby site of Jezreel, located less than ten miles to the east of Megiddo. The site was excavated in the 1990s by David Ussishkin of Tel Aviv University and John Woodhead of the British School of Archaeology in Jerusalem. They uncovered a large fortified enclosure, which they identified with the palace built by Ahab in the first half of the ninth century BCE. This palatial acropolis was destroyed a short while after it was built. This presumably happened either in the course of the revolt against the Omride dynasty led by the future Israelite king Jehu or as a result of the military campaign of Hazael, king of Damascus, in northern Israel. In either case, the date of abandonment of the Jezreel enclosure would be around the middle of the ninth century BCE. The surprise was that the pottery found in the Jezreel enclosure is identical to the pottery of the city of palaces at Megiddo. But the latter was supposed to have been destroyed by Pharaoh Shishak almost a century earlier! How can we bridge this gap? There are only two possibilities here: either we pull the building of Jezreel back to the time of Solomon, or we push the Megiddo palaces ahead to the time of the dynasty of Ahab. It goes without saying that in this case, there is only one solution, since there is no record of Solomonic occupation of Jezreel and since the Jezreel compound is similar in layout to the acropolis of Samaria, the capital of the northern kingdom, which was no doubt built by the Omrides. The city of ashlar palaces at Megiddo was destroyed in the mid-ninth century, probably by Hazael, and not in 926 BCE by Shishak.

But is there any other direct evidence about the date of Megiddo's city of palaces in addition to the domino effect we described above? In other words, is it still possible that it was *built* in the time of Solomon in the tenth century BCE, and only *destroyed* in the ninth century? The answer is apparently negative, for two reasons. The first clue comes from Samaria — the capital of the northern kingdom of Israel, which was built in the early ninth century. There are clear similarities in the building methods of the Samaria palace and the two Megiddo palaces and it seems, therefore, that they were built at the same time. Here too we face two options: either to argue that the Samaria palace and royal acropolis were both built by Solomon or to argue that the Megiddo palaces were built later than Solomon. The first option cannot be accepted, because there is hardly a doubt that the Samaria palace and the entire acropolis were built by Omri and Ahab in the early ninth century.

A word should be said here about the treatment of the biblical materials. Some of our colleagues wonder how we can dismiss the historicity of one verse in the Bible (1 Kings 9:15) and accept the historicity of others — relating to Ahab's construction of the palace at Jezreel (1 Kings 21:1) and to the construction of the palace at Samaria by Omri (1 Kings 16:24). The answer has to do with methodology. The biblical material cannot be treated as a monolithic block. It does not require a take-all-or-leave-all attitude. Two centuries of modern biblical scholarship have shown us that the biblical material must be evaluated chapter by chapter and sometimes verse by verse. The Bible includes historical, nonhistorical, and quasi-historical materials, which sometimes appear very close to one another in the text. The whole essence of biblical scholarship is to separate the historical parts from the rest of the text according to linguistic, literary, and extrabiblical historical considerations. So, yes, one may doubt the historicity of one verse and accept the validity of another, especially in the case of Omri and Ahab, whose kingdom is described in contemporary Assyrian, Moabite, and Aramean texts.

APPENDIX E

Identifying the Era of Manasseh in the Archaeological Record

It is not easy to pinpoint Manasseh archaeologically, that is, to identify the specific city levels built during his reign in sites throughout Judah. Although the pottery of the Late Iron II in Judah is known better than that of any other phase of the Iron Age, its dating is not yet precise enough to distinguish the styles of a specific generation. The main reason for this less-than-desired situation is that in order to date pottery assemblages in a precise way, we need to uncover destruction layers that can safely be assigned to a particular historical event. The entire pottery chronology of the last phase of the history of Judah after the fall of Israel is therefore based on one site, Lachish in the Shephelah, which twice provides this combination of an unambiguous archaeological destruction layer with rich finds and a reliable historical source. First, the Assyrian annals, the Nineveh relief, and the Bible leave no doubt that the city was devastated by Sennacherib in 701 BCE. Second, the biblical reference to Azekah and Lachish as the last strongholds to withstand the Babylonian assault (Jeremiah 34:7), confirmed by an ostracon found at the site, provides clear evidence that Lachish was annihilated by the Babylonians in 587/6 BCE.

These two destructions of Lachish were linked to the end of strata III and II at the site. Comparing Late Iron II assemblages that were exposed in other Judean sites to the two rich, well-dated pottery assemblages of

Lachish, scholars were able to distinguish two horizons in eighth–seventh centuries BCE Judah: sites that were destroyed by the Assyrians in the late eighth century BCE and those the Babylonians destroyed in the beginning of the sixth century.

The reign of Manasseh falls between these two horizons. Since Manasseh was a loyal vassal of Assyria there were no wars in his time; no great destructions took place. His days were peaceful times for Judah. Yet what was good for the people of Judah is, ironically, bad for archaeologists. We do not have even one stratum that can safely be dated to his days. Cities established by Manasseh survived until the final fall of Judah and therefore destruction layers feature the material culture of their last years rather than that of their early days. Hence the only way to pinpoint Manasseh is to outline the general settlement and demographic trends in Judah between 701 BCE and the late seventh century. Bearing in mind that the reign of Manasseh comes right after Sennacherib's campaign, and represents a significant period of economic recovery, even this very general information is of much value.

APPENDIX F

How Vast Was the Kingdom of Josiah?

The book of Chronicles suggests that Josiah's campaign of cultic purification and territorial conquest reached far to the north and south, into "the cities of Manasseh, Ephraim, and Simeon, and as far as Naphtali" (2 Chronicles 34:6). Accordingly, many biblical archaeologists have long taken the Chronicler's report at face value and have believed that Josiah's kingdom extended over most of the territory of western Palestine, from the Negev highlands in the south to the Galilee in the north. According to this view, Josiah took over large parts of the territories of the former northern kingdom, also expanding to the south and west, into areas which had never before been controlled by Jerusalem. Yet a new archaeological analysis suggests that the territorial advances of Josiah were much more limited.

The older, maximalist view regarding the northern border of Judah in the time of Josiah was based on the finds at Megiddo. With the fall of the northern kingdom, the Assyrians made Megiddo the capital of their province in the northern valleys and Galilee. They rebuilt the city in a completely new layout, with two typical Assyrian palaces and a new concept of an orthogonal city with sets of parallel streets crossing one another at right angles. This city—stratum III—is the best archaeological example of an Assyrian government center in the western provinces of their empire. It functioned until the Assyrian withdrawal from Palestine toward the end of the seventh century BCE.

The following layer at Megiddo, stratum II, is, in many parts of the mound, simply a continuation of the previous city with minimal rebuilding and additions. But there are two main differences between the cities of stratum III and stratum II: in the later level, the city wall went out of use and a massive building, which was identified by the team of the University of Chicago as a fort, was erected on the eastern side of the mound. There it dominates the valley and the international highway from Egypt to Mesopotamia. Stratum II was attributed by the same excavators to Josiah "in his efforts to unite the two kingdoms," and its partial destruction was attributed to the encounter that would ultimately end Josiah's life.

The Megiddo fort, therefore, presumably provided the missing link to explain the showdown with Necho. It was suggested that Josiah took over the entire hill country territories of the ex-northern kingdom and then expanded farther north to Megiddo and made it his strategic northern outpost. The control over the entire region from Jerusalem to the Jezreel valley made it possible for Josiah to advance to Megiddo with his army, possibly in an attempt to stop Necho from assisting the Assyrian army against the Babylonians.

As to the presumed western border of the kingdom of Judah at the time of Josiah, the prize find for the maximalists was Mesad Hashavyahu—a small site on the coast about fifteen miles south of Tel Aviv. This modest building, which has been identified as a fort (hence the name in Hebrew, *mesad,* or "fort"), yielded two exciting finds. First, the pottery assemblage, which is well dated to the seventh century BCE, included imported Greek pottery. Second, a number of ostraca found at the site were written in biblical Hebrew. They mention Yahwistic names with the ending *yahu:* Hoshayahu, Obadiahu, Hashavyahu. The site was therefore interpreted as a fort built by Josiah on the coast, with the aim to give Judah access to the sea. It was staffed with a Judahite commander and Greek mercenaries who served in the Judahite army, in a capacity similar to their role in the Egyptian army of the time. Contemporary ostraca found at the Judahite fort of Arad in the Beersheba valley seemed to support this idea. They mention allocation of food provisions to people named Kittim, a term that was interpreted as meaning "Greeks"—that is, a Greek mercenary contingent in the Judahite army.

The discussion of the border of the kingdom of Josiah in the south concentrated on the two great seventh century forts—Kadesh-barnea and Haseva—excavated by the Israeli archaeologist Rudolph Cohen in the desert far to the south of the southern line of Judahite cities in the Beersheba valley. Kadesh-barnea commands the largest oasis on the important trade road from southern Palestine to the head of the Gulf of Aqaba and, farther south, to Arabia. According to the excavator, a series of Judahite forts was built at the site. The last of the series was built in the days of Josiah and destroyed by the Babylonians in 586 BCE. This last structure was identified as a Judahite fort because of a certain resemblance to the Judahite forts in the Beersheba valley, because a few Hebrew ostraca were found there, and because the general historical evaluation of Josiah's reign suggested the likelihood of Judahite expansion into this area. At Haseva, about twenty miles to the south of the Dead Sea, a massive square casemate structure, about two and a half acres in size, with an elaborate four-chambered gate, was dated to the ninth–eighth centuries BCE. It was succeeded by a somewhat smaller fort in the late seventh century BCE, related to the activities of Josiah. A hoard of smashed Edomite cult vessels buried in a pit near the fort was also ascribed to the seventh century and connected with the cult reform of Josiah.

Despite these seeming archaeological indications of Josianic expansion, there were some scholars who believed that certain geographical material in the Bible clearly indicates that Josiah's territorial gains were minimal. The most important source is the lists of tribal towns in Joshua 15–19, several of which the German biblical scholar Albrecht Alt suggested should be dated to the seventh century. In particular, he suggested that the town lists of Judah, Benjamin, Dan, and Simeon reflect the administrative division of Judah in the time of Josiah. At that time the kingdom was divided into twelve districts, which encompassed the area from the Beersheba valley in the south to the plateau of Benjamin in the north, including the eastern Shephelah. Another indication came from the lists of those who returned from the Babylonian exile, which appear in the books of Ezra and Nehemiah. These lists apparently include places that were within the borders of Judah before the destruction of 586 BCE.

The Israeli biblical historian Benjamin Mazar added that the description of the geographical limits of the religious reform of Josiah in 2 Kings 23:8 also discloses the borders of his state: "And he brought all the priests out of the cities of Judah, and defiled the high places where the priests had burned incense, from Geba to Beersheba." Mazar identified this Geba with a site located about fifteen miles north of Jerusalem. The meaning of all this was apparently that Josiah's expansion in the north was minimal and included only the area of the much-hated cult center of Bethel.

Indeed, the archaeological finds that were used by the maximalists may be interpreted in a very different way. To start with Megiddo in the north, there is no evidence whatsoever to attribute the fort of stratum II to Josiah. Not a single Judahite item of the seventh century (which we shall describe below) has ever been found at Megiddo. We can safely accept the alternative view, that stratum II at Megiddo represents a peaceful takeover by the Egyptians. The Assyrian palaces probably continued to serve the Egyptian administration, and a fort was constructed on the eastern edge of the mound. This interpretation raises a somewhat similar problem, in that stratum II at Megiddo did not produce Egyptian finds. But the Egyptian rule in Palestine in the seventh century was very short—between ten and twenty years—and did not leave many finds even in the southern coastal plain.

As for Mesad Hashavyahu on the west, the Greek pottery that was found there is now known from a number of sites in the southern coastal plain and the Beersheba valley. The question is, should this pottery be understood as representing the physical presence of Greek merchants or mercenaries, or just the product of trade relations with the West? In general, the answer to a question like this depends, among other factors, on the quantity of this pottery found at a given site. The relatively high ratio of this pottery at Mesad Hashavyahu may indeed indicate the presence of Greeks. And if the site was indeed a fort, then we may be dealing with mercenaries. The next question would be, in which army did they serve? The Greek historian Herodotus tells us that Greek mercenaries served in the army of Psammetichus I, king of Egypt, and that they were stationed in his border fortresses. This has been confirmed in excavations in Egypt, including a dig of one of the places specifically mentioned by Herodotus. We can therefore quite safely accept the theory that Mesad Hashavyahu was an Egyptian coastal outpost staffed by, among others, Greek mercenaries.

But is it not possible that Greek mercenaries served also in the Judahite army? It is worth noting again in this connection the Kittim, who are mentioned in some of the late seventh century ostraca that were found in the southern Judahite fort of Arad. The commander of the fort was instructed to supply them with food provisions. Based on the Bible, which identifies Kittim with Greeks or Cypriots, and on the Greek pottery found in Mesad Hashavyahu (which was supposed to have been a Judahite fortress from the time of Josiah), Aharoni, the excavator of Arad, proposed that the Kittim were Greek or Cypriot mercenaries who served in the Judahite army. But other explanations are no less logical. Nadav Naaman suggested that the Arad ostraca should be understood as orders given to the Judahite commanders to provide supplies to Greek mercenaries in the Egyptian army, which at that time dominated Judah. Another biblical historian, Anson Rainey, proposed that the Kittim were not mercenaries but, rather, merchants who originated from the town of Kition in Cyprus. In any event, regarding Mesad Hashavyahu, there can be little doubt that Egypt, which expanded in the late seventh century along the coast of the Levant, was strong enough to prevent Josiah from building an isolated fort in the middle of an area in which Egypt had strong strategic interests.

If Mesad Hashavyahu was an Egyptian fort, we should ask what Judahites—that is, people carrying Yahwistic names—were doing there. The book of Jeremiah (44:1; 46:14) tells us that in his time Judahites lived in several places in Egypt, and from the finds at the island of Elephantine in the Nile, in Upper Egypt, combined with the references in the Bible to Syene (Aswan), we may assume that Judahites served as mercenaries in the Egyptian army as early as the late monarchic period. It is therefore quite reasonable that the unit stationed in the Egyptian fort of Mesad Hashavyahu included Judahite mercenaries. Naaman suggested that some of these Judahites may have been corvée workers who were sent there as part of Judah's obligation as a subordinate of Egypt. There is thus no reason to stretch the territory of Josiah as far west as the coast.

Now to the south. The two seventh century forts in the deep south—Kadesh-barnea in the west and Haseva in the east—were identified as Judahite according to some pottery types and (in the case of the former) a few Hebrew ostraca, but mainly according to the idea of the great expansion of Judah in the time of Josiah. But there is a no less appealing alternative, which was proposed by Naaman, that both were built in the early seventh century under Assyrian auspices with the assistance of the local vassal states—Judah (of Manasseh) and Edom—and that they were manned with local vassal troops. He further proposed that the ostraca written in Egyptian hieratic script found at Kadesh-barnea hint that in the late seventh century the site passed to the Egyptians. Indeed, the two forts, especially the huge fort of Haseva (which probably dates to the seventh century), look somewhat different from the Judahite forts in the Beersheba valley.

So far for the negative evidence. But do we have positive clues, that is, archaeological finds that can help us delineate the borders of Judah at the time of Josiah? The material culture of Judah in the late seventh century had several clear characteristics that are relatively easy to trace in the archaeological record. They represent various aspects of seventh century life in Judah—trade, cult, administration, and daily life. If we plot their distribution on a map we may be able to identify the borders of Judah. Though some of them appeared for the first time a few decades before Josiah's reign, they must have continued to be in use, and their popularity peaked in the late seventh century. In other words, we may speculate that if Josiah extended the borders of Judah, the typical Judahite finds must also have gradually expanded to the new territories.

The first characteristic of the archaeology of Judah in the seventh century is small inscribed weights made of limestone. They were apparently used for daily, private commercial activity. They appear mainly in the heartland of Judah, from the Beersheba valley in the south to the area just to the north of Jerusalem. They were also found in large quantities in the eastern Shephelah. Outside of these traditional borders of Judah they are found in meaningful quantities only in the west, that is, in the lower Shephelah and the coastal plain. But this can be a result of strong trade activity between Judah and this area.

Another typical seventh century find in Judah is seal impressions in the shape of a rosette, found on the handles of storage jars. These seals probably played some role, which is not yet fully understood, in the administration of Judah at that time. Their distribution encompasses the highlands of Judah, from the Beersheba valley in the south to the area a bit to the north of Jerusalem, with the main concentration in the area of the capital.

Figurines of a standing woman supporting her breasts with her hands are also found in large quantities in late monarchic Judah. They can be distinguished from similar figurines that appear in neighboring regions. Almost all of them were found in the heartland of Judah, between Beersheba and Bethel. In the west they appear in large numbers as far west as the Lachish–Beth-shemesh line. Another type of figurine, depicting a horse and a rider, is also popular in the Late Iron II in the region. In this case, too, a Judahite version can be isolated. Almost all figurines of the latter type were found within the borders of Judah proper.

At any rate, these objects and typical Judahite pottery types of the late seventh century are found mainly in the heartland of the southern kingdom. Their numbers decline when one goes west and north. They still appear in meaningful quantity on the plateau of Bethel, but farther north their share in the assemblages declines.

When all these items are individually plotted on a map, their distribution is quite similar. It extends from the Beersheba valley to the plateau of Bethel north of Jerusalem, and from the Dead Sea and Jordan valley to the upper Shephelah. The question is, were these the borders of Judah, and do they indicate that there was no expansion farther to the north? Or do they represent only the core territory of the kingdom? In this case too, we must remember that if the drive to the north was short-lived, it could be underrepresented in the archaeological record. But a permanent and far-reaching annexation of new territories into the kingdom of Judah is simply not suggested by the archaeological finds.

APPENDIX G

The Boundaries of the Province of Yehud

The Persian kings retained the general administrative division of the Near East that had been instituted by the earlier Assyrian and Babylonian empires. Under the Persians, the vast territories of the region were divided into satrapies, and each satrapy was further subdivided into provinces that were administered by governors. Palestine belonged to the satrapy called Beyond the River (that is, west of the Euphrates), which, according to Herodotus—the great Greek historian of the time—included the areas of Syria, Phoenicia, Cyprus, and Palestine.

The most detailed territorial data on the post-exilic province of Yehud come from the biblical text, from the list of exiles who returned from Babylonia (Ezra 2; Nehemiah 7) and from the list of the builders of the walls of Jerusalem (Nehemiah 3). In the south, the boundary between Yehud and the Edomite territory passed just to the south of Beth-zur, leaving Hebron—the second-most-important town in the highlands in late monarchic times and the location of the tombs of the patriarchs—outside the territory of the repatriates. In the north, the border of Yehud conformed to the late seventh century border of late monarchic Judah, passing to the north of Mizpah and Bethel. In the east, Jericho was included in Yehud. In the west, the area of Lod in the northern Shephelah is mentioned in the list of the exiles returning from Babylon, but there is no consensus among scholars as to whether it was included in the province. Yehud was therefore a small province, covering mainly the Judean hills approximately fifteen miles to the north and south of Jerusalem, an area not much bigger than eight hundred square miles. This was a much smaller territory even than the limited area of Judah in the late seventh century BCE. Unlike the latter, it did not include the southern Hebron hills, the Beersheba valley, and much of the Shephelah. The province was apparently subdivided into districts; the list of the builders of the wall (Nehemiah 3) mentions a few towns, among them Mizpah in the north and Beth-zur in the south, that served as district centers within the province of Yehud.

This textual reconstruction of the boundaries of the province of Yehud is confirmed by archaeological finds. The most indicative of these are various seal impressions found on pottery vessels from the Persian period, bearing Aramaic or Hebrew characters that spell out the Aramaic name of the province—Yehud. A few hundred examples have so far been found. Their distribution, at least in meaningful quantities, is identical to the boundaries of the province of Yehud as described above: from the area of Mizpah in the north to Beth-zur in the south, and from Jericho in the east to Gezer (near Lod) in the west. In fact, almost all the impressions were found in Jerusalem and in the sites immediately to its north and south. One type of these impressions carries, in addition to the name of the province, a personal name and the title "the governor." Such personal names are identified by most scholars as otherwise unknown governors of the province of Yehud, that is to say, officials who held the same post as Nehemiah.

Bibliography

Author's Note: Although there is a rich and relevant scholarly literature on the subjects covered in this book also in Hebrew and in German, French, and other European languages, we have selected the main sources in English for this bibliography. In a very few cases, German or French sources are cited when they are the only relevant references to a particular subject.

Introduction: Archaeology and the Bible

Reference encyclopedias:
I. The main archaeological sites in Israel and Jordan:
Stern, E. (editor). 1993. *The New Encyclopedia of Archaeological Excavations in the Holy Land.* Jerusalem.
II. Bible entries:
Freedman, D. N. (editor). 1992. *The Anchor Bible Dictionary.* New York.
III. The Ancient Near East:
Meyers, E. M. (editor). 1997. *The Oxford Encyclopedia of Archaeology in the Near East.* New York.
Sasson, J. M. (editor). 1995. *Civilizations of the Ancient Near East.* London.

On the physical geography of Canaan / Israel:
Orni, E. and Efrat, E. 1971. *Geography of Israel.* Jerusalem.

On archaeological method:
Renfrew, C. and Bahn, P. 1991. *Archaeology: Theories, Methods and Practice.* London.

On the history of archaeological research in Palestine:
Silberman, N. A. 1982. *Digging for God and Country: Exploration in the Holy Land 1799–1917.* New York.

Introductory books on the archaeology of the Levant:
Ben-Tor, A. (editor). 1992. *The Archaeology of Ancient Israel.* New Haven.
Levy, T. E. (editor). 1995. *The Archaeology of Society in the Holy Land.* London.
Mazar, A. 1990. *Archaeology of the Land of the Bible 10,000–586 B.C.E.* New York.

Stern, E. 2001. *Archaeology of the Land of the Bible, Vol. II: The Assyrian, Babylonian, and Persian Periods 732–332 BCE.* New York.

On the historical geography of the Land of Israel:
Aharoni, Y. 1979. *The Land of the Bible: A Historical Geography.* Philadelphia.

Translation of ancient Near Eastern texts:
Pritchard, J. B. 1969. *Ancient Near Eastern Texts Relating to the Old Testament.* Princeton.

On the Pentateuch:
Blenkinsopp, J. 1992. *The Pentateuch: An Introduction to the First Five Books of the Bible.* New York.
Friedman, R. E. 1987. *Who Wrote the Bible?* New York.
Gunkel, H. 1964. *The Legends of Genesis.* New York.
Noth, M. 1981. *A History of Pentateuchal Traditions.* Sheffield.
Van Seters, J. 1999. *The Pentateuch: A Social-Science Commentary.* Sheffield
Wellhausen, J. 1957. *Prolegomena to the History of Ancient Israel.* New York.
Whybray, R.N. 1987. *The Making of the Pentateuch.* Sheffield.

On the Deuteronomistic History:
I. General
McKenzie, S. L. and Graham, M. P. (editors). 1994. *The History of Israel's Traditions: The Heritage of Martin Noth.* Sheffield.
Knoppers, G.N. and McConville, J. G. (editors). 2000. *Reconsidering Israel and Judah: Recent Studies on the Deuteronomistic History.* Winona Lake.
Rofé, A. 1991. Ephraimite versus Deuteronomistic History. In: Garrone, D. and Felice, I. (editors). *Storia e tradizioni di Israele.*
II. The German (Martin Noth) School:
Noth, M. 1981. *The Deuteronomistic History.* Sheffield.
III. The Harvard (Frank M. Cross) School:
Cross, F. M. 1973. *Canaanite Myth and Hebrew Epic.* Cambridge, Mass.: 274–288.
Halpern, B. and Vanderhooft, D. 1991. The Editions of Kings in the 7th-6th Centuries B.C.E. *Hebrew Union College Annual* 62: 179–244.
McKenzie. S. L. 1991. *The Trouble with Kings: The Composition of the Book of Kings in the Deuteronomistic History.* Leiden.
Nelson, R. D. 1981. *The Double Redaction of the Deuteronomistic History.* Sheffield.

On the books of Chronicles:
Japhet, S. 1993. *I & II Chronicles: A Commentary.* London.
Noth, M. 1987. *The Chronicler's History.* Sheffield.
Williamson, H. G. M. 1982. *1 and 2 Chronicles.* London.

On historiography in the Bible:
Brettler, M. Z. 1995. *The Creation of History in Ancient Israel.* London.
Halpern, B. 1988. *The First Historians: The Hebrew Bible and History.* San Francisco.

Philips Long, V. (editor). 1999. *Israel's Past in Present Research, Essays on Ancient Israelite Historiography*. Winona Lake.

Van Seters, J. 1983. *In Search of History: Historiography in the Ancient World and the Origins of Biblical History*. New Haven.

On biblical chronology:

Cogan, M. 1992. Chronology. *Anchor Bible Dictionary*. New York.

Galil, G. 1996. *The Chronology of the Kings of Israel and Judah*. Leiden.

On the history of Israel:

I. Mainstream studies:

Alt, A. 1966. *Essays on Old Testament History and Religion*. Oxford.

Noth, M. 1965. *The History of Israel*. London.

Hayes, J. H. and Miller, M. J. 1977. *Israelite and Judaean History*. London.

Miller, M. J. and Hayes, J. H. 1986. *A History of Ancient Israel and Judah*. London.

De Vaux, R. 1978. *The Early History of Israel*. Philadelphia.

II. The Minimalist Approach:

Davies, P. 1992. *In Search of 'Ancient Israel'*. Sheffield.

Lemche, N. P. 1994. Is it Still Possible to Write a History of Ancient Israel? *Scandinavian Journal of Old Testament* 8:165–190.

Thompson, T. L. 1992. *Early History of the Israelite People*. Leiden.

Thompson, T. L. 1999. *The Mythic Past*. New York.

On the Annales school:

Braudel, F. 1980. *On History*. London.

Febvre, L. 1973. *A New Kind of History and Other Studies*. New York.

Chapter 1: Searching for the Patriarchs

On the book of Genesis:

See items in the Pentateuch bibliography to the Introduction.

Sarna, N. M. 1966. *Understanding Genesis*. New York.

Speiser, E. A. 1964. *Genesis: Introduction, Translation, and Notes*. Garden City.

On the J source:

See items in the Pentateuch bibliography to the Introduction.

Friedman, R. E. 1999. *The Hidden Book in the Bible*. San Francisco.

Van Seters, J. 1992. *Prologue to History: The Yahwist as Historian in Genesis*. Louisville.

On the E source:

Jenks, A. W. 1977. *The Elohist and North Israelite Traditions*. Missoula.

On the P source:

Haran, M. 1981. Behind the Scenes of History: Determining the Date of the Priestly Source. *Journal of Biblical Literature* 100: 321–333.

Hurvitz, A. 1988. Dating the Priestly Source in Light of the Historical Study of Biblical Hebrew a Century after Wellhausen. *Beihefte zur Zeitschrift für die alttestamentliche Wissenschaft* 100: 88–99

General reviews of the patriarchal traditions:

Dever, W. G. and Clark, M. W. 1977. The Patriarchal Traditions. In: Hayes and Miller in the bibliography to the introduction: 70–148.

Hendel, R. S. 1995. Finding Historical Memories in the Patriarchal Narratives. *Biblical Archaeology Review* 21/4: 52–59, 70–71.

McCarter, P. K. 1999. The Patriarchal Age: Abraham, Isaac and Jacob. In: Shanks, H. (editor). *Ancient Israel: From Abraham to the Roman Destruction of the Temple.* Washington, D.C.: 1–31.

Past theories on the historicity of the patriarchal traditions:

Albright, W. F. 1961. Abraham the Hebrew: A New Archaeological Interpretation. *Bulletin of the American Schools of Oriental Research* 163: 36–54.

Gordon, C. H. 1964. Biblical Customs and the Nuzi Tablets. In: Campbell, E. F. and Freedman, D. N. (editors). *The Biblical Archaeologist Reader.* Volume II. Garden City: 21–33.

Mazar, B. 1986. *The Early Biblical Period: Historical Studies.* Jerusalem: 49–62.

De Vaux, R. 161–287. See the bibliography to the Introduction.

Critical studies of the patriarchal traditions:

Thompson, T. L. 1974. *The Historicity of the Patriarchal Narratives: The Quest for the Historical Abraham.* Berlin.

Van Seters, J. 1975. *Abraham in History and Tradition.* New Haven.

Redford, D. B. 1970. *A Study of the Biblical Joseph Story.* Leiden.

On the archaeology of Transjordan:

Bienkowski, P. (editor). 1992. *Early Edom and Moab: The Beginning of the Iron Age in Southern Jordan.* Sheffield.

McDonald, B. and Younker, R.W. (editors). 1999. *Ancient Ammon.* Leiden.

On the early Arabs:

Ephal, I. 1982. *The Ancient Arabs.* Jerusalem.

Chapter 2: Did the Exodus Happen?

On the conventional theory of Exodus in the Late Bronze Age:

Frerichs, E. S. and Lesko, L. H. (editors). 1997. *Exodus: The Egyptian Evidence.* Winona Lake.

Sarna, N. M. 1999. Israel in Egypt: The Egyptian Sojourn and the Exodus. In: Shanks, H.

(editor). *Ancient Israel: From Abraham to the Roman Destruction of the Temple.* Washington: 33–54.

On Canaan in the Late Bronze Age:
Leonard, A. 1989. The Late Bronze Age. *Biblical Archaeologist* 52: 4–39.
Singer, I. 1994. Egyptians, Canaanites and Philistines in the Period of the Emergence of Israel. In: Finkelstein, I. and Naaman, N. (editors). *From Nomadism to Monarchy: Archaeological and Historical Aspects of Early Israel.* Jerusalem: 282–338.
Weinstein, J. M. 1981. The Egyptian Empire In Palestine: A Reassessment. *Bulletin of the American Schools of Oriental Research* 241: 1–28.

On the survey along the international road in northern Sinai:
Oren, E. D. 1987. The "Ways of Horus" in North Sinai. In: Rainey, A. F. (editor). *Egypt, Israel, Sinai: Archaeological and Historical Relationships in the Biblical Period.* Tel Aviv: 69–119.

On the Delta of the Nile, the "Period of the Hyksos" and the Exodus:
Bietak, M. 1996. *Avaris the Capital of the Hyksos: Recent Excavations at Tell el-Daba.* London.
Redford, D. B. 1987. An Egyptological Perspective on the Exodus Narrative. In: Rainey, A. F. (editor). *Egypt, Israel, Sinai: Archaeological and Historical Relationships in the Biblical Period.* Tel Aviv: 137–161.
Redford, D. B. 1992. *Egypt, Canaan and Israel in Ancient Times.* Princeton: 98–122.

On the Delta in the Saite Period and the Exodus tradition:
See Redford, above: 408–469.

Commentaries on Exodus:
Propp, W. H. C. 1999. *Exodus 1–18.* New York.
Sarna, N. M. 1986. *Exploring Exodus.* New York

Chapter 3: The Conquest of Canaan

On the military conquest theory:
Albright, W. F. 1939. The Israelite Conquest of Canaan in the Light of Archaeology. *Bulletin of the American Schools of Oriental Research* 74: 11–23.
Kaufman, Y. 1953. *The Biblical Account of the Conquest of Palestine.* Jerusalem.
Malamat, A. 1976. Conquest of Canaan: Israelite Conduct of War according to Biblical Tradition. *Encyclopedia Judaica Year Book* 1975/6: 166–182.
Wright, G. E. 1940. Epic of Conquest. *Biblical Archaeologist* 3: 25–40.
Yadin, Y. 1979. The Transition from a Semi-Nomadic to a Sedentary Society in the Twelfth Century BCE. In: Cross, F.M. (editor). *Symposia Celebrating the Seventy-Fifth Anniversary of the Foundation of the American Schools of Oriental Research (1900–1975).* Cambridge: 57–68.
Yadin, Y. 1982. Is the Biblical Account of the Israelite Conquest of Canaan Historically Reliable? *Biblical Archaeology Review* 8: 16–23.

On the current excavations of Hazor:
Ben-Tor, A. 1998. The Fall of Canaanite Hazor—the "Who" and "When" Questions. In: Gitin,
S., Mazar, A. and Stern, E. 1998. *Mediterranean Peoples in Transition: Thirteenth to Early Tenth
Centuries BCE.* Jerusalem: 456–467.

Critique of the military conquest theory:
Finkelstein, I. 1988. *The Archaeology of the Israelite Settlement.* Jerusalem: 295–302.

On etiological stories in Joshua:
Noth, M. 1935. Bethel und Ai. *Palästinajahrbuch* 31: 7–29.
Noth, M. 1937. Die fünf Könige in der Höhle von Makkeda. *Palästinajahrbuch* 33: 22–36.

Rationalization of the negative evidence regarding the Conquest of Canaan:
Albright, above: 16.
Glueck, N. 1959. *Rivers in the Desert.* New York: 114

On the biblical narrative of the Conquest:
Nelson, R. D. 1997. *Joshua: A Commentary.* Louisville.
Nelson, R. D. 1981. Josiah in the Book of Joshua. *Journal of Biblical Literature* 100: 531–540.

On the Sea Peoples:
Dothan, T. 1982. *The Philistines and Their Material Culture.* Jerusalem.
Dothan, T. and Dothan, M. 1992. *People of the Sea.* New York.
Oren, E. D. (editor). 2000. *The Sea Peoples and Their World: A Reassessment.* Philadelphia.
Singer, in the bibliography to Chapter 2.
Stager, L. E. 1995. The Impact of the Sea Peoples (1185–1050 BCE). In: Levy, T. E. *The Archaeol-
ogy of Society in the Holy Land.* London: 332–348.

On the date of the end of the Late Bronze Age:
Ussishkin, D. 1985. Levels VII and VI at Tel Lachish and the End of the Late Bronze Age in
Canaan. In: Tubb, J. N. (editor). *Palestine in the Bronze and Iron Ages: Papers in Honour of
Olga Tufnell.* London: 213–228.
Ussishkin, D. 1995. The Destruction of Megiddo at the End of the Late Bronze Age and Its His-
torical Significance. *Tel Aviv* 22: 240–267.

On the crisis years at the end of the Late Bronze Age:
Gitin, S., Mazar, A. and Stern, E. 1998. *Mediterranean Peoples in Transition: Thirteenth to Early
Tenth Centuries BCE.* Jerusalem.
Ward, W. A. and Sharp Joukowsky, M. (editors). 1992. *The Crisis Years: The 12th Century B.C.
From Beyond the Danube to the Tigris.* Dubuque.

On Canaan in the Amarna period in particular and the Late Bronze Age in general:
See above, in the bibliography to Chapter 2.
Finkelstein, I. 1996. The Territorio-Political System of Canaan in the Late Bronze Age, *Ugarit-
Forschungen* 28: 221–255.

Naaman, N. 1997. The Network of Canaanite Late Bronze Kingdoms and the City of Ashdod. *Ugarit-Forschungen* 29: 599–626.
Singer in the bibliography to Chapter 2.

Chapter 4: Who Were the Israelites?

On the Peaceful Infiltration theory:
Alt, A. 1966. *Essays on Old Testament History and Religion.* Oxford: 135–139.
Alt, A. 1953. *Kleine Schriften zur Geschichte des Volkes Israel, I.* München: 256–273.
Aharoni, Y. 1976. Nothing Early and Nothing Late. Re-writing Israel's Conquest. *Biblical Archaeologist* 39: 55–76.

On the Peasant Revolt theory:
Mendenhall, G. E. 1962. The Hebrew Conquest of Palestine. *Biblical Archaeologist* 25: 66–87.
Gottwald, N. K. 1979. *The Tribes of Yahweh.* New York.

Current views on the rise of early Israel:
Coote, R. B. and Whitelam, K. W. 1987. *The Emergence of Early Israel in Historical Perspective.* Sheffield.
Dever, W. G. 1995. Ceramics, Ethnicity, and the Question of Israel's Origins. *Biblical Archaeologist* 58: 200–13.
Finkelstein in the bibliography to Chapter 3, *The Archaeology.*
Finkelstein, I. 1995. The Great Transformation: The 'Conquest' of the Highlands Frontiers and the Rise of the Territorial States. In: Levy, T. E. (editor). *The Archaeology of Society in the Holy Land.* London: 349–365.
Finkelstein, I. 1996. Ethnicity and Origin of the Iron I Settlers in the Highlands of Canaan: Can the Real Israel Stand Up? *Biblical Archaeologist* 59: 198–212.
Finkelstein, I. and Naaman, N. (editors). 1994. *From Nomadism to Monarchy: Archaeological and Historical Aspects of Early Israel.* Jerusalem.
Lemche, N. P. 1985. *Early Israel.* Leiden.
Stager, L. E. 1985. The Archaeology of the Family in Ancient Israel. *Bulletin of the American Schools of Oriental Research* 260: 1–35.

On the Apiru and the Shosu:
Giveon, R. 1971. *Les bédouins Shosou des documents égyptiens.* Leiden.
Greenberg, M. 1955. *The Hab/piru.* New Haven.
Rowton, M. B. 1976. Dimorphic Structure and the Problem of the *Apiru-Ibrim. Journal of Near Eastern Studies* 35: 13–20.
Naaman, N. 1986. Habiru and Hebrews: The Transfer of a Social Term to the Literary Sphere. *Journal of Near Eastern Studies* 45: 271–288.
Rainey, A. F. 1995. Unruly Elements in Late Bronze Canaanite Society. In: Wright, D.P., Freedman, D.N. and Hurvitz, A. (editors). *Pomegranates and Golden Bells.* Winona Lake: 481–496.

Ward, W. A. 1972. The Shasu "Bedouin". Notes on a Recent Publication. *Journal of the Economy and Social History of the Orient* 15: 35–60.

Commentary on the book of Judges:
Boling, R. G. 1975. *Judges.* New York.

Chapter 5: Memories of a Golden Age

Commentaries on the books of Samuel and I Kings:
McCarter, K. P. 1980. *I Samuel.* Garden City.
McCarter, K. P. 1984. *II Samuel.* Garden City.
Gray, J. 1970. *I and II Kings, A Commentary.* London.

On the united monarchy, David and Solomon:
Fritz, V. and Davies, P. 1996. *The Origins of the Ancient Israelite States.* Sheffield.
Halpern, B. 2001. *David's Secret Demons: Messiah, Murderer, Traitor, King.* Grand Rapids.
Handy, L. K. (editor) 1997. *The Age of Solomon.* Leiden.
Knauf, E. A. 1991. King Solomon's Copper Supply. In: Lipinski, E. (editor). *Phoenicia and the Bible.* Leuven: 167–186.
Niemann, H. M. 2000. Megiddo and Solomon—A Biblical Investigation in Relation to Archaeology. *Tel Aviv* 27: 59–72.

The "minimalist" view on the united monarchy:
See in the bibliography to the Introduction

The conventional theory on the archaeology of the United Monarchy:
Dever, W. G. 1990. *Recent Archaeological Discoveries and Biblical Research.* Seattle: 85–117.
Kenyon, K. 1971. *Royal Cities of the Old Testatment.* New York: 53–70.
Mazar, A. 1997. Iron Age Chronology: A Reply to I. Finkelstein. *Levant* 29: 155–165.
Ussishkin, D. 1973. King Solomon's Palaces. *Biblical Archaeologist* 36: 78–105.
Yadin, Y. 1970. Megiddo of the Kings of Israel. *Biblical Archaeologist* 33: 66–96.
Yadin, Y. 1972. *Hazor.* London: 147–164.
Yadin, Y. 1975. *Hazor: The Discovery of a Great Citadel of the Bible.* London: 147–248.

On the "Low Chronology" for the Iron Age strata:
Finkelstein, I. 1996. The Archaeology of the United Monarchy: An Alternative View. *Levant* 28: 177–187.
Finkelstein, I. 1998. Bible Archaeology or Archaeology of Palestine in the Iron Age? A Rejoinder. *Levant* 30: 167–174.

On the settlement patterns in Judah:
Ofer, A. 1994. 'All the Hill Country of Judah': From Settlement Fringe to a Prosperous Monarchy. In: Finkelstein, I. and Naaman, N. (editors). *From Nomadism to Monarchy, Archaeological and Historical Aspects of Early Israel.* Jerusalem: 92–121.

On Jerusalem in the period of the united monarchy:

Cahill, J. 1998. David's Jerusalem, Fiction or Reality? The Archaeological Evidence Proves it. *Biblical Archaeology Review* 24/4: 34–41.

Steiner, M. 1998. David's Jerusalem, Fiction or Reality? It's Not There: Archaeology Proves a Negative. *Biblical Archaeology Review* 24/4: 26–33, 62.

Ussishkin, D. Forthcoming. Solomon's Jerusalem: The Text and the Facts on the Ground. *Tel Aviv.*

Knauf, E. A. 2000. Jerusalem in the Late Bronze and Early Iron Periods: A Proposal. *Tel Aviv* 27: 73–89.

On the Tel Dan inscription:

Biran, A. and Naveh, J. 1995. The Tel Dan Inscription: A New Fragment. *Israel Exploration Journal* 45: 1–18.

Halpern, B. 1994. The Stela from Dan: Epigraphic and Historical Considerations. *Bulletin of the American Schools of Oriental Research* 296:63–80.

Lemaire, A. 1998. The Tel Dan Stela as a Piece of Royal Historiography. *Journal for the Study of the Old Testament* 81: 3–14.

Schniedewind, W. M. 1996. Tel Dan Stela: New Light on Aramaic and Jehu's Revolt. *Bulletin of the American Schools of Oriental Research* 302:75–90.

Yamada, S. 1995. Aram-Israel Relations as Reflected in the Aramaic Inscription from Tel Dan. *Ugarit-Forschungen* 27:611–625.

On the Philistines:

See bibliography on the Sea Peoples in Chapter 3 above.

Chapter 6: One State, One Nation, One People?

On North vs. South in the central hill country during the millennia:

See Finkelstein 1995 in the bibliography to Chapter 4.

On the hill country in the Amarna period:

See Finkelstein 1996 and Naaman 1997 in the bibliography to Chapter 3 above.

Naaman, N. 1992. Canaanite Jerusalem and its Central Hill Country Neighbours in the Second Millennium B.C.E. *Ugarit-Forschungen* 24: 277–291.

On state formation in the Levant:

Finkelstein, I. 1999. State Formation in Israel and Judah: A Contrast in Context, A Contrast in Trajectory. *Near Eastern Archaeology* 62: 35–52.

Marfoe, L. 1979. The Integrative Transformation: Patterns of Socio-political Organization in Southern Syria. *Bulletin of the American Schools of Oriental Research* 234: 1–42.

On the campaign of Pharaoh Shishak:

Kitchen, K. A. 1973. *The Third Intermediate Period in Egypt.* Warminster: 293–300.

Mazar in the bibliography to Chapter 1: 139–150.

Chapter 7: Israel's Forgotten First Kingdom

Commentary on II Kings:
Cogan, M. and Tadmor, H. 1988. *II Kings*. Garden City.

On the Mesha stele:
Dearman, J. A. (editor). 1989. *Studies in the Mesha Inscription and Moab*. Atlanta.
Naaman, N. 1997. King Mesha and the Foundation of the Moabite Monarchy. *Israel Exploration Journal* 47: 83–92.
Smelik, K. A. D. 1992. *Converting the Past, Studies in Ancient Israelite and Moabite Historiography*. Leiden: 59–92.

On the Tel Dan inscription:
See the bibliography to Chapter 5.

On Samaria:
See Kenyon, *Royal Cities,* the bibliography to Chapter 5.

On ninth century Megiddo and Hazor according to Yadin:
Yadin's items in the bibliography to Chapter 5.

On the Iron II water systems:
Shiloh, Y. 1992. Underground Water Systems in the Land of Israel in the Iron Age. In: Kempinski, A. and Reich, R. (editors). *The Architecture of Ancient Israel from the Prehistoric to the Persian Periods*. Jerusalem: 275–293.

On the bit-hilani *palaces:*
See Ussishkin, King Solomon's Palaces, in the bibliography to Chapter 5.

On Jezreel:
Naaman, N. 1997. Historical and Literary Notes on the Excavations of Tel Jezreel. *Tel Aviv* 24: 122–128.
Ussishkin, D. and Woodhead, J. 1992. Excavations at Tel Jezreel 1990–1991: Preliminary Report, *Tel Aviv* 19: 3–56.
Ussishkin, D. and Woodhead, J. 1994. Excavations at Tel Jezreel 1992–1993: Second Preliminary Report, *Levant* 26: 1–71.
Ussishkin, D. and Woodhead, J. 1997. Excavations at Tel Jezreel 1994–1996: Third Preliminary Report, *Tel Aviv* 24: 6–72.
Williamson, H. G. M. 1991. Jezreel in the Biblical Texts. *Tel Aviv* 18: 72–92.
Zimhoni, O. 1997. *Studies in the Iron Age Pottery of Israel: Typological, Archaeological and Chronological Aspects*. Tel Aviv: 13–56.

On Proto-Aeolic capitals:
Shiloh, Y. 1979. *The Proto-Aeolic Capital and Israelite Ashlar Masonry (Qedem* 11). Jerusalem.

On the Omride state:
Olivier, H. 1983. In Search of a Capital for the Northern Kingdom, *Journal of Northwest Semitic Languages* 11: 117–132.
Schulte, H. 1994. The End of the Omride Dynasty: Social-Ethical Observations on the Subject of Power and Violence. In: Knight, D. A. (editor). *Ethics and Politics in the Hebrew Bible.* Atlanta: 133–148.
Timm, S. 1982. *Die Dynastie Omri.* Göttingen.
Williamson, H. G. M. 1996. Tel Jezreel and the Dynasty of Omri, *Palestine Exploration Quarterly* 128: 41–51.

On the representation of the Omrides in the Deuteronomistic History:
Ishida, T. 1975. The House of Ahab, *Israel Exploration Journal* 25: 135–137.
Whitley, C. F. 1952. The Deuteronomic Presentation of the House of Omri, *Vetus Testamentum* 2: 137–152.

Chapter 8: In the Shadow of Empire

On Aram Damascus and the Arameans:
Dion, P.-E. 1997. *Les araméens à l'âge du fer.* Paris.
Lipinski, E. 2000. *The Arameans: Their Ancient History, Culture, Religion.* Leuven.
Pitard, W. T. 1987. *Ancient Damascus.* Winona Lake.

On Hazael and his war against Israel:
Lemaire, A. 1991. Hazaël de Damas, roi d'Aram. In: Charpin, D. and Joannès, F. (editors). *Marchands, diplomates et empereurs.* Paris: 91–108.
See bibliography on the Dan Stele in Chapter 5.

On Hazor and the north in the Iron Age II:
Finkelstein, I. 1999. Hazor and the North in the Iron Age: A Low Chronology Perspective. *Bulletin of the American Schools of Oriental Research* 314: 55–70.

On the excavations of Dan and Bethsaida:
Biran, A. 1994. *Biblical Dan.* Jerusalem.
Arav, R., Freund, R.A. and Shroder, J.F. 2000. Bethsaida Rediscovered: Long Lost City Found North of Galilee Shore. *Biblical Archaeology Review* 26/1: 45–56.

On the Samaria ostraca:
Lemaire, A. 1977. *Inscriptions hébraiques I: Les ostraca.* Paris.
Rainey, A. F. 1967. The Samaria Ostraca in the Light of Fresh Evidence. *Palestine Exploration Quarterly* 99: 32–41.
Shea, W.H. 1977. The Date and Significance of the Samaria Ostraca. *Israel Exploration Journal* 27: 16–27.

On the population of Iron II Israel and Judah:
Broshi, M. and Finkelstein, I. 1992. The Population of Palestine in Iron Age II. *Bulletin of the American Schools of Oriental Research* 287: 47–60.

On the Megiddo "stables":
Davies, A. I. 1988. Solomonic Stables at Megiddo After All? *Palestine Exploration Quarterly* 120: 130–141.
Herr, L. G. 1988. Tripartite Pillared Buildings and the Market Place in Iron Age Palestine. *Bulletin of the American Schools of Oriental Research* 272: 47–67.
Herzog, Z. 1973. The Storehouses. In: Aharoni, Y. (editor). *Beer-sheba I.* Tel Aviv: 23–30.
Pritchard, J. B. 1970. The Megiddo Stables: A Reassessment. In: Sanders, J. A. (editor). *Near Eastern Archaeology in the Twentieth Century.* Garden City: 268–275.
Yadin, Y. 1976. The Megiddo Stables. *Magnalia Dei: the Mighty Acts of God. Essays on the Bible and Archaeology in Memory of G.E. Wright.* Garden City: 249–252.

On the Assyrian "horse lists":
Dalley, S. 1985. Foreign Chariotry and Cavalry in the Armies of Tiglath-pileser III and Sargon II. *Iraq* 47: 31–48.

On the Samaria ivories:
Crowfoot, J. W. and Crowfoot, G. M. 1938. *Early Ivories from Samaria.* London.

On the Assyrian campaigns:
Tadmor, H. 1966. Philistia under Assyrian Rule. *Biblical Archaeologist* 29: 86–102.

On the fall of Samaria:
Becking, B. 1992. *The Fall of Samaria.* Leiden.
Naaman, N. 1990. The Historical Background to the Conquest of Samaria (720 BC). *Biblica* 71: 206–225.

On the deportation of the Israelites:
Naaman, N. 1993. Population Changes in Palestine Following Assyrian Deportations. *Tel Aviv* 20: 104–124.
Oded, B. 1979. *Mass Deportations and Deportees in the Neo-Assyrian Empire.* Wiesbaden.
Younger, L. K. 1998. The Deportations of the Israelites. *Journal of Biblical Literature* 117: 201–227.

Chapter 9: The Transformation of Judah

On the rise of Judah in the eighth century:
Jamieson-Drake, D. W. 1991. *Scribes and Schools in Monarchic Judah: A Socio-Archaeological Approach.* Sheffield.

Finkelstein 1999 in the bibliography to Chapter 6.

Finkelstein, I. 2001. The Rise of Jerusalem and Judah: The Missing Link. *Levant* 33: 105–115.

On Ahaz in history and in the Deuteronomistic History:

Naaman, N. 1995. The Deuteronomist and Voluntary Servitude to Foreign Powers. *Journal for the Study of the Old Testament* 65: 37–53.

Nelson, R. D. 1986. The Altar of Ahaz: A Revisionist View. *Hebrew Annual Review* 10: 267–276.

Smelik, K. A. D. 1997. The New Altar of King Ahaz (2 Kings 16); Deuteronomistic Reinterpretation of a Cult Reform. In: Vervenne, M. and Lust, J. (editors). *Deuteronomy and Deuteronomic Literature.* Leuven: 263–278.

Tadmor, H. and Cogan, M. 1979. Ahaz and Tiglath-Pileser in the Book of Kings: Historiographic Considerations. *Biblica* 60: 491–508.

On the dating of the list of cities fortified by Rehoboam:

Naaman, N. 1986. Hezekiah's Fortified Cities and the *LMLK* Stamps. *Bulletin of the American Schools of Oriental Research* 261: 5–21

Fritz, V. 1981. The 'List of Rehoboam's Fortresses' in 2 Chr. 11:5–12—A Document from the Time of Josiah. *Eretz-Israel* 15: 46–53.

On Iron Age II inscriptions, including seals:

Avigad, N. and Sass, B. 1997. *Corpus of West Semitic Stamp Seals.* Jerusalem.

McCarter, K. P. 1996. *Ancient Inscriptions: Voices from the Biblical World.* Washington.

Naveh, J. 1982. *Early History of the Alphabet.* Leiden.

On mass production of pottery in Iron II Judah:

Zimhoni, *Studies in Iron Age Pottery* in the bibliography to Chapter 7: 57–178.

On the settlement history of Judah:

Ofer in the bibliography to Chapter 5.

On the similarity between Late Bronze and early Iron Age Jerusalem:

Naaman, N. 1996. The Contribution of the Amarna Letters to the Debate on Jerusalem's Political Position in the Tenth Century B.C.E. *Bulletin of the American Schools of Oriental Research* 304: 17–27.

On the religion of Judah:

Ackerman, S. 1992. *Under Every Green Tree: Popular Religion in Sixth Century Judah.* Atlanta.

Albertz, R. 1994. *A History of Israelite Religion in the Old Testament Period.* Louisville.

Miller, P. D. 2000. *Israelite Religion and Biblical Theology.* Sheffield.

Smith, M. 1971. *Palestinian Parties and Politics that Shaped the Old Testament.* New York.

On the expansion of Jerusalem in the eighth century:

Avigad, N. 1984. *Discovering Jerusalem.* Oxford: 31–60.

Broshi, M. 1974. The Expansion of Jerusalem in the Reigns of Hezekiah and Manasseh. *Israel Exploration Journal* 24: 21–26.

On the Jerusalem Iron Age II cemeteries:
Barkay, G. and Kloner, A. 1986. Jerusalem Tombs from the Days of the First Temple. *Biblical Archaeology Review* 12/2: 22–39.
Ussishkin, D. 1993. *The Village of Silwan: The Necropolis from the Period of the Judean Kingdom.* Jerusalem.

On the religious reform of Hezekiah:
Naaman, N. 1995. The Debated Historicity of Hezekiah's Reform in the Light of Historical and Archaeological Research. *Zeitschrift für die alttestamentliche Wissenschaft* 107: 179–195.
Rosenbaum, J. 1979. Hezekiah's Reform and the Deuteronomistic Tradition. *Harvard Theological Review* 72: 23–43.

On the possibility of an early Deuteronomistic History in the time of Hezekiah:
Halpern and Vanderhooft in the bibliography to the introduction.
Provan, I. W. 1988. *Hezekiah and the Books of Kings: A Contribution to the Debate about the Composition of the Deuteronomistic History.* Berlin.

Chapter 10: Between War and Survival

On Hezekiah's revolt:
Halpern, B. 1991. Jerusalem and the Lineages in the Seventh Century BCE: Kinship and the Rise of Individual Moral Liability. In: Halpern, B. and Hobson, D. W. (editors). *Law and Ideology in Monarchic Israel.* Sheffield: 11–107.
Naaman, N. 1994. Hezekiah and the Kings of Assyria. *Tel Aviv* 21: 235–254.

On the foreign relations of Judah in the Days of Hezekiah and Manasseh:
Evans, C. D. 1980. Judah's Foreign Policy from Hezekiah to Josiah. In: Evans, C. D., Hallo, W. W. and White, J. B. (editors). *Scripture in Context: Essays on the Comparative Method.* Pittsburgh: 157–178.
Nelson, R. 1983. Realpolitik in Judah (687–609 B.C.E.). In: Hallo, W. W., Moyer, J. C. and Perdue, L. G. (editors). *Scripture in Context II: More Essays on the Comparative Method.* Winona Lake: 177–189.

On the westward expansion of Jerusalem:
See Avigad and Broshi in the bibliography to Chapter 9.

On Lachish and its conquest by Sennacherib:
Ussishkin, D. 1982. *The Conquest of Lachish by Sennacherib.* Tel Aviv.

On the LMLK storage jars and Hezekiah's administration:
Naaman, N. 1979. Sennacherib's Campaign to Judah and the Date of the *LMLK* Stamps. *Vetus Testamentum* 29: 61–86.
Ussishkin, D. 1977. The Destruction of Lachish by Sennacherib and the Dating of the Royal Judean Storage Jars. *Tel Aviv* 4: 28–60.

Vaughn, A. G. 1999. *Theology, History, and Archaeology in the Chronicler's Account of Hezekiah.* Atlanta.

On the days of Manasseh:
Finkelstein, I. 1994. The Archaeology of the Days of Manasseh. In: Coogan, M. D., Exum, J. C. and Stager, L. E. (editors), *Scripture and Other Artifacts: Essays on the Bible and Archaeology in Honor of Philip J. King.* Louisville: 169–187.

On the biblical evaluation of Manasseh:
Ben-Zvi, E. 1991. The Account of the Reign of Manasseh in II Reg 21:1–18 and the Redactional History of the Book of Kings. *Zeitschrift für die alttestamentliche Wissenschaft* 103: 355–374.
Eynikel, E. 1997. The Portrait of Manasseh and the Deuteronomistic History. In: Vervene, M. and Lust, J. (editors). *Deuteronomy and Deuteronomic Literature.* Leuven: 233–261.
Halpern, B. 1998. Why Manasseh was Blamed for the Babylonian Exile: The Revolution of a Biblical Tradition. *Vetus Testamentum* 48: 473–514.
Schniedewind, W. M. 1991. The Source Citations of Manasseh: King Manasseh in History and Homily. *Vetus Testamentum* 41: 450–461.
Van Keulen, P. 1996. *Manasseh through the Eyes of the Deuteronomists.* Leiden.

On the prosperity in the south in the seventh century:
Finkelstein, I. 1992. Horvat Qitmit and the Southern Trade in the Late Iron Age II. *Zeitschrift des Deutschen Palästina-Vereins* 108: 156–170.
Bienkowski, in the bibliography to Chapter 1, various articles.

On the Tel Miqne oil production:
Eitam, D. and Shomroni, A. 1987. Research of the Oil Industry during the Iron Age at Tel Miqne. In: Heltzer, M. and Eitam, D. (editors). *Olive Oil in Antiquity.* Haifa: 37–56.
Gitin, S. 1987. Tel Miqne-Ekron in the 7th c. BC: City Plan, Development and the Oil Industry. In: Heltzer, M. and Eitam, D. (editors). *Olive Oil in Antiquity.* Haifa: 81–97.

On the evaluation of the kings of Judah in late-monarchic times:
Naaman 1994 above.
Schniedewind, W. 1999. *Society and the Promise to David.* Oxford.

Chapter 11: In the Days of King Josiah

On Josiah and his reform in the Deuteronomistic History:
Eynikel, E. 1996. *The Reform of King Josiah and the Composition of the Deuteronomistic History.* Leiden.
Laato, A. 1992. *Josiah and David Redivivus: The Historical Josiah and the Messianic Expectations of Exilic and Postexilic Times.* Stockholm.
Lohfink, N. 1987. The Cult Reform of Josiah: 2 Kings 22–23 as a Source for the History of Israelite Religion. In: Miller, P. D., Hanson, P. D. and McBride, S. D. (editors). *Ancient Israelite Religion.* Philadelphia: 459–475.

Naaman, N. 1991. The Kingdom of Judah under Josiah. *Tel Aviv* 18:3–71.

Talshir, Z. 1996. The Three Deaths of Josiah and the Strata of Biblical Historiography (2 Kings XXIII 29–30; 2 Chronicles XXXV 20–5; 1 Esdras I 23–31). *Vetus Testamentum* 46: 213–236.

On the book of Deuteronomy:

Tigay, J. 1996. *Deuteronomy.* Philadelphia.

Von Rad in the bibliography to the Introduction.

Von Rad, G. 1966. *Deuteronomy: A Commentary.* London.

Weinfeld, M. 1972. *Deuteronomy and the Deuteronomic School.* Oxford.

On the international scene in the last decades of the history of Judah:

Malamat, A. 1973. Josiah's Bid for Armageddon. *Journal of the Ancient Near Eastern Society* 5: 267–279.

Malamat, A. 1988. The Kingdom of Judah between Egypt and Babylon: A Small State within a Great Power Confrontation. In: Classen, W. (editor). *Text and Context.* Sheffield: 117–129.

On Egypt and the Levant in the days of the Twenty-Sixth Dynasty:

Redford, *Egypt and Canaan,* in the bibliography to Chapter 2.

On Dtr[1]:

See bibliography to the Introduction.

On iconism and aniconism in ancient Israel:

Keel, O. and Uehlinger, C. 1998. *Gods, Goddesses, and Images of God in Ancient Israel.* Edinburgh.

Mettinger, T. 1995. *No Graven Image? Israelite Aniconism in Its Ancient Near Eastern Context.* Lund.

Chapter 12: Exile and Return

On Dtr[2]:

See bibliography on the Deuteronomistic History (the Harvard School) in the introduction, especially Halpern and Vanderhooft.

See the items on King Manasseh in the bibliography to Chapter 10.

On the Babylonian period:

Lipschits, O. Forthcoming. *The Fall and Rise of Jerusalem.*

Vanderhooft, D. S. 1999. *The Neo-Babylonian Empire and Babylon in the Latter Prophets.* Atlanta.

On the last four verses in the book of Kings (the release of Jehoiachin from jail):

Becking, B. 1990. Jehoiachin's Amnesty, Salvation for Israel? Notes on 2 Kings 25, 27–30. In:

Brekelmans, C. and Lust, J. (editors). *Pentateuchal and Deuteronomistic Studies*. Leuven: 283–293.

Levenson, J. D. 1984. The Last Four Verses in Kings. *Journal of Biblical Literature*. 103: 353–361. Von Rad in the bibliography to the introduction.

On the myth of the empty land and the settlement and demography of Yehud:
Barstad, H. M. 1996. *The Myth of the Empty Land*. Oslo.

Carter, C. E. 1999. *The Emergence of Yehud in the Persian Period*. Sheffield.

On the province of Yehud and the emergence of Second Temple Judaism:
Berquist, J. L. 1995. *Judaism in Persia's Shadow*. Minneapolis.

Davies, P. R. (editor). 1991. *Second Temple Studies 1. The Persian Period*. Sheffield.

Eskenazi, T. C. and Richards, K. H. (editors). 1994. *Second Temple Studies 2. Temple and Community in the Persian Period*. Sheffield.

Hanson, P. D. 1987. Israelite Religion in the Early Postexilic Period. In: Miller, P. D., Hanson, P. D. and McBride, S. D. (editors). *Ancient Israelite Religion*. Philadelphia: 485–508.

Williamson, H. 1998. Judah and the Jews. In: Brosius, M. and Kuhrt, A. (editors). *Studies in Persian History: Essays in Memory of David M. Lewis*. Leiden: 145–163.

On the material culture of the Persian period in general and the province of Yehud in particular:
Stern, E. 1982. *Material Culture of the Land of the Bible in the Persian Period, 538–332 B.C.* Warminster.

On exilic and post-exilic realities behind the Pentateuchal narratives:
Clines, D. J. A. 1997. *The Theme of the Pentateuch*. Sheffield.

Hoffman, Y. 1998. The Exodus—Tradition and Reality. The Status of the Exodus Tradition in Ancient Israel. In: Shirun-Grumach, I. (editor). *Jerusalem Studies in Egyptology*. Wiesbaden: 193–202.

Van Seters 1975, in the bibliography for Chapter 1.

Index

Aaron, 35, 50

Abdi-Heba, king of Jerusalem, 155, 238–39

Abijah, 165

Abijam, king of Judah, 232, 236

Abraham, 8, 27, 28–30, 43, 44

    as Amorite, 320–21

    failed search for historical, 33–36

    post-exilic Yehud and story of, 312

    war with Mesopotamian kings, 46n

Absalom, 127

Adad-nirari III, king of Assyria, 205

Adbeel, 41

Adonizedek, king of Jerusalem, 75

Agriculture, in northern kingdom (Israel), 207

Ahab, king of Israel, 140, 169, 171, 172, 173, 206, 210, 211, 232

Aharoni, Yohanan, 106, 250n, 332–33, 334, 351

Ahaz, king of Judah, 233–34, 237, 240, 243, 246, 270–71

Ahaziah, king of Israel, 171, 174

Ahaziah, king of Judah, 232, 236

Ahijah (prophet), 164–66, 170

Ahmose, pharaoh, 56

Ai, city of, 75, 154

    conquest of Canaan and, 82–83

    Josianic "conquest" of, 93

Akhenaten, pharaoh, 77

Akhetaten, city of, 238

Alashiya, kingdom of, 86

Albright, William F., 19, 34, 35, 79, 82–83, 320–21, 329, 333

Alt, Albrecht, 91, 102, 192, 329–33, 334, 349

Altars, open-air. *See* High places

Amalekites (people), 99

Amarna tablets (Tell el-Amarna letters), 60, 155, 238, 335

    conquest of Canaan and, 77–78

Amaziah, king of Judah, 233, 237

Amenhotep III, pharaoh, 77

Ammon, kingdom of, 39

    settlement history of, 119

Ammonites, 99, 127

Amon, king of Judah, 272, 273

Amorite hypothesis, 319–21

Amorites (Amurru), 35, 320

Amos (prophet), 212–13

Anatolia, 85

Anthropology of ancient Israel, 21–22

Aphek, city of, 90

Apiru (people), 102–3, 104, 239, 240, 335–36

Aqaba, Gulf of, 143–44

Arabian trade

    caravan, 41, 267–70, 320

    Judah and, 267–68

    in 7th c. BCE, 143

Arad, Tel, 64, 250

Arad, town of, 82

Arad site, 64, 250

Aram-Damascus, kingdom of, 39, 193

    Jehoshaphat's war against, 174

    northern kingdom and, 174–75, 177–78, 197, 200, 201–5, 206

Aramean presence in northern kingdom, 201–5

Arameans, 10, 39, 127, 324

Archaeological periods, 20